EUREKA MATH™

A Story of Ratios

Grade 7, Module 4
Percent and Proportional Relationships

JB JOSSEY-BASS™
A Wiley Brand

Cover design by Chris Clary

Published by Jossey-Bass
A Wiley Brand
One Montgomery Street, Suite 1200, San Francisco, CA 94104-4594—www.josseybass.com

ISBN: 978-1-118-81113-9

Printed in the United States of America
FIRST EDITION
PB Printing   10 9 8 7 6 5 4 3 2

When do you know you really understand something? One test is to see if you can explain it to someone else—well enough that *they* understand it. Eureka Math routinely requires students to "turn and talk" and explain the math they learned to their peers.

That is because the goal of Eureka Math (which you may know as the EngageNY math modules) is to produce students who are not merely literate, but fluent, in mathematics. By fluent, we mean not just knowing what process to use when solving a problem but understanding why that process works.

Here's an example. A student who is fluent in mathematics can do far more than just name, recite, and apply the Pythagorean theorem to problems. She can explain why $a^2 + b^2 = c^2$ is true. She not only knows the theorem can be used to find the length of a right triangle's hypotenuse, but can apply it more broadly—such as to find the distance between any two points in the coordinate plane, for example. She also can see the theorem as the glue joining seemingly disparate ideas including equations of circles, trigonometry, and vectors.

By contrast, the student who has merely memorized the Pythagorean theorem does not know why it works and can do little more than just solve right triangle problems by rote. The theorem is an abstraction—not a piece of knowledge, but just a process to use in the limited ways that she has been directed. For her, studying mathematics is a chore, a mere memorizing of disconnected processes.

Eureka Math provides much more. It offers students math knowledge that will serve them well beyond any test. This fundamental knowledge not only makes wise citizens and competent consumers, but it gives birth to budding physicists and engineers. Knowing math deeply opens vistas of opportunity.

A student becomes fluent in math—as they do in any other subject—by following a course of study that builds their knowledge of the subject, logically and thoroughly. In Eureka Math, concepts flow logically from PreKindergarten through high school. The "chapters" in the story of mathematics are "A Story of Units" for the elementary grades, followed by "A Story of Ratios" in middle school and "A Story of Functions" in high school.

This sequencing is joined with a mix of new and old methods of instruction that are proven to work. For example, we utilize an exercise called a "sprint" to develop students' fluency with standard algorithms (routines for adding, subtracting, multiplying, and dividing whole numbers and fractions). We employ many familiar models and tools such as the number line and tape diagrams (aka bar diagrams). A newer model highlighted in the curriculum is the number bond (illustrated below), which clearly shows how numbers are comprised of other numbers.

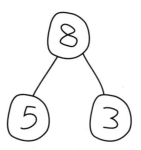

Eureka Math is designed to help accommodate different types of classrooms and serve as a resource for educators, who make decisions based on the needs of students. The "vignettes" of teacher-student interactions included in the curriculum are not scripts, but exemplars illustrating methods of instruction recommended by the teachers who have crafted our curricula.

Eureka Math has been adopted by districts from East Meadows, NY to Lafayette, LA to Chula Vista, CA. At Eureka Math we are excited to have created the most transparent math curriculum in history—every lesson, all classwork, and every problem is available online.

Many of us have less than joyful memories of learning mathematics: lots of memorization, lots of rules to follow without understanding, and problems that didn't make any sense. What if a curriculum came along that gave children a chance to avoid that math anxiety and replaced it with authentic understanding, excitement, and curiosity? Like a NY educator attending one of our trainings said: "Why didn't I learn mathematics this way when I was a kid? It is so much easier than the way I learned it!"

Eureka!

Lynne Munson
Washington DC
September 2014

Mathematics Curriculum

GRADE 7
GRADE 7 • MODULE 4

Table of Contents[1]

Percent and Proportional Relationships

---

[1] Each lesson is ONE day and ONE day is considered a 45-minute period.

Grade 7 • Module 4

Percent and Proportional Relationships

OVERVIEW

In Module 4, students deepen their understanding of ratios and proportional relationships from Module 1 (**7.RP.A.1**, **7.RP.A.2**, **7.RP.A.3**, **7.EE.B.4**, **7.G.A.1**) by solving a variety of percent problems. They convert between fractions, decimals, and percents to further develop a conceptual understanding of percent (introduced in Grade 6 Module 1) and use algebraic expressions and equations to solve multi-step percent problems (**7.EE.B.3**). An initial focus on relating 100% to "the whole" serves as a foundation for students. Students begin the module by solving problems without using a calculator to develop an understanding of the reasoning underlying the calculations. Material in early lessons is designed to reinforce students' understanding by having them use mental math and basic computational skills. To develop a conceptual understanding, students will use visual models and equations, building on their earlier work with these. As the lessons and topics progress and students solve multi-step percent problems algebraically with numbers that are not as compatible, teachers may let students use calculators so that their computational work does not become a distraction. This will also be noted in the teacher's lesson materials.

Topic A builds on students' conceptual understanding of percent from Grade 6 (**6.RP.3c**), and relates 100% to "the whole." Students represent percents as decimals and fractions and extend their understanding from Grade 6 to include percents greater than 100%, such as 225%, and percents less than 1%, such as $\frac{1}{2}$% or 0.5%. They understand that, for instance, 225% means $\frac{225}{100}$, or equivalently, $\frac{2.25}{1} = 2.25$ (**7.RP.A.1**).

Students use complex fractions to represent non-whole number percents (e.g., $12\frac{1}{2}\% = \frac{12\frac{1}{2}}{100} = \frac{1}{8} = 0.125$).

Module 3's focus on algebra prepares students to move from the visual models used for percents in Grade 6 to algebraic equations in Grade 7. They write equations to solve multi-step percent problems and relate their conceptual understanding to the representation: $Quantity = Percent \times Whole$ (**7.RP.A.2c**). Students solve percent increase and decrease problems with and without equations (**7.RP.A.3**). For instance, given a multi-step word problem where there is an increase of 20% and "the whole" equals $200, students recognize that $200 can be multiplied by 120%, or 1.2, to get an answer of $240. They use visual models, such as a double number line diagram, to justify their answers. In this case, 100% aligns to $200 in the diagram and intervals of fifths are used (since 20% = $\frac{1}{5}$) to partition both number line segments to create a scale indicating that 120% aligns to $240. Topic A concludes with students representing 1% of a quantity using a ratio, and then using that ratio to find the amounts of other percents. While representing 1% of a quantity and using it to find the amount of other percents is a strategy that will always work when solving a problem, students recognize that when the percent is a factor of 100, they can use mental math and proportional reasoning to find the amount of other percents.

In Topic B, students create algebraic representations and apply their understanding of percent from Topic A to interpret and solve multi-step word problems related to markups or markdowns, simple interest, sales tax, commissions, fees, and percent error (**7.RP.A.3**, **7.EE.B.3**). They apply their understanding of proportional relationships from Module 1, creating an equation, graph, or table to model a tax or commission rate that is represented as a percent (**7.RP.A.1**, **7.RP.A.2**). Students solve problems related to changing percents and use their understanding of percent and proportional relationships to solve the following: *A soccer league has* 300 *players, 60% of whom are boys. If some of the boys switch to baseball, leaving only 52% of the soccer players as boys, how many players remain in the soccer league?* Students determine that, initially, $100\% - 60\% = 40\%$ of the players are girls and 40% of 300 equals 120. Then, after some boys switched to baseball, $100\% - 52\% = 48\%$ of the soccer players are girls, so $0.48p = 120$, or $p = \frac{120}{0.48}$. Therefore, there are now 250 players in the soccer league.

In Topic B, students also apply their understanding of absolute value from Module 2 (**7.NS.A.1b**) when solving percent error problems. To determine the percent error for an estimated concert attendance of 5,000 people, when actually 6,372 people attended, students calculate the percent error as:
$\frac{|5000-6372|}{|6372|} \cdot 100\%$, which is about 21.5%.

Students revisit scale drawings in Topic C to solve problems in which the scale factor is represented by a percent (**7.RP.A.2b**, **7.G.A.1**). They understand from their work in Module 1, for example, that if they have two drawings where if Drawing 2 is a scale model of Drawing 1 under a scale factor of 80%, then Drawing 1 is also a scale model of Drawing 2, and that scale factor is determined using inverse operations. Since $80\% = \frac{4}{5}$, the scale factor is found by taking the complex fraction $1 / \frac{4}{5}$, or $\frac{5}{4}$, and multiplying it by 100%, resulting in a scale factor of 125%. As in Module 1, students construct scale drawings, finding scale lengths and areas given the actual quantities and the scale factor (and vice-versa); however, in this module the scale factor is represented as a percent. Students are encouraged to develop multiple methods for making scale drawings. Students may find the multiplicative relationship between figures; they may also find a multiplicative relationship among lengths within the same figure.

The problem-solving material in Topic D provides students with further applications of percent and exposure to problems involving population, mixtures, and counting, in preparation for later topics in middle school and high school mathematics and science. Students apply their understanding of percent (**7.RP.A.2c**, **7.RP.A.3**, **7.EE.B.3**) to solve word problems in which they determine, for instance, when given two different sets of 3-letter passwords and the percent of 3-letter passwords that meet a certain criteria, which set is the correct set. Or, given a 5-gallon mixture that is 20% pure juice, students determine how many gallons of pure juice must be added to create a 12-gallon mixture that is 40% pure juice by writing and solving the equation $0.2(5) + j = 0.4(12)$, where j is the amount of pure juice added to the original mixture.

This module spans 25 days and includes 18 lessons. Seven days are reserved for administering the assessments, returning the assessments, and remediating or providing further applications of the concepts. The Mid-Module Assessment follows Topic B and the End-of-Module Assessment follows Topic D.

Focus Standards

Analyze proportional relationships and use them to solve real-world and mathematical problems.

7.RP.A.1 Compute unit rates associated with ratios of fractions, including ratios of lengths, areas and other quantities measured in like or different units. *For example, if a person walks 1/2 mile in each 1/4 hour, compute the unit rate as the complex fraction ½ / ¼ miles per hour, equivalently 2 miles per hour.*

7.RP.A.2 Recognize and represent proportional relationships between quantities.

   a. Decide whether two quantities are in a proportional relationship, e.g., by testing for equivalent ratios in a table or graphing on a coordinate plane and observing whether the graph is a straight line through the origin.

   b. Identify the constant of proportionality (unit rate) in tables, graphs, equations, diagrams, and verbal descriptions of proportional relationships.

   c. Represent proportional relationships by equations. *For example, if total cost t is proportional to the number n of items purchased at a constant price p, the relationship between the total cost and the number of items can be expressed at t = pn.*

   d. Explain what a point (x,y) on the graph of a proportional relationship means in terms of the situation, with special attention to the points (0,0) and (1,r), where r is the unit rate.

7.RP.A.3 Use proportional relationships to solve multistep ratio and percent problems. *Examples: simple interest, tax, markups and markdowns, gratuities and commissions, fees, percent increase and decrease, percent error.*

Solve real-life and mathematical problems using numerical and algebraic expressions and equations.[2]

7.EE.B.3 Solve multi-step real-life and mathematical problems posed with positive and negative rational numbers in any form (whole numbers, fractions, and decimals), using tools strategically. Apply properties of operations to calculate with numbers in any form; convert between forms as appropriate; and assess the reasonableness of answers using mental computation and estimation strategies. *For example: If a woman making $25 an hour gets a 10% raise, she will make an additional 1/10 of her salary an hour, or $2.50, for a new salary of $27.50. If you want to place a towel bar 9 3/4 inches long in the center of a door that is 27 ½ inches wide, you will need to place the bar about 9 inches from each edge. This estimate can be used as a check on the exact computation.*

Draw, construct, and describe geometrical figures and describe the relationships between them.

7.G.A.1[3] Solve problems involving scale drawings of geometric figures, including computing actual lengths and areas from a scale drawing and reproducing a scale drawing at a different scale.

---

[2] 7.EE.3 is introduced in Module 3. The balance of this cluster was taught in the first three modules.
[3] 7.G.1 is introduced in Module 1. The balance of this cluster is taught in Module 6.

EUREKA MATH™ | Module 4: Percent and Proportional Relationships

Foundational Standards

Understand ratio concepts and use ratio reasoning to solve problems.

6.RP.A.1 Understand the concept of a ratio and use ratio language to describe a ratio relationship between two quantities. *For example, "The ratio of wings to beaks in the bird house at the zoo was 2:1, because for every 2 wings there was 1 beak." Or, "For every vote candidate A received, candidate C received nearly three votes."*

6.RP.A.2 Understand the concept of a unit rate a/b associated with a ratio $a:b$ with $b \neq 0$, and use rate language in the context of a ratio relationship. *For example, "This recipe has a ratio of 3 cups of flour to 4 cups of sugar, so there is 3/4 cup of flour for each cup of sugar." Or, "We paid $75 for 15 hamburgers, which is a rate of $5 per hamburger."*[4]

6.RP.A.3 Use ratio and rate reasoning to solve real-world and mathematical problems, e.g., by reasoning about tables of equivalent ratios, tape diagrams, double number line diagrams, or equations.

　　a. Make tables of equivalent ratios relating quantities with whole-number measurements, find missing values in the tables, and plot the pairs of values on the coordinate plane. Use tables to compare ratios.

　　b. Solve unit rate problems including those involving unit pricing and constant speed. *For example, if it took 7 hours to mow 4 lawns, then at that rate, how many lawns could be mowed in 35 hours? At what rate were lawns being mowed?*

　　c. Find a percent of a quantity as a rate per 100 (e.g., 30% of a quantity means 30/100 times the quantity); solve problems involving finding the whole, given a part and the percent.

　　d. Use ratio reasoning to convert measurement units; manipulate and transform units.

Solve real-world and mathematical problems involving area, surface area, and volume.

6.G.A.1 Find the area of right triangles, other triangles, special quadrilaterals, and polygons by composing into rectangles or decomposing into triangles and other shapes; apply these techniques in the context of solving real-world and mathematical problems.

Apply and extend previous understandings of operations with fractions to add, subtract, multiply, and divide rational numbers.

7.NS.A.1b Apply and extend previous understandings of addition and subtraction to add and subtract rational numbers; represent addition and subtraction on a horizontal or vertical number line diagram.

　　b. Understand $p + q$ as the number located a distance $|q|$ from p, in the positive or negative direction depending on whether q is positive or negative. Show that a number and its opposite have a sum of 0 (are additive inverses). Interpret sums of rational numbers by describing real-world contexts.

---

[4] Expectations for unit rates in this grade are limited to non-complex fractions.

Module 4:　　Percent and Proportional Relationships

7.NS.A.3   Solve real-world and mathematical problems involving the four operations with rational numbers.[5]

Solve real-life and mathematical problems using numerical and algebraic expressions and equations.

7.EE.B.4a   Use variables to represent quantities in a real-world or mathematical problem, and construct simple equations and inequalities to solve problems by reasoning about the quantities.

  a.   Solve word problems leading to equations of the form $px + q = r$ and $p(x + q) = r$, where p, q, and r are specific rational numbers. Solve equations of these forms fluently. Compare an algebraic solution to an arithmetic solution, identifying the sequence of the operations used in each approach. *For example, the perimeter of a rectangle is 54 cm. Its length is 6 cm. What is its width?*

Focus Standards for Mathematical Practice

MP.1   **Make sense of problems and persevere in solving them**. Students make sense of percent problems by modeling the proportional relationship using an equation, a table, a graph, a double number line diagram, mental math, and factors of 100. When solving a multi-step percent word problem, students use estimation and math sense to determine if their steps and logic lead to a reasonable answer. Students know they can always find one percent of a quantity by dividing it by 100 or multiplying it by $\frac{1}{100}$, and they also know that finding 1% first allows them to then find other percents easily. For instance, if students are trying to *find the amount of money after 4 years in a savings account with an annual interest rate of* $\frac{1}{2}$*% on an account balance of* $300, they use the fact that 1% of 300 equals $\frac{300}{100}$, or \$3, thus $\frac{1}{2}$% of 300 equals $\frac{1}{2}$ of \$3, or \$1.50. \$1.50 multiplied by 4 is \$6 interest, and adding \$6 to \$300 makes the total balance with interest equal to \$306.

MP.2   **Reason abstractly and quantitatively**. Students use proportional reasoning to recognize that when they find a certain percent of a given quantity, the answer must be greater than the given quantity if they found more than 100% of it and less than the given quantity if they found less than 100% of it. Double number line models are used to quantitatively represent proportional reasoning related to percents. For instance, *if a father has 70% more money in his savings account than his 25-year-old daughter has in her account, and the daughter has* \$4,500 *in her savings account*; students represent this information with a visual model by equating 4,500 to 100% and the father's unknown savings amount to 170% of 4,500. Students represent the amount of money in the father's savings account by writing the expression: $\frac{170}{100} \times 4,500$, or $1.7(4500)$. When working with scale drawings, given an original two-dimensional picture and a scale factor as a percent, students generate a scale

---

[5] Computations with rational numbers extend the rules for manipulating fractions to complex fractions.

drawing so that each corresponding measurement is the given percentage of the original drawing's measurements. Students work backwards to create a new scale factor and scale drawing from a given scale drawing and scale factor given as a percent. For instance, given a scale drawing with a scale factor of 25%, students create a new scale drawing with a scale factor of 10%. They relate working backwards in their visual model to the following steps:

(1) multiplying all lengths in the original scale drawing by $\frac{1}{0.25}$ (or dividing by 25%) to get back to their original lengths, and then (2) multiplying each original length by 10% to get the new scale drawing.

MP.5   **Use appropriate tools strategically**. Students solve word problems involving percents using a variety of tools, including equations and double number line models. They choose their model strategically. For instance, given that 75% of a class of learners is represented by 21 students; they recognize that since 75 is $\frac{3}{4}$ of 100, and 75 and 21 are both divisible by 3, a double number line diagram can be used to establish intervals of 25's and 7's to show that 100% would correspond to $21 + 7$, which equals 28. For percent problems that do not involve benchmark fractions, decimals, or percents, students use math sense and estimation to assess the reasonableness of their answers and computational work. For instance, a bicycle is marked up 18%, and it retails for $599; students determine that approximately 120% equals $600 and so the wholesale price must be close to $600 \div 1.2$, or equivalently $6{,}000 \div 12$, to arrive at an estimate of $500 for their answer.

MP.6   **Attend to precision**. Students pay close attention to the context of the situation when working with markups, markdowns, percent increase, and percent decrease problems. They construct models based on the language of a word problem. For instance, a markdown of 15% on an $88 item, can be represented by the following expression: $0.85(88)$, whereas a markup of 15% is represented by: $1.15(88)$. Students attend to precision when writing their answer to a percent problem. If they are finding a percent, they use the "%" sign in their answer or write their answer as a fraction with "100" as the denominator (or in an equivalent form). Double number line diagrams display correct segment lengths, and if a line in the diagram represents percents, it is either labeled as such or the percent sign is shown after each number. When stating the area of a scale drawing or actual drawing, students include the square units along with the numerical part of their answer.

MP.7   **Look for and make use of structure**. Students understand percent to be a rate per hundred and express p percent as $\frac{p}{100}$. They know that, for instance, 5% means 5 for every 100, 1% means 1 for every 100, and 225% means 225 for every 100. They use their number sense to find benchmark percents. Since 100% is a whole, then 25% is one-fourth, 50% is a half, and 75% is three-fourths. So, to find 75% of 24, they find $\frac{1}{4}$ of 24, which is 6, and multiply it by 3 to arrive at 18. They use factors of 100 and mental math to solve problems involving other benchmark percents as well. Students know that 1% of a quantity represents $\frac{1}{100}$ of it and use place value and the structure of the base-ten number system to find 1% or $\frac{1}{100}$ of a quantity. They use "finding 1%" as a method to solve percent problems. For instance, to find 14% of 245, students first find 1% of 245 by dividing 245 by 100, which equals 2.45. Since 1% of 245 equals 2.45, 14% of 245 would equal $2.45 \times 14 = 34.3$. Students observe the steps involved in finding a discount price or price including sales tax and use the properties of operations to efficiently find the answer. To find the discounted price of a $73 item that is on sale for 15% off, students realize that the distributive property allows them to arrive at an answer in one step, by multiplying $73 by 0.85, since $73(100\%) - 73(15\%) = 73(1) - 73(0.15) = 73(0.85)$.

Terminology

New or Recently Introduced Terms

- **Absolute Error** (Given the exact value x of a quantity and an approximate value a of it, the absolute error is $|a - x|$.)
- **Percent Error** (The percent error is the percent the absolute error is of the exact value: $\frac{|a-x|}{|x|} \cdot 100\%$, where x is the exact value of the quantity and a is an approximate value of the quantity.)

Familiar Terms and Symbols[6]

- Area
- Circumference
- Coefficient of the Term
- Complex Fraction
- Constant of Proportionality
- Discount Price
- Expression
- Equation
- Equivalent Ratios
- Fee
- Fraction
- Greatest Common Factor
- Length of a Segment
- One-to-One Correspondence
- Original Price
- Percent
- Perimeter
- Pi

---

[6] These are terms and symbols students have seen previously.

- Proportional To
- Proportional Relationship
- Rate
- Ratio
- Rational Number
- Sales Price
- Scale Drawing
- Scale Factor
- Unit Rate

Suggested Tools and Representations

- Calculator
- Coordinate Plane
- Double Number Line Diagrams
- Equations
- Expressions
- Geometric Figures
- Ratio Tables
- Tape Diagrams

Assessment Summary

Assessment Type	Administered	Format	Standards Addressed
Mid-Module Assessment Task	After Topic B	Constructed response with rubric	7.RP.A.1, 7.RP.A.2, 7.RP.A.3. 7.EE.B.3
End-of-Module Assessment Task	After Topic D	Constructed response with rubric	7.RP.A.1, 7.RP.A.2, 7.RP.A.3, 7.EE.B.3, 7.G.A.1

Mathematics Curriculum

GRADE 7

Topic A:

Finding the Whole

7.RP.A.1, 7.RP.A.2c, 7.RP.A.3

Focus Standard:	7.RP.A.1	Compute unit rates associated with ratios of fractions, including ratios of lengths, areas and other quantities measured in like or different units. *For example, if a person walks 1/2 mile in each 1/4 hour, compute the unit rate as the complex fraction ½ / ¼ miles per hour, equivalently 2 miles per hour.*
	7.RP.A.2c	Recognize and represent proportional relationships between quantities.
		c. Represent proportional relationships by equations. *For example, if total cost t is proportional to the number n of items purchased at a constant price p, the relationship between the total cost and the number of items can be expressed as t = pn.*
	7.RP.A.3	Use proportional relationships to solve multistep ratio and percent problems. *Examples: simple interest, tax, markups and markdowns, gratuities and commissions, fees, percent increase and decrease, percent error.*
Instructional Days:	6	
Lesson 1:	Percent (P)[1]	
Lesson 2:	Part of a Whole as a Percent (P)	
Lesson 3:	Comparing Quantities with Percent (P)	
Lesson 4:	Percent Increase and Decrease (P)	
Lesson 5:	Finding One-Hundred Percent Given Another Percent (P)	
Lesson 6:	Fluency with Percents (P)	

In Topic A, students build on their conceptual understanding of percent from Grade 6. They realize that a percent can be greater than 100%, less than 1%, or a non-whole number, such as $33\frac{1}{3}\%$, which can be represented with a complex fraction as $\frac{33\frac{1}{3}}{100}$, which is equivalent to $\frac{1}{3}$. They know 100% to be the whole and also equal to one. They use this conceptualization along with their previous understandings of ratios and

---

[1] Lesson Structure Key: **P**-Problem Set Lesson, **M**-Modeling Cycle Lesson, **E**-Exploration Lesson, **S**-Socratic Lesson

proportional relationships from Module 1 to solve percent problems (**7.RP.A.2c**, **7.RP.A.3**). In Lesson 1, students revisit the meaning of the word *percent* and convert between fractions, decimals, and percents with a Sprint to open the lesson. In this lesson, students use complex fractions to represent non-whole number percents; they also recognize that any percent greater than 100% is a number greater than one and any percent less than 1% is a number less than one-hundredth. Students realize that, for instance, 350% means 350 for every 100, which equals 3.5, or $3\frac{1}{2}$, for every 1 (**7.RP.A.1**). In Lessons 2 and 3, students deepen their conceptual understanding of percent and the relationship between the part and the whole. They use a variety of models, including fractional representations, visual models (i.e., 10 by 10 grids and double number line diagrams), and algebraic models. As an algebraic representation, they use the formula $Part = Percent \times Whole$ to solve percent problems when given two terms out of three from the part, percent, and whole. Students continue to use this algebraic representation in Lesson 3 and write $Quantity = Percent \times Whole$ in situations where the part is larger than the whole. For instance, when expressing 250 as a percent of 200, they identify 200 as the whole, write $250 = p \cdot 200$, and solve the equation to reach a value of $p = 1.25$, which equals 125%. They relate their solution to a visual model, such as a double number line diagram, where 200 represents 100%, so 250 would represent 125%. Lesson 3 includes a percent Sprint, where students use mental math, patterns, place value, and the meaning of percent as "per hundred" to find specified percents of quantities, such as 15% of 20, 30% of 20, etc.

Students advance their work with percents in Lesson 4 when they solve problems related to percent increase and decrease (**7.RP.A.3**). They continue to use algebraic representations and identify the whole in the context of the situation. In Lesson 5, students find one-hundred percent given another percent. They recognize that they can always find 1% of a quantity (by dividing it by 100 or multiplying it by $\frac{1}{100}$) and use 1% to find quantities represented by other percents. Students understand that an algebraic equation may not always be the most efficient way to solve a percent problem. They recognize factors of 100 and use mental math, proportional reasoning, and double number line diagrams to problem-solve as well. Topic A culminates with Lesson 6, where students solve various percent problems using the different strategies and complete a Sprint as they work towards fluency in finding the part, whole, and percent.

Lesson 1: Percent

Student Outcomes

- Students understand that P percent is the number $\frac{P}{100}$ and that the symbol % means percent.
- Students convert between a fraction, decimal, and percent, including percents that are less than 1% or greater than 100%.
- Students write a non-whole number percent as a complex fraction.

Classwork

Fluency Exercise (9 minutes): Sprint

Students complete a two-round Sprint exercise where they practice their knowledge of converting percents, fractions and decimals. Provide one minute for each round of the Sprint. Follow the established protocol for delivering a Sprint exercise. Be sure to provide any answers not completed by the students. (The Fluency Sprint and answer keys are provided at the end of this lesson.)

Opening Exercise 1 (4 minutes): Matching

Students will use mental math and their knowledge of percents to match the percent with the word problem/clue. Allow students to share their answers with their neighbors and discuss the correct answers as a class.

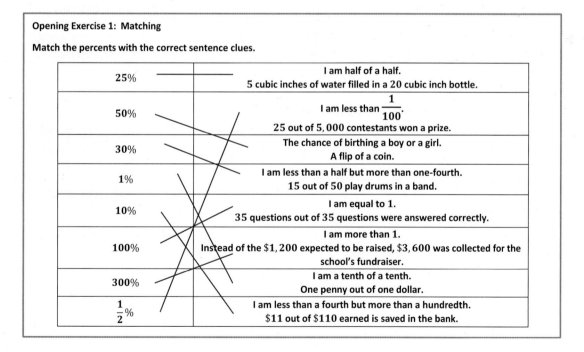

Opening Exercise 1: Matching

Match the percents with the correct sentence clues.

Percent	Clue
25%	I am half of a half. 5 cubic inches of water filled in a 20 cubic inch bottle.
50%	I am less than $\frac{1}{100}$. 25 out of 5,000 contestants won a prize.
30%	The chance of birthing a boy or a girl. A flip of a coin.
1%	I am less than a half but more than one-fourth. 15 out of 50 play drums in a band.
10%	I am equal to 1. 35 questions out of 35 questions were answered correctly.
100%	I am more than 1. Instead of the $1,200 expected to be raised, $3,600 was collected for the school's fundraiser.
300%	I am a tenth of a tenth. One penny out of one dollar.
$\frac{1}{2}$%	I am less than a fourth but more than a hundredth. $11 out of $110 earned is saved in the bank.

Opening Exercise 2 (4 minutes)

Opening Exercise 2

Color in the grids to represent the following fractions:

a. $\dfrac{30}{100}$　　　　　　b. $\dfrac{3}{100}$　　　　　　c. $\dfrac{\frac{1}{3}}{100}$

　　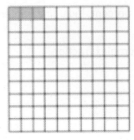　　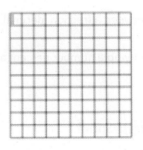

Discussion (4 minutes)

- How are these fractions and representations related to percents?
    - *Percent means out of one hundred and can be written as a fraction with a denominator of* 100.
- What are equivalent representations of $\dfrac{30}{100}$?
    - $\dfrac{3}{10}, \dfrac{15}{50}, 30\%, 0.3.$
- What do these have in common?
    - *They are all equal to 30%. The first two are equivalent fractions reduced by a common factor. The 30% is in percent form and the last is in decimal form.*
- Why do these all equal to 30%?
    - *Because the numerator-denominator is a part-to-whole relationship and 3 out of 10 is 30%. The decimal 0.3 represents 3-tenths, which is also equivalent to 30%.*
- What are other equivalent representations of $\dfrac{\frac{1}{3}}{100}$?
    - $\dfrac{1}{3}\%, \ 0.33\ldots\%, \ 0.0033\ldots, \ \dfrac{1}{300}$

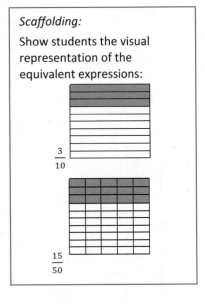

Scaffolding:

Show students the visual representation of the equivalent expressions:

$\dfrac{3}{10}$

$\dfrac{15}{50}$

Example 1 (6 minutes)

Example 1

Use the definition of the word "percent" to write each percent as a fraction and then a decimal.

Percent	Fraction	Decimal
37.5%	$\dfrac{37.5}{100}$	0.375
100%	$\dfrac{100}{100}$	1.0
110%	$\dfrac{110}{100}$	1.10
1%	$\dfrac{1}{100}$	0.01
$\dfrac{1}{2}\%$	$\dfrac{\frac{1}{2}}{100}$	0.005

- What is the pattern or process that you recall or notice when converting percents to fractions?
  - *Place the percent value over* 100 *and reduce if possible.*
- If I gave you a number as a fraction, could you tell me what percent the fraction represents? How would you do this?
  - *Find the equivalent fraction with the denominator of* 100.
- *What mathematical process is occurring for the percent to convert to a decimal?*
  - *The percent is being divided by* 100.
- If I gave you a number as a decimal, could you tell me what percent the decimal represents? How would you do this?
  - *Yes, multiply by* 100.

Scaffolding:

For example, to convert a fraction, $\dfrac{7}{20}$, to a percent:

$$\frac{7}{20} = \frac{?}{100}$$

$$\frac{7 \times 5}{20 \times 5} = \frac{35}{100}$$

Example 2 (5 minutes)

Example 2

Fill in the chart by converting between a fraction, decimal, and percent. Show your work in the space below.

Fraction	Decimal	Percent
$\dfrac{7}{2}$	3.5	350%
$\dfrac{2\frac{1}{2}}{100}$	0.025	$2\frac{1}{2}\%$ or 2.5%
$\dfrac{1}{8}$	0.125	$12\frac{1}{2}\%$ or 12.5%

350% *as a fraction:* $350\% = \dfrac{350}{100} = \dfrac{35}{10} = \dfrac{7}{2}$

350% *as a decimal:* $350\% = \dfrac{350}{100} = 3.50$

0.025 *as a fraction:* $0.025 = \dfrac{2.5}{100}$ *or* $\dfrac{2\frac{1}{2}}{100}$

0.025 *as a percent:* $0.025 = \dfrac{2.5}{100} = 2.5\%$ *or* $2\frac{1}{2}\%$

$\dfrac{1}{8}$ *as a percent:* $\dfrac{1}{8} = \dfrac{12.5}{100} = 12.5\%$ *or* $12\frac{1}{2}\%$

$\dfrac{1}{8}$ *as a decimal:* $\dfrac{1}{8} = \dfrac{12.5}{100} = 0.125$

Exercise 1 (6 minutes): Class Card Activity

Prior to class, copy and cut out the cards found at the end of the lesson. Mix up the cards and pass out one card per student. *Ask* any student to begin by asking the class the question on his/her card in bold face. The student with the equivalent value on his card should respond by reading his sentence, and then read his question for another student to respond. Students will attend to precision when reading the clues and answers, using the correct place value terms when reading decimal numbers. Provide half sheets of blank paper so students can work out the problems that are being read. This will continue until the first person to read his/her question answers somebody's equivalent value.

> *Scaffolding:*
>
> If there are less than 30 students in the class, pass out more than one card to the advanced learners.

Exercise 1: Class Card Activity

Read your card to yourself (each student will have a different card) and work out the problem. When the exercise begins, listen carefully to the questions being read. When you have the card with the equivalent value, respond by reading your card aloud.

Examples:

0.22 should be read "twenty two-hundredths".

$\dfrac{\frac{1}{5}}{1000}$ should be read "one-fifth thousandths" or "one-fifth over one thousand".

$\dfrac{7}{300}$ should be read " seven-three hundredths" or "seven over three hundred".

$\dfrac{200}{100}$ should be read "two hundred-hundredths" or "two hundred over 100".

Closing (3 minutes)

- What does percent mean?
  - *It means "per hundred" or "each hundred".*

- Is the value of $\dfrac{7}{10}$ less than or greater than the value of $\dfrac{7}{10}\%$? Why?
  - *The value of $\dfrac{7}{10}$ will always be greater than $\dfrac{7}{10}\%$ because the percent means it is over 100.*

- How are the fraction and decimal representations related to the percent?
  - *They are related to the ratio of percent over 100.*

- What do percents greater than 1 look like? Why?
  - *They look like numbers that are bigger than 100% because they are bigger than the ratio $\dfrac{100}{100}$.*

Lesson Summary

- *Percent* means "per hundred". *P* percent is the same as $\dfrac{P}{100}$. Write % as short for percent.
- Usually there are three ways to write a number: a percent, a fraction, and a decimal. Fractions and decimals are related to the ratio of percent over 100.

Exit Ticket (4 minutes)

Lesson 1:   Percent

Name _____   Date _____

Lesson 1: Percent

Exit Ticket

1. Fill in the chart converting between fractions, decimals and percents. Show work in the space provided.

Fraction	Decimal	Percent
$\dfrac{1}{8}$		
	1.125	
		$\dfrac{2}{5}\%$

2. Using the values from the chart in Problem 1, which is the least and which is the greatest? Explain how you arrived at your answers.

Exit Ticket Sample Solutions

1. Fill in the chart converting between fractions, decimals and percentages. Show work in the space provided.

Fraction	Decimal	Percent
$\dfrac{1}{8}$	$1 \div 8 = 0.125$	$0.125 \times 100 = 12.5\%$
$1\dfrac{125}{1000} = 1\dfrac{1}{8}$	1.125	$1.125 \times 100 = 112.5\%$
$\dfrac{\frac{2}{5}}{100} = \dfrac{1}{250}$	$(2 \div 5) \div 100 = 0.004$	$\dfrac{2}{5}\%$

2. Using the values from the chart in Problem 1, which is the least and which is the greatest?

   The least of the values is $\dfrac{2}{5}\%$ *and the greatest is* 1.125.

Problem Set Sample Solutions

1. Use a visual model to represent the following percents:

   a. 90%

   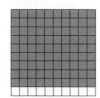

   b. 0.9%

   c. 900%

   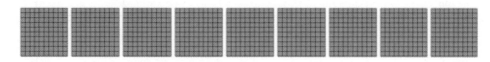

   d. $\dfrac{9}{10}\%$

   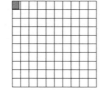

2. Benjamin believes that $\frac{1}{2}\%$ is equivalent to 50%. Is he correct? Why or why not?

Benjamin is not correct because $\frac{1}{2}\%$ is equivalent to 0.50%, which is equal to $\frac{\frac{1}{2}}{100}$. The second percent is equivalent to $\frac{50}{100}$. These percents are not equivalent.

3. Order the following from least to greatest:

$100\%, \frac{1}{100}, 0.001\%, \frac{1}{10}, 0.001, 1.1, 10, \frac{10,000}{100}$

$0.001\%, 0.001, \frac{1}{100}, \frac{1}{10}, 100\%, 1.1, 10, \frac{10,000}{100}$

4. Fill in the chart by converting between a fraction, decimal, and percent. Show work in the space below.

Fraction	Decimal	Percent
$\frac{1}{1}$	1	100%
$\frac{33}{400}$	0.0825	8.25%
$6\frac{1}{4}$	6.25	625%
$\frac{\frac{1}{8}}{100}$	0.00125	$\frac{1}{8}\%$
$\frac{2}{300}$	$0.00666\ldots$	$\frac{2}{3}\%$
$\frac{333}{1,000}$	0.333	33.3%
$\frac{\frac{3}{4}}{100}$	0.0075	$\frac{3}{4}\%$
$2\frac{1}{2}$	2.50	250%
$\frac{1}{200}$	0.005	$\frac{1}{2}\%$
$\frac{150}{100}$	1.5	150%
$\frac{5\frac{1}{2}}{100}$	0.055	$5\frac{1}{2}\%$

Exercise 1 Cards

I have the equivalent value 0.11. Who has the card equivalent to 350%?	I have the equivalent value 3.5. Who has the card equivalent to $\dfrac{3}{8}$?	I have the equivalent value 37.5%. Who has the card equivalent to $\dfrac{\frac{1}{4}}{100}$?	I have the equivalent value 0.0025%. Who has the card equivalent to 5?	I have the equivalent value 500%. Who has the card equivalent to $1\dfrac{2}{5}$?
I have the equivalent value $.4\%$. Who has the card equivalent to $\dfrac{1}{5}\%$?	I have the equivalent value 0.002. Who has the card equivalent to 100%?	I have the equivalent value 1. Who has the card equivalent to $\dfrac{210}{100}$?	I have the equivalent value 210%. Who has the card equivalent to $\dfrac{\frac{3}{4}}{100}$?	I have the equivalent value 0.75%. Who has the card equivalent to $35\dfrac{1}{2}\%$?
I have the equivalent value 0.355. Who has the card equivalent to 2%?	I have the equivalent value $\dfrac{1}{50}$. Who has the card equivalent to 0.5%?	I have the equivalent value $\dfrac{1}{200}$. Who has the card equivalent to 0.37?	I have the equivalent value 37%. Who has the card equivalent to 90%?	I have the equivalent value $\dfrac{9}{10}$. Who has the card equivalent to $\dfrac{\frac{1}{10}}{100}$?
I have the equivalent value 0.10%. Who has the card equivalent to $\dfrac{1}{2}$?	I have the equivalent value 50%. Who has the card equivalent to 300?	I have the equivalent value $30,000\%$. Who has the card equivalent to $\dfrac{3}{5}\%$?	I have the equivalent value $\dfrac{3}{500}$. Who has the card equivalent to 75%?	I have the equivalent value $\dfrac{3}{4}$. Who has the card equivalent to $\dfrac{180}{100}$?
I have the equivalent value 180%. Who has the card equivalent to 5%?	I have the equivalent value 0.05. Who has the card equivalent to $\dfrac{1}{100}\%$?	I have the equivalent value $\dfrac{1}{10,000}$. Who has the card equivalent to 1.1?	I have the equivalent value 110%. Who has the card equivalent to 250%?	I have the equivalent value 2.5. Who has the card equivalent to 18%?
I have the equivalent value $\dfrac{9}{50}$. Who has the card equivalent to $\dfrac{15}{4}$?	I have the equivalent value 375%. Who has the card equivalent to 0.06?	I have the equivalent value 6%. Who has the card equivalent to 0.4?	I have the equivalent value $\%$. Who has the card equivalent to 1.5%?	I have the equivalent value $\dfrac{3}{200}$. Who has the card equivalent to 11%?

Sprint: Fractions, Decimals, and Percents – Round 1

Number Correct: _____

Directions: Write each number in the alternate form indicated.

1.	$\frac{20}{100}$ as a percent	
2.	$\frac{40}{100}$ as a percent	
3.	$\frac{80}{100}$ as a percent	
4.	$\frac{85}{100}$ as a percent	
5.	$\frac{95}{100}$ as a percent	
6.	$\frac{100}{100}$ as a percent	
7.	$\frac{10}{10}$ as a percent	
8.	$\frac{1}{1}$ as a percent	
9.	$\frac{1}{10}$ as a percent	
10.	$\frac{2}{10}$ as a percent	
11.	$\frac{4}{10}$ as a percent	
12.	75% as a decimal	
13.	25% as a decimal	
14.	15% as a decimal	
15.	10% as a decimal	
16.	5% as a decimal	
17.	30% as a fraction	
18.	60% as a fraction	
19.	90% as a fraction	
20.	50% as a fraction	
21.	25% as a fraction	
22.	20% as a fraction	

23.	$\frac{9}{10}$ as a percent	
24.	$\frac{9}{20}$ as a percent	
25.	$\frac{9}{25}$ as a percent	
26.	$\frac{9}{50}$ as a percent	
27.	$\frac{9}{75}$ as a percent	
28.	$\frac{18}{75}$ as a percent	
29.	$\frac{36}{75}$ as a percent	
30.	96% as a fraction	
31.	92% as a fraction	
32.	88% as a fraction	
33.	44% as a fraction	
34.	22% as a fraction	
35.	3% as a decimal	
36.	30% as a decimal	
37.	33% as a decimal	
38.	33.3% as a decimal	
39.	3.3% as a decimal	
40.	0.3% as a decimal	
41.	$\frac{1}{3}$ as a percent	
42.	$\frac{1}{9}$ as a percent	
43.	$\frac{2}{9}$ as a percent	
44.	$\frac{8}{9}$ as a percent	

Lesson 1:   Percent

Sprint: Fractions, Decimals, and Percents – Round 1 [KEY]

Directions: Write each number in the alternate form indicated.

1.	$\dfrac{20}{100}$ as a percent	20%	23.	$\dfrac{9}{10}$ as a percent	90%
2.	$\dfrac{40}{100}$ as a percent	40%	24.	$\dfrac{9}{20}$ as a percent	45%
3.	$\dfrac{80}{100}$ as a percent	80%	25.	$\dfrac{9}{25}$ as a percent	36%
4.	$\dfrac{85}{100}$ as a percent	85%	26.	$\dfrac{9}{50}$ as a percent	18%
5.	$\dfrac{95}{100}$ as a percent	95%	27.	$\dfrac{9}{75}$ as a percent	12%
6.	$\dfrac{100}{100}$ as a percent	100%	28.	$\dfrac{18}{75}$ as a percent	24%
7.	$\dfrac{10}{10}$ as a percent	100%	29.	$\dfrac{36}{75}$ as a percent	48%
8.	$\dfrac{1}{1}$ as a percent	100%	30.	96% as a fraction	$\dfrac{72}{75}$ or $\dfrac{24}{25}$
9.	$\dfrac{1}{10}$ as a percent	10%	31.	92% as a fraction	$\dfrac{23}{25}$
10.	$\dfrac{2}{10}$ as a percent	20%	32.	88% as a fraction	$\dfrac{22}{25}$
11.	$\dfrac{4}{10}$ as a percent	40%	33.	44% as a fraction	$\dfrac{11}{25}$
12.	75% as a decimal	0.75	34.	22% as a fraction	$\dfrac{11}{50}$
13.	25% as a decimal	0.25	35.	3% as a decimal	0.03
14.	15% as a decimal	0.15	36.	30% as a decimal	0.3
15.	10% as a decimal	0.1	37.	33% as a decimal	0.33
16.	5% as a decimal	0.05	38.	33.3% as a decimal	0.333
17.	30% as a fraction	$\dfrac{3}{10}$	39.	3.3% as a decimal	0.033
18.	60% as a fraction	$\dfrac{3}{5}$	40.	0.3% as a decimal	0.003
19.	90% as a fraction	$\dfrac{9}{10}$	41.	$\dfrac{1}{3}$ as a percent	$33\dfrac{1}{3}\%$
20.	50% as a fraction	$\dfrac{1}{2}$	42.	$\dfrac{1}{9}$ as a percent	$11\dfrac{1}{9}\%$
21.	25% as a fraction	$\dfrac{1}{4}$	43.	$\dfrac{2}{9}$ as a percent	$22\dfrac{2}{9}\%$
22.	20% as a fraction	$\dfrac{1}{5}$	44.	$\dfrac{8}{9}$ as a percent	$88\dfrac{8}{9}\%$

Sprint: Fractions, Decimals, and Percents – Round 2

Directions: Write each number in the alternate form indicated.

Number Correct: _____

Improvement: _____

1.	$\frac{30}{100}$ as a percent		23.	$\frac{6}{10}$ as a percent	
2.	$\frac{60}{100}$ as a percent		24.	$\frac{6}{20}$ as a percent	
3.	$\frac{70}{100}$ as a percent		25.	$\frac{6}{25}$ as a percent	
4.	$\frac{75}{100}$ as a percent		26.	$\frac{6}{50}$ as a percent	
5.	$\frac{90}{100}$ as a percent		27.	$\frac{6}{75}$ as a percent	
6.	$\frac{50}{100}$ as a percent		28.	$\frac{12}{75}$ as a percent	
7.	$\frac{5}{10}$ as a percent		29.	$\frac{24}{75}$ as a percent	
8.	$\frac{1}{2}$ as a percent		30.	64% as a fraction	
9.	$\frac{1}{4}$ as a percent		31.	60% as a fraction	
10.	$\frac{1}{8}$ as a percent		32.	56% as a fraction	
11.	$\frac{3}{8}$ as a percent		33.	28% as a fraction	
12.	60% as a decimal		34.	14% as a fraction	
13.	45% as a decimal		35.	9% as a decimal	
14.	30% as a decimal		36.	90% as a decimal	
15.	6% as a decimal		37.	99% as a decimal	
16.	3% as a decimal		38.	99.9% as a decimal	
17.	3% as a fraction		39.	9.9% as a decimal	
18.	6% as a fraction		40.	0.9% as a decimal	
19.	60% as a fraction		41.	$\frac{4}{9}$ as a percent	
20.	30% as a fraction		42.	$\frac{5}{9}$ as a percent	
21.	45% as a fraction		43.	$\frac{2}{3}$ as a percent	
22.	15% as a fraction		44.	$\frac{1}{6}$ as a percent	

Sprint: Fractions, Decimals, and Percents – Round 2 [KEY]

Directions: Write each number in the alternate form indicated.

1.	$\frac{30}{100}$ as a percent	30%	23.	$\frac{6}{10}$ as a percent	60%
2.	$\frac{60}{100}$ as a percent	60%	24.	$\frac{6}{20}$ as a percent	30%
3.	$\frac{70}{100}$ as a percent	70%	25.	$\frac{6}{25}$ as a percent	24%
4.	$\frac{75}{100}$ as a percent	75%	26.	$\frac{6}{50}$ as a percent	12%
5.	$\frac{90}{100}$ as a percent	90%	27.	$\frac{6}{75}$ as a percent	8%
6.	$\frac{50}{100}$ as a percent	50%	28.	$\frac{12}{75}$ as a percent	16%
7.	$\frac{5}{10}$ as a percent	50%	29.	$\frac{24}{75}$ as a percent	32%
8.	$\frac{1}{2}$ as a percent	50%	30.	64% as a fraction	$\frac{48}{75}$ or $\frac{16}{25}$
9.	$\frac{1}{4}$ as a percent	25%	31.	60% as a fraction	$\frac{15}{25}$ or $\frac{3}{5}$
10.	$\frac{1}{8}$ as a percent	12.5%	32.	56% as a fraction	$\frac{14}{25}$
11.	$\frac{3}{8}$ as a percent	37.5%	33.	28% as a fraction	$\frac{7}{25}$
12.	60% as a decimal	0.6	34.	14% as a fraction	$\frac{7}{50}$
13.	45% as a decimal	0.45	35.	9% as a decimal	0.09
14.	30% as a decimal	0.3	36.	90% as a decimal	0.9
15.	6% as a decimal	0.06	37.	99% as a decimal	0.99
16.	3% as a decimal	0.03	38.	99.9% as a decimal	0.999
17.	3% as a fraction	$\frac{3}{100}$	39.	9.9% as a decimal	0.099
18.	6% as a fraction	$\frac{3}{50}$	40.	0.9% as a decimal	0.009
19.	60% as a fraction	$\frac{3}{5}$	41.	$\frac{4}{9}$ as a percent	$44\frac{4}{9}\%$
20.	30% as a fraction	$\frac{3}{10}$	42.	$\frac{5}{9}$ as a percent	$55\frac{5}{9}\%$
21.	45% as a fraction	$\frac{9}{20}$	43.	$\frac{2}{3}$ as a percent	$66\frac{2}{3}\%$
22.	15% as a fraction	$\frac{3}{20}$	44.	$\frac{1}{6}$ as a percent	$16\frac{2}{3}\%$

Lesson 2: Part of a Whole as Percent

Student Outcomes

- Students understand that the whole is 100% and use the formula $Part = Percent \times Whole$ to problem-solve when given two terms out of three from the part, whole, and percent.
- Students solve word problems involving percent using expressions, equations, and numeric and visual models.

Lesson Notes

This lesson serves as an introduction to general percent problems by considering problems of which a part of a whole is represented as a percent of the whole. Students solve percent problems using visual models and proportional reasoning then make connections to solving percent problems using numeric and algebraic methods. This lesson focuses on the relationship: $Part = Percent \times Whole$.

Classwork

Opening (2 minutes)

One of the challenges students face when solving word problems involving percents is deciding which of the given quantities represents the whole unit and which represents the part of that whole unit. Discuss with the students how the value of a nickel coin ($0.05) compares to the value of a dollar ($1.00) using percents.

- As a percent, how does the value of a nickel coin compare to the value of a dollar?
    - *A dollar is* 100 *cents; therefore, the quantity* 100 *cents is* 100% *of a dollar. A nickel coin has a value of* 5 *cents, which is* 5 *of* 100 *cents, or* $\frac{5}{100}$ = 5% *of a dollar.*
- Part-of-a-whole percent problems involve:
    - *A comparison of generic numbers (e.g.,* 25% *of* 12 *is* 3*) or;*
    - *A comparison of a quantity that is a part of another quantity (e.g., the number of boys in a classroom **is part of the** total number of students in the classroom).*
- The number or quantity that another number or quantity **is being compared to** is called the **whole**. The number or quantity that is **compared to the whole** is called the **part** because it is *part* (or a piece) of the whole quantity.
- In our comparison of the value of a nickel coin to the value of a dollar, which quantity is considered the part and which is considered the whole? Explain your answer.
    - *The value of the nickel coin is the part because it is being compared to the value of the whole dollar. The dollar represents the whole because the value of the nickel coin is being compared to the value of the dollar.*

Opening Exercise (4 minutes)

Part (a) of the Opening Exercise asks students to practice identifying the whole in given percent scenarios. In part (b), students are presented with three different approaches to a given scenario but need to make sense of each approach to identify the part, the whole, and the percent.

Opening Exercise

a.   What is the whole unit in each scenario?

Scenario	Whole Unit
15 is what percent of 90?	*The number* 90
What number is 10% of 56?	*The number* 56
90% of a number is 180.	*The unknown number*
A bag of candy contains 300 pieces, and 25% of the pieces in the bag are red.	*The* 300 *pieces of candy*
Seventy percent (70%) of the students earned a B on the test.	*All the students in the class*
The 20 girls in the class represented 55% of the students in the class.	*All the students in the class*

After students complete part (a) with a partner, ask the following question:

- How did you decide on the whole unit in each of the given scenarios?

  □   *In each case we looked for the number or quantity that another number or quantity was being compared to.*

---

b.   Read each problem and complete the table to record what you know.

Problem	Part	Percent	Whole
40% of the students on the field trip love the museum. If there are 20 students on the field trip, how many love the museum?	?	40%	20 students
40% of the students on the field trip love the museum. If 20 students love the museum, how many are on the field trip?	20 students	40%	?
20 students on the field trip love the museum. If there are 40 students on the field trip, what percent love the museum?	20 students	?	40 students

---

When students complete part (b), encourage them to share how they decided which number in the problem represents the whole and which represents the part.

Example 1 (5 minutes): Visual Approaches to Finding a Part, Given a Percent of the Whole

Present the following problem to students. Show how to solve the problem using visual models then generalize a numeric method through discussion. Have students record each method in their student materials.

Example 1: Visual Approaches to Finding a Part, Given a Percent of the Whole

In Ty's math class, 20% of students earned an A on a test. If there were 30 students in the class, how many got an A?

- Is 30 the whole unit or part of the whole?
  - *It is the whole unit; the number of students that earned an A on the test is compared to the total number of students in the class.*
- What percentage of Ty's class does the quantity "30 students" represent?
  - *100% of Ty's class.*

Solve the problem first using a tape diagram.

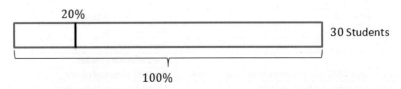

> **Scaffolding:**
> Some students may recognize that there are five intervals of 20% in the tape diagram and want to divide 30 students into 5 groups. That is okay! However, if students do not immediately recognize this, do not force it upon them. Further practice scaffolds this shortcut while also supporting primary understanding of how the percent problems work.

- 30 students make up 100% of the class. Let's divide the 100% into 100 slices of 1%, and also divide the quantity of 30 students into 100 slices. What number of students does each 1% correspond to?
  - $\frac{30}{100} = 0.3$; *0.3 of a student represents 1% of Ty's class.*
- If this is 1% of Ty's class, then how do we find 20% of Ty's class?
  - *(1%) × 20 = 20% so we can multiply (0.3) × 20 = 6; 6 students are 20% of Ty's class, therefore 6 students got an A on the test.*

Revisit the problem using a double number line.

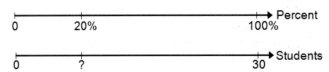

- 30 students represent the whole class, so 30 aligns with 100%. There are 100 intervals of 1% on the percent number line. What number of students does each 1% correspond to?
  - $\frac{30}{100} = 0.3$; *0.3 of a student represents 1% of Ty's class.*
- To help us keep track of quantities and their corresponding percents, we can use arrows to show the correspondences in our sequences of reasoning:

$$\div 100 \overset{\displaystyle 30 \to 100\%}{\underset{\displaystyle 0.3 \to 1\%}{}} \div 100$$

- If this is 1% of Ty's class, how do we find 20% of Ty's class?
  - *Multiply by 20; 0.3 · 20 = 6; 6 students are 20% of Ty's class, so 6 students got an A on the test.*

$$\times 20 \overset{\displaystyle 0.3 \to 1\%}{\underset{\displaystyle 6 \to 20\%}{}} \times 20$$

- What similarities do you notice in each of these visual models?
  - *In both models, 30 corresponds with the 100% and we divided 30 by 100 to get the number of students that correspond with 1%, and then multiplied that by 20 to get the number of students that correspond with 20%.*

Exercise 1 (3 minutes)

Students use visual methods to solve a problem similar to Example 1. After completing the exercise, initiate a discussion about the similarities of the problems and generalize a numeric approach to the problems. This numeric approach will be used to generalize an algebraic equation that can be used in solving percent problems.

Exercise 1

In Ty's art class, 12% of the Flag Day art projects received a perfect score. There were 25 art projects turned in by Ty's class. How many of the art projects earned a perfect score? (Identify the whole.)

The whole is the number of art projects turned in by Ty's class.

$\frac{25}{100} = 0.25; \ 0.25 \cdot 12 = 3; \ 12\%$ *of 25 is 3, so 3 art projects in Ty's class received a perfect score.*

Discussion (2 minutes)

- What similarities do you recognize in Example 1 and Exercise 1?
  - *In each case the whole corresponded with 100% and dividing the whole by 100 resulted in 1% of the whole. Multiplying this number by the percent resulted in the part.*
- Describe and show how the process seen in the visual models can be generalized into a numeric approach?
  - *Divide the whole by 100 to get 1%, and then multiply by the percent needed.*
  - *Whole → 100%.*

Example 1

$$\div 100 \begin{cases} 30 \to 100\% \\ \frac{30}{100} \to 1\% \\ \times 20 \end{cases} \div 100$$
$$\times 20 \begin{cases} \\ 20\left(\frac{30}{100}\right) \to 20\% \\ 6 \to 20\% \end{cases} \times 20$$

Exercise 1

$$\div 100 \begin{cases} 25 \to 100\% \\ \frac{25}{100} \to 1\% \\ \times 20 \end{cases} \div 100$$
$$\times 20 \begin{cases} \\ 12\left(\frac{25}{100}\right) \to 12\% \\ 3 \to 12\% \end{cases} \times 20$$

Example 2 (3 minutes): A Numeric Approach to Finding a Part, Given a Percent of the Whole

Present the following problem to students. Have them guide you through solving the problem using the arithmetic method from the previous discussion. When complete, generalize an arithmetic method through further discussion.

Example 2: A Numeric Approach to Finding a Part, Given a Percent of the Whole

In Ty's English class, 70% of the students completed an essay by the due date. There are 30 students in Ty's English class. How many completed the essay by the due date?

- First, identify the whole quantity in the problem.
  - *The number of students that completed the essay by the due date is being compared to the total number of students in Ty's class, so the total number of students in the class is the whole.*

$whole \rightarrow 100\%$

$30 \rightarrow 100\%$

$\dfrac{30}{100} \rightarrow 1\%$

$70 \cdot \dfrac{30}{100} \rightarrow 70\%$

$21 \rightarrow 70\%$

70% of 30 is 21, so 21 of the students in Ty's English class completed their essays on time.

Discussion (2 minutes)

This discussion is an extension of Example 2 and serves as a bridge to Example 3.

- Is the expression $\dfrac{70}{100} \cdot 30$ equivalent to $70 \cdot \dfrac{30}{100}$ from the steps above? Why or why not?
  - *The expressions are equivalent by the any order, any grouping property of multiplication.*
- What does $\dfrac{70}{100}$ represent? What does 30 represent? What does their product represent?
  - $\dfrac{70}{100} = 70\%$, *30 represents the whole, and their product (21) represents the part, or 70% of the students in Ty's English class.*
- Write a true multiplication sentence relating the part (21), the whole (30), and the percent ($\dfrac{70}{100}$) in this problem?
  - $21 = \dfrac{70}{100} \cdot (30)$
- Translate your sentence into words. Is the sentence valid?
  - *Twenty-one is seventy percent of thirty. Yes the sentence is valid because 21 students represent 70% of the 30 students in Ty's English class.*
- Generalize the terms in your multiplication sentence by writing what each term represents.
  - $Part = Percent \times Whole$

MP.7

Example 3 (4 minutes): An Algebraic Approach to Finding a Part, Given a Percent of the Whole

In percent problems, the percent equation ($Part = Percent \times Whole$) can be used to solve the problem when given two of its three terms. To solve a percent word problem, first identify the whole quantity in the problem, and then the part and percent. Use a letter (variable) to represent the term whose value is unknown.

Example 3: An Algebraic Approach to Finding a Part, Given a Percent of the Whole

A bag of candy contains 300 pieces of which 28% are red. How many pieces are red?

Which quantity represents the whole?

The total number of candies in the bag, 300, is the whole because the number of red candies is being compared to it.

Which of the terms in the percent equation is unknown? Define a letter (variable) to represent the unknown quantity.

We do not know the part, the number of red candies in the bag. Let r represent the number of red candies in the bag.

Write an expression using the percent and the whole to represent the number of pieces of red candy.

$\frac{28}{100} \cdot (300)$ *or* $0.28 \cdot (300)$ *is the amount of red candy since the number of red candies is* 28% *of the* 300 *pieces of candy in the bag.*

Write and solve an equation to find the unknown quantity.

$Part = Percent \times Whole$

$r = \frac{28}{100} \cdot (300)$

$r = 28 \cdot 3$

$r = 84$

There are 84 *red pieces of candy in the bag.*

Exercise 2 (4 minutes)

This exercise is a continuation of Example 3.

Exercise 2

A bag of candy contains 300 pieces of which 28% are red. How many pieces are *NOT* red?

    a.   Write an equation to represent the number of pieces that are not red, n.

$$Part = Percent \times Whole$$
$$n = (100\% - 28\%)(300)$$

    b.   Use your equation to find the number of pieces of candy that are not red.

If 28% *of the candies are red, then the difference of* 100% *and* 28% *must be candies that are not red.*

$$n = (100\% - 28\%)(300)$$
$$n = (72\%)(300)$$
$$n = \frac{72}{100}(300)$$
$$n = 72 \cdot 3$$
$$n = 216$$

There are 216 *pieces of candy in the bag that are not red.*

    c.   Jah-Lil told his math teacher that he could use the answer from part (b) and mental math to find the number of pieces of candy that are not red. Explain what Jah-Lil meant by that.

He meant that once you know there are 84 *red pieces of candy, if there are* 300 *pieces of candy in the bag, you just subtract* 84 *from* 300, *to know that* 216 *pieces of candy are not red.*

> **Note to teacher:**
>
> Students saw in Module 3 that we can find a solution to a formula, or algebraic equation, by using the properties of operations and if-then moves to rewrite the expressions in an equation in a form in which a solution can be easily seen. Examples 4 and 5 use the algebraic formula $Part = Percent \times Whole$ to solve percent word problems where they are given two of the three terms: part, percent, and whole.

Example 4 (5 minutes): Comparing Part of a Whole to the Whole with the Percent Formula

Students use the percent formula and algebraic reasoning to solve a percent problem in which they are given the part and the percent.

Example 4: Comparing Part of a Whole to the Whole with the Percent Formula

Zoey inflated 24 balloons for decorations at the middle school dance. If Zoey inflated 15% of the balloons that are inflated for the dance, how many balloons are there in total? Solve the problem using the percent formula, and verify your answer using a visual model.

- What is the whole quantity? How do you know?
  - *The total number of balloons is the whole quantity because the number of balloons that Zoey inflated is compared to the total number of balloons for the dance.*
- What do the 24 balloons represent?
  - *24 balloons are part of the total number of balloons for the dance.*
- Write the percent formula and determine which term is unknown.

$Part = Percent \times Whole$; *The part is 24 balloons, and the percent is 15%, so let t represent the unknown total number of balloons.*

$$24 = \frac{15}{100}t$$

If $a = b$, then $ac = bc$

$$\frac{100}{15}(24) = \frac{100}{15}\left(\frac{15}{100}\right)t$$

Multiplicative Inverse

$$\frac{2400}{15} = 1t$$

Multiplicative Identity property of 1 and equivalent fractions

$$160 = t$$

The total number of balloons to be inflated for the dance was 160 balloons.

$$15\% \rightarrow 24$$

$$1\% \rightarrow \frac{24}{15}$$

$$100\% \rightarrow \frac{24}{15} \cdot 100$$

We want the quantity that corresponds with 100%, so first we find 1%.*

$$100\% \rightarrow \frac{24}{3} \cdot 20 = 160$$

*May also find 5% as is shown in the tape diagram above.

- Is the solution from the equation consistent with the visual and numeric solution?
  - *Yes!*

Example 5 (5 minutes): Finding the Whole given a Part of the Whole and the Corresponding Percent

Students use the percent formula and algebraic reasoning to solve a percent problem in which they are given the part and the whole.

Example 5

Haley is making admission tickets to the middle school dance. So far she has made 112 tickets, and her plan is to make 320 tickets. What percent of the admission tickets has Haley produced so far? Solve the problem using the percent formula, and verify your answer using a visual model.

- What is the whole quantity? How do you know?
  - *The total number of admission tickets, 320, is the whole quantity because the number of tickets that Haley has already made is compared to the total number of tickets that she needs to make.*
- What does the quantity "112 tickets" represent?
  - *112 tickets is part of the total number of tickets for the dance.*
- Write the percent formula and determine which term is unknown.

$Part = Percent \times Whole$; **The part is 112 tickets, and the whole is 320 tickets, so let p represent the unknown percent.**

$112 = p(320)$ 　　　　　　　　　　*If $a = b$, then $ac = bc$*

$112 \cdot \dfrac{1}{320} = p(320) \cdot \dfrac{1}{320}$ 　　　　*Multiplicative Inverse*

$\dfrac{112}{320} = p(1)$ 　　　　　　　　*Multiplicative Identity property of 1*

$\dfrac{7}{20} = p$

$0.35 = p$ 　　　　　　$0.35 = \dfrac{35}{100} = 35\%$**, so Haley has made 35% of the tickets for the dance.**

0%	?%	100%
0	112	320

We need to know the percent that corresponds with 112, so first we find the percent that corresponds with 1 ticket.

$320 \rightarrow 100\%$

$1 \rightarrow \left(\dfrac{100}{320}\right)\%$

$112 \rightarrow 112 \cdot \left(\dfrac{100}{320}\right)\%$

$112 \rightarrow 112 \cdot \left(\dfrac{5}{16}\right)\%$

$112 \rightarrow 7 \cdot (5)\% = 35\%$

- Is the solution from the equation consistent with the visual and numeric solution?
  - *Yes!*

Closing (2 minutes)

- What formula can we use to relate the part, the whole, and the percent of the whole? Translate the formula into words.

  □ *$Part = Percent \times Whole$. The part is some percent of the whole.*

- What are the advantages of using an algebraic representation to solve percent problems?

  □ *If you can identify the whole, part, and percent, the algebraic approach is very fast and efficient.*

- Explain how to use a visual model and an equation to find the total number of calories from sugar in a candy bar if 75% of its 200 calories is from sugar.

  □ *Use a double number line or tape diagram. The whole (total calories) corresponds with 100%. 200 calories divided into 100 intervals show that every 1% will be 2 calories. That means there are 150 calories from sugar in the candy bar.*

Lesson Summary

- **Visual models or numeric methods can be used to solve percent problems.**
- **Equations can be used to solve percent problems using the basic equation:**

$$Part = Percent \times Whole.$$

Exit Ticket (4 minutes)

Note to the teacher: Students using the visual or numeric approaches for problems in the problem set do not necessarily need to find 1% first. Alternatively, if they recognize that they can instead find 4%, 5%, 10%, 20%, or other factors of 100%, then they can multiply by the appropriate factor to obtain 100%.

Name _____   Date _____

Lesson 2: Part of a Whole as Percent

Exit Ticket

1. On a recent survey, 60% of those surveyed indicated that they preferred walking to running.

    a. If 540 people preferred walking, how many people were surveyed?

    b. How many people preferred running?

2. Which is greater: 25% of 15 or 15% of 25? Explain your reasoning using algebraic representations or visual models.

Exit Ticket Sample Solutions

1. On a recent survey, 60% of those surveyed indicated that they preferred walking to running.

    a. If 540 people preferred walking, how many people were surveyed?

    Let n represent the number of people surveyed.

    $0.60n$ *is the number of people who preferred walking.*

    Since 540 *people preferred walking,*

    $0.60n = 540$

    $$n = \frac{540}{0.6} = \frac{5400}{6} = 900$$

    900 *people were surveyed.*

    b. How many people preferred running?

    Subtract 540 *from* 900.

    $900 - 540 = 360$

    360 *people preferred running.*

2. Which is greater: 25% of 15 or 15% of 25? Explain your reasoning using algebraic representations or visual models.

    They are the same.

    $$0.25 \times 15 = \frac{25}{100} \times 15 = 3.75$$

    $$0.15 \times 25 = \frac{15}{100} \times 25 = 3.75$$

    Also, you can see they are the same without actually computing the product because of any order, any grouping of multiplication.

    $$\frac{25}{100} \times 15 = 25 \times \frac{1}{100} \times 15 = 25 \times \frac{15}{100}$$

Problem Set Sample Solutions

Students should be encouraged to solve these problems using an algebraic approach.

1. Represent each situation using an equation. Check your answer with a visual model or numeric method.

    a. What number is 40% of 90?

    $n = 0.40(90)$
    $n = 36$

    b. What number is 45% of 90?

    $n = 0.45(90)$
    $n = 40.5$

c.   27 is 30% of what number?

$$27 = 0.3n$$
$$\frac{27}{0.3} = 1n$$
$$90 = n$$

  d.   18 is 30% of what number?

$$0.30n = 18$$
$$1n = \frac{18}{0.3}$$
$$n = 60$$

  e.   25.5 is what percent of 85?

$$25.5 = p(85)$$
$$\frac{25.5}{85} = 1p$$
$$0.3 = p$$
$$0.3 = \frac{30}{100} = 30\%$$

  f.   21 is what percent of 60?

$$21 = p(60)$$
$$0.35 = p$$
$$0.35 = \frac{35}{100} = 35\%$$

2.   Forty percent of the students on a field trip love the museum. If there are 20 students on the field trip, how many love the museum?

Let s represent the number of students who love the museum.

$$s = 0.40(20)$$
$$s = 8$$

Eight students love the museum.

3.   Maya spent 40% of her savings to pay for a bicycle that cost her $85.

  a.   How much money was in her savings to begin with?

Let s represent the unknown amount of money in Maya's savings.

$$85 = 0.4s$$
$$212.5 = s$$

Maya originally had $212.50 in her savings.

  b.   How much money does she have left in her savings after buying the bicycle?

$$\$212.50 - \$85 = \$127.5$$

She has $127.5 left in her savings after buying the bicycle.

4.   Curtis threw 15 darts at a dart board. 40% of his darts hit the bull's-eye. How many darts did not hit the bull's-eye?

6 darts hit the bull's-eye. $15 - 6 = 9$, *so 9 darts did not hit the bull's-eye.*

5. A tool set is on sale for $424.15. The original price of the tool set was $499. What percent of the original price is the sale price?

    The sale price is 85% of the original price.

6. Matthew's total points scored in basketball this season were 168 points. He scored 147 of those points in the regular season and the rest were scored in his only playoff game. What percent of his total points did he score in the playoff game?

    The points that Matthew scored in the playoff game were 12.5% of his total points scored in basketball this year.

7. Brad put 10 crickets in his pet lizard's cage. After one day, Brad's lizard had eaten 20% of the crickets he had put in the cage. By the end of the next day, the lizard had eaten 25% of the remaining crickets. How many crickets were left in the cage at the end of the second day?

    Day 1:

    $n = 0.2(10)$
    $n = 2$ *At the end of the first day, Brad's lizard had eaten 2 of the crickets.*

    Day 2:
    $n = 0.75(10 - 2)$
    $n = 0.75(8)$
    $n = 6$ *At the end of the second day, Brad's lizard had eaten a total of 4 crickets leaving 6 crickets in the cage.*

8. A furnace used 40% of the fuel in its tank in the month of March, then used 25% of the remaining fuel in the month of April. At the beginning of March, there were 240 gallons of fuel in the tank. How much fuel (in gallons) was left at the end of April?

    There were 144 gallons of fuel remaining in the tank at the end of March and 108 gallons of fuel remaining at the end of April.

9. In Lewis County, there were 2,277 student athletes competing in spring sports in 2014. That was 110% of the number from 2013, which was 90% of the number from the year before. How many student athletes signed up for a spring sport in 2012?

    There were 2,070 students competing in spring sports in 2013 and 2,300 students in 2012.

10. Write a real world word problem that could be modeled by the equation below. Identify the elements of the percent equation and where they appear in your word problem, and then solve the problem.

    $57.5 = p(250)$

    Greig is buying sliced almonds for a baking project. According to the scale, his bag contains 57.5 grams of almonds. Greig needs 250 grams of sliced almonds for his project. What percent of his total weight of almonds does Greig currently have?

    The quantity 57.5 represents the part of the almonds that Greig currently has on the scale, the quantity 250 represents the 250 grams of almonds that he plans to purchase, and the variable p represents the unknown percent of the whole quantity that corresponds to the quantity 57.5.

    $$57.5 = p(250)$$
    $$\frac{1}{250}(57.5) = p\left(\frac{1}{250}\right)(250)$$
    $$\frac{57.5}{250} = p(1)$$
    $$0.23 = p$$
    $$0.23 = \frac{23}{100} = 23\%$$

    Greig currently has 23% of the total weight of almonds that he plans to buy.

Lesson 3: Comparing Quantities with Percent

Student Outcomes

- Students use the context of a word problem to determine which of two quantities represents the whole.
- Students understand that the whole is 100% and think of one quantity as a percent of another using the formula $Quantity = Percent \times Whole$ to problem-solve when given two terms out of three from a quantity, whole, and percent.
- When comparing two quantities, students compute percent more or percent less using algebraic, numeric, and visual models.

Lesson Notes

In this lesson, students compare two quantities using a percent. They will build on their understanding of the relationship between the part, whole, and percent. It is important for students to understand that the part in a percent problem may be greater than the whole, especially in problems that compare two disjoint (or separate) quantities (for example, a quantity of dogs versus a quantity of cats). For this reason, the formula $Part = Percent \times Whole$ will be changed to $Quantity = Percent \times Whole$ from this point forward. This wording will work for problems that compare a part to the whole and in problems comparing one quantity to another. Students continue to relate the algebraic model to visual and arithmetic models and come to understand that an algebraic model will always work for any numbers and is often more efficient than constructing a visual model. Students are prompted to consider percent more than a quantity and percent less than a quantity in this lesson as a bridge to percent increase and percent decrease in Lesson 4.

Classwork

Opening Exercises (3 minutes)

Since many of the problems in this lesson represent percents greater than 100, these exercises will review different models that represent percents greater than 100.

> *Scaffolding:*
>
> Some students may recognize that 125% contains exactly 5 regions of 25%. In this case, they would simply multiply $10 \cdot 5 = 50$ to show that the shaded region represents 50 students. This recognition is okay, but allow the students to make this observation for themselves.

Opening Exercise

If each 10×10 unit square represents one whole, then what percent is represented by the shaded region?

    125%

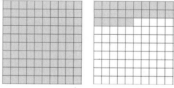

In the model above, 25% represents a quantity of 10 students. How many students does the shaded region represent?

If 25% *represents* 10 *students, then* 1% *represents* $\frac{10}{25}$ *or* $\frac{2}{5}$ *of a student. The shaded region covers* 125 *square units, or* 125%, *so since* $\frac{2}{5} \cdot 125 = 50$, *the shaded region represents* 50 *students.*

Example 1 (20 minutes)

Model Example 1, part (a) with students using a visual model, then shift to numeric and algebraic approaches in parts (b) and (c). To highlight MP.1, give students an opportunity to engage with the parts of Example 1 before modeling with them. Students are equipped to understand the problems based on knowledge of percents. Use scaffolding questions as needed to assist students in their reasoning.

Example 1

a.   The members of a club are making friendship bracelets to sell to raise money. Anna and Emily made 54 bracelets over the weekend. They need to produce 300 bracelets by the end of the week. What percent of the bracelets were they able to produce over the weekend?

- What quantity represents the whole, and how do you know?
    - *The total number of bracelets is the whole because the number of bracelets that Anna and Emily produced is being compared to it.*

It will often be helpful to include a percent number line in visual models to show that 100% corresponds with the whole quantity. This will be used to a greater extent in future lessons.

$300 \rightarrow 100\%$

$1 \rightarrow \dfrac{100}{300}\%$

$54 \rightarrow 54 \cdot \dfrac{100}{300}\%$

$54 \rightarrow 54 \cdot \dfrac{1}{3}\%$

$54 \rightarrow 18\%$ *Anna and Emily were able to produce 18% of the total number of bracelets over the weekend.*

0%   ?%   100%

54

300

- In the previous steps, we included $54 \rightarrow 54 \cdot \dfrac{100}{300}\%$. Is the expression $\dfrac{54}{300} \cdot 100\%$ equivalent to the expression to the right of the arrow? Explain why or why not.
    - *The expressions are equivalent by the any order, any grouping property of multiplication.*

Next, solve the problem using the percent formula. Compare the steps used to solve the equation to the arithmetic steps previously used with the tape diagram.

Quantity = Percent × Whole. Let *p* represent the unknown percent.

$$54 = p(300)$$
$$\frac{1}{300}(54) = \frac{1}{300}(300)p$$
$$\frac{54}{300} = 1p$$
$$0.18 = p$$
$$0.18 = \frac{18}{100} = 18\%$$

Anna and Emily were able to produce 18% of the total bracelets over the weekend.

- What similarities do you observe between the arithmetic method and the algebraic method?
  - *In both cases we divided the part (54) by the whole quantity (300) to get the quotient 0.18.*
  - *In the arithmetic approach we multiplied 0.18 × 100% to obtain the percent, and in the algebraic method we converted 0.18 to a percent by moving the decimal 2 places to the right which is equivalent to multiplying by 100% .*

> **b.** Anna produced 32 bracelets of the 54 bracelets produced by Emily and Anna over the weekend. **Compare the number of bracelets that Emily produced as a percent of those that Anna produced.**

- What is the whole quantity, and how do you know?
  - *The whole quantity is the number of bracelets that Anna produced because the problem asks us to compare the number of bracelets that Emily produced to the number that Anna produced.*
- How does the context of part (b) differ from the context of part (a)?
  - *The whole quantity is not the same. In part (a) the whole quantity was the total number of bracelets to be produced, and in part (b) the whole quantity was the number of bracelets that Anna produced over the weekend.*
  - *In part (a) the number of bracelets that Anna and Emily produced was a part of the whole quantity of bracelets. In part (b) the number of bracelets that Emily produced was NOT part of the whole quantity. The quantities being compared are separate quantities.*
- Why are we able to compare one of these quantities to the other?
  - *Because the quantities are measured using the same unit, the number of bracelets.*

Solve part (b) using both the arithmetic method and the algebraic method.

> **Arithmetic Method:**
>
> $$32 \rightarrow 100\%$$
> $$1 \rightarrow \frac{100}{32}\%$$
> $$22 \rightarrow 22 \cdot \frac{100}{32}\%$$
> $$22 \rightarrow 100 \cdot \frac{22}{32}\%$$
> $$22 \rightarrow 100 \cdot 0.6875\%$$
> $$22 \rightarrow 68.75\%$$
>
> **Algebraic Method:**
>
> $Quantity = Percent \times Whole.$ **Let p represent the unknown percent.**
>
> $$22 = p(32)$$
> $$\frac{1}{32}(22) = \frac{1}{32}(32)p$$
> $$\frac{22}{32} = 1p$$
> $$0.6875 = p$$
> $$0.6875 = 68.75\%$$
>
> **22 bracelets are 68.75% of the number of bracelets that Anna produced. Emily produced 22 bracelets; therefore, she produced 68.75% of the number of bracelets that Anna produced.**

- How does each method compare?
  - *In each case we divided the part by the whole quantity, and then converted the quotient to a percent.*
- Do you prefer one method over another? Why?
  - *Answers will vary.*

Ask student to solve part (c) using either the arithmetic or the algebraic method.

> c.   Compare the number of bracelets that Anna produced as a percent of those that Emily produced.

- What is the whole quantity, and how do you know?
  - *The whole quantity is the number of bracelets that Emily produced over the weekend because the problems asks us to compare the number of bracelets that Anna produced to the number that Emily produced.*
- How do you think this will affect the percent and why?
  - *The percent should be greater than 100% because the part (Anna's 32 bracelets) is greater than the whole (Emily's 22 bracelets).*

MP.2

Arithmetic method:

$22 \rightarrow 100\%$

$1 \rightarrow \dfrac{100}{22}\%$

$32 \rightarrow 32 \cdot \dfrac{100}{22}\%$

$32 \rightarrow 100 \cdot \dfrac{32}{22}\%$

$32 \rightarrow 100 \cdot \dfrac{16}{11}\%$

$32 \rightarrow \dfrac{1600}{11}\%$

$32 \rightarrow 145\dfrac{5}{11}\%$

$32 \rightarrow 145\dfrac{5}{11}\%$

Algebraic method:

$Quantity = Percent \times Whole.$

Let p represent the unknown percent.

$32 = p(22)$

$\dfrac{1}{22}(32) = \dfrac{1}{22}(22)p$

$\dfrac{32}{22} = 1p$

$\dfrac{16}{11} = p$

$1\dfrac{5}{11} = p$

$1\dfrac{5}{11} = 1\dfrac{5}{11} \times 100\%$

$= 145\dfrac{5}{11}\%$

Scaffolding:

- The following progression can help students understand why $1\dfrac{5}{11} = 145\dfrac{5}{11}\%$:

$1\dfrac{5}{11} \cdot 1$ *multiplicative identity*

$1\dfrac{5}{11} \cdot 100\%$ *Since* $100\% = 1$

$\left(1 + \dfrac{5}{11}\right) \cdot 100\%$ *Since* $1 + \dfrac{5}{11} = 1\dfrac{5}{11}$

$1(100\%) + \dfrac{5}{11}(100\%)$ *distributive property*

$100\% + \left(\dfrac{500}{11}\right)\%$

$100\% + 45\dfrac{5}{11}\% = 145\dfrac{5}{11}\%$

32 bracelets are $145\dfrac{5}{11}$% of the number of bracelets that Emily produced. Anna produced 32 bracelets over the weekend, so Anna produced $145\dfrac{5}{11}$% of the number of bracelets that Emily produced.

- What percent more did Anna produce in bracelets than Emily? What percent fewer did Emily produce than Anna? Are these numbers the same? Why?
  - *Anna produced $45\dfrac{5}{11}$% more bracelets than Emily. This is because Anna produced more than Emily did, so her quantity is 100% of Emily's quantity plus an additional $45\dfrac{5}{11}$% more.*
  - *Emily produced 31.25% fewer bracelets than Anna. This is because the difference of what Anna produced and what Emily produced is $100\% - 68.75\% = 31.25\%$.*
  - *The numbers are not the same because in each case the percent is calculated using a different whole quantity.*

Exercise 1 (12 minutes): Fluency Sprint

Students complete two rounds of the Fluency Sprint provided at the end of this lesson (Part, Whole, or Percent). Provide one minute for each round of the sprint exercise. Follow your regular protocol for delivering sprint exercises.

Note to the teacher: The end of this lesson is designed for teacher flexibility. The sprint exercise enriches the students' fluencies with percents and helps them to be more efficient in future work with percents. However, an alternate set of exercises (Exercises 1–4) is included below if the teacher assesses that students need further practice before attempting problems independently.

Alternate Exercises 1–4 (12 minutes)

Have students use an equation for each problem and justify their solution with a visual or numeric model. After 10 minutes, ask students to present their solutions to the class. Compare and contrast different methods and emphasize how the algebraic, numeric, and visual models are related. This also provides an opportunity for differentiation.

Exercises

1. There are 750 students in the 7th grade class and 625 students in the 8th grade class at Kent Middle School.

a. What percent is the 7th grade class of the 8th grade class at Kent Middle School?

The number of 8th graders is the whole amount. Let p represent the percent of 7th graders compared to 8th graders.

$Quantity = Percent \times Whole.$ *Let p represent the unknown percent.*

$$750 = p(625)$$
$$750\left(\frac{1}{625}\right) = p(625)\left(\frac{1}{625}\right)$$
$$1.2 = p$$
$$1.2 = 120\%$$

The number of 7th graders is 120% of the number of 8th graders.

(Teacher may choose to ask what percent more are 7th graders than 8th graders.)

There are 20% more 7th graders than 8th graders.

Alternate solution: There are 125 more 7th graders. $125 = p(625), p = 0.20.$ There are 20% more 7th graders than 8th graders.

b. The principal will have to increase the number of 8th grade teachers next year if the 7th grade enrollment exceeds 110% of the current 8th grade enrollment. Will she need to increase the number of teachers? Explain your reasoning.

The principal will have to increase the number of teachers next year. In part (a), we found out that the 7th grade enrollment was 120%, which is greater than 110%.

---

2. At Kent Middle School, there are 104 students in the band and 80 students in the choir. What percent of the number of students in the choir is the number of students in the band?

The number of students in the choir is the whole. Let b represent the number of students in the band.

Quantity = Percent × Whole. Let p represent the unknown percent.

$$104 = p(80)$$
$$p = 1.3$$
$$1.3 = 130\%$$

The number of students in the band is 130% of the number of students in the choir.

3. At Kent Middle School, breakfast costs $1.25 and lunch costs $3.75. What percent of the cost of lunch is the cost of breakfast?

Quantity = Percent × Whole. Let p represent the unknown percent.

$$1.25 = p(3.75)$$
$$1.25\left(\frac{1}{3.75}\right) = p(3.75)\left(\frac{1}{3.75}\right)$$
$$p = \frac{1.25}{3.75}$$
$$p = \frac{1}{3}$$
$$\frac{1}{3} = \frac{1}{3}(100\%) = 33\frac{1}{3}\%$$

÷ 3 ⟨ $3.75   *lunch*   →   100% ⟩ ÷ 3
      $1.25   *breakfast*   → $33\frac{1}{3}\%$

The cost of breakfast is $33\frac{1}{3}$% of the cost of lunch.

(Teacher may ask students what percent less than the cost of lunch is the cost of breakfast.)

The cost of breakfast is $66\frac{2}{3}$% less than the cost of lunch.

(Teacher may ask what percent more is the cost of lunch than the cost of breakfast.)

Let p represent the percent of lunch to breakfast.

$$3.75 = p(1.25)$$
$$3.75\left(\frac{1}{1.25}\right) = p(1.25)\left(\frac{1}{1.25}\right)$$
$$p = \frac{3.75}{1.25} = 3 = 300\%$$

× 3 ⟨ $1.25   *breakfast*   →   100% ⟩ × 3
      $3.75   *lunch*   →   300%

The cost of lunch is 300% of the cost of breakfast.

4. Describe a real world situation that could be modeled using the equation: $398.4 = 0.83(x)$. Describe how the elements of the equation correspond with the real world quantities in your problem. Then solve your problem.

Word problems will vary.

Sample problem: A new tablet is on sale for 83% of its original sale price. The tablet is currently priced at $398.40. What was the original price of the tablet?

$0.83 = \frac{83}{100} = 83\%$, *so* 0.83 *represents the percent that corresponds with the current price. The current price ($398.40) is part of the original price; therefore, it is represented by* 398.4. *The original price is represented by* x *and is the whole quantity in this problem.*

$$398.4 = 0.83x$$
$$\frac{1}{0.83}(398.4) = \frac{1}{0.83}(0.83)x$$
$$\frac{398.4}{0.83} = 1x$$
$$480 = x$$

The original price of the tablet was $480.

Closing (5 minutes)

- What formula can we use to relate the part, whole, and percent?
  - $Quantity = Percent \times Whole$
- Why did the word "part" change to "quantity" in the percent formula?
  - *When we compare two separate quantities, one quantity is not a part of the other.*
- What are the advantages of using an algebraic representation to solve percent problems?
  - *It can be a quicker way to solve the problem. Sometimes the numbers do not divide evenly, which makes the visual model more complex.*
- Explain how to decide on which quantity in a problem should represent the whole.
  - *You need to focus on identifying the quantity that we are finding a percent "of". That quantity will be the whole in the equation or equal to 100% when you use a visual or arithmetic model.*

Lesson Summary

- Visual models or arithmetic methods can be used to solve problems that compare quantities with percents.
- Equations can be used to solve percent problems using the basic equation:
  $Quantity = Percent \times Whole.$
- "Quantity" in the new percent formula is the equivalent of "part" in the original percent formula.

Exit Ticket (5 minutes)

Name _____   Date _____

Lesson 3: Comparing Quantities with Percent

Exit Ticket

Solve each problem below using at least two different approaches.

1. Jenny's great grandmother is 90 years old. Jenny is 12 years old. What percent of Jenny's great grandmother's age is Jenny's age?

2. Jenny's mom is 36 years old. What percent of Jenny's mother's age is Jenny's great grandmother's age?

Exit Ticket Sample Solutions

Solve each problem below using at least two different approaches.

1. Jenny's great grandmother is 90 years old. Jenny is 12 years old. What percent of Jenny's great grandmother's age is Jenny's age?

Algebraic Solution:

$Quantity = Percent \times Whole$. **Let p represent the unknown percent. Jenny's age is the whole.**

$$12 = p(90)$$
$$12 \cdot \frac{1}{90} = p(90) \cdot \frac{1}{90}$$
$$2 \cdot \frac{1}{15} = p(1)$$
$$\frac{2}{15} = p$$
$$\frac{2}{15} = \frac{2}{15}(100\%) = 13\frac{1}{3}\%$$

Jenny's age is $13\frac{1}{3}\%$ of her great grandmother's age.

Numeric Solution:

$$90 \rightarrow 100\%$$
$$1 \rightarrow \frac{100}{90}\%$$
$$12 \rightarrow \left(12 \cdot \frac{100}{90}\right)\%$$
$$12 \rightarrow \left(100 \cdot \frac{12}{90}\right)\%$$
$$12 \rightarrow 100\left(\frac{2}{15}\right)\%$$
$$12 \rightarrow 20\left(\frac{2}{3}\right)\% = \left(\frac{40}{3}\right)\% = 13\frac{1}{3}\%$$

Alternative Numeric Solution:

$$90 \rightarrow 100\%$$
$$9 \rightarrow 10\%$$
$$3 \rightarrow \frac{10}{3}\%$$
$$12 \rightarrow 4\left(\frac{10}{3}\right)\%$$
$$12 \rightarrow \left(\frac{40}{3}\right)\%$$
$$12 \rightarrow 13\frac{1}{3}\%$$

2. Jenny's mom is 36 years old. What percent of Jenny's mother's age is Jenny's great grandmother's age?

$Quantity = Percent \times Whole$ **Let p represent the unknown percent. Jenny's mother's age is the whole.**

$$90 = p(36)$$
$$90 \cdot \frac{1}{36} = p(36) \cdot \frac{1}{36}$$
$$5 \cdot \frac{1}{2} = p(1)$$
$$2.5 = p$$
$$2.5 = 250\%$$

Jenny's great grandmother's age is 250% of Jenny's mother's age.

Problem Set Sample Solutions

Encourage students to solve these problems using an equation. They can check their work with a visual or arithmetic model if needed. Problem 2, part (e) is a very challenging problem, and most students will likely solve it using arithmetic reasoning rather than an equation.

1. Solve each problem using an equation.

   a. 49.5 is what percent of 33?

   $$49.5 = p(33)$$
   $$p = 1.5$$
   $$1.5 = 150\%$$

   b. 72 is what percent of 180?

   $$72 = p(180)$$
   $$p = 0.4$$
   $$0.4 = 40\%$$

   c. What percent of 80 is 90?

   $$90 = p(80)$$
   $$p = 1.125$$
   $$1.125 = 112.5\%$$

2. This year, Benny is 12 years old and his mom is 48 years old.

   a. What percent of his mom's age is Benny's age?

   Let p represent the percent of Benny's age to his mom's age.

   $$12 = p(48)$$
   $$p = 0.25 = 25\%$$

   Benny's age is 25% of his mom's age.

   b. What percent of Benny's age is his mom's age?

   Let p represent the percent of his mom's age to Benny's age.

   $$48 = p(12)$$
   $$p = 4 = 400\%$$

   Benny's mom's age is 400% of Benny's age.

   c. In two years, what percent of his age will Benny's mom's age be at that time?

   In two years, Benny will be 14 and his mom will be 50.

   Let p represent the percent that Benny's mom's age is of his age.

   $$14 \rightarrow 100\%$$
   $$1 \rightarrow \left(\frac{100}{14}\right)\%$$
   $$50 \rightarrow 50\left(\frac{100}{14}\right)\%$$
   $$50 \rightarrow 25\left(\frac{100}{7}\right)\%$$
   $$50 \rightarrow \left(\frac{2500}{7}\right)\%$$
   $$50 \rightarrow 357\frac{1}{7}\%$$

   His mom's age will be $357\frac{1}{7}\%$ of Benny's age at that time.

d.   In 10 years, what percent will Benny's mom's age be of his age?

In 10 years, Benny will be 22 years old, and his mom will be 58 years old.

Let p represent the percent that Benny's mom's age is of his age.

$$22 \rightarrow 100\%$$
$$1 \rightarrow \left(\frac{100}{22}\right)\%$$
$$58 \rightarrow 58\left(\frac{100}{22}\right)\%$$
$$58 \rightarrow 29\left(\frac{100}{11}\right)\%$$
$$58 \rightarrow \left(\frac{2900}{11}\right)\%$$
$$58 \rightarrow 263\frac{7}{11}\%$$

In ten years, Benny's mom's age will be $263\frac{7}{11}\%$ of Benny's age at that time.

e.   In how many years will Benny be 50% of his mom's age?

Benny will be 50% of his mom's age when she is 100% of his age (or twice his age). Benny and his mom are always 36 years apart. When Benny is 36, his mom will be 72, and he will be 50% of her age. So, in 24 years, Benny will be 50% of his mom's age.

f.   As Benny and his mom get older, Benny thinks they are getting closer in age. Do you agree or disagree? Explain your reasoning.

Student responses will vary. Some students might argue that they are not getting closer since they are always 36 years apart. However, if you compare the percents, you can see that Benny's age is getting closer to 100% of his mom's age, even though their ages are not getting any closer.

3.   This year, Benny is 12 years old. His brother Lenny's age is 175% of Benny's age. How old is Lenny?

Let L represent Lenny's age. Benny's age is the whole.

$$L = 1.75(12)$$
$$L = 21$$

4.   When Benny's sister Penny is 24, Benny's age will be 125% of her age.
   a.   How old will Benny be then?
   Let b represent Benny's age when Penny is 24.

$$b = 1.25(24)$$
$$b = 30$$

   b.   If Benny is 12 years old now, how old is Penny now? Explain your reasoning.
   Penny is 6 years younger than Benny. If Benny is 12 now, then Penny is 6.

5.   Benny's age is currently 200% of his sister Jenny's age. What percent of Benny's age will Jenny's age be in 4 years?

If Benny is 200% of Jenny's age, then he is twice her age, and she is half of his age. Half of 12 is 6. Jenny is currently 6 years old. In 4 years, Jenny will be 10 years old, and Benny will be 16 years old.

$Quantity = Percent \times Whole$. Let p represent the unknown percent. Benny's age is the whole.

$$10 = p(16)$$
$$p = 0.625 = 62.5\%$$

In 4 years, Jenny will be 62.5% of Benny's age.

6. At the animal shelter there were 15 dogs, 12 cats, 3 snakes, and 5 parakeets.

    a. What percent of the number of cats is the number of dogs?

    $\frac{15}{12} = 1.25.$ *That is* $125\%.$ *The number of dogs is* 125% *the number of cats.*

    b. What percent of the number of cats is the number of snakes?

    $\frac{3}{12} = \frac{1}{4} = 0.25.$ *There are* 25% *as many snakes as cats.*

    c. What percent less parakeets are there than dogs?

    $\frac{5}{15} = \frac{1}{3}.$ *That is* $33\frac{1}{3}\%.$ *There are* $66\frac{1}{3}\%$ *less parakeets than dogs.*

    d. Which animal has 80% of the number of another animal?

    $\frac{12}{15} = 0.8.$ *The number of cats is* 80% *the number of dogs.*

    e. Which animal makes up approximately 14% of the animals in the shelter?

    $Quantity = Percent \times Whole.$ *The total number of animals is the whole.*

    $$q = 0.14(35)$$
    $$q = 4.9$$

    The quantity closest to 4.9 *is* $5,$ *the number of parakeets.*

7. Is 2 hours and 30 minutes more or less than 10% of a day? Explain your answer.

    2 hr. 30 min. $\rightarrow$ *2.5 hr.; 24 hours are a whole day and represent the whole quantity in this problem.*

    10% of 24 hours is 2.4 hours.

    2.5 > 2.4, so 2 hours and 30 minutes is more than 10% of a day.

8. A club's membership increased from 25 to 30 members.

    a. Express the new membership as a percent of the old membership.

    The old membership is the whole.

    $Quantity = Percent \times Whole$. *Let p represent the unknown percent.*

    $$30 = p(25)$$
    $$p = 1.2 = 120\%$$

    The new membership is 120% *of the old membership.*

b.   **Express the old membership as a percent of the new membership.**

The new membership is the whole.

$$30 \rightarrow 100\%$$
$$1 \rightarrow \frac{100}{30}\%$$
$$25 \rightarrow 25 \cdot \frac{100}{30}\%$$
$$25 \rightarrow 5 \cdot \frac{100}{6}\%$$
$$25 \rightarrow \frac{500}{6}\% = 83\frac{1}{3}\%$$

The old membership is $83\frac{1}{3}\%$ of the new membership.

9.   **The number of boys in a school is 120% the number of girls at the school.**

    a.   **Find the number of boys if there are 320 girls.**

The number of girls is the whole.

$Quantity = Percent \times Whole$. Let b represent the unknown number of boys at the school.

$$b = 1.2(320)$$
$$b = 384$$

If there are 320 girls, then there are 384 boys at the school.

    b.   **Find the number of girls if there are 360 boys.**

The number of girls is still the whole.

$Quantity = Percent \times Whole$. Let g represent the unknown number of girls at the school.

$$360 = 1.2(g)$$
$$g = 300$$

If there are 360 boys at the school, then there are 300 girls.

10.   **The price of a bicycle was increased from \$300 to \$450.**

    a.   **What percent of the original price is the increased price?**

The original price is the whole.

$Quantity = Percent \times Whole$. Let p represent the unknown percent.

$$450 = p(300)$$
$$p = 1.5$$
$$1.5 = \frac{150}{100} = 150\%$$

The increased price is 150% of the original price.

b.   **What percent of the increased price is the original price?**

       The increased price is the whole.

$$450 \to 100\%$$
$$1 \to \left(\frac{100}{450}\right)\%$$
$$300 \to 300\left(\frac{100}{450}\right)\%$$
$$300 \to 2\left(\frac{100}{3}\right)\%$$
$$300 \to \frac{200}{3}\% = 66\frac{2}{3}\%$$

       The original price is $66\frac{2}{3}\%$ of the increased price.

11.   The population of Appleton is 175% of the population of Cherryton.

    a.   Find the population in Appleton if the population in Cherryton is $4,000$ people.

       The population of Cherryton is the whole.

       $Quantity = Percent \times Whole$. Let a represent the unknown population of Appleton.

       $a = 1.75(4,000)$
       $a = 7,000$

       If the population of Cherryton is $4,000$ people, the the population of Appleton is $7,000$ people.

    b.   Find the population in Cherryton if the population in Appleton is $10,500$ people.

       The population of Cherryton is still the whole.

       $Quantity = Percent \times Whole$. Let c represent the unknown population of Cherryton.

$$10,500 = 1.75c$$
$$c = 6000$$

       If the population of Appleton is $10,500$ people, then the population of Cherryton is $6,000$ people.

12. A statistics class collected data regarding the number of boys and the number of girls in each classroom at their school during homeroom. Some of their results are shown in the table below:

a. Complete the blank cells of the table using your knowledge about percent.

Number of Boys (x)	Number of Girls (y)	Number of Girls as a Percent of the Number of Boys
10	5	50%
4	1	25%
18	12	$66\frac{2}{3}\%$
5	10	200%
4	2	50%
20	18	90%
4	10	250%
10	6	60%
11	22	200%
15	5	$33\frac{1}{3}\%$
15	3	20%
20	15	75%
6	18	300%
25	10	40%
10	11	110%
20	2	10%
16	12	75%
14	7	50%
3	6	200%
12	10	$83\frac{1}{3}\%$

b. Using a coordinate plane and grid paper, locate and label the points representing the ordered pairs (x, y).

See graph to the right.

c. Locate all points on the graph that would represent classrooms in which the number of girls y is 100% of the number of boys x. Describe the pattern that these points make.

The points lie on a line that includes the origin; therefore, it is a proportional relationship.

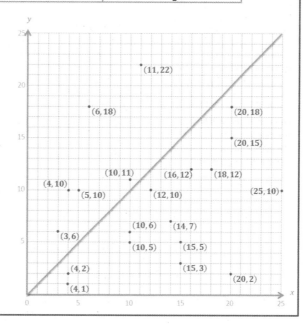

d.   Which points represent the classrooms in which the number of girls is greater than 100% of the number of boys? Which points represent the classrooms in which the number of girls is less than 100% of the number of boys? Describe the locations of the points in relation to the points in part (c).

All points where $y > x$ are above the line and represent classrooms where the number of girls is greater than 100% of the number of boys. All points where $y < x$ are below the line and represent classrooms where the number of girls is less than 100% of the boys.

e.   Find three ordered pairs from your table representing classrooms where the number of girls is the same percent of the number of boys. Do these points represent a proportional relationship? Explain your reasoning?

There are two sets of points that satisfy this question:

$\{(3, 6), (5, 10), and (11, 22)\}$: The points do represent a proportional relationship because there is a constant of proportionality $k = \frac{y}{x} = 2$.

$\{(4, 2), (10, 5), and (14, 7)\}$: The points do represent a proportional relationship because there is a constant of proportionality $k = \frac{y}{x} = \frac{1}{2}$.

f.   Show the relationship(s) from part (e) on the graph, and label them with the corresponding equation(s).

g.   What is the constant of proportionality in your equation(s), and what does it tell us about the number of girls and the number of boys at each point on the graph that represents it? What does the constant of proportionality represent in the table in part (a)?

In the equation $y = 2x$, the constant of proportionality is 2, and it tells us that the number of girls will be twice the number of boys or 200% of the number of boys as shown in the table in part (a).

In the equation $y = \frac{1}{2}x$, the constant of proportionality is $\frac{1}{2}$, and it tells us that the number of girls will be half the number of boys or 50% of the number of boys as shown in the table in part (a).

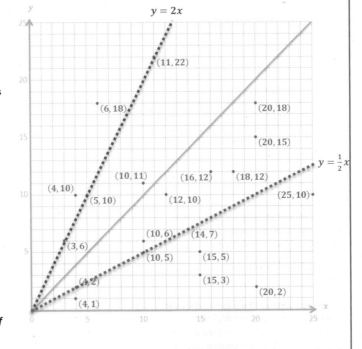

Sprint: Part, Whole, or Percent – Round 1

Number Correct: _____

Directions: Find each missing value.

1.	1% of 100 is?	
2.	2% of 100 is?	
3.	3% of 100 is?	
4.	4% of 100 is?	
5.	5% of 100 is?	
6.	9% of 100 is?	
7.	10% of 100 is?	
8.	10% of 200 is?	
9.	10% of 300 is?	
10.	10% of 500 is?	
11.	10% of 550 is?	
12.	10% of 570 is?	
13.	10% of 470 is?	
14.	10% of 170 is?	
15.	10% of 70 is?	
16.	10% of 40 is?	
17.	10% of 20 is?	
18.	10% of 25 is?	
19.	10% of 35 is?	
20.	10% of 36 is?	
21.	10% of 37 is?	
22.	10% of 37.5 is?	

23.	10% of 22 is?	
24.	20% of 22 is?	
25.	30% of 22 is?	
26.	50% of 22 is?	
27.	25% of 22 is?	
28.	75% of 22 is?	
29.	80% of 22 is?	
30.	85% of 22 is?	
31.	90% of 22 is?	
32.	95% of 22 is?	
33.	5% of 22 is?	
34.	15% of 80 is?	
35.	15% of 60 is?	
36.	15% of 40 is?	
37.	30% of 40 is?	
38.	30% of 70 is?	
39.	30% of 60 is?	
40.	45% of 80 is?	
41.	45% of 120 is?	
42.	120% of 40 is?	
43.	120% of 50 is?	
44.	120% of 55 is?	

Sprint: Part, Whole, or Percent – Round 1 **[KEY]**

Directions: Find each missing value.

1.	1% of 100 is?	1	23.	10% of 22 is?	2.2
2.	2% of 100 is?	2	24.	20% of 22 is?	4.4
3.	3% of 100 is?	3	25.	30% of 22 is?	6.6
4.	4% of 100 is?	4	26.	50% of 22 is?	11
5.	5% of 100 is?	5	27.	25% of 22 is?	5.5
6.	9% of 100 is?	9	28.	75% of 22 is?	16.5
7.	10% of 100 is?	10	29.	80% of 22 is?	17.6
8.	10% of 200 is?	20	30.	85% of 22 is?	18.7
9.	10% of 300 is?	30	31.	90% of 22 is?	19.8
10.	10% of 500 is?	50	32.	95% of 22 is?	20.9
11.	10% of 550 is?	55	33.	5% of 22 is?	1.1
12.	10% of 570 is?	57	34.	15% of 80 is?	12
13.	10% of 470 is?	47	35.	15% of 60 is?	9
14.	10% of 170 is?	17	36.	15% of 40 is?	6
15.	10% of 70 is?	7	37.	30% of 40 is?	12
16.	10% of 40 is?	4	38.	30% of 70 is?	21
17.	10% of 20 is?	2	39.	30% of 60 is?	18
18.	10% of 25 is?	2.5	40.	45% of 80 is?	36
19.	10% of 35 is?	3.5	41.	45% of 120 is?	54
20.	10% of 36 is?	3.6	42.	120% of 40 is?	48
21.	10% of 37 is?	3.7	43.	120% of 50 is?	60
22.	10% of 37.5 is?	3.75	44.	120% of 55 is?	66

Sprint: Part, Whole, or Percent – Round 2

Number Correct: _____

Directions: Find each missing value.

Improvement: _____

1.	20% of 100 is?	
2.	21% of 100 is?	
3.	22% of 100 is?	
4.	23% of 100 is?	
5.	25% of 100 is?	
6.	25% of 200 is?	
7.	25% of 300 is?	
8.	25% of 400 is?	
9.	25% of 4000 is?	
10.	50% of 4000 is?	
11.	10% of 4000 is?	
12.	10% of 4700 is?	
13.	10% of 4600 is?	
14.	10% of 4630 is?	
15.	10% of 463 is?	
16.	10% of 46.3 is?	
17.	10% of 18 is?	
18.	10% of 24 is?	
19.	10% of 3.63 is?	
20.	10% of 0.336 is?	
21.	10% of 37 is?	
22.	10% of 37.5 is?	

23.	10% of 4 is?	
24.	20% of 4 is?	
25.	30% of 4 is?	
26.	50% of 4 is?	
27.	25% of 4 is?	
28.	75% of 4 is?	
29.	80% of 4 is?	
30.	85% of 4 is?	
31.	90% of 4 is?	
32.	95% of 4 is?	
33.	5% of 4 is?	
34.	15% of 40 is?	
35.	15% of 30 is?	
36.	15% of 20 is?	
37.	30% of 20 is?	
38.	30% of 50 is?	
39.	30% of 90 is?	
40.	45% of 90 is?	
41.	90% of 120 is?	
42.	125% of 40 is?	
43.	125% of 50 is?	
44.	120% of 60 is?	

Sprint: Part, Whole, or Percent – Round 2 [KEY]

Directions: Find each missing value.

1.	20% of 100 is?	20		23.	10% of 4 is?	0.4
2.	21% of 100 is?	21		24.	20% of 4 is?	0.8
3.	22% of 100 is?	22		25.	30% of 4 is?	1.2
4.	23% of 100 is?	23		26.	50% of 4 is?	2
5.	25% of 100 is?	25		27.	25% of 4 is?	1
6.	25% of 200 is?	50		28.	75% of 4 is?	3
7.	25% of 300 is?	75		29.	80% of 4 is?	3.2
8.	25% of 400 is?	100		30.	85% of 4 is?	3.4
9.	25% of 4000 is?	1000		31.	90% of 4 is?	3.6
10.	50% of 4000 is?	2000		32.	95% of 4 is?	3.8
11.	10% of 4000 is?	400		33.	5% of 4 is?	0.2
12.	10% of 4700 is?	470		34.	15% of 40 is?	6
13.	10% of 4600 is?	460		35.	15% of 30 is?	4.5
14.	10% of 4630 is?	463		36.	15% of 20 is?	3
15.	10% of 463 is?	46.3		37.	30% of 20 is?	6
16.	10% of 46.3 is?	4.63		38.	30% of 50 is?	15
17.	10% of 18 is?	1.8		39.	30% of 90 is?	27
18.	10% of 24 is?	2.4		40.	45% of 90 is?	40.5
19.	10% of 3.63 is?	0.363		41.	90% of 120 is?	108
20.	10% of 0.336 is?	0.0363		42.	125% of 40 is?	50
21.	10% of 37 is?	3.7		43.	125% of 50 is?	62.5
22.	10% of 37.5 is?	3.75		44.	120% of 60 is?	72

Lesson 3:   Comparing Quantities with Percent

Lesson 4: Percent Increase and Decrease

Student Outcomes

- Students solve percent problems when one quantity is a certain percent more or less than another.
- Students solve percent problems involving a percent increase or decrease.

Lesson Notes

Students begin the lesson by reviewing the prerequisite understanding of percent. Following this are examples and exercises related to percent increase and decrease. Throughout the lesson, students should continue to relate 100% to the whole and identify the original whole each time they solve a percent increase or decrease problem. When students are working backwards, a common mistake is to erroneously represent the whole as the amount *after* the increase or decrease, *rather than the original amount.* Be sure to address this common mistake during whole-group instruction.

Classwork

Opening Exercise (4 minutes)

Opening Exercise

Cassandra likes jewelry. She has five rings in her jewelry box.

    a.   In the box below, sketch Cassandra's five rings.

    b.   Draw a double number line diagram relating the number of rings as a percent of the whole set of rings.

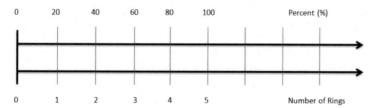

    c.   What percent is represented by the whole collection of rings? What percent of the collection does each ring represent?

    100%, 20%

Discussion (2 minutes)

Whole-group discussion of the Opening Exercise ensues. Students' understanding of Opening Exercise part (c) will be critical for their understanding of percent increase and decrease. A document camera may be used for a student to present work to the class, or a student may use the board to draw a double number line diagram to explain.

- How did you arrive at your answer for Opening Exercise part (c)?
    - *I knew that there were five rings. I knew that the five rings represented the whole, or* 100%. *So, I divided* 100% *and the total number of rings into five pieces on each number line. Each piece (or ring) represents* 20%.

> **Scaffolding:**
> - For tactile learners, provide students with counters to represent the rings. Include six counters. The 6th counter should be transparent or a different color so that it can be atop one of the original five to indicate $\frac{1}{5}$, or 20%.
> - Consider providing premade double number lines for struggling students.

Example 1 (4 minutes): Finding a Percent Increase

Let's look at some additional information related to Cassandra's ring collection.

> **Example 1**
>
> Cassandra's aunt said she will buy Cassandra another ring for her birthday.
>
> If Cassandra gets the ring for her birthday, what will be the percent increase in her ring collection?

- Looking back at our answers to the Opening Exercise, what percent is represented by one ring? If Cassandra gets the ring for her birthday, by what percent did her ring collection increase?
    - 20% *represents one ring, so her ring collection would increase by* 20%.
- Compare the number of new rings to the original total:
    - $\frac{1}{5} = \frac{20}{100} = 0.20 = 20\%$
- Use an algebraic equation to model this situation. The quantity is represented by the number of new rings.

> $Quantity = Percent \times Whole.$ **Let p represent the unknown percent.**
> $$1 = p \cdot 5$$
> $$\frac{1}{5} = p$$
> $$\frac{1}{5} = \frac{20}{100} = 0.2 = 20\%$$

Exercise 1 (3 minutes)

Students work independently to answer this question.

Exercise 1

a. Jon increased his trading card collection by 5 cards. He originally had 15 cards. What is the percent increase? Use the equation: $Quantity = Percent \times Whole$ to arrive at your answer, and then justify your answer using a numeric or visual model.

$Quantity = Percent \times Whole$. **Let p represent the unknown percent.**

$$5 = p\,(15)$$
$$5\left(\frac{1}{15}\right) = p\,(15)\left(\frac{1}{15}\right)$$
$$\frac{5}{15} = \frac{1}{3} = 0.3333\ldots$$
$$0.3333\ldots = \frac{33}{100} + \frac{0.3333\ldots}{100} = 33\% + \frac{1}{3}\% = 33\frac{1}{3}\%$$

b. Suppose instead of increasing the collection by 5 cards, John increased his 15-card collection by just 1 card. Will the percent increase be the same as when Cassandra's ring collection increased by 1 ring (in Example 1)? Why or why not? Explain.

No, it would not be the same because the part to whole relationship is different. Cassandra's additional ring compared to the original whole collection was 1 to 5, which is equivalent to 20 to 100, which is 20%. John's additional trading card compared to his original card collection is 1 out of 15, which is less than 10%, since $\frac{1}{15} < \frac{1}{10}$, and $\frac{1}{10} = 10\%$.

c. Based on your answer to part (b) how is displaying change as a percent useful?

Representing change as a percent helps us to understand how large the change is compared to the whole.

Discussion (4 minutes)

Ask the class for an example of a situation that involves a percent decrease or use the sample given below, and conduct a brief whole-group discussion about the meaning of the percent decrease. Then, using whole-group instruction, complete Example 2.

Provide each student (or pair of students) with a small piece of paper or index card to answer the following question. Read the question aloud:

- Consider the following statement: "A sales representative is taking 10% off of your bill as an apology for any inconveniences". Write down what you think this statement implies? Collect the responses to the question and scan for examples that look like the following:
  - *I will only pay 90% of my bill.*
  - *10% of my bill will be subtracted from the original total.*
- How does this example differ from the percent increase problems?
  - *In percent increase problems, the final value or quantity is greater than the original value or quantity; therefore, it is greater than 100% of the original value or quantity. In this problem, the final value is less than the original value or quantity; therefore, it is less than 100% of the original value or quantity.*
- Let's examine these statements more closely. What will they look like in equation form?

"I will only pay 90% of my bill."	"10% of my bill will be subtracted from the original total."
The new bill is part of the original bill, so the original bill is the whole. $new\ bill = 0.9(original\ bill)$	*The new bill is the part of the original bill left over after 10% has been removed, so the original bill is the whole.* $new\ bill = (original\ bill) - 0.1(original\ bill)$

- These expressions are equivalent. Can you show and explain why?

Note to teacher: If students are not able to provide the reasoning, provide scaffolding questions to help them through the following progression:

  □ *Let n represent the amount of money due on the new bill, and let b represent the amount of money due on the original bill.*

$n = b - 0.1(b)$	*10% of the original bill is subtracted from the original bill;*
$n = 1b - 0.1(b)$	*multiplicative identity property of 1*
$n = b(1 - 0.1)$	*distributive property*
$n = b(0.9)$	
$n = 0.9(b)$	*Any order (commutative property of multiplication)*

  The new bill is 90% of the original bill.

Example 2 (3 minutes): Percent Decrease

> **Example 2: Percent Decrease**
>
> Ken said that he is going to reduce the number of calories that he eats during the day. Ken's trainer asked him to start off small and reduce the number of calories by no more than 7%. Ken estimated and consumed 2,200 calories per day instead of his normal 2,500 calories per day until his next visit with the trainer. Did Ken reduce his calorie intake by 7%? Justify your answer.

Scaffolding:

- Provide examples of the words increase and decrease in real-world situations. Provide opportunities for learners struggling with the language to identify situations involving an increase or decrease, distinguishing between the two.
- Create two lists of words: one listing synonyms for "increase" and one listing synonyms for "decrease", so students can recognize key words in word problems.

- Using mental math and estimation, was Ken's estimate close? Why or why not?
  □ *No. 10% of 2,500 is 250, and 5% of 2,500 is 125 because $5\% = \frac{1}{2}(10\%)$. So mentally, Ken should have reduced his calorie intake between 125 and 250 calories per day, but he reduced his calorie intake by 300 calories per day. $300 > 250$, which is more than a 10% decrease; therefore, it is greater than a 7% decrease.*

- How can we use an equation to determine whether Ken made a 7% decrease in his daily calories?
  □ *We can use the equation $Quantity = Percent \times Whole$ and substitute the values into the equation to see if it is a true statement.*

*NOTE: Either of the following approaches (A or B) could be used per previous discussion.

---

a.   *Ken reduced his daily calorie intake by 300 calories. Does 7% of 2,500 calories equal 300 calories?*

$$Quantity = Percent \times Whole$$

$$300 \overset{?}{=} \frac{7}{100}(2,500)$$

$$300 \overset{?}{=} (0.07)(2,500)$$

$$300 \overset{?}{=} 175$$

False, because $300 \neq 175$.

b.   *A 7% decrease means Ken would get 93% of his normal daily calorie intake since* $100\% - 7\% = 93\%$. *Ken consumed 2,200 calories, so does 93% of 2,500 equal 2,200?*

$$Quantity = Percent \times Whole$$

$$2,200 \overset{?}{=} \frac{93}{100}(2,500)$$

$$2,200 \overset{?}{=} 93(25)$$

$$2,200 \overset{?}{=} 2,325$$

False, because $2,200 \neq 2,325$; *therefore, Ken's estimation was wrong.*

Exercise 2 (5 minutes)

Students complete the exercise with a learning partner. The teacher should move around the room providing support where needed. After 3 minutes have elapsed, select students to share their work with the class.

Exercise 2

Skylar is answering the following math problem:

"The value of an investment decreased by 10%. *The original amount of the investment was* $75. *What is the current value of the investment?"*

a.   Skylar said 10% of $75 is $7.50, and since the investment decreased by that amount, you have to subtract $7.50 from $75 to arrive at the final answer of $67.50. Create one algebraic equation that can be used to arrive at the final answer of $67.50. Solve the equation to prove it results in an answer of $67.50. Be prepared to explain your thought process to the class.

Let F represent the final value of the investment.

The final value is 90% *of the original investment, since* $100\% - 10\% = 90\%$.

$$F = Percent \times Whole$$
$$F = (0.90)(75)$$
$$F = 67.5$$

The final value of the investment is $67.50.

---

b. Skylar wanted to show the proportional relationship between the dollar value of the original investment, x, and its value after a 10% decrease, y. He creates the table of values shown below. Does it model the relationship? Explain. Then provide a correct equation for the relationship Skylar wants to model.

x	y
75	7.5
100	10
200	20
300	30
400	40

No. The table only shows the proportional relationship between the amount of the investment and the amount of the decrease, which is 10% of the amount of the investment. To show the relationship between the value of the investment before and after the 10% decrease, he needs to subtract each value currently in the y-column from each value in the x-column, so that the y-column shows the following values: $67.5, 90, 180, 270, 360$. The correct equation is: $y = x - 0.10x$, or $y = 0.90x$.

- Let's talk about Skylar's thought process. Skylar's approach to finding the value of a $75 investment after a 10% decline was to find 10% of 75, and then subtract it from 75. He generalized this process and created a table of values to model a 10% decline in the value of an investment. Did his table of values represent his thought process? Why or why not?

Example 3 (4 minutes): Finding a Percent Increase or Decrease

Students understand from earlier lessons how to convert a fraction to a percent. A common error in finding a percent increase or decrease (given the before and after amounts) is that students do not correctly identify the quantity (or part) and the whole (the original amount). Example 3 may reveal students' misunderstandings related to this common error which will allow the teacher to pinpoint misconceptions and correct them early on.

Example 3: Finding a Percent Increase or Decrease

Justin earned 8 badges in Scouts as of the Scout Master's last report. Justin wants to complete 2 more badges so that he will have a total of 10 badges earned before the Scout Master's next report.

a. If Justin completes the additional 2 badges, what will be the percent increase in badges?

$Part = Percent \times Whole$. *Let p represent the unknown percent.*

$$2 = p \cdot 8$$
$$2\left(\frac{1}{8}\right) = p\left(\frac{1}{8}\right)(8)$$
$$\frac{2}{8} = \frac{1}{4} = \frac{25}{100} = 25\% = p$$

There would be a 25% increase in the number of badges.

b. Express the 10 badges as a percent of the 8 badges.

8 badges are the whole or 100%, 2 badges represent 25% of the badges, so 10 badges represent $100\% + 25\% = 125\%$ of the 8 badges.

Check:

$$10 = p \cdot 8$$
$$10\left(\frac{1}{8}\right) = p\left(\frac{1}{8}\right)(8)$$
$$\frac{10}{8} = \frac{5}{4} = \frac{125}{100} = 125\% = p$$

c. Does 100% plus your answer in part (a) equal your answer in part (b)? Why or why not?

Yes. My answer makes sense because 8 badges are the whole or 100%, 2 badges represent 25% of the badges, so 10 badges represent $100\% + 25\% = 125\%$ of the 8 badges.

Examples 4–5 (9 minutes): Finding the Original Amount given a Percent Increase or Decrease

Note that upcoming lessons will focus on finding the whole given a percent change as students often are challenged by these problem types.

> **Example 4: Finding the Original Amount given a Percent Increase or Decrease**
>
> The population of cats in a rural neighborhood has declined in the past year by roughly 30%. Residents hypothesize that this is due to wild coyotes preying on the cats. The current cat population in the neighborhood is estimated to be 12. Approximately how many cats were there originally?

- Do we know the part or the whole?
  - *We know the part (how many cats are left), but we do not know the original whole.*
- Is this a percent increase or decrease problem? How do you know?
  - *Percent decrease because the word "declined" means decreased.*
- If there was about a 30% decline in the cat population, then what percent of cats remain?
  - $100\% - 30\% = 70\%$, *so about 70% of the cats remain.*
- How do we write an equation to model this situation?
  - *12 cats represent the quantity that is about 70% of the original amount of cats. We are trying to find the whole, which equals the original number of cats. So, using $Quantity = Percent \times Whole$ and substituting the known values into the equation, we have $12 = 70\% \cdot W$.*

> $$Quantity = Percent \times Whole$$
> $$12 = \left(\frac{7}{10}\right) \cdot W$$
> $$(12)\left(\frac{10}{7}\right) = \left(\frac{7}{10}\right)\left(\frac{10}{7}\right) \cdot W$$
> $$\frac{120}{7} = W$$
> $$17.1 \approx 17 = W$$
>
> *There must have been 17 cats originally.*

Lesson 4:   Percent Increase and Decrease

- Let's relate our algebraic work to a visual model.

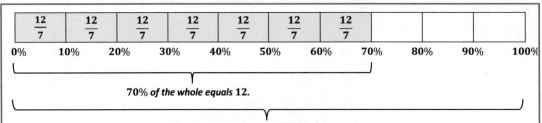

70% of the whole equals 12.

What quantity represents 100% of the cats?

To find the original amount of cats or the whole (100% of the cats), we need to add three more twelve-sevenths to 12.

$$12 + 3\left(\frac{12}{7}\right) = \frac{84}{7} + \frac{36}{7} = \frac{120}{7} \approx 17$$

The decrease was given as approximately 30%, so there must have been 17 cats originally.

Example 5

Lu's math level on her achievement test in 7th grade was a level 650. Her math teacher told her that her test level went up by 25% from her 6th-grade test score level. What was Lu's test score level in 6th grade?

- Does this represent a percent increase or decrease? How do you know?
  - *Percent increase because the word "up" means increase.*
- Using the equation: *Quantity = Percent × Whole*, what information do we know?
  - *We know Lu's test score level in 7th grade after the change, which is the quantity, and we know the percent. But we do not know the whole (her test score level from 6th grade).*
- If Lu's 6th grade test score level represents the whole, then what percent represents the 7th grade level?
  - $100\% + 25\% = 125\%$
- How do we write an equation to model this situation?

Quantity = Percent × Whole

$$650 = 125\% \times W$$

$$650 = 1.25W$$

$$650\left(\frac{1}{1.25}\right) = 1.25\left(\frac{1}{1.25}\right)W$$

$$\frac{650}{1.25} = \frac{65,000}{125} = 520 = W$$

Lu's 6th grade test score level was 520.

Closing (2 minutes)

- How does the context of a problem determine whether there is percent increase or decrease?

- Using the equation $Quantity = Percent \times Whole$, what does the whole represent in a percent increase or decrease problem? What does the quantity represent?

- For each phrase, identify the whole unit: (Read each phrase aloud to class and ask for student responses.)

Phrase	Whole Unit (100%)
"Mary has 20% more money than John."	John's money
"Anne has 15% less money than John."	John's money
"What percent more (money) does Anne have than Bill?"	Bill's money
"What percent less (money) does Bill have than Anne?	Anne's money

Exit Ticket (5 minutes)

Name _____   Date _____

Lesson 4: Percent Increase and Decrease

Exit Ticket

Erin wants to raise her math grade to a 95 to improve her chances of winning a math scholarship.   Her math average for the last marking period was an 81. Erin decides she must raise her math average by 15% to meet her goal. Do you agree? Why or why not? Support your written answer by showing your math work.

Exit Ticket Sample Solutions

Erin wants to raise her math average to a 95 to improve her chances of winning a math scholarship. Her math average for the last marking period was an 81. Erin decides she must raise her math average by 15% to meet her goal. Do you agree? Why or why not? Support your written answer by showing your math work.

No, I do not agree. 15% of 81 is 12.15. 81 + 12.15 = 93.15, which is less than 95. I arrived at my answer using the equation below to find 15% of 81.

$Quantity = Percent \times Whole$

Let G stand for the number of points Erin must raise her math average by. The whole is 81, and the percent is 15%. First, I need to find 15% of 81 to arrive at the number of points represented by a 15% increase. Then I will add that to 81 to see if it equals 95, which is Erin's goal.

$$G = 0.15 \times 81$$
$$G = 12.15$$

Adding the points onto her average: $81.00 + 12.15 = 93.15$

Comparing it to her goal: $93.15 < 95$

Problem Set Sample Solutions

1. A store advertises 15% off an item that regularly sells for $300.

    a. What is the sale price of the item?

    $(0.85)300 = 255$; *the sale price is* $255.

    b. How is a 15% discount similar to a 15% decrease? Explain.

    In both cases, you are subtracting 15% of the whole from the whole, or finding 85% of the whole.

    c. If 8% sales tax is charged on the sale price, what is the total with tax?

    $(1.08)(255) = 275.40$; *the total with tax is* $275.40.

    d. How is 8% sales tax like an 8% increase? Explain.

    In both cases, you are adding 8% of the whole to the whole or finding 108% of the whole.

2. An item that was selling for $72 is reduced to $60. Find the percent decrease in price. Round your answer to the nearest tenth.

    The whole is 72. 72 − 60 = 12. 12 *is the part. Using* $Quantity = Percent \times Whole$, *I get*

    $12 = p \times 72$, *and working backwards, I arrive at* $\dfrac{12}{72} = \dfrac{1}{6} = 0.1\overline{6} = p$.   *So, it is about a* 16.7% *decrease.*

3. A baseball team had 80 players show up for tryouts last year and this year had 96 players show up for tryouts. Find the percent increase in players from last year to this year.

    The number of players that showed up last year is the whole; 16 players are the quantity of change since 96 − 80 = 16.

    Quantity = Percent × Whole. Let p represent the unknown percent.

    $$16 = p(80)$$
    $$p = 0.2$$
    $$0.2 = \frac{20}{100} = 20\%$$

    The number of players this year was a 20% increase from last year.

4. At a student council meeting, there were a total of 60 students present. Of those students, 35 were female.

    a. By what percent is the number of females greater than the number of males?

        The number of males at the meeting is the whole. The part (quantity) can be represented by the number of females or how many more females there are than the number of males.

        $$Quantity = Percent \times Whole$$
        $$35 = p(25)$$
        $$p = 1.4$$

        1.4 = 140% which is 40% more than 100%. Therefore, there were 40% more females than males at the student council meeting.

    b. By what percent is the number of males less than the number of females?

        The number of females at the meeting is the whole. The part quantity can be represented by the number of males, or the number less of males than females.

        $$Quantity = Percent \times Whole$$
        $$10 = p(35)$$
        $$p \approx 0.29$$
        $$0.29 = 29\%$$

        so the number of males at the meeting is approximately 29% less than the number of females.

    c. Why are the percent increase and percent decrease in parts (a) and (b) different?

        The difference in the number of males and females is the same in each case, but the whole quantities in parts (a) and (b) are different.

5. Once each day, Darlene writes in her personal diary and records whether the sun is shining or not. When she looked back though her diary she found that over a period of 600 days, the sun was shining 60% of the time. She kept recording for another 200 days and then found that the total number of sunny days dropped to 50%. How many of the final 200 days were sunny days?

    To find the number of sunny days in the first 600 days, the total number of days is the whole.

    $Quantity = Percent \times Whole$. Let s represent the number of sunny days.

    $$s = 0.6(600)$$
    $$s = 360$$

    so there were 360 sunny days in the first 600 days.

    The total number of days that Darlene observed was 800 days because $600 + 200 = 800$.

    $$d = 0.5(800)$$
    $$d = 400$$

    so there were a total of 400 sunny days out of the 800 days.

    The number of sunny days in the final 200 days is the difference of 400 days and 360 days.

    $400 - 360 = 40$, so there were 40 sunny days of the last 200 days.

6. Henry is considering purchasing a mountain bike. He likes two bikes: one costs $500 and the other costs $600. He tells his dad that the bike that is more expensive is 20% more than the cost of the other bike. Is he correct? Justify your answer.

    Yes. $Quantity = Percent \times Whole$, and substituting in the values of the bikes and percent, I arrive at the following equation: $500 = 1.2(600)$, which is a true equation.

7. State two numbers such that the lesser number is 25% less than the greater number.

    Answers will vary. One solution is as follows: Greater number is 100, lesser number is 75.

8. State two numbers such that the greater number is 75% more than the lesser number.

    Answers will vary. One solution is as follows: Greater number is 175 , lesser number is 100.

9. Explain the difference in your thought process for Problems 7 and 8. Can you use the same numbers for each problem? Why or Why not?

    No. The whole is different in each problem. In Problem 7, the greater number is the whole. In Problem 8, the lesser number is the whole.

10. In each of the following expressions, c represents the original cost of an item.

    i. $\boxed{0.90c}$

    ii. $\enclose{circle}{0.10c}$

    iii. $\boxed{c - 0.10c}$

    a. Circle the expression(s) that represents 10% of the original cost. If more than one answer is correct, explain why the expressions you chose are equivalent.

b. Put a box around the expression(s) that represents the final cost of the item after a 10% decrease. If more than one is correct, explain why the expressions you chose are equivalent.

$c - 0.10c$

$1c - 0.10c$ *multiplicative identity property of 1*

$(1 - 0.10)c$ *distributive property (writing a sum (or difference) as a product)*

$0.90c$

Therefore, $c - 0.10c = 0.90c$.

c. Create a word problem involving a percent decrease, so that the answer can be represented by expression (ii).

The store's cashier told me I would get a 10% discount on my purchase. How can I find the amount of the 10% discount?

d. Create a word problem involving a percent decrease, so that the answer can be represented by expression (i).

An item is on sale for 10% off. If the original price of the item is, c, what is the final price after the 10% discount?

e. Tyler wants to know if it matters if he represents a situation involving a 25% decrease as $0.25x$ or $(1 - 0.25)x$. In the space below, write an explanation that would help Tyler understand how the context of a word problem often determines how to represent the situation.

If the word problem asks you to find the amount of the 25% decrease, then $0.25x$ would represent it. If the problem asks you to find the value after a 25% decrease, then $(1 - 0.25)x$ would be a correct representation.

Lesson 5: Find One Hundred Percent Given Another Percent

Student Outcomes

- Students find 100% of a quantity (the whole) when given a quantity that is a percent of the whole by using a variety of methods including finding 1%, equations, mental math using factors of 100, and double number line models.
- Students solve word problems involving finding 100% of a given quantity with and without using equations.

Classwork

Opening Exercise (5 minutes)

Students recall factors of 100 and their multiples to complete the table below. The discussion that follows introduces students to a means of calculating whole quantities through the use of a double number line.

Opening Exercise

What are the whole number factors of 100? What are the multiples of those factors? How many multiples are there of each factor (up to 100)?

Factors of 100	Multiples of the Factors of 100	Number of Multiples
100	100	1
50	50, 100	2
25	25, 50, 75, 100	4
20	20, 40, 60, 80, 100	5
10	10, 20, 30, 40, 50, 60, 70, 80, 90, 100	10
5	5, 10, 15, 20, 25, 30, 35, 40, 45, 50, ..., 75, 80, 85, 90, 95, 100	20
4	4, 8, 12, 16, 20, 24, 28, 32, 36, 40, ..., 80, 84, 88, 92, 96, 100	25
2	2, 4, 6, 8, 10, 12, 14, 16, 18, 20, 22, ..., 88, 90, 92, 94, 96, 98, 100	50
1	1, 2, 3, 4, 5, 6, ..., 98, 99, 100	100

- How do you think we can use these whole number factors in calculating percents on a double number line?
  - *The factors represent all ways by which we could break 100% into equal sized intervals. The multiples listed would be the percents representing each cumulative interval. The number of multiples would be the number of intervals.*

Example 1 (5 minutes): Using a Modified Double Number Line with Percents

The use of visual models is a powerful strategy for organizing and solving percent problems. In this example (and others that follow) the double number line is modified so that it is made up of a percent number line and a bar model. This model provides a visual representation of how quantities compare and what percent they correspond with. We use the greatest common factor of the given percent and 100 to determine the number of equal size intervals to use.

> **Example 1**
>
> The 42 students who play wind instruments represent 75% of the students who are in band. How many students are in band?

- Which quantity in this problem represents the whole?
    - *The total number of students in band is the whole or 100%.*

- Draw the visual model shown with a percent number line and a tape diagram.

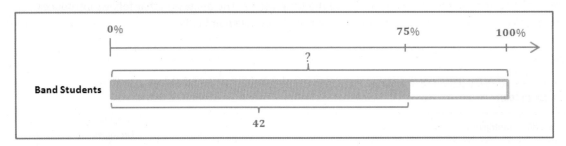

- Use the double number line to find the total number of students in band.
    - *100% represents the total number of students in band, and 75% is $\frac{3}{4}$ of 100%. The greatest common factor of 75 and 100 is 25.*

$$42 \rightarrow 75\%$$
$$\frac{42}{3} \rightarrow 25\%$$
$$4\left(\frac{42}{3}\right) \rightarrow 100\%$$
$$4(14) \rightarrow 100\%$$
$$56 \rightarrow 100\%$$

There are 56 students in the band.

Exercises 1–3 (10 minutes)

Solve Exercises 1–3 using a modified double number line.

Exercises 1–3

1. Bob's Tire Outlet sold a record number of tires last month. One salesman sold 165 tires, which was 60% of the tires sold in the month. What was the record number of tires sold?

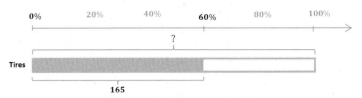

The salesman's total is being compared to the total number of tires sold by the store, so the total number of tires sold is the whole quantity. The greatest common factor of 60 and 100 is 20, so I divided the percent line into five equal sized intervals of 20%. 60% is three of the 20% intervals, so I divided the salesman's 165 tires by 3 and found that 55 tires corresponds with each 20% interval. 100% consists of five 20% intervals which corresponds to five groups of 55 tires. Since 5 · 55 = 275, the record number of tires sold was 275 tires.

2. Nick currently has 7,200 points in his fantasy baseball league, which is 20% more points than Adam. How many points does Adam have?

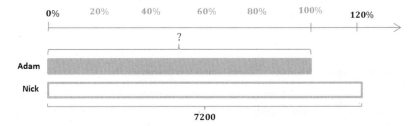

Nick's points are being compared to Adam's points so Adam's points are the whole quantity. Nick has 20% more points than Adam, so Nick really has 120% of Adam's points. The greatest common factor of 120 and 100 is 20, so I divided the 120% on the percent line into six equal sized intervals. I divided Nick's 7,200 points by 6 and found that 1,200 points correspond to each 20% interval. Five intervals of 20% make 100%, and five intervals of 1,200 points totals 6,000 points. Adam has 6,000 points in the fantasy baseball league.

3. Kurt has driven 276 miles of his road trip but has 70% of the trip left to go. How many more miles does Kurt have to drive to get to his destination?

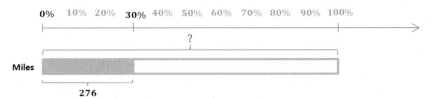

With 70% of his trip left to go, Kurt has only driven 30% of the way to his destination. The greatest common factor of 30 and 100 is 10, so I divided the percent line into ten equal size intervals. 30% is three of the 10% intervals, so I divided 276 miles by 3 and found that 92 miles corresponds to each 10% interval. Ten intervals of 10% make 100%, and 10 intervals of 92 miles total 920 miles. Kurt has already driven 276 miles, and 920 − 276 = 644, so Kurt has 644 miles left to get to his destination.

EUREKA MATH™

Lesson 5:   Find One Hundred Percent Given Another Percent

Example 2 (10 minutes): Mental Math Using Factors of 100

Students use mental math and factors of 100 to determine the whole quantity when given a quantity that is a percent of that whole.

Example 2

Answer each part below using only mental math and describe your method.

   a.   If 39 is 1% of a number, what is that number? How did you find your answer?

   39 *is* 1% *of* 3,900; *I found my answer by multiplying* 39 · 100 *because* 39 *corresponds with each* 1% *in* 100% *and* 1% · 100 = 100%, *so* 39 · 100 = 3,900.

   b.   If 39 is 10% of a number, what is that number? How did you find your answer?

   39 *is* 10% *of* 390; 10 *is a factor of* 100 *and there are ten* 10% *intervals in* 100%. *The quantity* 39 *corresponds to* 10%, *so there are* 39 · 10 *in the whole quantity, and* 39 · 10 = 390.

   c.   If 39 is 5% of a number, what is that number? How did you find your answer?

   39 *is* 5% *of* 780; 5 *is a factor of* 100 *and there are twenty* 5% *intervals in* 100%. *The quantity* 39 *corresponds to* 5%, *so there are twenty intervals of* 39 *in the whole quantity.*

   39 · 20

   39 · 2 · 10   *Factor* 20 *for easier mental math*

   78 · 10 = 780

   d.   If 39 is 15% of a number, what is that number? How did you find your answer?

   39 *is* 15% *of* 260; 15 *is not a factor of* 100, *but* 15 *and* 100 *have a common factor of* 5. *If* 15% *is* 39, *then because* $5 = \frac{15}{3}$, 5% *is* $13 = \frac{39}{3}$. *There are twenty* 5% *intervals in* 100%, *so there are twenty intervals of* 13 *in the whole.*

   13 · 20

   13 · 2 · 10   *Factored* 20 *for easier mental math*

   26 · 10 = 260

   e.   If 39 is 25% of a number, what is that number? How did you find your answer?

   39 is 25% of 156; 25 *is a factor of* 100 *and there are four intervals of* 25% *in* 100%. *The quantity* 39 *corresponds with* 25%, *so there are* 39 · 4 *in the whole quantity.*

   39 · 4

   39 · 2 · 2   *Factored* 4 *for easier mental math*

   78 · 2 = 156

Exercises 4–5 (8 minutes)

Solve Exercises 4 and 5 using mental math and factors of 100. Describe your method with each exercise.

Exercises 4–5

4. Derrick had a 0.250 batting average at the end of his last baseball season, which means that he got a hit 25% of the times he was up to bat. If Derrick had 47 hits last season, how many times did he bat?

The decimal 0.250 is 25%, which means that Derrick had a hit 25% of the times that he batted. His number of hits is being compared to the total number of times he was up to bat. The 47 hits corresponds with 25% and since 25 is a factor of 100, $100 = 25 \cdot 4$, I used mental math to multiply the following:

$47 \cdot 4$

$(50 - 3) \cdot 4$ *using the distributive property for easier mental math*

$200 - 12 = 188$

Derrick was up to bat 188 times last season.

5. Nelson used 35% of his savings account for his class trip in May. If he used $140 from his savings account while on his class trip, how much money was in his savings account before the trip?

35% of Nelson's account was spent on the trip which was $140. The amount that he spent is being compared to the total amount of savings, so the total savings represents the whole. The greatest common factor of 35 and 100 is 5. 35% is seven intervals of 5%, so I divided $140 by seven to find that $20 corresponds to 5%. $100\% = 5\% \cdot 20$, so the whole quantity is $20 \cdot 20 = $400. Nelson's savings account had $400 in it before his class trip.

Closing (2 minutes)

- What did the modified double number line method and the factors of 100 method have in common?
    - *Both methods involved breaking 100% into equal sized intervals using the greatest common factor of 100 and the percent corresponding to the part.*
- Can you describe a situation where you would prefer using the modified double number line?
- Can you describe a situation where you would prefer using the factors of 100?

Exit Ticket (5 minutes)

    Lesson 5:   Find One Hundred Percent Given Another Percent

Name _____   Date _____

Lesson 5: Finding One Hundred Percent Given Another Percent

Exit Ticket

1. A tank that is 40% full contains 648 gallons of water. Use a double number line to find the capacity of the water tank.

2. Loretta picks apples for her grandfather to make apple cider. She brings him her cart with 420 apples. Her grandfather smiles at her and says, "Thank you Loretta. That is 35% of the apples that we need."

   Use mental math to find how many apples Loretta's grandfather needs. Describe your method.

Exit Ticket Sample Solutions

1. A water tank currently contains 648 gallons of water, but the tank is only 40% filled. Use a double number line to find the capacity of the water tank.

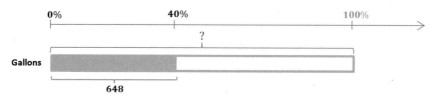

I divided the percent line into intervals of 20% making 5 intervals of 20% in 100%. I know that I have to divide $\frac{40}{2}$ to get 20, so I divided $\frac{648}{2}$ to get 324 that corresponds with 20%. Since there are five 20% intervals in 100%, there are five 324 gallon intervals in the whole quantity, and $324 \cdot 5 = 1,620$. The capacity of the tank is 1,620 gallons.

2. Loretta picks apples for her grandfather to make apple cider. She brings him her cart with 420 apples. Her grandfather smiles at her and says "Thank you Loretta. That is 35% of the apples that we need."

   Use mental math to find how many apples Loretta's grandfather needs. Describe your method.

   420 is 35% of 1,200. 35 is not a factor of 100, but 35 and 100 have a common factor of 5. There are seven intervals of 5% in 35%, so I divided 420 apples into seven intervals; $\frac{420}{7} = 60$. There are 20 intervals of 5% in 100%, so I multiplied

   $60 \cdot 20$

   $60 \cdot 2 \cdot 10$

   $120 \cdot 10 = 1,200$

   Loretta's grandfather needs a total of 1,200 apples to make apple cider.

Problem Set Sample Solutions

Use a double number line to answer Problems 1–5.

1. Tanner collected 360 cans and bottles while fundraising for his baseball team. This was 40% of what Reggie collected. How many cans and bottles did Reggie collect?

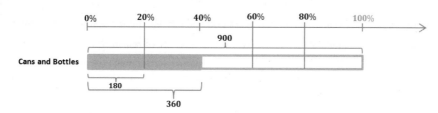

The greatest common factor of 40 and 100 is 20.

$\frac{1}{2}(40\%) = 20\%$, *and* $\frac{1}{2}(360) = 180$, *so 180 corresponds with 20%. There are five intervals of 20% in 100%, and $5(180) = 900$, so Reggie collected 900 cans and bottles.*

2. Emilio paid $287.50 in taxes to the school district that he lives in this year. This year's taxes were a 15% increase from last year. What did Emilio pay in school taxes last year?

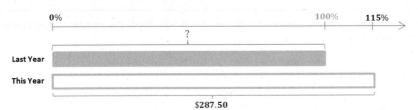

The greatest common factor of 100 and 115 is 5. There are 23 intervals of 5% in 115%, and $\frac{287.5}{23} = 12.5$, so 12.5 corresponds with 5%. There are 20 intervals of 5% in 100%, and $20(12.5) = 250$, so Emilio paid $250 in school taxes last year.

3. A snowmobile manufacturer claims that its newest model is 15% lighter than last year's model. If this year's model weighs 799 lb., how much did last year's model weigh?

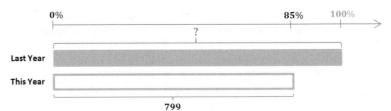

15% lighter than last year's model means 15% less than 100% of last year's model's weight, which is 85%. The greatest common factor of 85 and 100 is 5. There are 17 intervals of 5% in 85%, and $\frac{799}{17} = 47$, so 47 corresponds with 5%. There are 20 intervals of 5% in 100%, and $20(47) = 940$, so last year's model weighed 940 pounds.

4. Student enrollment at a local school is concerning the community because the number of students has dropped to 504, which is a 20% decrease from the previous year. What was the student enrollment the previous year?

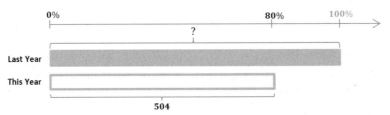

A 20% decrease implies that this year's enrollment is 80% of last year's enrollment. The greatest common factor of 80 and 100 is 20. There are 4 intervals of 20% in 80%, and $\frac{504}{4} = 126$, so 126 corresponds to 20%. There are 5 intervals of 20% in 100%, and $5(126) = 630$, so the student enrollment from the previous year was 630 students.

5. A color of paint used to paint a race car includes a mixture of yellow and green paint. Scotty wants to lighten the color by increasing the amount of yellow paint 30%. If a new mixture contains 3.9 liters of yellow paint, how many liters of yellow paint did he use in the previous mixture?

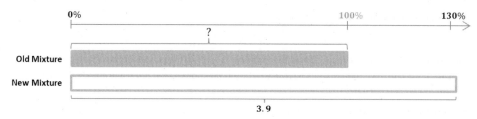

The greatest common factor of 130 and 100 is 10. There are 13 intervals of 10% in 130%, and $\frac{3.9}{13} = 0.3$, so 0.3 corresponds to 10%. There are 10 intervals of 10% in 100%, and 10(0.3) = 3, so the previous mixture included 3 liters of yellow paint.

Use factors of 100 and mental math to answer Problems 6–10. Describe the method you used.

6. Alexis and Tasha challenged each other to a typing test. Alexis typed 54 words in 1-minute, which was 120% of what Tasha typed. How many words did Tasha type in 1-minute?

The greatest common factor of 120 and 100 is 20, and there are 6 intervals of 20% in 120%, so I divided 54 into 6 equal size intervals to find that 9 corresponds to 20%. There are 5 intervals of 20% in 100%, so there are 5 intervals of 9 words in the whole quantity. 9 · 5 = 45, so Tasha typed 45 words in 1 minute.

7. Yoshi is 5% taller today than she was one year ago. Her current height is 168 cm. How tall was she one year ago?

5% taller means that Yoshi's height is 105% of her height one year ago. The greatest common factor of 5 and 100 is 5, and there are 21 intervals of 5% in 105%, so I divided 168 into 21 equal size intervals to find that 8 cm corresponds to 5%. There are 20 intervals of 5% in 100%, so there are 20 intervals of 8 cm in the whole quantity. 20 · 8 cm = 160 cm, so Yoshi was 160 cm tall one year ago.

8. Toya can run one lap of the track in 1 min. 3 sec., which is 90% of her younger sister Niki's time. What is Niki's time for one lap of the track?

1 min. 3 sec= 63 sec. The greatest common factor of 90 and 100 is 10, and there are 9 intervals of 10 in 90, so I divided 63 sec. by 9 to find that 7 sec. corresponds to 10%. There are 10 intervals of 10% in 100%, so 10 intervals of 7 sec. represents the whole quantity which is 70 sec. 70 sec.= 1 min. 10 sec. Niki can run one lap of the track in 1 min. 10 sec.

9. An animal shelter houses only cats and dogs, and there are 25% more cats than dogs. If there are 40 cats, how many dogs are there, and how many animals are there total?

25% more cats means that the number of cats is 125% the number of dogs. The greatest common factor of 125 and 100 is 25. There are 5 intervals of 25% in 125%, so I divided the number of cats into 5 intervals to find that 8 corresponds to 25%. There are 4 intervals of 25% in 100%, so there are 4 intervals of 8 in the whole quantity. 8 · 4 = 32. There are 32 dogs in the animal shelter.

The number of animals combined is 32 + 40 = 72, so there are 72 animals in the animal shelter.

10. Angie scored 91 points on a test but only received a 65% grade on the test. How many points were possible on the test?

The greatest common factor of 65 and 100 is 5. There are 13 intervals of 5% in 65%, so I divided 91 points into 13 intervals and found that 7 points corresponds to 5%. There are 20 intervals of 5% in 100%, so I multiplied 7 points times 20 which is 140 points. There were 140 points possible on Angie's test.

For Problems 11–17, find the answer using any appropriate method.

11. Robbie owns 15% more movies than Rebecca, and Rebecca owns 10% more movies than Joshua. If Rebecca owns 220 movies, how many movies do Robbie and Joshua each have?

Robbie owns 253 movies, and Joshua owns 200 movies.

12. 20% of the seventh grade students have math class in the morning. $16\frac{2}{3}\%$ of those students also have science class in the morning. If 30 seventh grade students have math class in the morning but not science class, find how many seventh grade students there are.

There are 180 seventh grade students.

13. The school bookstore ordered three-ring notebooks. They put 75% of the order in the warehouse and sold 80% of the rest in the first week of school. There are 25 notebooks left in the store to sell. How many three-ring notebooks did they originally order?

The store originally ordered 500 three-ring notebooks.

14. In the first game of the year, the modified basketball team made 62.5% of their foul shot free throws. Matthew made all 6 of his free throws, which made up for 25% of the team's free throws. How many free throws did the team miss altogether?

The team attempted 24 free throws, made 15 of them, and missed 9.

15. Aiden's mom calculated that in the previous month, their family had used 40% of their monthly income for gasoline, and 63% of that gasoline was consumed by the family's SUV. If the family's SUV used $\$261.45$ worth of gasoline last month, how much money was left after gasoline expenses?

The amount of money spent on gasoline was $\$415$; the monthly income was $\$1037.50$. The amount left over after gasoline expenses was $\$622.50$.

16. Rectangle A is a scale drawing of Rectangle B and has 25% of its area. If Rectangle A has side lengths of 4 cm and 5 cm, what are the side lengths of Rectangle B?

$Area_A = length \times width$

$Area_A = (5\ cm)(4\ cm)$

$Area_A = 20\ cm^2$

The area of Rectangle A is 25% of the area of Rectangle B.

$20 \rightarrow 25\%$

$80 \rightarrow 100\%$. *So, the area of Rectangle B is $80\ cm^2$*

The value of the ratio of area $A{:}B$ is the square of the scale factor of the side lengths $A{:}B$.

The value of the ratio of area $A{:}B$ is $\dfrac{20}{80} = \dfrac{1}{4}$, and $\dfrac{1}{4} = \left(\dfrac{1}{2}\right)^2$, so the scale factor of the side lengths $A{:}B$ is $\dfrac{1}{2}$.

So using the scale factor:

$\dfrac{1}{2}\left(length_B\right) = 5\ cm;\ length_B = 10\ cm$

$\dfrac{1}{2}\left(width_B\right) = 4\ cm;\ width_B = 8\ cm$

The dimensions of Rectangle B are 8 cm and 10 cm.

17. Ted is a supervisor and spends 20% of his typical work day in meetings and 20% of that meeting time in his daily team meeting. If he starts each day at 7:30 a.m., and his daily team meeting is from 8:00 a.m. to 8:20 a.m., when does Ted's typical work day end?

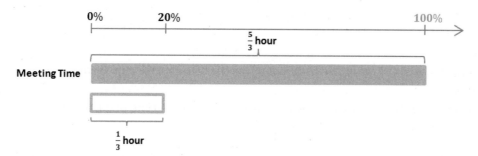

20 minutes is $\frac{1}{3}$ of an hour since $\frac{20}{60} = \frac{1}{3}$.

Ted spends $\frac{1}{3}$ hour in his daily team meeting so $\frac{1}{3}$ corresponds to 20% of his meeting time. There are 5 intervals of 20% in 100%, and $5\left(\frac{1}{3}\right) = \frac{5}{3}$, so Ted spends $\frac{5}{3}$ hours in meetings.

$\frac{5}{3}$ of an hour corresponds to 20% of Ted's work day.

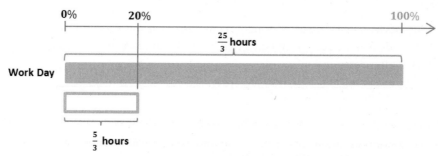

There are 5 intervals of 20% in 100%, and $5\left(\frac{5}{3}\right) = \frac{25}{3}$, so Ted spends $\frac{25}{3}$ hours working. $\frac{25}{3}$ hours $= 8\frac{1}{3}$ hours.

Since $\frac{1}{3}$ hour $= 20$ minutes, Ted works a total of 8 hours 20 minutes. If he starts at 7:30 a.m., he works 4 hours 30 minutes until 12:00 p.m., and since $8\frac{1}{3} - 4\frac{1}{2} = 3\frac{5}{6}$, Ted works another $3\frac{5}{6}$ hours after 12:00 p.m.

$\frac{1}{6}$ hour $= 10$ minutes, and $\frac{5}{6}$ hour $= 50$ minutes, so Ted works 3 hours 50 minutes after 12:00 p.m., which is 3:50 p.m. Ted's typical work day ends at 3:50 p.m.

Lesson 6: Fluency with Percents

Student Outcomes

- Students solve various types of percent problems by identifying the type of percent problem and applying appropriate strategies.
- Students extend mental math practices to mentally calculate the part, the percent, or the whole in percent word problems.

Lesson Notes

This lesson provides further development of mental math strategies with percents, additional exercises involving a variety of percent problems from Lessons 2–5, and includes a sprint exercise.

Classwork

Opening Exercise (4 minutes)

The Opening Exercise reviews concepts learned in Lesson 5; students continue to use mental math strategies with other percent problems in Example 1. Provide two minutes for students to find a solution to the problem, and then ask for students to share their strategies with the class.

Opening Exercise

Solve the following problem using mental math only. Be prepared to discuss your method with your classmates.

Cory and Everett have collected model cars since the third grade. Cory has 80 model cars in his collection, which is 25% more than what Everett has. How many model cars does Everett have?

The number of cars that Everett has is the whole; 25% more than Everett would be 125% of Everett's cars. 125% → 80. There are 5 intervals of 25% in 125%, so if I divide both 125% and 80 by 5, then 25% → 16, and then 100% → 64. Everett has 64 model cars.

- What made this problem fairly easy to solve in our head?
    - *The numbers were easily compatible and shared factors with 100.*

Example 1 (10 minutes): Mental Math and Percents

In Lesson 5, students practiced using mental math strategies to calculate the whole when given the part and its corresponding percent. In this example, students extend those strategies to mentally calculate (a) the part when given its corresponding percent and the whole and (b) the percent when given the whole and the part of that whole.

Example 1: Mental Math and Percents

    a.   75% of the students in Jesse's class are 60 inches or taller. If there are 20 students in her class, how many students are 60 inches or taller?

- Is this question a comparison of two separate quantities, or is it part of the whole? How do you know?
  - *The problem says that the students make up 75% of Jesse's class which means they are part of the whole class; this is a part of the whole problem.*
- What numbers represent the part, whole, and percent?
  - *The part is the number of students that are 60 inches or taller, the percent is 75%, and the whole is the 20 students that make up Jesse's class.*

Instruct students to discuss the problem with a partner, and challenge them to solve it using mental math only. After 1–2 minutes of discussion, ask for students to share their mental strategies with the class.

- *Possible strategies:*
  - *75% is the same as $\frac{3}{4}$ of 100%; 20 → 100% and 20 = 4(5), so 3(5) = 15, which means 15 is $\frac{3}{4}$ of 20.*
  - *100% → 20*
    25% → 5
    75% → 15

> **Scaffolding:**
> For struggling students, the teacher may want to challenge students to solve these problems by writing down as little as possible, and then trying to internalize their strategy and repeat it without paper.

Have students write a description of how to mentally solve the problem (including the math involved) in their student materials.

- Was this problem easy to solve mentally? Why?
  - *The numbers involved in the problem shared factors with 100 that were easy to work with.*

> **Note to Teacher:**
> You may need to explain the meaning of "tip" in this problem. Gratuity is covered in later lessons.

> **b.** Bobbie wants to leave a tip for her waitress equal to 15% of her bill. Bobbie's bill for her lunch was $18. How much money represents 15% of the bill?

- Is this question a comparison of two separate quantities, or is it part of a whole? How do you know?
  - *She is leaving a quantity that is equal to 15% of her bill, so this is a comparison of two separate quantities.*
- What numbers represent the part, the whole, and the percent? Is the part actually part of her lunch bill?
  - *The part is the amount that she plans to leave for her waitress and is not part of her lunch bill but is calculated as if it is a part of her bill; the whole is the $18 lunch bill, and the percent is 15%.*

Instruct students to discuss the problem with a partner and challenge them to solve it using mental math only. After 1–2 minutes of discussion, ask for students to share their mental strategies with the class.

- *Possible strategies include:*
  - *15% = 10% + 5%; 10% of $18 is $1.80; half of 10% is 5%, so 5% → $\frac{1}{2}$($1.80) = $0.90; $1.80 + $0.90 = $2.70.*
- Was this problem easy to solve mentally? Why?
  - *The numbers involved in the problem shared factors with 100 that were easy to work with.*

- Could you use this strategy to find 7% of Bobbie's bill?
  - *Yes; 7% = 5% + 2(1%); 1% of* $18 *is* $0.18, *so* 2% → $0.36; $0.90 + $0.36 = $1.26, *so* 7% → $1.26.

Have students write a description of how to mentally solve the problem in their student materials including the math involved.

Exercises 1–6 (12 minutes)

The following exercises should be completed independently or with a partner. Students must apply their understanding of percents from previous lessons and choose an appropriate strategy to solve each problem. (If exercises are not completed within the time frame, assign the remainder with the problem set.)

Exercises 1–6

1. **Express 9 hours as a percentage of 3 days.**

   3 days is the equivalent of 72 hours since $3(24) = 72$.

   72 hours represents the whole.

   $Quantity = Percent \times Whole$. Let p represent the unknown percent.

   $$9 = p(72)$$
   $$\frac{1}{72}(9) = p(72) \cdot \frac{1}{72}$$
   $$\frac{9}{72} = p(1)$$
   $$\frac{1}{8} = p$$
   $$\frac{1}{8}(100\%) = 12.5\%$$

2. **Richard works from $11{:}00$ a.m. to $3{:}00$ a.m. His dinner break is 75% of the way through his work shift. What time is Richard's dinner break?**

   The total amount of time in Richard's work shift is 14 hours since $1 + 12 + 3 = 16$.

   16 hours represents the whole.

   $Quantity = Percent \times Whole$. Let b represent the number of hours until Richard's dinner break.

   $$b = 0.75(16)$$
   $$b = 12$$

   Richard's dinner break is 12 hours after his shift begins.

   12 hours after $11{:}00$ a.m. is $11{:}00$ p.m.

   Richard's dinner break is at $11{:}00$ p.m.

---

3.   At a playoff basketball game, there were 370 fans cheering for school A and 555 fans cheering for school B.

   a.   Express the number of fans for school A as a percent of the number of fans for school B.

   The number of fans for school B is the whole.

   Quantity = Percent × Whole. *Let p represent the unknown percent.*

$$370 = p(555)$$
$$\frac{1}{555}(370) = p(555)\left(\frac{1}{555}\right)$$
$$\frac{370}{555} = p(1)$$
$$\frac{2}{3} = p$$
$$\frac{2}{3}(100\%) = 66\frac{2}{3}\%$$

   The number of fans for school A is $66\frac{2}{3}\%$ of the number of fans for school B.

   b.   Express the number of fans for school B as a percent of the number of fans for school A.

   The number of fans for school A is the whole.

   Quantity = Percent × Whole. *Let p represent the unknown percent.*

$$555 = p(370)$$
$$\frac{1}{370}(555) = p(370)\left(\frac{1}{370}\right)$$
$$\frac{555}{370} = p(1)$$
$$\frac{3}{2} = p$$
$$\frac{3}{2}(100\%) = 150\%$$

   The number of fans for school B is 150% of the number of fans for school A.

   c.   What percent more fans were there for school B than for school A?
   There are 50% more fans for school B than for school A.

4. Rectangle A has a length of 8 cm and a width of 16 cm. Rectangle B has the same area as the first, but its width is 62.5% of the length of the first rectangle. Express the width of Rectangle B as a percent of the area of Rectangle A. What percent more or less is the width Rectangle B than the width of Rectangle A?

To find the length of Rectangle B:

   The length of Rectangle A is the whole

   $Quantity = Percent \times Whole$. *Let l represent the unknown length of Rectangle B.*

   $l = 0.625(8) = 5$ *The length of Rectangle B is 5 cm.*

To find the width of Rectangle B:

   The area of Rectangle B is 100% of the area of Rectangle A because the problem says the areas are the same.

   $Area = length \times width.$ *Let A represent the unknown area of Rectangle A.*

   $Area = 8\ cm(16\ cm) = 128\ cm^2$

   $Area = length \times width.$ *Let w represent the unknown width of Rectangle B.*

   $128\ cm^2 = 5\ cm\ (w)$

   $25.6\ cm = w.$ *The width of Rectangle B is 25.6 cm.*

To express the width of Rectangle B as a percent of the width of Rectangle A:

   The width of Rectangle A is the whole.

   $Quantity = Percent \times Whole.$ *Let p represent the unknown percent.*

   $25.6\ cm = p(16)$

   $1.6 = p$ $1.6(100\%) = 160\%.$ *The width of Rectangle B is 160% of the width of Rectangle A.*

The width of Rectangle B is 60% more than the width of Rectangle A.

5. A plant in Mikayla's garden was 40 inches tall one day and was 4 feet tall one week later. By what percent did the plant's height increase over one week?

4 feet is equivalent to 48 inches since $4(12) = 48$.

40 inches is the whole;

$Quantity = Percent \times Whole.$ *Let p represent the unknown percent.*

$$8 = p(40)$$
$$\frac{1}{5} = p$$
$$\frac{1}{5} = \frac{20}{100} = 20\%$$

The plant's height increased by 20% in one week.

6. Loren must obtain a minimum number of signatures on a petition before it can be submitted. She was able to obtain 672 signatures, which is 40% more than she needs. How many signatures does she need?

The number of signatures needed represents the whole;

$Quantity = Percent \times Whole.$ *Let s represent the number of signatures needed.*

$$672 = 1.4(s)$$
$$480 = s$$

Loren needed to obtain 480 signatures on her petition.

Exercise 7 (12 minutes): Fluency Sprint

Students complete two rounds of a sprint exercise included at the end of this lesson (Percent More or Less) that focuses on finding the whole, the part, and the percent more or percent less. Please provide one minute for each round of the Sprint, and follow your normal protocol for delivering sprint exercises. The sprint exercises and answer keys are provided at the end of the lesson.

Closing (2 minutes)

- Describe how to find the percent that 12 is of 60.

  Since 12 *and* 60 *have a common factor of* 6 *(or* 12*),* $\frac{12}{60} = \frac{2}{10}$ *and* $\frac{2}{10} = \frac{20}{100} = 20\%.$

- Describe how you can mentally determine the whole given that 15 is 30% of a number.

  Divide both 15 *and* 30% *by* 3 *to get* 5 *and* 10%. *If* $5 \rightarrow 10\%,$ *then* $50 \rightarrow 100\%.$

Exit Ticket (5 minutes)

The use of a calculator is recommended for the Exit Ticket.

Name _____   Date _____

Lesson 6: Fluency with Percents

Exit Ticket

1. Parker was able to pay for 44% of his college tuition with his scholarship. The remaining $10,054.52 he paid for with a student loan. What was the cost of Parker's tuition?

2. Two bags contain marbles. Bag A contains 112 marbles and Bag B contains 140 marbles. What percent fewer marbles does Bag A have than Bag B?

3. There are 42 students on a large bus and the rest are on a smaller bus. If 40% of the students are on the smaller bus, how many total students are on the two buses?

Exit Ticket Sample Solutions

1. Parker was able to pay for 44% of his college tuition with his scholarship. The remaining $10,054.52 he paid for with a student loan. What was the cost of Parker's tuition?

   Parker's tuition is the whole; 56% represents the amount paid by student loan.

   Quantity = Percent × Whole. Let t represent the cost of Parker's tuition.

$$10,054.52 = 0.56(t)$$
$$\frac{10,054.52}{0.56} = t$$
$$17,954.50 = t$$

   Parker's tuition is $17,954.50.

2. Two bags contain marbles. Bag A contains 112 marbles and Bag B contains 140 marbles. What percent fewer marbles does Bag A have than Bag B?

   The number of marbles in Bag B is the whole.

   There are 28 fewer marbles in Bag A.

   Quantity = Percent × Whole. Let p represent the unknown percent.

$$28 = p(140)$$
$$\frac{2}{10} = p$$
$$\frac{2}{10} = \frac{20}{100} = 20\%$$

   Bag A contains 20% fewer marbles than Bag B.

3. There are 42 students on a large bus and the rest are on a smaller bus. If 40% of the students are on the smaller bus, how many total students are on the two buses?

   The 42 students on the larger bus represent 60% of the students. If I divide both 60% and 42 by 6, then I get 7 → 10%. Multiplying both by 10, I get 70 → 100%. There are 70 total students on the buses.

Problem Set Sample Solutions

This problem set is a compilation of all types of percent problems from Lessons 2–6. For each problem, students should choose an appropriate strategy to find a solution. Students may also be asked to describe the mental math they used to solve the problem.

1. Micah has 294 songs stored in his phone which is 70% of the songs that Jorge has stored in his phone. How many songs are stored on Jorge's phone?

   Quantity = Percent × Whole. Let s represent the number of songs on Micah's phone.

$$294 = \frac{70}{100} \cdot s$$
$$294 = \frac{7}{10} \cdot s$$
$$294 \cdot \frac{10}{7} = \frac{7}{10} \cdot \frac{10}{7} \cdot s$$
$$42 \cdot 10 = 1 \cdot s$$
$$420 = s$$

   There are 420 songs stored on Micah's phone.

2. Lisa sold 81 magazine subscriptions, which was 27% of her class' fundraising goal. How many magazine subscriptions does her class hope to sell?

$Quantity = Percent \times Whole$. *Let s represent the number of magazine subscriptions Lisa's class wants to sell.*

$$81 = \frac{27}{100} \cdot s$$

$$81 \cdot \frac{100}{27} = \frac{27}{100} \cdot \frac{100}{27} \cdot s$$

$$3 \cdot 100 = 1 \cdot s$$

$$300 = s$$

Lisa's class hopes to sell 300 *magazine subscriptions.*

3. Theresa and Isaiah are comparing the number of pages that they read for pleasure over the summer. Theresa read 2210 pages, which was 85% of the number of pages that Isaiah read. How many pages did Isaiah read?

$Quantity = Percent \times Whole$. *Let p represent the number of pages that Isaiah read.*

$$2,210 = \frac{85}{100} \cdot p$$

$$2,210 = \frac{17}{20} \cdot p$$

$$2,210 \cdot \frac{20}{17} = \frac{17}{20} \cdot \frac{20}{17} \cdot p$$

$$130 \cdot 20 = 1 \cdot p$$

$$2,600 = p$$

Isaiah read 2,600 *pages over the summer.*

4. In a parking garage, the number of SUVs is 40% greater than the number of non-SUVs. Gina counted 98 SUVs in the parking garage. How many automobiles were parked in the garage?

40% *greater means* 100% *of the non-SUVs plus another* 40% *of that number, or* 140%.

$Quantity = Percent \times Whole$. *Let d represent the number of non-SUVs in the parking garage.*

$$98 = \frac{140}{100} \cdot d$$

$$98 = \frac{7}{5} \cdot d$$

$$98 \cdot \frac{5}{7} = \frac{7}{5} \cdot \frac{5}{7} \cdot d$$

$$14 \cdot 5 = 1 \cdot d$$

$$70 = d$$

There are 70 *non-SUVs in the parking garage.*

The total number of vehicles is the sum of the number of the SUVs and non-SUVs.

$70 + 98 = 168$. *There are a total of* 168 *vehicles in the parking garage.*

5. The price of a tent was decreased by 15% and sold for $\$76.49$. What was the original price of the tent in dollars?

If the price was decreased by 15%, then the sale price is 15% less than 100% of the original price, or 85%. $Quantity = Percent \times Whole$. Let p represent the original price of the tent.

$$76.49 = \frac{85}{100} \cdot p$$
$$76.49 = \frac{17}{20} \cdot p$$
$$76.49 \cdot \frac{20}{17} = \frac{17}{20} \cdot \frac{20}{17} \cdot p$$
$$\frac{1,529.8}{17} = 1 \cdot p$$
$$89.988 \approx p$$

Because this quantity represents money, the original price was $\$89.99$ after rounding to the nearest hundredth.

6. 40% of the students at Rockledge Middle School are musicians. 75% of those musicians have to read sheet music when they play their instruments. If 38 of the students can play their instruments without reading sheet music, how many students are there at Rockledge Middle School?

Let m represent the number of musicians at the school, and let s represent the number of students. There are two whole quantities in this problem. The first whole quantity is the number of musicians. The 38 students that can play an instrument without reading sheet music represent 25% of the musicians.

$Quantity = Percent \times Whole$
$$38 = \frac{25}{100} \cdot m$$
$$38 = \frac{1}{4} \cdot m$$
$$38 \cdot \frac{4}{1} = \frac{1}{4} \cdot \frac{4}{1} \cdot m$$
$$\frac{152}{1} = 1 \cdot m$$
$$152 = m$$

There are 152 musicians in the school.

$Quantity = Percent \times Whole$
$$152 = \frac{40}{100} \cdot s$$
$$152 = \frac{2}{5} \cdot s$$
$$152 \cdot \frac{5}{2} = \frac{2}{5} \cdot \frac{5}{2} \cdot s$$
$$\frac{760}{2} = 1 \cdot s$$
$$380 = s$$

There are a total of 380 students at Rockledge Middle School.

7. At Longbridge Middle School, 240 students said that they are an only child, which is 48% of the school's student enrollment. How many students attend Longbridge Middle School?

$$Quantity \rightarrow \%$$
$$240 \rightarrow 48\%$$
$$\frac{240}{48} \rightarrow 1\%$$
$$\frac{240}{48} \cdot 100 \rightarrow 100\%$$
$$5 \cdot 100 \rightarrow 100\%$$
$$500 \rightarrow 100\%$$

There are 500 students attending Longbridge Middle School.

8. Grace and her father spent $4\frac{1}{2}$ hours over the weekend restoring their fishing boat. This time makes up 6% of the time needed to fully restore the boat. How much total time is needed to fully restore the boat?

$$Quantity \rightarrow \%$$

$$4\frac{1}{2} \rightarrow 6\%$$

$$\frac{9}{2} \rightarrow 6\%$$

$$\frac{\frac{9}{2}}{6} \rightarrow 1\%$$

$$\frac{\frac{9}{2}}{6} \cdot 100 \rightarrow 100\%$$

$$\frac{9}{2} \cdot \frac{1}{6} \cdot 100 \rightarrow 100\%$$

$$\frac{9}{12} \cdot 100 \rightarrow 100\%$$

$$\frac{3}{4} \cdot 100 \rightarrow 100\%$$

$$\frac{300}{4} \rightarrow 100\%$$

$$75 \rightarrow 100\%$$

The total amount of time to restore the boat is 75 hours.

9. Bethany's mother was upset with her because Bethany's text messages from the previous month were 218% of the amount allowed at no extra cost under her phone plan. Her mother had to pay for each text message over the allowance. Bethany had $5,450$ text messages last month. How many text messages is she allowed under her phone plan at no extra cost?

$$Quantity \rightarrow \%$$

$$5,450 \rightarrow 218\%$$

$$\frac{5,450}{218} \rightarrow 1\%$$

$$\frac{5,450}{218} \cdot 100 \rightarrow 100\%$$

$$25 \cdot 100 \rightarrow 100\%$$

$$2,500 \rightarrow 100\%$$

Bethany is allowed $2,500$ text messages without extra cost.

10. Harry used 84% of the money in his savings account to buy a used dirt bike that cost him $\$1,050$. How much money is left in Harry's savings account?

$$Quantity \rightarrow \%$$

$$1,050 \rightarrow 84\%$$

$$\frac{1,050}{84} \rightarrow 1\%$$

$$\frac{1,050}{84} \cdot 100 \rightarrow 100\%$$

$$12.5 \cdot 100 \rightarrow 100\%$$

$$1250 \rightarrow 100\%$$

Harry started with $\$1,250$ in his account, but then spent $\$1,050$ of it on the dirt bike.
$1,250 - 1,050 = 200$. Harry has $\$200$ left in his savings account.

EUREKA
MATH™

Lesson 6:   Fluency with Percents

11. 15% of the students in Mr. Riley's social studies classes watch the local news every night. Mr. Riley found that 136 of his students do not watch the local news. How many students are in Mr. Riley's social studies classes?

If 15% of his students do watch their local news, then 85% do not.

$$Quantity \rightarrow \%$$
$$136 \rightarrow 85\%$$
$$\frac{136}{85} \rightarrow 1\%$$
$$\frac{136}{85} \cdot 100 \rightarrow 100\%$$
$$1.6 \cdot 100 \rightarrow 100\%$$
$$160 \rightarrow 100\%$$

There are 160 total students in Mr. Riley's social studies classes.

12. Grandma Bailey and her children represent about 9.1% of the Bailey family. If Grandma Bailey has 12 children, how many members are there in the Bailey family?

$$13 \rightarrow 9.1\%$$
$$\frac{1}{9.1}(13) \rightarrow 1\%$$
$$100\left(\frac{13}{9.1}\right) \rightarrow 100\%$$
$$\frac{1,300}{9.1} \rightarrow 100\%$$
$$142.857\ldots \rightarrow 100\%$$

The Bailey family has 143 members.

13. Shelley earned 20% more money waitressing this week than last week. This week she earned $72 waitressing. How much money did she earn last week?

Let m represent the number of dollars Shelley earned waitressing last week.

$$72 = \frac{120}{100}\, m$$
$$72\left(\frac{100}{120}\right) = \frac{120}{100}\left(\frac{100}{120}\right)m$$
$$60 = m$$

Shelley earned $60 in tips last week.

14. Lucy's savings account has 35% more money than her sister Edy's. Together the girls have saved a total of $206.80. How much money has each girl saved?

The money in Edy's account corresponds to 100%. Lucy has 35% more than Edy, so the money in Lucy's account corresponds to 135%. Together the girls have a total of $206.80, which is 235% of Edy's account balance.

Quantity = Pecent × Whole. Let b represent Edy's savings account balance in dollars.

$$206.8 = \frac{235}{100} \cdot b$$
$$206.8 = \frac{47}{20} \cdot b$$
$$206.8 \cdot \frac{20}{47} = \frac{47}{20} \cdot \frac{20}{47} \cdot b$$
$$\frac{4,136}{47} = 1 \cdot b$$
$$88 = b$$

Edy has saved $88 in her account. Lucy has saved the remainder of the $206.80, so:

206.8 − 88 = 118.8; Lucy has $118.80 saved in her account.

15. Bella spent 15% of her paycheck at the mall, and 40% of that was spent at the movie theatre. Bella spent a total of $13.74 at the movie theater for her movie ticket, popcorn, and a soft drink. How much money was in Bella's paycheck?

$$\$13.74 \to 40\%$$
$$\$3.435 \to 10\%$$
$$\$34.35 \to 100\%$$

Bella spent $34.35 at the mall.

$$\$34.35 \to 15\%$$
$$\$11.45 \to 5\%$$
$$\$229 \to 100\%$$

Bella's paycheck was $229.

16. On a road trip, Sara's brother drove 47.5% of the trip and Sara drove 80% of the remainder. If Sara drove for 4 hours and 12 minutes, how long was the road trip?

There are two whole quantities in this problem. First, Sara drove 80% of the remainder of the trip; the remainder is the first whole quantity. 4 hr. 12 min. is equivalent to $4\frac{12}{60}$ hr. $= 4.2$ hr.

$$Quantity \to \%$$
$$4.2 \to 80\%$$
$$\frac{4.2}{80} \to 1\%$$
$$\frac{4.2}{80} \cdot 100 \to 100\%$$
$$\frac{420}{80} \to 100\%$$
$$\frac{42}{8} \to 100\%$$
$$5.25 \to 100\%$$

The remainder of the trip that Sara's brother did not drive was 5.25 hours. He drove 47.5% of the trip, so the remainder of the trip was 52.5% of the trip, and the whole quantity is the time for the whole road trip.

$$Quantity \to \%$$
$$5.25 \to 52.5\%$$
$$\frac{5.25}{52.5} \to 1\%$$
$$\frac{5.25}{52.5} \cdot 100 \to 100\%$$
$$\frac{525}{52.5} \to 100\%$$
$$10 \to 100\%$$

The road trip was a total of 10 hours.

Sprint: Percent More or Less – Round 1

Number Correct: _____

Directions: Find each missing value.

1.	100% of 10 is __?	
2.	10% of 10 is __?	
3.	10% more than 10 is __?	
4.	11 is ___ % more than 10?	
5.	11 is ___% of 10?	
6.	11 is 10% more than ___ ?	
7.	110% of 10 is __?	
8.	10% less than 10 *is* __?	
9.	9 is ___% less than 10?	
10.	9 is ___% of 10?	
11.	9 is 10% less than ___?	
12.	10% of 50 is __?	
13.	10% more than 50 is __?	
14.	55 is ___% of 50?	
15.	55 is ___% more than 50?	
16.	55 is 10% more than ___?	
17.	110% of 50 is __?	
18.	10% less than 50 is __?	
19.	45 is ___% of 50?	
20.	45 is ___% less than 50?	
21.	45 is 10% less than ___?	
22.	40 is ___% less than 50?	

23.	15% of 80 is __?	
24.	15% more than 80 is __?	
25.	What is 115% of 80?	
26.	92 is 115% of __?	
27.	92 is ___% more than 80?	
28.	115% of 80 is __?	
29.	What is 15% less than 80?	
30.	What % of 80 is 68?	
31.	What % less than 80 is 68?	
32.	What % less than 80 is 56?	
33.	What % of 80 is 56?	
34.	What is 20% more than 50?	
35.	What is 30% more than 50?	
36.	What is 140% of 50?	
37.	What % of 50 is 85?	
38.	What % more than 50 is 85?	
39.	What % less than 50 is 35?	
40.	What % of 50 is 35?	
41.	1 is what % of 50?	
42.	6 is what % of 50?	
43.	24% of 50 is?	
44.	24% more than 50 is?	

Sprint: Percent More or Less – Round 1 [KEY]

Directions: Find each missing value.

1.	100% of 10 is ___?	**10**	23.	15% of 80 is ___?	**12**
2.	10% of 10 is ___?	**1**	24.	15% more than 80 is ___?	**92**
3.	10% more than 10 is ___?	**11**	25.	What is 115% of 80?	**92**
4.	11 is ___ % more than 10?	**10%**	26.	92 is 115% of ___?	**80**
5.	11 is ___% of 10?	**110%**	27.	92 is ___% more than 80?	**15%**
6.	11 is 10% more than ___ ?	**10**	28.	115% of 80 is ___?	**92**
7.	110% of 10 is ___?	**11**	29.	What is 15% less than 80?	**68**
8.	10% less than 10 *is* ___?	**9**	30.	What % of 80 is 68?	**85%**
9.	9 is ___% less than 10?	**10%**	31.	What % less than 80 is 68?	**15%**
10.	9 is ___% of 10?	**90%**	32.	What % less than 80 is 56?	**30%**
11.	9 is 10% less than ___?	**10**	33.	What % of 80 is 56?	**70%**
12.	10% of 50 is ___?	**5**	34.	What is 20% more than 50?	**60**
13.	10% more than 50 is ___?	**55**	35.	What is 30% more than 50?	**65**
14.	55 is ___% of 50?	**110%**	36.	What is 140% of 50?	**70**
15.	55 is ___% more than 50?	**10%**	37.	What % of 50 is 85?	**130%**
16.	55 is 10% more than ___?	**50**	38.	What % more than 50 is 85?	**30%**
17.	110% of 50 is ___?	**55**	39.	What % less than 50 is 35?	**30%**
18.	10% less than 50 is ___?	**45**	40.	What % of 50 is 35?	**70%**
19.	45 is ___% of 50?	**90%**	41.	1 is what % of 50?	**2%**
20.	45 is ___% less than 50?	**10%**	42.	6 is what % of 50?	**12%**
21.	45 is 10% less than ___?	**50**	43.	24% of 50 is?	**12**
22.	40 is ___% less than 50?	**20%**	44.	24% more than 50 is?	**62**

Sprint: Percent More or Less – Round 2

Number Correct: _____

Directions: Find each missing value.

Improvement: _____

1.	100% of 20 is ___?	
2.	10% of 20 is ___?	
3.	10% more than 20 is ___?	
4.	22 is ___ % more than 20?	
5.	22 is ___% of 20?	
6.	22 is 10% more than ___ ?	
7.	110% of 20 is ___?	
8.	10% less than 20 is ___?	
9.	18 is ___% less than 20?	
10.	18 is ___% of 20?	
11.	18 is 10% less than ___?	
12.	10% of 200 is ___?	
13.	10% more than 200 is ___?	
14.	220 is ___% of 200?	
15.	220 is ___% more than 200?	
16.	220 is 10% more than ___?	
17.	110% of 200 is ___?	
18.	10% less than 200 is ___?	
19.	180 is ___% of 200?	
20.	180 is ___% less than 200?	
21.	180 is 10% less than ___?	
22.	160 is ___% less than 200?	

23.	15% of 60 is ___?	
24.	15% more than 60 is ___?	
25.	What is 115% of 60?	
26.	69 is 115% of ___?	
27.	69 is ___% more than 60?	
28.	115% of 60 is ___?	
29.	What is 15% less than 60?	
30.	What % of 60 is 51?	
31.	What % less than 60 is 51?	
32.	What % less than 60 is 42?	
33.	What % of 60 is 42?	
34.	What is 20% more than 80?	
35.	What is 30% more than 80?	
36.	What is 140% of 80?	
37.	What % of 80 is 104?	
38.	What % more than 80 is 104?	
39.	What % less than 80 is 56?	
40.	What % of 80 is 56?	
41.	1 is what % of 200?	
42.	6 is what % of 200?	
43.	24% of 200 is?	
44.	24% more than 200 is?	

Sprint: Percent More or Less – Round 2 **[KEY]**

Directions: Find each missing value.

1.	100% of 20 is __?	20
2.	10% of 20 is __?	2
3.	10% more than 20 is __?	22
4.	22 is __ % more than 20?	10%
5.	22 is __% of 20?	110%
6.	22 is 10% more than __ ?	20
7.	110% of 20 is __?	22
8.	10% less than 20 is __?	18
9.	18 is __% less than 20?	10%
10.	18 is __% of 20?	90%
11.	18 is 10% less than __?	20
12.	10% of 200 is __?	20
13.	10% more than 200 is __?	220
14.	220 is __% of 200?	110%
15.	220 is __% more than 200?	10%
16.	220 is 10% more than __?	200
17.	110% of 200 is __?	220
18.	10% less than 200 is __?	180
19.	180 is __% of 200?	90%
20.	180 is __% less than 200?	10%
21.	180 is 10% less than __?	200
22.	160 is __% less than 200?	20%

23.	15% of 60 is __?	9
24.	15% more than 60 is __?	69
25.	What is 115% of 60?	69
26.	69 is 115% of __?	60
27.	69 is __% more than 60?	15%
28.	115% of 60 is __?	69
29.	What is 15% less than 60?	51
30.	What % of 60 is 51?	85%
31.	What % less than 60 is 51?	15%
32.	What % less than 60 is 42?	30%
33.	What % of 60 is 42?	70%
34.	What is 20% more than 80?	96
35.	What is 30% more than 80?	104
36.	What is 140% of 80?	112
37.	What % of 80 is 104?	130%
38.	What % more than 80 is 104?	30%
39.	What % less than 80 is 56?	30%
40.	What % of 80 is 56?	70%
41.	1 is what % of 200?	$\frac{1}{2}$%
42.	6 is what % of 200?	3%
43.	24% of 200 is?	48
44.	24% more than 200 is?	248

GRADE 7 • MODULE 4

Mathematics Curriculum

Topic B:

Percent Problems Including More than One Whole

7.RP.A.1, 7.RP.A.2, 7.RP.A.3, 7.EE.B.3

Focus Standard:	7.RP.A.1	Compute unit rates associated with ratios of fractions, including ratios of lengths, areas and other quantities measured in like or different units. *For example, if a person walks 1/2 mile in each 1/4 hour, compute the unit rate as the complex fraction ½ / ¼ miles per hour, equivalently 2 miles per hour.*
	7.RP.A.2	Recognize and represent proportional relationships between quantities.
		a. Decide whether two quantities are in a proportional relationship, e.g., by testing for equivalent ratios in a table or graphing on a coordinate plane and observing whether the graph is a straight line through the origin.
		b. Identify the constant of proportionality (unit rate) in tables, graphs, equations, diagrams, and verbal descriptions of proportional relationships.
		c. Represent proportional relationships by equations. *For example, if total cost t is proportional to the number n of items purchased at a constant price p, the relationship between the total cost and the number of items can be expressed as t = pn.*
		d. Explain what a point *(x, y)* on the graph of a proportional relationship means in terms of the situation, with special attention to the points (0, 0) and *(1, r)*, where *r* is the unit rate.
	7.RP.A.3	Use proportional relationships to solve multistep ratio and percent problems. *Examples: simple interest, tax, markups and markdowns, gratuities and commissions, fees, percent increase and decrease, percent error.*
	7.EE.B.3	Solve multi-step real-life and mathematical problems posed with positive and negative rational numbers in any form (whole numbers, fractions, and decimals), using tools strategically. Apply properties of operations to calculate with numbers in any form; convert between forms as appropriate; and assess the reasonableness of answers using mental computation and estimation

strategies. *For example: If a woman making $25 an hour gets a 10% raise, she will make an additional 1/10 of her salary an hour, or $2.50, for a new salary of $27.50. If you want to place a towel bar 9 3/4 inches long in the center of a door that is 27 ½ inches wide, you will need to place the bar about 9 inches from each edge; this estimate can be used as a check on the exact computation.*

Instructional Days: 5

Lesson 7:   Markup and Markdown Problems (P)[1]

Lesson 8:   Percent Error Problems (S)

Lesson 9:   Problem-Solving when the Percent Changes (P)

Lesson 10: Simple Interest (P)

Lesson 11: Tax, Commissions, Fees, and Other Real-World Percent Problems (M)

In Topic B, students understand and interpret the elements of increasingly complex real-world problems and directly connect elements in these contexts to the concept of the *part*, *whole*, and *percent* from Topic A (**7.RP.A.2**, **7.RP.A.3**, **7.EE.B.3**). The topic begins in Lesson 7, with students solving markup and markdown problems. They understand that the markup price will be more than the whole or more than 100% of the original price. And similarly, they know that the markdown price or discount price will be less than 100% of the whole. This conceptual understanding supports students' algebraic representations. To find a markup price, they multiply the whole by $(1 + m)$, where m is the markup rate, and to find a markdown price, they multiply the whole by $(1 - m)$, where m is the markdown rate. They write and solve algebraic equations, working backwards, for instance, to find a price before a markup when given the percent increase and markup price. Students relate percent markup or markdown to proportional relationships as they consider cases where items of varying initial prices undergo a markup (or markdown). They create an equation, a table, and a graph relating the initial prices to the prices after markup (or markdown). They relate the constant of proportionality to the markup or markdown rate, m, using the value of $(1 + m)$ in the case of a markup or $(1 - m)$ in the case of a markdown. Students also identify and describe in context the meaning of the point $(1, (1 + m))$ or $(1, (1 - m))$ on the graph.

Students continue to apply their conceptual understanding of the *part*, *whole*, and *percent* as they are introduced to *percent error* in Lesson 8. Additionally, they draw upon prior experiences with absolute value to make sense of the percent error formula and relate it to the elements of a word problem. Given an exact value, x, of a quantity and an approximate value, a, of the quantity, students use absolute value to represent the *absolute error* as $|a - x|$, and then use that to compute the *percent error* with the formula: $\frac{|a-x|}{|x|} \cdot 100\%$. Students understand that even when an exact value is not known, an estimate of the percent error can still be computed when given an inclusive range of values in which the exact value lies.

In Lesson 9, students solve word multi-step problems related to percents that change. They identify the quantities that represent the part and the whole and recognize when the whole changes based on the context of a word problem. For instance, to find the sale price of a $65 item that is discounted 20%, and then an extra 15% discount is applied, students create more than one equation to solve the problem. First,

---

[1] Lesson Structure Key: **P**-Problem Set Lesson, **M**-Modeling Cycle Lesson, **E**-Exploration Lesson, **S**-Socratic Lesson

they identify 65 as the whole, then write and solve the equation $Q = (1 - 0.20)(65)$ to arrive at a price of $52 before they apply the extra discount of 15%. They then identify 52 as the whole, then write and solve the equation $Q = (1 - 0.15)(52)$ to arrive at a final sale price of $44.20.

In lesson 10, students use the formula $interest = principal \times rate \times time$ to solve problems involving simple interest, and they relate principal to the whole, the interest rate to the percent, and the amount of interest to the part. When solving an interest problem, students pay close attention to the interest rates' units, the units for time, and convert when necessary so they are compatible. Topic B concludes with Lesson 11, which involves percents related to other rates, such as tax, commission, and fees. Students apply their conceptual understanding of the part, whole, and percent to a real-life scenario related to the formation of a new sports team in a school district. In Lessons 10–11 students interpret and represent these proportional relationships through equations, graphs, and tables (**7.RP.A.1**, **7.RP.A.2**), recognizing where the constant of proportionality is present in their equations and graphs and connecting it to the value $(1 + m)$ or $(1 - m)$, where m is the rate given as a percentage.

Lesson 7: Markup and Markdown Problems

Student Outcomes

- Students understand the terms *original price, selling price, markup, markdown, markup rate,* and *markdown rate*.
- Students identify the original price as the whole and use their knowledge of percent and proportional relationships to solve multistep markup and markdown problems.
- Students understand equations for markup and markdown problems and use them to solve markup and markdown problems.

Lesson Notes

- In this lesson, students use algebraic equations to solve multi-step word problems involving markups and markdowns. This lesson extends the mathematical practices and terminology students were exposed to in Module 1, Lesson 14.
- New finance terms such as *retail price, consumer, cost price,* and *wholesale price* are introduced. Although students are not required to memorize these terms, they do provide a solid foundational knowledge for financial literacy. To make the lesson more meaningful to students, use examples from an actual newspaper circular.
- Students have had significant exposure to creating tables and graphs to determine proportional relationships in Module 3. Before the lesson, the teacher may need to review past student performance data to target students who might potentially struggle with discovering proportional relationships using percent problems in Exercise 4.

Definitions:

- A **markup** is the amount of increase in a price.
- A **markdown** is the amount of decrease in a price.
- The **original price** is the starting price. It is sometimes called the cost or wholesale price.
- The **selling price** is the original price plus the markup or minus the markdown.
- The **markup rate** is the percent increase in the price, and the markdown rate (discount rate) is the percent decrease in the price.
- Most markup problems can be solved by the equation: $Selling\ Price = (1 + m)(Whole)$, where m is the markup rate, and the whole is the original price.
- Most markdown problems can be solved by the equation: $Selling\ Price = (1 - m)(Whole)$, where m is the markdown rate, and the whole is the original price.

Classwork

Opening (3 minutes)

Pose the question to the class. Students, who have been placed in groups, discuss possible answers. Teacher asks a few students to share out.

- A brand of sneakers costs $29.00 to manufacture in Omaha, Nebraska. The shoes are then shipped to shoe stores across the country. When you see them on the shelves, the price is $69.99. How do you think the price you pay for the sneakers is determined? Use percent to describe the markup. Explain your reasoning.

   □ *The store makes up a new price so they can make money. The store has to buy the sneakers and pay for any transportation costs to get the sneakers to the store.*

   □ *The store marks up the price to earn a profit because they had to buy the shoes from the company.*

   □ *Markup is the amount of increase in a price from the original price.*

Close the discussion by explaining how the price of an item sold in a store is determined. For example, in order for the manufacturer to make a profit, it has to pay for the cost to make the item. This is the first markup. Then, a store purchases the item at a *cost price* from the manufacturer. The store then increases the price of the item by a percent called the *markup rate* before it is sold to the store's customers. Stores do this in order to earn a *profit*.

Example 1 (5 minutes): A Video Game Markup

Students construct an algebraic equation based on a word problem. They express the markup rate of 40% on a video game that costs $30.00 as 1.40(30) to show that a markup means a percent increase. Students identify the quantity that corresponds with 100% (the whole).

> **Scaffolding:**
> - Use sentence strips to create a word wall for student reference throughout the lesson to avoid confusion over financial terms.
>
>   Some words can be written on the same sentence strip to show they are synonyms, such as *discount price* and *sales price*, and *cost price* and *wholesale price*.

Example 1

Games Galore Super Store buys the latest video game at a wholesale price of $30.00. The markup rate at Game's Galore Super Store is 40%. You use your allowance to purchase the game at the store. How much will you pay, not including tax?

   a. Write an equation to find the price of the game at Games Galore Super Store. Explain your equation.

   Let P represent the price of the video game.

   $$Quantity = Percent \times Whole$$

   $$P = (100\% + 40\%)(30)$$

   b. Solve the equation from part (a).

   $$P = (100\% + 40\%)(30)$$

   $$P = (1.40)(30)$$

   $$P = 42 \qquad \text{I would pay \$42 if I bought it from Games Galore Super Store.}$$

   c. What was the total markup of the video game? Explain.

   The markup was $12 because $42 − $30 = $12.

> d. You and a friend are discussing markup rate. He says that an easier way to find the total markup is by multiplying the wholesale price of $30 by 40%. Do you agree with him? Why or why not?
>
> *Yes, I agree with him because $(0.40)(30) = 12$. The markup rate is a percent of the wholesale price. Therefore, it makes sense to multiply them together because $Quantity = Percent \times Whole$.*

- Which quantity is the "whole" quantity in this problem?
    - *The wholesale price is the whole quantity.*
- How do 140% and 1.4 correspond in this situation?
    - *The markup price of the video game is 140% times the wholesale price. 140% and 1.4 are equivalent forms. In order to find the markup price, convert the percent to a decimal or fraction and multiply it by the whole.*
- What does a "markup" mean?
    - *A markup is the amount of increase in a price.*

Example 2 (7 minutes): Black Friday

Students discuss the greatest American shopping day of the year, Black Friday—the day after Thanksgiving. The teacher could share the history of Black Friday to engage students in the lesson by reading the article at http://www.marketplace.org/topics/life/commentary/history-black-friday. Students make the connection that markdown is a percent decrease.

 Students realize that the distributive property allows them to arrive at an answer in one step. They learn that in order to apply an additional discount, a new whole must be found first.

> **Scaffolding:**
> - Provide newspaper circulars from Black Friday sales, or print one from the Internet to access prior knowledge of discounts for all learners.
> - Choose an item from the circular in lieu of the one provided in Example 1.

- Does it matter in what order we take the discount? Why or why not? Allow students time to conjecture in small groups or with elbow partners before problem solving. Monitor student conversations, providing clarification as needed.
    - *I think the order does matter because applying the first discount will lower the price. Then, you would multiply the second discount to the new lower price.*
    - *I do not think order matters because both discounts will be multiplied to the original price anyway and multiplication is commutative. For example, $2 \times 3 \times 4$ is the same as $3 \times 4 \times 2$.*

Example 2: Black Friday

A $300 mountain bike is discounted by 30% and then discounted an additional 10% for shoppers who arrive before 5:00 a.m.

a. Find the sales price of the bicycle.

Find the price with 30% discount.

Let D represent the discount price of the bicycle with the 30% discount rate.

$$Quantity = Percent \times Whole$$
$$D = (100\% - 30\%)(300)$$
$$D = (0.70)(300)$$
$$D = 210$$

$210 is the discount price of the bicycle with the 30% discount rate.

- Which quantity is the new whole?

  □ *The discounted price of 30% off, which is* $210.

Find the price with the additional 10% discount.

Let A represent the discount price of the bicycle with the additional 10% discount.

$$A = (100\% - 10\%)(210)$$
$$= (1 - 0.10)(210)$$
$$= (0.90)(210)$$
$$= 189$$

$189 *is the discount price of the bicycle with the additional 10% discount.*

    b.   **In all, by how much has the bicycle been discounted in dollars? Explain.**

        $300 − $189 = $111. ***The bicycle has been discounted*** $111 *because the original price was* $300. ***With both discounts applied, the new price is*** $189.

    c.   **After both discounts were taken, what was the total percent discount?**

        A final discount of 40% means that you would add 30% + 10% and apply it to the same whole. This is not the case because the additional 10% discount is taken after the 30% discount has been applied, so you are only receiving that 10% discount on 70% of the original price. A 40% discount would make the final price $180 *because* $180 = (0.60)(300).

        However, the actual final discount as a percent is 37%.

        Let P be the percent the sales price is of the original price. Let F represent the actual final discount as a percent.

$$Part = Percent \times Whole$$
$$189 = P \times Whole$$
$$189 = P \times 300$$
$$\left(\frac{1}{300}\right)189 = P \times 300\left(\frac{1}{300}\right)$$
$$0.63 = 63\% = P$$

$$F = 100\% - 63\% = 37\%$$

- Teacher could also show students that a 30% discount means to multiply by 0.70, and an extra 10% means to multiply by 0.90. $(0.70)(0.90) = 0.63$, so it is the same as $100\% - 63\% = 37\%$ discount. This can help students perform the mathematics more efficiently.

---

    d.   **Instead of purchasing the bike for** $300, **how much would you save if you bought it before 5:00 a.m.?**

        You would save $111 *if you bought the bike before 5:00 a.m. because* $300 − $189 *is* $111.

Exercises 1–3 (6 minutes)

Students complete the following exercises independently or in groups of two using $Quantity = Percent \times Whole$. Review the correct answers before moving to Example 3. The use of a calculator is recommended for the exercises.

Exercises 1–3

1. Sasha went shopping and decided to purchase a set of bracelets for 25% off of the regular price. If Sasha buys the bracelets today, she will receive an additional 5%. Find the sales price of the set of bracelets with both discounts. How much money will Sasha save if she buys the bracelets today?

   Let B be the sales price with both discounts in dollars.

   $B = (0.95)(0.75)(44) = 31.35.$ *The sales price of the set of bracelets with both discounts is $31.35. Sasha will save $12.65.*

   $44.00

2. A golf store purchases a set of clubs at a wholesale price of $250. Mr. Edmond learned that the clubs were marked up 200%. Is it possible to have a percent increase greater than 100%? What is the retail price of the clubs?

   Yes, it is possible. Let C represent the retail price of the clubs in dollars.

   $$C = (100\% + 200\%)(250)$$
   $$= (1 + 2)(250)$$
   $$= (3)(250)$$
   $$= 750$$

   The retail price of the clubs is $750.

3. Is a percent increase of a set of golf clubs from $250 to $750 the same as a markup rate of 200%? Explain.

   Yes, it is the same. In both cases, the percent increase and markup rate show by how much (in terms of percent) the new price is over the original price. The whole is $250 and corresponds to 100%. $\frac{750}{250} = \frac{3}{1} \times 100\% = 300\%.$ $750 is 300% of $250. 300% − 100% = 200%. From question 1, the markup is 200%. So, percent increase is the same as markup.

Example 3 (5 minutes): Working Backwards

Teacher refers to an item in the newspaper circular displayed to the class. Students find the markdown rate (discount rate) given an original price (regular price) and a sales price (discount price). Students find the total or final price, including sales tax.

Example 3: Working Backwards

A car that normally sells for $20,000 is on sale for $16,000. The sales tax is 7.5%.

- What is the "whole quantity" in this problem?
  - *The whole quantity is $20,000.*

a.   What percent of the original price of the car is the final price?

$$Quantity = Percent \times Whole$$
$$16,000 = P(20,000)$$
$$16,000 \left(\frac{1}{20,000}\right) = P(20,000)\left(\frac{1}{20,000}\right)$$
$$0.8 = P$$
$$0.8 = \frac{80}{100} = 80\%$$

The final price is 80% *of the original price.*

b.   Find the discount rate.

The discount rate is 20% *because* $100\% - 80\% = 20\%$.

c.   By law, sales tax has to be applied to the discount price. However, would it be better for the consumer if the 7.5% sales tax were calculated before the 20% discount was applied? Why or why not?

Apply Sales Tax First

Apply the sales tax to the whole.

$(100\% + 7.5\%)(20,000)$

$(1 + 0.075)(20,000)$

$(1.075)(20,000)$

$\$21,500$ *is the price of the car, including tax, before the discount.*

Apply the discount to the new whole.

$(100\% - 20\%)(21,500)$

$(1 - 0.2)(21,500) = 17,200$

$\$17,200$ *is the final price, including the discount.*

Apply the Discount First

$(100\% + 7.5\%)(16,000)$

$(1 + 0.075)(16,000)$

$(1.075)(16,000)$

$\$17,200$ *is the final price, including the tax.*

Because both final prices are the same, it doesn't matter which is applied first. This is because multiplication is commutative. The discount rate and sales tax rate are both being applied to the whole, $\$20,000$.

d.   Write an equation applying the commutative property to support your answer to part (c).

$$20,000(1.075)(0.8) = 20,000(0.8)(1.075)$$

Exercises 4–5 (9 minutes)

Students write a markup or markdown equation based on the context of the problem. They use algebraic equations of the form: $Quantity = (1 + m) \cdot Whole$ for markups, or $Quantity = (1 - m) \cdot Whole$ for markdowns. Students will use their equations to make a table and graph in order to interpret the unit rate (**7.RP.A.2**). Students may use a calculator for calculations, but their equations and steps should be shown for these exercises.

Exercise 4

a. Write an equation to determine the selling price, p, on an item that is originally priced s dollars after a markup of 25%.

$$p = 1.25s \ \ or \ \ p = (0.25 + 1)s$$

b. Create a table (and label it) showing five possible pairs of solutions to the equation.

Price of Item before Markup, s (in dollars)	Price of Item after Markup, p (in dollars)
10	12.50
20	25.00
30	37.50
40	50.00
50	62.50

c. Create a graph (and label it) of the equation.

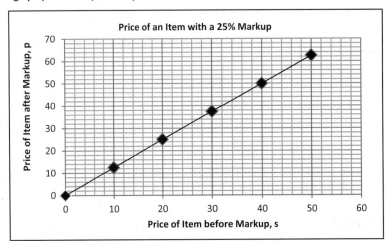

d. Interpret the points $(0, 0)$ and $(1, r)$.

The point $(0, 0)$ means that a $0 (free) item will cost $0 because the 25% markup is also $0. The point $(1, r)$ is $(1, 1.25)$. It means that a $1.00 item will cost $1.25 after it is marked up by 25%; r is the unit rate.

Exercise 5

Use the following table to calculate the markup or markdown rate. Show your work. Is the relationship between the original price and selling price proportional or not? Explain.

Original Price, m (in dollars)	Selling Price, p (in dollars)
$1,750	$1,400
$1,500	$1,200
$1,250	$1,000
$1,000	$800
750	600

Because the selling price is less than the original price, use the equation: $Selling\ Price = (1 - m) \times Whole.$

$$1400 = (1 - m)(1750)$$
$$\frac{1400}{1750} = (1 - m)\frac{1750}{1750}$$
$$0.80 = 1 - m$$
$$0.20 = m$$

The markdown rate is 20%. The relationship between the original price and selling price is proportional because the table shows the ratio $\frac{p}{m} = \frac{0.80}{1}$ *for all possible pairs of solutions.*

Closing (3 minutes)

- How do you find the markup and markdown of an item?
  - *To find the markup of an item, you multiply the whole by $(1 + m)$, where m is the markup rate.*
  - *To find the markdown of an item, you multiply the whole by $(1 - m)$, where m is the markdown rate.*
- Discuss two ways to apply two discount rates to the price of an item when one discount follows the other.
  - *In order to apply two discounts, you must first multiply the original price (whole) by 1 minus the first discount rate to get the discount price (new whole). Then, you must multiply by 1 minus the second discount rate to the new whole to get the final price. For example, to find the final price of an item discounted by 25%, and then discounted by another 10%, you would first have to multiply by 75% to get a new whole. Then, you multiply the new whole by 90% to find the final price.*

Exit Ticket (7 minutes)

Name _____   Date _____

Lesson 7: Markup and Markdown Problems

Exit Ticket

1. A store that sells skis buys them from a manufacturer at a wholesale price of $57. The store's markup rate is 50%.

    a. What price does the store charge its customers for the skis?

    b. What percent of the original price is the final price? Show your work.

    c. What is the percent increase from the original price to the final price?

Exit Ticket Sample Solutions

---

1. A store that sells skis buys them from a manufacturer at a wholesale price of $57. The store's markup rate is 50%.

   a. What price does the store charge its customers for the skis?

   $57 \times (1 + 0.50) = 85.50$. *The store charges* $85.50 *for the skis.*

   b. What percent of the original price is the final price? Show your work.

   $$Quantity = Percent \times Whole$$
   $$85.50 = P(57)$$
   $$85.50\left(\frac{1}{57}\right) = P(57)\left(\frac{1}{57}\right)$$
   $$01.50 = P$$

   $1.50 = \dfrac{150}{100} = 150\%$. *The final price is* 150% *of the original price.*

   c. What is the percent increase from the original price to the final price?

   The percent increase is 50% *because* $150\% - 100\% = 50\%$.

Problem Set Sample Solutions

In the following problems, students solve markup problems by multiplying the whole by $(1 + m)$, where m is the markup rate, and work backwards to find the whole by dividing the markup price by $(1 + m)$. They also solve markdown problems by multiplying the whole by $(1 - m)$, where m is the markdown rate, and work backwards to find the whole by dividing the markdown price by $(1 - m)$. Students also solve percent problems learned so far in the module.

---

1. You have a coupon for an additional 25% off the price of any sale item at a store. The store has put a robotics kit on sale for 15% off the original price of $40. What is the price of the robotics kit after both discounts?

   $(0.75)(0.85)(40) = 25.50$. *The price of the robotics kit after both discounts is* $25.50.

2. A sign says that the price marked on all music equipment is 30% off the original price. You buy an electric guitar for the sale price of $315.

   a. What is the original price?

   $\dfrac{315}{1-0.30} = \dfrac{315}{0.70} = 450$. *The original price is* $450.

   b. How much money did you save off the original price of the guitar?

   $450 - 315 = 135$. *I saved* $135 *off the original price of the guitar.*

   c. What percent of the original price is the sale price?

   $\dfrac{315}{450} = \dfrac{70}{100} = 70\%$

---

3. The cost of a New York Yankees baseball cap is $24.00. The local sporting goods store sells it for $30.00. Find the markup rate.

    $30 = P(24)$

    $P = \frac{30}{24} = 1.25 = (100\% + 25\%)$. *The markup rate is* 25%.

4. Write an equation to determine the selling price, p, on an item that is originally priced s dollars after a markdown of 15%.

    $p = 0.85s$ *or* $p = (1 - 0.15)s$

    a. Create a table (and label it) showing five possible pairs of solutions to the equation.

Price of Item before Markdown, s (in dollars)	Price of Item after Markdown, p (in dollars)
10	8.50
20	17.00
30	25.50
40	34.00
50	42.50

    b. Create a graph (and label it) of the equation.

    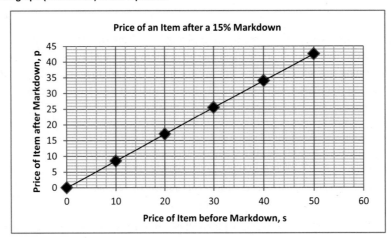

    c. Interpret the points $(0, 0)$ and $(1, r)$.

    The point $(0, 0)$ *means that a* $\$0$ *(free) item will cost* $\$0$ *because the* 15% *markdown is also* $\$0$*. The point* $(1, r)$ *is* $(1, 0.85)$*, which represents the unit rate. It means that a* $\$1.00$ *item will cost* $\$0.85$ *after it is marked down by* 15%*.*

5. At the amusement park, Laura paid $6.00 for a small cotton candy. Her older brother works at the park, and he told her they mark up the cotton candy by 300%. Laura does not think that is mathematically possible. Is it possible, and if so, what is the price of the cotton candy before the markup?

    Yes, it is possible. $\frac{6.00}{1+3} = \frac{6}{4} = 1.50$. *The price of the cotton candy before the markup is* $\$1.50$*.*

6. **A store advertises that customers can take 25% off the original price and then take an extra 10% off. Is this 35% off? Explain.**

    No, because the 25% is taken first off the original price to get a new whole. Then, the extra 10% off is multiplied to the new whole. For example, $(1 - 0.25)(1 - 0.10) = 0.675$ or $(0.75)(0.90) = 0.675$. This is multiplied to the whole, which is the original price of the item. This is not the same as adding 25% and 10% to get 35%, then multiplying by $(1 - 0.35)$.

7. **An item that costs \$50 is marked 20% off. Sales tax for the item is 8%. What is the final price, including tax?**

    a.   **Solve the problem with the discount applied before the sales tax.**

        $(1.08)(0.80)(50) = 43.20$. *The final price is $\$43.20$.*

    b.   **Solve the problem with discount applied after the sales tax.**

        $(0.80)(1.08)(50) = 43.20$. *The final price is $\$43.20$.*

    c.   **Compare your answers in parts (a) and (b). Explain.**

        My answers are the same. The final price is $\$43.20$. This is because multiplication is commutative.

8. **The sale price for a bicycle is \$315 dollars. The original price was first discounted by 50% and then discounted an additional 10%. Find the original price of the bicycle.**

    $(315 \div 0.9) \div 0.5 = 700$. *The original price was $\$700$.*

9. **A ski shop has a markup rate of 50%. Find the selling price of skis that cost the storeowner \$300.**

    Solution 1: Use the original price of $\$300$ as the whole. The markup rate is 50% of $\$300 = \$150$. The selling price is $\$300 + \$150 = \$450$.

    Solution 2: Multiply $\$300$ by 1 plus the markup rate (i.e., the selling price is $(1.5)(\$300) = \$450$).

10. **A tennis supply store pays a wholesaler \$90 for a tennis racquet and sells it for \$144. What is the markup rate?**

    Solution 1: Let the original price of $\$90$ be the whole. $Quantity = Percent \times Whole$.

    $144 = Percent(90)$

    $\dfrac{144}{90} = Percent = 0.6 = 160\%$. *This is a 60% increase. The markup rate is 60%.*

    Solution 2:

    $$Selling\ Price = (1 + m)(Whole)$$
    $$144 = (1 + m)90$$
    $$1 + m = \frac{144}{90} = 1.6$$
    $$m = 0.6 = 60\%$$

11. A shoe store is selling a pair of shoes for $60 that has been discounted by 25%. What was the original selling price?

   Solution 1:

   $60 → 75\%$
   $20 → 25\%$
   $80 → 100\%$

   The original price was $80.

   Solution 2: Let x be the original cost in dollars.

   $(1 - 0.25)x = 60$
   $\frac{3}{4}x = 60$
   $\left(\frac{4}{3}\right)\left(\frac{3}{4}x\right) = \frac{4}{3}(60) = 80$
   The original price was $80.

12. A shoe store has a markup rate of 75% and is selling a pair of shoes for $133. Find the price the store paid for the shoes.

   Solution 1:

   $133 → 175\%$
   $19 → 25\%$
   $76 → 100\%$

   The store paid $76.

   Solution 2: Divide the selling price by 1.75.

   $\frac{133}{1.75} = 76$

   The store paid $76.

13. Write $5\frac{1}{4}\%$ as a simple fraction.

   $\frac{21}{400}$

14. Write $\frac{3}{8}$ as a percent.

   37.5%

15. If 20% of the 70 faculty members at John F. Kennedy Middle School are male, what is the number of male faculty members?

   14

16. If a bag contains 400 coins, and $33\frac{1}{2}\%$ are nickels, how many nickels are there? What percent of the coins are not nickels?

   There are 134 nickels. The percent of coins that are not nickels is $66\frac{1}{2}\%$.

17. The temperature outside is 60 degrees Fahrenheit. What would be the temperature if it is increased by 20%?

   72 degrees Fahrenheit.

Lesson 8: Percent Error Problems

Student Outcomes

- Given the exact value, x, of a quantity and an approximate value, a, of the quantity, students use the absolute error, $|a - x|$, to compute the percent error by using the formula $\frac{|a-x|}{|x|} \times 100\%$.
- Students understand the meaning of percent error as the percent the absolute error is of the exact value.
- Students understand that when an exact value is not known, an estimate of the percent error can still be computed when given a range determined by two inclusive values (e.g., if there are known to be between 6,000 and 7,000 black bears in New York, but the exact number is not known, the percent error can be estimated to be $\left(\frac{1,000}{6,000}\right)(100\%)$ at most, which is $16\frac{2}{3}\%$).

Lesson Notes

There are two cases in which percent error is discussed in the seventh grade curriculum. The first case is when the exact value is known, and the second case is when the exact value is not known. The following definitions are used throughout this module as the teacher presents students with examples and exercises for both cases.

Absolute Error: Given the exact value, x, of a quantity and an approximate value, a, of the quantity, the absolute error is $|a - x|$.

Percent Error: The percent error is the percent the absolute error is of the exact value, $\frac{|a-x|}{|x|} \times 100\%$, where x is the exact value of the quantity and a is an approximate value of the quantity.

In order to teach percent error, both cases should be addressed individually. In the first case, when absolute error and exact value are known, percent error can be computed precisely. In the second case, when the exact value is not known, percent error can only be estimated. Problems in this lesson will emphasize the first case. Review with students how to calculate absolute value if necessary.

Classwork

Discussion (10 minutes)

The class will discuss the dimensions of a computer monitor's size. The length of the diagonal of the screen tells the screen's size. Before discussion, select three students to measure the diagonal of a 15-inch screen (in inches) using a ruler. A sample list of each student's measurement is recorded in a list below. If a 15-inch monitor is not available, use another size. If no computer monitor is available, present the sample data below and pose discussion questions to the class.

> *Scaffolding:*
> 1. Record student data on chart paper or a projection device for visual learners.
> 2. If necessary, remind students how to record measurements that fall between whole numbers on a ruler.
> 3. Have all students record the data in their notes to aid kinesthetic learners and to increase participation throughout the discussion.

Student	Measurement 1 (in.)	Measurement 2 (in.)
Taylor	$15\frac{2}{8}$	$15\frac{3}{8}$
Connor	$15\frac{4}{8}$	$14\frac{7}{8}$
Jordan	$15\frac{4}{8}$	$14\frac{6}{8}$

Possible discussion questions:

- Do you believe that the stated size of the screen, printed on the box, is the actual size of the screen?
  - *Yes, because it would not be right to print one thing when the actual size is something else.*

- Using our sample data, how could you determine the error of each student's measurement to the actual measurement?
  - *You could subtract the actual measurement from the student measurement.*
  - *You could subtract the student measurement from the actual measurement.*

- What is the difference between Connor's Measurement 2 and the actual measurement?
  - $\left(14\frac{7}{8} - 15\right)$ *in.* $= -0.125$ *in.*
  - $\left(15 - 14\frac{7}{8}\right)$ *in.* $= 0.125$ *in.*

- Which one is correct? Why?
  - *I think the second one is correct because you cannot have* -0.125 *in. Measurements have to be positive.*
  - *The error,* $a - x$, *is positive if the approximation is too big and negative if the approximation is too small.*

- How can we make sure that the difference is always positive? Elaborate.
  - *You could use the absolute value. Using the absolute value will tell you how far the actual measurement is below or above your measurement.*

At this point, introduce the definition of *absolute error*. Project the definition for students to copy in their notes. Explain to the class that in this case, the *exact value* is the advertised or printed screen size, and the *approximate value* is each student's measurement.

Absolute Error: Given the exact value, x, of a quantity and an approximate value, a, of the quantity, the *absolute error* is $|a - x|$.

Example 1 (5 minutes): How Far Off?

Continue to use the sample data to introduce the concept of absolute error. Students will calculate how far off the trial measurements are from the actual length of the diagonal of the screen using the absolute error formula.

Example 1: How Far Off?

Find the absolute error for the following problems. Explain what the absolute error means in context.

   a.   Taylor's Measurement 1

$$\left| 15\frac{2}{8} \ in. - 15 \ in. \right| = |0.25 \ in| = 0.25 \ in.$$

   Taylor's Measurement 1 was 0.25 inches away from the actual value of 15 inches.

   b.   Connor's Measurement 1

$$\left| 15\frac{4}{8} \ in. - 15 \ in. \right| = |0.5 \ in.| = 0.5 \ in.$$

   Connor's Measurement 1 was 0.5 inches away from the actual value of 15 inches.

   c.   Jordan's Measurement 2

$$\left| 14\frac{6}{8} \ in. - 15 \ in. \right| = 0.25 \ in.$$

   Jordan's Measurement 2 was 0.25 inches away from the actual value of 15 inches.

Teacher should continue with Socratic questioning:

- Do you think the absolute error should be large or small? Why or why not?
  - *I think the absolute value should be small because you want the approximate value to be as close to the exact value as possible. If it is too large, then the student made an error in reading the measurement or a better measurement tool is needed.*
- If we wanted to know the percent that our absolute error is of the exact value, what would this tell us?
  - *This would tell us by how much our measurement (approximation) differs from the real (exact) measurement. We could use this to know how well we did or did not estimate.*
- Can you derive a formula or rule to calculate the percent that our absolute error is of the exact value?
  - $\frac{|x-a|}{|x|} \times 100\%$
  - $\frac{|a-x|}{|x|} \times 100\%$

Percent Error: The *percent error* is the percent the absolute error is of the exact value, $\frac{|a-x|}{|x|} \times 100\%$, where x is the exact value of the quantity and a is an approximate value of the quantity.

Students should realize that percent error is always positive because of the use of absolute value in the formula.
MP.6 Students should still pay careful attention to the ordering of the values in the numerator (a and x) even though the absolute value will produce a positive difference.

Example 2 (5 minutes): How Right is Wrong?

Use sample data to introduce the concept of percent error. Students will learn that the percent error is the percent the absolute error is of the real value.

Example 2: How Right is Wrong?

    a.   Find the percent error for Taylor's Measurement 1. What does this mean?

$$\frac{\left|15\frac{2}{8} \ in. - 15 \ in.\right|}{|15 \ in.|} \times 100\%$$

$$\frac{|0.25|}{|15|} \times 100\%$$

$$\frac{1}{60} \times 100\%$$

$$1\frac{2}{3}\%$$

          This means that Taylor's measurement of 15.25 inches has an error that is $1\frac{2}{3}\%$ of the actual value.

    b.   From Example 1, part (b), find the percent error for Connor's Measurement 1. What does this mean?

$$\frac{0.5 \ in.}{15 \ in.} \times 100\% = 3\frac{1}{3}\%$$

          This means that Connor's measurement of $15\frac{4}{8}$ inches has an error that is $3\frac{1}{3}\%$ of the actual value.

    c.   From Example 1, part (c), find the percent error for Jordan's Measurement 2. What does it mean?

$$\frac{0.25 \ in.}{15 \ in.} \times 100\% = 1\frac{2}{3}\%$$

          This means that Jordan's measurement of $14\frac{6}{8}$ inches has an error that is $1\frac{2}{3}\%$ of the actual value.

    d.   What is the purpose of finding percent error?

          It tells you how big your error is compared to the true value. An error of 1 cm is very small when measuring the distance for a marathon, but an error of 1 cm is very large if you are a heart surgeon. In evaluating the seriousness of an error, we usually compare it to the exact value.

Exercises 1–3 (7 minutes)

In these exercises, students will solve a variety of real-world percent error problems when absolute error and exact value are known, which means that percent error can be computed precisely. They will show their work by substituting the appropriate values into the percent error formula and performing calculations with or without a calculator.

Exercises 1–3

Calculate the percent error for Problems 1–3. Leave your final answer in fraction form, if necessary.

1. A realtor expected 18 people to show up for an open house, but 25 attended.

$$\frac{|18 - 25|}{|25|} \times 100\% = 28\%$$

2. In science class, Mrs. Moore's students were directed to weigh a 300 gram mass on the balance scale. Tina weighed the object and reported 328 grams.

$$\frac{|328 - 300|}{|300|} \times 100\% = 9\frac{1}{3}\%$$

3. Darwin's coach recorded that he had bowled 250 points out of 300 in a bowling tournament. However, the official scoreboard showed that Darwin actually bowled 225 points out of 300.

$$\frac{|250 - 225|}{|225|} \times 100\% = 11\frac{1}{9}\%$$

Continue with Socratic questioning:

- Determine if this statement is always, sometimes, or never true: "The greater the difference between an approximate value and the exact value, the greater the percent error." Justify your response with an example.
  - *This statement is sometimes true. In measuring the length of a piece of string, the exact value of 2 inches and an approximate value of 1 inch will give a percent error of 50% because $\frac{|1-2|}{2} \times 100\% = 50\%$. The measurements are 1 inch apart. In measuring the length of a football field, the exact value of 100 yards and an approximate value of 90 yards will give a percent error of 10% because $\frac{|90-100|}{100} \times 100\% = 10\%$. The measurements are 10 yards apart.*

- Is it possible to calculate the percent error if you do not know the exact value?
  - *No. The formula requires the exact value.*

- What if you know the exact value is between 100 and 110, and your estimate is 103. Is it possible to estimate the absolute error?
  - *Yes. The absolute error would be 7, at most.*

- Is it now possible to estimate the percent error?
  - *Yes. The percent error is 7 divided by a number between 100 and 110. The largest the percent error could be is $\frac{7}{100} = 7\%$. The percent error is 7%, at most.*

Example 3 (5 minutes): Estimating Percent Error

In this example, students learn that the percent error can only be estimated, not calculated, if the exact value is not known but is known to lie in an interval between two numbers. They will show their work by substituting the appropriate values into the percent error formula. In reviewing the example with the class, the teacher should explain that the most the percent error could be occurs when the numerator is as big as possible (16) and the denominator is as small as possible (573). The least the percent error could be is 0%. This occurs if the actual count is the same as the actual attendance.

Example 3: Estimating Percent Error

The attendance at a musical event was counted several times. All counts were between 573 and 589. If the actual attendance number is between 573 and 589, inclusive, what is the most the percent error could be? Explain your answer.

The most the absolute error could be is $|589 - 573| = 16$*. The percent error will be largest when the exact value is smallest. Therefore, the most the percent error could be is* $\frac{16}{573} \times 100\% < 2.8\%$*. In this case, the percent error is less than* 2.8%*.*

Closing (2 minutes)

- Explain the difference between absolute error and percent error.
  - *Absolute error is the magnitude of the difference between the approximate value and the exact value. It tells you how far away in units the approximate value is from the exact value. Percent error is the percent that the absolute error is of the exact value.*

- Can either the absolute error or percent error be negative? Why or why not?
  - *No, neither can be negative because finding the absolute value of each will cause the final result to be positive.*

- What is the benefit of calculating or using the percent error?
  - *The absolute error tells how big your error is, but the percent error tells how big it is compared to the actual value. All measurements have some error. A good measurement will have a small percent error.*

Exit Ticket (6 minutes)

Name _____   Date _____

Lesson 8: Percent Error Problems

Exit Ticket

1. The veterinarian weighed Oliver's new puppy, Boaz, on a defective scale. He weighed 36 pounds. However, Boaz weighs exactly 34.5 pounds. What is the percent of error in measurement of the defective scale to the nearest tenth?

2. Use the π key on a scientific or graphing calculator to compute the percent of error of the approximation of pi, 3.14, to the value π. Show your steps, and round your answer to the nearest hundredth of a percent.

3. Connor and Angie helped take attendance during their school's practice fire drill. If the actual count was between 77 and 89, inclusive, what is the most the absolute error could be? What is the most the percent error could be? Round your answer to the nearest tenth of a percent.

Exit Ticket Sample Solutions

1. The veterinarian weighed Oliver's new puppy, Boaz, on a defective scale. He weighed 36 pounds. However, Boaz weighs exactly 34.5 pounds. What is the percent of error in measurement of the defective scale to the nearest tenth?

$$\frac{|36 - 34.5|}{|34.5|} \times 100\% = 4\frac{8}{23}\%$$

2. Use the π key on a scientific or graphing calculator to compute the percent of error of the approximation of pi, 3.14, to the value π. Show your steps, and round your answer to the nearest hundredth of a percent.

$$\frac{|3.14 - \pi|}{|\pi|} \times 100\% = 0.05\%$$

3. Connor and Angie helped take attendance during their school's practice fire drill. If the actual count was between 77 and 89, inclusive, what is the most the absolute error could be? What is the most the percent error could be? Round your answer to the nearest tenth of a percent.

The most the absolute error could be is $|89 - 77| = |12| = 12$.

The percent error will be largest when the exact value is smallest. The most the percent error could be is

$$\frac{|12|}{|77|} \times 100\% < 15.6\%. \text{ The percent error is less than } 15.6\%.$$

Problem Set Sample Solutions

Students may choose any method to solve problems.

1. The odometer in Mr. Washington's car does not work correctly. The odometer recorded 13.2 miles for his last trip to the hardware store, but he knows the distance traveled is 15 miles. What is the percent error? Use a calculator and the percent error formula to help find the answer. Show your steps.

15 is the exact value and 13.2 is the approximate value. Using the percent error formula, $\frac{|a-x|}{|x|} \times 100\%$, the percent error is:

$$= \frac{|13.2 - 15|}{|15|} \times 100\%$$
$$= \frac{|-1.8|}{|15|} \times 100\%$$
$$= \frac{1.8}{15} \times 100\%$$
$$= 0.12\,(100\%)$$
$$= 12\%$$

The percent error is equal to 12%.

2.   The actual length of a soccer field is 500 feet. A measuring instrument shows the length to be 493 feet. The actual width of the field is 250 feet, but the recorded width is 246.5 feet. Answer the following questions based on this information. Round all decimals to the nearest tenth.

   a.   Find the percent error for the length of the soccer field.

   $$\frac{|493 - 500|}{|500|} \times 100 = 1.4\%$$

250 feet

500 feet

   b.   Find the percent error of the area of the soccer field.

   Actual area:

   $A = l \times w$

   $A = (500)(250) = 125,000$ *square feet*

   Approximate area:

   $A = l \times w$

   $A = (493)(246.5) = 121,524.5$ *square feet*

   Percent Error of the Area:

   $$\frac{|121,524.5 - 125,000|}{|125,000|} \times 100 = 2.8\%$$

   c.   Explain why the values from parts (a) and (b) are different.

   In part (a), 1.4% is the percent error for the length, which is one dimension of area. Part (b) is the percent error for the area, which includes two dimensions—length and width. The percent error for the width of the soccer field should be the same as the percent error for the length if the same measuring tool is used. So, 2.8% = 1.4% × 2. However, this is not always the case. Percent error for the width is not always the same as the percent error for the length. It is possible to have an error for both the length and the width, yet the area has no error. For example: actual length = 100 ft., actual width = 90 ft., measured length = 150 ft., and measured width = 60 ft.

3.   Kayla's class went on a field trip to an aquarium. One tank had 30 clown fish. She miscounted the total number of clown fish in the tank and recorded it as 24 fish. What is Kayla's percent error?

   $$\frac{|24 - 30|}{|30|} \times 100\% = 20\%$$

4.   Sid used geometry software to draw a circle of radius 4 units on a grid. He estimated the area of the circle by counting the squares that were mostly inside the circle and got an answer of 52 square units.

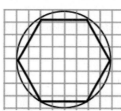

   a.   Is his estimate too large or too small?

   The exact area of the circle is 16π square units. 16π is approximately 50.3. His estimate is too large.

   b.   Find the percent error in Sid's estimation to the nearest hundredth using the π key on your calculator.

   3.45%

5. The exact value for the density of aluminum is 2.699 g/cm^3. Working in the science lab at school, Joseph finds the density of a piece of aluminum to be 2.75 g/cm^3. What is Joseph's percent error? (Round to the nearest hundredths.)

$$\frac{|2.75 - 2.699|}{|2.699|} \times 100\% = 1.89\%$$

6. The world's largest marathon, The New York City Marathon, is held on the first Sunday in November each year. It is estimated that anywhere between 2 million and 2.5 million spectators will line the streets to cheer on Marathon runners. At most, what is the percent error?

$$\frac{|2.5 - 2|}{|2|} \times 100\% = \frac{0.5}{2}(100\%) = 25\%$$

7. A circle is inscribed inside a square, which has a side length of 12.6 cm. Jared estimates the area of the circle to be about 80% of the area of the square and comes up with an estimate of 127 cm^2.

    12.6 cm

    a. Find the absolute error from Jared's estimate to two decimal places.

    2.31 cm

    b. Find the percent error of Jared's estimate to two decimal places.

    $$\frac{|127 - \pi 6.3^2|}{|\pi 6.3^2|} \times 100 \approx 1.85\%. \; \textbf{\textit{Approximately equals }} 1.85\%$$

    c. Do you think Jared's estimate was reasonable?

    Yes, the percent error is less than 2%.

    d. Would this method of computing the area of a circle always be too large?

    Yes. If the circle has radius r, ***then the area of the circle is*** πr^2, ***and the area of the square is*** $4r^2$.

    $$\frac{\pi r^2}{4r^2} = \frac{\pi}{4}. \; \textbf{\textit{The area approximately equals }} 0.785 = 78.5\% < 80\%.$$

8. In a school library, 52% of the books are paperback. If there are $2,658$ books in the library, how many of them are not paperback to the nearest whole number?

    About $1,276$ ***books are not paperback.***

9. Shaniqua has 25% less money than her older sister Jennifer. If Shaniqua has $\$180$, how much money does Jennifer have?

    Jennifer has $\$240$.

10. An item that was selling for $\$1,102$ is reduced to $\$806$. To the nearest whole, what is the percent decrease?

    27%

11. If 60 calories from fat is 75% of the total number of calories in a bag of chips, find the total number of calories in the bag of chips.

    80 ***calories.***

Lesson 9: Problem Solving when the Percent Changes

Student Outcomes

- Students solve percent problems where quantities and percents change.
- Students use a variety of methods to solve problems where quantities and percents change, including double number lines, visual models, and equations.

Lesson Notes

In this lesson, students solve multi-step word problems related to percents that change. They identify the quantities that represent the *part* and the *whole* and recognize when the whole changes based on the context of a word problem. They will build on their understanding of the relationship between the part, whole, and percent. All of the problems can be solved with a visual model. Students may solve some of the problems with an equation, but often the equation will require eighth grade methods for a variable on both sides of the equation. If students generalize and solve such equations, they should be given full credit.

Classwork

Example 1 (5 minutes)

Begin class by displaying Example 1. Have the students work in groups or pairs to try to start the problem on their own.

- Based on the words in the example, which person's money should represent the whole?
  - *The first whole is Sally's beginning money. The second whole is Sally's ending money.*

> **Scaffolding:**
> - Students that had difficulty solving equations in earlier modules may need additional practice working with these one-step equations. Students should continue to use calculators where appropriate throughout the lesson.
> - Where appropriate, provide visual models with equations to show an alternative problem-solving strategy for visual learners.

Example 1

Tom's money is 75% of Sally's money. After Sally spent $120 and Tom saved all his money, Tom's money is 50% more than Sally's. How much money did each have at the beginning? Use a visual model and a percent line to solve the problem.

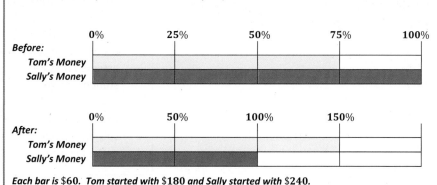

Each bar is $60. Tom started with $180 and Sally started with $240.

Example 2 (10 minutes)

Following the discussion of Example 1, have students try to start Example 2 without modeling. Students will solve the example using a visual model and an equation to show the change in percent. Pose possible discussion questions to the class as you solve the problem.

- Which person's candy represents the whole?
  - *Erin's candy represents the whole.*

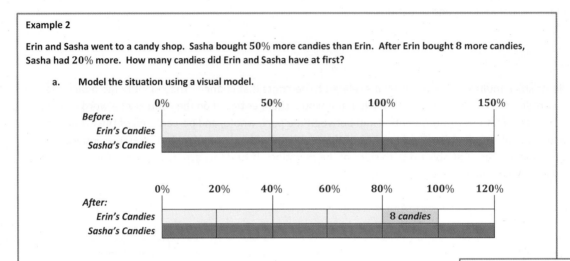

Example 2

Erin and Sasha went to a candy shop. Sasha bought 50% more candies than Erin. After Erin bought 8 more candies, Sasha had 20% more. How many candies did Erin and Sasha have at first?

a. Model the situation using a visual model.

b. How many candies did Erin have at first? Explain.

Each bar in the "after" tape diagram is 8 candies. Sasha has 48 candies. Each bar in the "before" tape diagram is 16 candies. Erin started with 32 candies.

Example 3 (7 minutes)

The previous example presented a visual model approach. In this example, allow students to choose their preferred method to solve the problem. It is important for students to first write an algebraic expression that represents each person's money before they can form an equation. Students should also remember that adding to a whole percent is represented as $1 + m$, where m is the percent increase.

MP.4

- Point out that since Kimberly and Mike have an equal amount of money in the beginning, the same variable can be used to represent the amount.

Scaffolding:

- Teacher could have some groups solve the problem using a visual model and other groups using an equation.

- Have students explain their models to other groups and look for comparisons for problem solving.

- For the exercises, the teacher could select specific individuals to solve problems using an assigned method to allow students to get comfortable with choosing and utilizing problem-solving methods of choice and efficiency.

Example 3

Kimberly and Mike have an equal amount of money. After Kimberly spent $50 and Mike spent $25, Mike's money is 50% more than Kimberly's. How much did Kimberly and Mike have at first?

    a.   Use an equation to solve the problem.

        Equation Method:

        Let x be Kimberly's money in dollars after she spent $50. *After Mike spent* $25, *his money is* 50% *more than Kimberly's. Mike's money is also* $25 *more than Kimberly's.*

$$0.5x = 25$$
$$x = 50$$

        Kimberly started with $100 *because* $100 − $50 = $50. *Mike has* $75 *because* (1.5)50 = 75.

        They each started with $100.

    b.   Use a visual model to solve the problem.

Teacher should lead the class through constructing a visual model for part (b). Since we are subtracting money, first create the *after picture,* then, add the money to get the *before picture*.

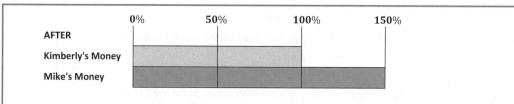

        Each bar is $25. *They both started with* $100.

    c.   Which method do you prefer and why?

        Answers will vary. I prefer the visual method because it is easier for me to draw the problem out instead of using the algebraic properties.

Exercise (13 minutes)

This exercise allows students to choose any method they would like to solve the problem. Then, they must justify their answer by using a different method. After about 10 minutes, ask students to present their solutions to the class. Compare and contrast different methods and emphasize how the algebraic, numeric, and visual models are related.

Exercise

Todd has 250% more video games than Jaylon. Todd has 56 video games in his collection. He gives Jaylon 8 of his games. How many video games did Todd and Jaylon have in the beginning? How many do they have now?

Answers may vary. Sample answer provided.

Visual Model:

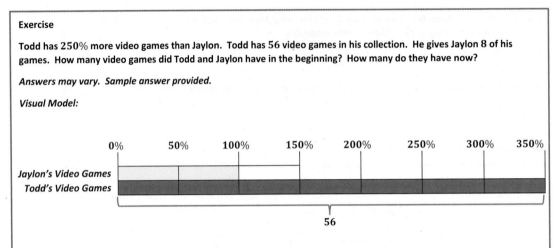

Equation Method:

Let z be the number of video games that Jaylon had at the beginning. Then, Todd started with $3.5z$ *video games.*

$$3.5z = 56$$
$$z = 16$$

In the beginning, Jaylon had 16 *and Todd had* 56. *After Todd gave Jaylon 8 of his games, Jaylon had* 24 *and Todd had* 48.

Closing (3 minutes)

- What formula can we use to relate the part, whole, and percent?
  - $Quantity = Percent \times Whole$
- Describe at least two strategies for solving a changing percent problem using an equation.
  - *You must identify the first whole and then identify what would represent the second whole.*
  - *You must use algebraic properties such as the distributive property to solve the problem.*

Exit Ticket (7 minutes)

Name _____   Date _____

Lesson 9: Problem Solving When the Percent Changes

Terrence and Lee were selling magazines for a charity. In the first week, Terrance sold 30% more than Lee. In the second week, Terrance sold 8 magazines, but Lee did not sell any. If Terrance sold 50% more than Lee by the end of the second week, how many magazines did Lee sell?

Choose any model to solve the problem. Show your work to justify your answer.

Exit Ticket Sample Solutions

Terrence and Lee were selling magazines for a charity. In the first week, Terrence sold 30% more than Lee. In the second week, Terrence sold 8 magazines, but Lee did not sell any. If Terrence sold 50% more than Lee by the end of the second week, how many magazines did Lee sell?

Choose any model to solve the problem. Show your work to justify your answer.

Answers may vary.

Equation Model:

Let m be the number of magazines Lee sold.

$50\% - 30\% = 20\%$, *so* $0.2m = 8$ *and* $m = 40$

Visual Model:

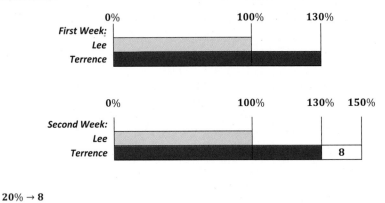

$20\% \to 8$

$100\% \to 40$

Problem Set Sample Solutions

1. Solve each problem using an equation.

   a. What is 150% of 625?

      $n = 1.5(625)$
      $n = 937.5$

   b. 90 is 40% of what number?

      $90 = 0.4(n)$
      $n = 225$

   c. What percent of 520 is 40? Round to the nearest hundredth of a percent.

      $40 = p(520)$
      $p \approx 0.0769 = 7.69\%$

2. The actual length of a machine is 12.25 cm. The measured length is 12.2 cm. Round to the nearest hundredth of a percent.

    a. Find the absolute error.   b. Find the percent error.

        0.05 cm   percent error ≈ 0.41%

3. A rowing club has 600 members. 60% of them are women. After 200 new members joined the club, the percentage of women was reduced to 50%. How many of the new members are women?

    Solutions will vary. (40 of the new members are women.)

4. 40% of the marbles in a bag are yellow. The rest are orange and green. The ratio of the number of orange to the number of green is 4: 5. If there are 30 green marbles, how many yellow marbles are there? Use a visual model to show your answer.

    5 *units* = 30 *marbles*

    1 *unit* = 30 ÷ 5 *marbles* = 6 *marbles*   4 *units* = 4 × 6 *marbles* = 24 *marbles*

    30 + 24 = 54 → 60%

    18 → 20%

    36 → 40%

    There are 36 yellow marbles because 40% of the marbles are yellow.

    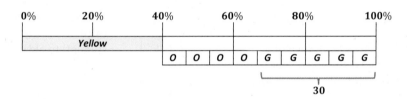

5. Susan has 50% more books than Michael. Michael has 40 books. If Michael buys 8 more books, will Susan have more or less books? What percent more or less will Susan's books be? Use any method to solve the problem.

    Solutions will vary. (Susan has 25% more.)

6. Harry's money is 75% of Kayla's money. After Harry earned $30 and Kayla earned 25% more of her money, Harry's money is 80% of Kayla's money. How much money did each have at the beginning? Use a visual model to solve the problem.

    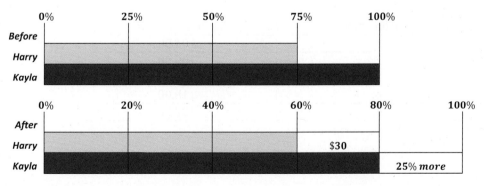

    Each bar is $30. Harry started with $90, and Kayla started with $120.

Lesson 10: Simple Interest

Student Outcomes

- Students solve simple interest problems using the formula $I = Prt$, where I = interest, P = principal, r = interest rate, and t = time.

- When using the formula $I = Prt$, students recognize that units for both interest rate and time must be compatible; students convert the units when necessary.

Opening Exercise (10 minutes): Fluency Sprint

Students complete a two-round sprint exercise provided at the end of this lesson (Fractional Percents) to practice finding the percent, including fractional percents, of a number. Provide one minute for each round of the sprint. Follow the established protocol for delivering a sprint exercise. Be sure to provide any answers not completed by the students. Sprint exercises and answer key are provided at the end of the lesson.

Classwork

Example 1 (7 minutes): Can Money Grow? A Look at Simple Interest

MP.1

Students solve a simple interest problem to find the new balance of a savings account that earns interest. Students model the interest earned over time (in years) by constructing a graph and table to show that a proportional relationship exists between the t, number of years, and I, interest.

Begin class discussion by displaying and reading the following problem to the whole class. Teacher should allow students time to process the information presented. Small group discussion should be encouraged before soliciting individual feedback.

> *Scaffolding:*
> - Teacher could allow one calculator per group (or student) to aid with discovering the mathematical pattern from the table.
> - Also, consider using a simpler percent value, such as 2%.

- Larry invests $100 in a savings plan. The plan pays $4\frac{1}{2}$% interest each year on his $100 account balance. The following chart shows the balance on his account after each year for the next five years. He did not make any deposits or withdrawals during this time.

Time (in years)	Balance (in dollars)
1	104.50
2	109.00
3	113.50
4	118.00
5	122.50

Possible discussion questions:

- What is simple interest?
- How is it calculated?
- What pattern(s) do you notice from the table?
- Can you create a formula to represent the pattern from the table?
- Display the interest formula to the class and explain each variable.

$$Interest = Principal \times Rate \times Time$$

$$I = P \times r \times t$$
$$I = Prt$$

- r is the percent of the principal that is paid over a period of time (usually per year).
- t is the time.
- r and t must be compatible. For example, if r is an annual interst rate, then t must be written in years.

- Model for the class how to substitute the given information into the interest formula to find the amount of interest owned.

Example 1: Can Money Grow? A Look at Simple Interest

Larry invests $100 in a savings plan. The plan pays $4\frac{1}{2}\%$ interest each year on his $100 account balance.

     a.   How much money will Larry earn in interest after 3 years? After 5 years?

        3 years:

$$I = Prt$$
$$I = 100\,(0.045)(3)$$
$$I = 13.50$$

        Larry will earn $13.50 in interest after 3 years.

        5 years:

$$I = Prt$$
$$I = 100\,(0.045)(5)$$
$$I = 22.50$$

        Larry will earn $22.50 in interest after 5 years.

     b.   How can you find the balance of Larry's account at the end of 5 years?

        You would add the interest earned after 5 years to the beginning balance. $22.50 + $100 = $122.50.

- Show the class that the relationship between the amount of interest earned each year can be represented in a table or graph by posing the question, "The interest earned can be found using an equation. How else can we represent the amount of interest earned other than an equation?"

- Draw a table and call on students to help you complete the table. Start with finding the amount of interest earned after one year.

t (in years)	I (interest earned after t years, in dollars)	
1	$I = (100)(0.045)(1) = 4.50$	Increase of $4.50
2	$I = (100)(0.045)(2) = 9.00$	Increase of $4.50
3	$I = (100)(0.045)(3) = 13.50$	Increase of $4.50
4	$I = (100)(0.045)(4) = 18.00$	Increase of $4.50
5	$I = (100)(0.045)(5) = 22.50$	

> The amount of interest earned increases by the same amount each year, $4.50. Therefore, the ratios in the table are equivalent. This means that the relationship between time and the interest earned is proportional.

Possible discussion questions:

- Using your calculator, what do you observe when you divide the I by t for each year?
    - *The ratio is 4.5.*
- What is the constant of proportionality in this situation? What does it mean? What evidence from the table supports your answer?
    - *The constant of proportionality is 4.5. This is the principal times the interest rate because $(100)(0.045) = 4.5$. This means that for every year, the interest earned on the savings account will increase by $4.50. The table shows that the principal and interest rate are not changing; they are constant.*
- What other representation could we use to show the relationship between time and the amount of interest earned is proportional?

Scaffolding:
Use questioning strategies to review graphing data in the coordinate plane for all learners. Emphasize the importance of an accurate scale and making sure variables are graphed along the correct axes.

    - *We could use a graph.*

Display to the class a graph of the relationship.

- What are some characteristics of the graph?
    - *It has a title.*
    - *The axes are labeled.*
    - *The scale for the x-axis is 1 year.*
    - *The scale for the y-axis is 5 dollars.*
- By looking at the graph of the line, can you draw a conclusion about the relationship between time and the amount of interest earned?
    - *All pairs from the table are plotted, and a straight line passes through those points and the origin. This means that the relationship is proportional.*

Lesson 10:	Simple Interest

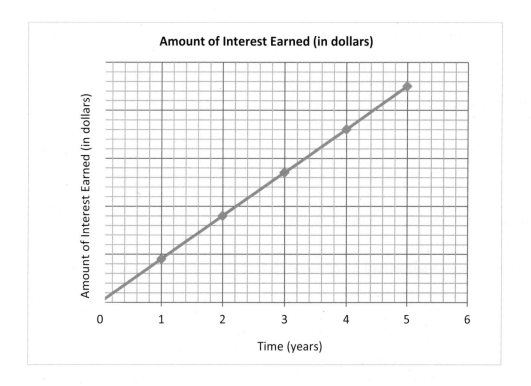

Amount of Interest Earned (in dollars)

- What does the point, $(4, 18)$ mean in terms of the situation?
  - *It means that at the end of four years, Larry would have earned $18 in interest.*

- What does the point $(0, 0)$ mean?
  - *It means that when Larry opens the account, no interest is earned.*

- What does the point $(1, 4.50)$ mean?
  - *It means that at the end of the first year, Larry's account earned $4.50. 4.5 is also the constant of proportionality.*

- What equation would represent the amount of interest earned at the end of a given year in this situation?
  - $I = 4.5t$

Scaffolding:
- Provide a numbered coordinate plane to help build confidence for students who struggle with creating graphs by hand.
- If time permits, allow advanced learners to practice graphing the interest formula using the $y =$ *editor* in a graphing calculator and scrolling the table to see how much interest is earned for x number of years.

Exercise 1 (3 minutes)

Students will practice using the interest formula independently, with or without technology. Review answers as a whole class.

Exercise 1

Find the balance of a savings account at the end of 10 years if the interest earned each year is 7.5%. The principal is $500.

$I = Prt$
$I = 500\,(0.075)(10)$
$I = 375$

The interest earned after 10 *years is* $375. *So, the balance at the end of* 10 *years is* $375 + $500 = $875.

| Lesson 10: | Simple Interest |

Example 2 (5 minutes): Time Other Than One Year

MP.1 In this example, students learn to recognize that units for both interest rate and time must be compatible. If not, they must convert the units when necessary.

Remind the class of how to perform a unit conversion from months to years. Because 1 year $=$ 12 months, the number of months given can be divided by 12 to get the equivalent year.

> *Scaffolding:*
>
> Provide a poster with the terms *semi*, *quarterly*, and *annual*. Write an example next to each word, showing an example of a conversion.

Example 2: Time Other Than One Year

A $1,000 savings bond earns simple interest at the rate of 3% each year. The interest is paid at the end of every month. How much interest will the bond have earned after three months?

Step 1: Convert 3 months to a year.

12 months $=$ 1 year. So, divide both sides by 4 to get 3 months $= \frac{1}{4}$ year.

Step 2: Use the interest formula to find the answer.

$I = Prt$
$I = (\$1000)(0.03)(0.25)$
$I = \$7.50$

The interest earned after three months is $7.50.

Example 3 (5 minutes): Solving for P, r, or t

Students practice working backwards to find the interest rate, principal, or time by dividing the interest earned by the product of the other two values given.

- Teacher could have students annotate the word problem by writing the corresponding variable above each given quantity. Have students look for keywords to identify the appropriate variable. For example, the words *investment*, *deposit*, and *loan* refer to principal. Students will notice that time is not given; therefore, they must solve for t.

Example 3: Solving for P, r, or t

Mrs. Williams wants to know how long it will take an investment of $\overset{P}{\$450}$ to earn $\overset{I}{\$200}$ in interest if the yearly interest rate is $\underset{r}{6.5\%}$, paid at the end of each year.

$$I = Prt$$
$$\$200 = (\$450)(0.065)t$$
$$\$200 = \$29.25t$$
$$\$200\left(\frac{1}{\$29.25}\right) = \left(\frac{1}{\$29.25}\right)\$29.25t$$
$$6.8376 = t$$

Six years is not enough time to earn $20. *At the end of seven years, the interest will be over* $20. *It will take seven years since the interest is paid at the end of each year.*

Exercises 2–3 (7 minutes)

Students complete the following exercise independently, or in groups of two, using the simple interest formula.

Exercise 2

Write an equation to find the amount of simple interest, A, earned on a $600 investment after $1\frac{1}{2}$ years if the semi-annual (six month) interest rate is 2%.

$1\frac{1}{2}$ years is the same as

6 months	6 months	6 months

Interest = Principal × Rate × Time

$A = 600\,(0.02)(3)$ *1.5 years is 1 year and 6 months, so $t = 3$.*

$A = 36$ *The amount of interest earned is $36.*

Exercise 3

A $1,500$ loan has an annual interest rate of $4\frac{1}{4}\%$ on the amount borrowed. How much time has elapsed if the interest is now 127.50?

Interest = Principal × Rate × Time

Let t be time in years.

$$127.50 = (1,500)(0.0425)t$$
$$127.50 = \$63.75t$$
$$(127.50)\left(\frac{1}{63.75}\right) = \left(\frac{1}{63.75}\right)(63.75)t$$
$$2 = t$$

Two years have elapsed.

Closing (2 minutes)

- Explain each variable of the simple interest formula.
  - *I is the amount of interest earned or owed.*
  - *P is the principal, or the amount invested or borrowed.*
  - *r is the interest rate for a given time period (yearly, quarterly, monthly).*
  - *t is time.*
- What would be the value of the time for a two-year period for a quarterly interest rate? Explain.
  - *T would be written as 8 because a quarter means every 3 months, and there are four quarters in one year. So, $2 \times 4 = 8$.*

Exit Ticket (6 minutes)

Name _____   Date _____

Lesson 10: Simple Interest

Exit Ticket

1. Erica's parents gave her $500 for her high school graduation. She put the money into a savings account that earned 7.5% annual interest. She left the money in the account for nine months before she withdrew it. How much interest did the account earn if interest is paid monthly?

2. If she would have left the money in the account for another nine months before withdrawing, how much interest would the account have earned?

3. About how many years and months would she have to leave the money in the account if she wants to reach her goal of saving $750?

Exit Ticket Sample Solutions

1. Erica's parents gave her $500 for her high school graduation. She put the money into a savings account that earned 7.5% annual interest. She left the money in the account for nine months before she withdrew it. How much interest did the account earn if interest is paid monthly?

$I = Prt$

$I = (500)(0.075)\left(\dfrac{9}{12}\right)$

$I = 28.125$

The interest earned is $28.13.

2. If she would have left the money in the account for another nine months before withdrawing, how much interest would the account have earned?

$I = Prt$

$I = (500)(0.075)\left(\dfrac{18}{12}\right)$

$I = 56.25$

The account would have earned $56.25.

3. About how many years and months would she have to leave the money in the account if she wants to reach her goal of saving $750?

$750 - 500 = 250$ *She would need to earn $250 in interest.*

$I = Prt$

$250 = (500)(0.075)t$

$250 = 37.5t$

$250\left(\dfrac{1}{37.5}\right) = \left(\dfrac{1}{37.5}\right)(37.5)t$

$6\dfrac{2}{3} = t$

It would take her six years and eight month to reach her goal because $\dfrac{2}{3} \times 12$ months is 8 months.

Problem Set Sample Solutions

1. Enrique takes out a student loan to pay for his college tuition this year. Find the interest on the loan if he borrowed $2,500 at an annual interest rate of 6% for 15 years.

$2,250

2. Your family plans to start a small business in your neighborhood. Your father borrows $10,000 from the bank at an annual interest rate of 8% rate for 36 months. What is the amount of interest he will pay on this loan?

$I = 2,400.$ *He will pay $2,400 in interest.*

3. Mr. Rodriguez invests $2,000 in a savings plan. The savings account pays an annual interest rate of 5.75% on the amount he put in at the end of each year.

   a. How much will Mr. Rodriguez earn if he leaves his money in the savings plan for 10 years?

   He will earn $1,150.

b.   How much money will be in his savings plan at the end of 10 years?

At the end of 10 *years, he will have* $3,150.

c.   Create (and label) a graph in the coordinate plane to show the relationship between time and the amount of interest earned for 10 years. Is the relationship proportional? Why or why not? If so, what is the constant of proportionality?

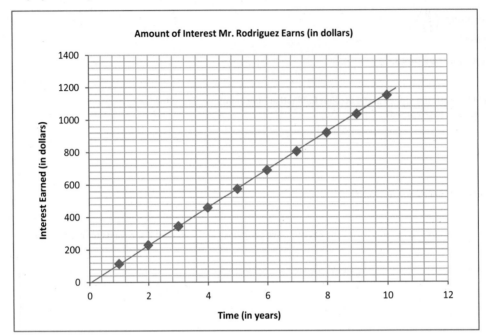

Yes, the relationship is proportional because the graph shows a straight line touching the origin. The constant of proportionality is 115 *because the amount of interest earned increases by* $115 *for every one year.*

d.   Explain what the points $(0,0)$ and $(1,115)$ mean on the graph.

$(0,0)$ *means that no time has elapsed and no interest has been earned.*

$(1,115)$ *means that after 1 year, the savings plan would have earned* $115. 115 *is also the constant of proportionality.*

e.   Using the graph, find the balance of the savings plan at the end of seven years.

From the table, the point $(7,805)$ *means that the balance would be* $2,000 + $805 = $2,805.

f.   After how many years will Mr. Rodriguez have increased his original investment by more than 50%? Show your work to support your answer.

$Quantity = Percent \times Whole$

Let Q be the account balance that is 50% *more than the original investment.*

$Q > (1 + 0.50)(2,000)$
$Q > 3,000$

The balance will be greater than $3,000 *beginning between 8 and 9 years because the graph shows* $(8,920)$ *and* $(9,1035)$, *so* $2,000 + $920 = $2,920 < $3,000, *and* $2,000 + $1,035 = $3,035 > $3,000.

4. Use a table to prove that the relationship between time and the balance is or is not proportional. **Explain your reasoning.**

Time (in years)	Balance (in dollars)
2	575
4	650
6	725
8	800
10	875

The table shows that the balance of the account increased by $\$37.50$ each year. But, the ratio of balance to time is different for each year. For example, $\dfrac{575}{2} = 287.50$, but $\dfrac{650}{4} = 162.50$. This means that the relationship is not proportional because the ratios in the table are not equivalent.

5. Without actually graphing, describe the graph of the relationship between the time and the balance.

I think the graph would be a straight line, but it wouldn't touch the origin because $(0,0)$ means that when the account was open less than a year, the balance was zero. This isn't true because the principal was $\$500$; so, there was $\$500$ in the account.

6. **Challenge Problem**

George went on a game show and won $\$60,000$. He wanted to invest it and found two funds that he liked. Fund 250 earns 15% interest annually, and Fund 100 earns 8% interest annually. George does not want to earn more than $\$7,500$ in interest income this year. He made the table below to show how he could invest the money.

	I	P	r	t
Fund 100	$0.08x$	x	0.08	1
Fund 250	$0.15(60000 - x)$	$60,000 - x$	0.15	1
Total	$7,500$	$60,000$		

a. Explain what value x is in this situation.

   x is the principal, in dollars, that George could invest in Fund 100.

b. Explain what the expression $60,000 - x$ represents in this situation.

   $60,000 - x$ is the principal, in dollars, that George could invest in Fund 250. It's the money he would have leftover once he invests in Fund 100.

c. Using the simple interest formula, complete the table for the amount of interest earned.

d. Write an equation to show the total amount of interest earned from both funds.

   $0.08x + 0.15(60,000 - x) = 7,500$

e. Use algebraic properties to solve the equation for x and the principal, in dollars, George could invest in Fund 100. Show your work.

$$0.08x + 9,000 - 0.15x = 7,500$$
$$9,000 - 0.07x = 7,500$$
$$9,000 - 9,000 - 0.07x = 7,500 - 9,000$$
$$-0.07x = -1,500$$
$$\left(\dfrac{1}{-0.07}\right)(-0.07x) = \left(\dfrac{1}{-0.07}\right)(-1,500)$$
$$x \approx 21,428.37$$

   x approximately equals $\$21,428.57$. George could invest $\$21,428.57$ in Fund 100.

f.   Use your answer from part (e) to determine how much George could invest in Fund 250.

He could invest $38,571.43 *in Fund* 250 *because* $60,000 - 21,428.57 = 38,571.43.$

g.   Using your answers to parts (e) and (f), how much interest would George earn from each fund?

Fund 100: $0.08 \times 21,428.57 \times 1$ *approximately equals* $1,714.29.$

Fund 250: $0.15 \times 38,571.43 \times 1$ *approximately equals* $= \$5,785.71$ *or* $7,500 - 1,714.29.$

Sprint: Fractional Percents – Round 1

Number Correct: _____

Directions: Find the part that corresponds with each percent.

1.	1% of 100	
2.	1% of 200	
3.	1% of 400	
4.	1% of 800	
5.	1% of 1,600	
6.	1% of 3,200	
7.	1% of 5,000	
8.	1% of 10,000	
9.	1% of 20,000	
10.	1% of 40,000	
11.	1% of 80,000	
12.	$\frac{1}{2}$% of 100	
13.	$\frac{1}{2}$% of 200	
14.	$\frac{1}{2}$% of 400	
15.	$\frac{1}{2}$% of 800	
16.	$\frac{1}{2}$% of 1,600	
17.	$\frac{1}{2}$% of 3,200	
18.	$\frac{1}{2}$% of 5,000	
19.	$\frac{1}{2}$% of 10,000	
20.	$\frac{1}{2}$% of 20,000	
21.	$\frac{1}{2}$% of 40,000	
22.	$\frac{1}{2}$% of 80,000	

23.	$\frac{1}{4}$% of 100	
24.	$\frac{1}{4}$% of 200	
25.	$\frac{1}{4}$% of 400	
26.	$\frac{1}{4}$% of 800	
27.	$\frac{1}{4}$% of 1,600	
28.	$\frac{1}{4}$% of 3,200	
29.	$\frac{1}{4}$% of 5,000	
30.	$\frac{1}{4}$% of 10,000	
31.	$\frac{1}{4}$% of 20,000	
32.	$\frac{1}{4}$% of 40,000	
33.	$\frac{1}{4}$% of 80,000	
34.	1% of 1,000	
35.	$\frac{1}{2}$% of 1,000	
36.	$\frac{1}{4}$% of 1,000	
37.	1% of 4,000	
38.	$\frac{1}{2}$% of 4,000	
39.	$\frac{1}{4}$% of 4,000	
40.	1% of 2,000	
41.	$\frac{1}{2}$% of 2,000	
42.	$\frac{1}{4}$% of 2,000	
43.	$\frac{1}{2}$% of 6,000	
44.	$\frac{1}{4}$% of 6,000	

Sprint: Fractional Percents – Round 1 **[KEY]**

Directions: Find the part that corresponds with each percent.

1.	1% of 100	**1**	23.	$\frac{1}{4}$% of 100	$\frac{1}{4}$
2.	1% of 200	**2**	24.	$\frac{1}{4}$% of 200	$\frac{1}{2}$
3.	1% of 400	**4**	25.	$\frac{1}{4}$% of 400	**1**
4.	1% of 800	**8**	26.	$\frac{1}{4}$% of 800	**2**
5.	1% of 1,600	**16**	27.	$\frac{1}{4}$% of 1,600	**4**
6.	1% of 3,200	**32**	28.	$\frac{1}{4}$% of 3,200	**8**
7.	1% of 5,000	**50**	29.	$\frac{1}{4}$% of 5,000	$12\frac{1}{2}$
8.	1% of 10,000	**100**	30.	$\frac{1}{4}$% of 10,000	**25**
9.	1% of 20,000	**200**	31.	$\frac{1}{4}$% of 20,000	**50**
10.	1% of 40,000	**400**	32.	$\frac{1}{4}$% of 40,000	**100**
11.	1% of 80,000	**800**	33.	$\frac{1}{4}$% of 80,000	**200**
12.	$\frac{1}{2}$% of 100	$\frac{1}{2}$	34.	1% of 1,000	**10**
13.	$\frac{1}{2}$% of 200	**1**	35.	$\frac{1}{2}$% of 1,000	**5**
14.	$\frac{1}{2}$% of 400	**2**	36.	$\frac{1}{4}$% of 1,000	**2.5**
15.	$\frac{1}{2}$% of 800	**4**	37.	1% of 4,000	**40**
16.	$\frac{1}{2}$% of 1,600	**8**	38.	$\frac{1}{2}$% of 4,000	**20**
17.	$\frac{1}{2}$% of 3,200	**16**	39.	$\frac{1}{4}$% of 4,000	**10**
18.	$\frac{1}{2}$% of 5,000	**25**	40.	1% of 2,000	**20**
19.	$\frac{1}{2}$% of 10,000	**50**	41.	$\frac{1}{2}$% of 2,000	**10**
20.	$\frac{1}{2}$% of 20,000	**100**	42.	$\frac{1}{4}$% of 2,000	**5**
21.	$\frac{1}{2}$% of 40,000	**200**	43.	$\frac{1}{2}$% of 6,000	**30**
22.	$\frac{1}{2}$% of 80,000	**400**	44.	$\frac{1}{4}$% of 6,000	**15**

Sprint: Fractional Percents – Round 2

Number Correct: _____
Improvement: _____

Directions: Find the part that corresponds with each percent.

1.	10% of 30	
2.	10% of 60	
3.	10% of 90	
4.	10% of 120	
5.	10% of 150	
6.	10% of 180	
7.	10% of 210	
8.	20% of 30	
9.	20% of 60	
10.	20% of 90	
11.	20% of 120	
12.	5% of 50	
13.	5% of 100	
14.	5% of 200	
15.	5% of 400	
16.	5% of 800	
17.	5% of 1,600	
18.	5% of 3,200	
19.	5% of 6,400	
20.	5% of 600	
21.	10% of 600	
22.	20% of 600	

23.	$10\frac{1}{2}$% of 100	
24.	$10\frac{1}{2}$% of 200	
25.	$10\frac{1}{2}$% of 400	
26.	$10\frac{1}{2}$% of 800	
27.	$10\frac{1}{2}$% of 1,600	
28.	$10\frac{1}{2}$% of 3,200	
29.	$10\frac{1}{2}$% of 6,400	
30.	$10\frac{1}{4}$% of 400	
31.	$10\frac{1}{4}$% of 800	
32.	$10\frac{1}{4}$% of 1,600	
33.	$10\frac{1}{4}$% of 3,200	
34.	10% of 1,000	
35.	$10\frac{1}{2}$% of 1,000	
36.	$10\frac{1}{4}$% of 1,000	
37.	10% of 2,000	
38.	$10\frac{1}{2}$% of 2,000	
39.	$10\frac{1}{4}$% of 2,000	
40.	10% of 4,000	
41.	$10\frac{1}{2}$% of 4,000	
42.	$10\frac{1}{4}$% of 4,000	
43.	10% of 5,000	
44.	$10\frac{1}{2}$% of 5,000	

Sprint: Fractional Percents – Round 2 **[KEY]**

Directions: Find the part that corresponds with each percent.

1.	10% of 30	3		23.	$10\frac{1}{2}$% of 100	10.5
2.	10% of 60	6		24.	$10\frac{1}{2}$% of 200	21
3.	10% of 90	9		25.	$10\frac{1}{2}$% of 400	42
4.	10% of 120	12		26.	$10\frac{1}{2}$% of 800	84
5.	10% of 150	15		27.	$10\frac{1}{2}$% of 1,600	168
6.	10% of 180	18		28.	$10\frac{1}{2}$% of 3,200	336
7.	10% of 210	21		29.	$10\frac{1}{2}$% of 6,400	672
8.	20% of 30	6		30.	$10\frac{1}{4}$ % of 400	41
9.	20% of 60	12		31.	$10\frac{1}{4}$ % of 800	82
10.	20% of 90	18		32.	$10\frac{1}{4}$ % of 1,600	164
11.	20% of 120	24		33.	$10\frac{1}{4}$ % of 3,200	328
12.	5% of 50	2.5		34.	10% of 1,000	100
13.	5% of 100	5		35.	$10\frac{1}{2}$% of 1,000	105
14.	5% of 200	10		36.	$10\frac{1}{4}$% of 1,000	102.5
15.	5% of 400	20		37.	10% of 2,000	200
16.	5% of 800	40		38.	$10\frac{1}{2}$% of 2,000	210
17.	5% of 1,600	80		39.	$10\frac{1}{4}$% of 2,000	205
18.	5% of 3,200	160		40.	10% of 4,000	400
19.	5% of 6,400	320		41.	$10\frac{1}{2}$% of 4,000	420
20.	5% of 600	30		42.	$10\frac{1}{4}$% of 4,000	410
21.	10% of 600	60		43.	10% of 5,000	500
22.	20% of 600	120		44.	$10\frac{1}{2}$% of 5,000	525

Lesson 11: Tax, Commissions, Fees, and Other Real-World Percent Problems

Student Outcomes

- Students solve real-world percent problems involving tax, gratuities, commissions, and fees.
- Students solve word problems involving percent using equations, tables, and graphs.
- Students identify the constant of proportionality (tax rate, commission rate, etc.) in graphs, equations, tables, and in the context of the situation.

Lesson Notes

The purpose of this modeling lesson is to create a real-world scenario related to a school budget and student programs. Prior to this lesson, consider inviting a school board member to speak about the math involved in school finances. Encourage students to participate in school government and attend school board meetings to learn more about their school's finances, student programs, and the role of the taxpayers.

Students should work in cooperative learning groups of three or four students for Exercise 5. Exercise 5, part (b) allows students to work together to make predictions based on a situation involving several variables. Encourage students to think critically and use all of the information provided to come up with one or more possible scenarios. Students should provide a detailed explanation of their thought process when justifying their answer.

Classwork

Discussion (3 minutes)

Inform students that the scenarios in today's lesson, although fictitious, are realistic. (If the data in the lesson has been replaced with actual data from the students' school district, inform them of that.) Post the following information on the board, and discuss the meaning of each.

- Gratuity is another word for tip. It is an amount of money (typically ranging from 5%–20%) that is computed on the total price of a service. For which types of services do we typically leave a gratuity for the service provider?
    - *We tip a waiter for a meal, a barber for a haircut, and a cab or limo driver for the transportation service provided.*
- Commission on sales is money earned by a sales person (as a reward for selling a high-priced item). For which types of items might a sales person earn a commission based on the amount of his sales?
    - *A car salesperson earns a commission for selling car; a real estate agent earns a commission for selling homes; an electronics salesperson earns a commission for selling computers and televisions; a jeweler earns a commission for selling expensive jewelry; etc.*

- Taxes come in many forms, such as sales tax. A public school district is tax-exempt.
  - *That means, for instance, if the school buys textbooks, they do not have to pay sales tax on the books.*
- A public school district gets its money from the taxpayers. If you are a homeowner, you pay property taxes and school taxes. What does this mean?
  - *That means that if you are a homeowner in the school district, you must pay school tax to the district.*
- What is a school budget?
  - *The budget shows how the school intends to uses the taxpayer's money. The taxpayers must approve the school budget. Percents are used in creating the budget to determine how much money is allocated to certain areas. Percent increase and decrease are also used to compare the current year's budget's total dollar amount to previous years' budgets' total dollar amounts.*

Opening Exercise: Tax, Commission, Gratuity, and Fees (5 minutes)

The purpose of this Opening Exercise is to associate contextual meaning to the vocabulary used in this lesson; students must also understand the commonalities in the solution process to percent problems when the vocabulary is used. While each student should complete the exercise, a group discussion should also take place to solidify the understanding that each scenario, although different, involves the same solution process—finding 10% of the whole. Finding 10% of a quantity should be mental math for students based upon their foundational work with place value in earlier grades, with percents in Grade 6, and with Topic A of this module.

Opening Exercise

How are each of the following percent applications different, and how are they the same? First, describe how percents are used to solve each of the following problems. Then, solve each problem. Finally, compare your solution process for each.

a. Silvio earns 10% for each car sale he makes while working at a used car dealership. If he sells a used car for $2,000, what is his commission?

His commission is $200.

b. Tu's family stayed at a hotel for 10 nights on their vacation. The hotel charged a 10% room tax, per night. How much did they pay in room taxes if the room cost $200 per night?

They paid $200.

c. Eric bought a new computer and printer online. He had to pay 10% in shipping fees. The items totaled $2,000. How much did the shipping cost?

The shipping cost $200.

d. Selena had her wedding rehearsal dinner at a restaurant. The restaurant's policy is that gratuity is included in the bill for large parties. Her father said the food and service were exceptional, so he wanted to leave an extra 10% tip on the total amount of the bill. If the dinner bill totaled $2,000, how much money did her father leave as the extra tip?

Her father left $200 as the extra tip.

For each problem, I had to find 10% of the total ($2,000). Even though each problem was different—one was a commission, one was a tax, one was a fee, and one was a gratuity—I arrived at the answer in the same manner, by taking 10% of $2,000 means $\frac{1}{10}$ of $2,000, which is $200.

Exercises 1–4 (16 minutes)

Each student will need a calculator, a ruler, and a sheet of graph paper.

Exercises 1–4

Show all work; a calculator may be used for calculations.

The school board has approved the addition of a new sports team at your school.

1. The district ordered 30 team uniforms and received a bill for $2,992.50$. The total included a 5% discount.

   a. The school needs to place another order for two more uniforms. The company said the discount will not apply because the discount only applies to orders of $1,000$ or more. How much will the two uniforms cost?

   $$Part = Percent \cdot Whole$$
   $$2,992.50 = 0.95W$$
   $$2,992.50\left(\frac{1}{0.95}\right) = 0.95\left(\frac{1}{0.95}\right)W$$
   $$3,150 = W$$

   30 uniforms cost $3,150$ before the discount. $\frac{\$3,150}{30}$ *per uniform = 105 per uniform.* $\$105 \times 2 = \$210$, *so it will cost 210 for 2 uniforms without a discount.*

   b. The school district does not have to pay the 8% sales tax on the $2,992.50$ purchase. Estimate the amount of sales tax the district saved on the $2,992.50$ purchase. Explain how you arrived at your estimate.

   $\$2,992.50 \approx \$3,000$. *To find 8% of $3,000$, I know 8% of 100 is 8, since percent means per hundred. 8% of $1,000$ is ten times as much, since $1,000$ is ten times as much as 100. $8(10) = 80$. Then, I multiplied that by 3 since it is $3,000$, so $3(80) = 240$. The district saved about 240 in sales tax.*

   c. A student who loses a uniform must pay a fee equal to 75% of the school's cost of the uniform. For a uniform that cost the school 105, will the student owe more or less than 75 for the lost uniform? Explain how to use mental math to determine the answer.

   75% means 75 per hundred. Since the uniform cost more than 100, a 75% fee will be more than 75.

   d. Write an equation to represent the proportional relationship between the school's cost of a uniform and the amount a student must pay for a lost uniform. Use u to represent the uniform cost and s to represent the amount a student must pay for a lost uniform. What is the constant of proportionality?

   $s = 0.75\,u$. *The constant of proportionality is $75\% = 0.75$.*

2. A taxpayer claims the new sports team caused his school taxes to increase by 2%.

   a. Write an equation to show the relationship between the school taxes before and after a 2% increase. Use b to represent the dollar amount of school tax before the 2% increase and t to represent the dollar amount of school tax after the 2% increase.

   $t = 1.02\,b$

   b. Use your equation to complete the table below, listing at least 5 pairs of values.

b	t
0	0
1,000	1,020
2,000	2,040
3,000	3,060
6,000	6,120

---

c.   On graph paper, graph the relationship modeled by the equation in part (a). Be sure to label the axes and scale.

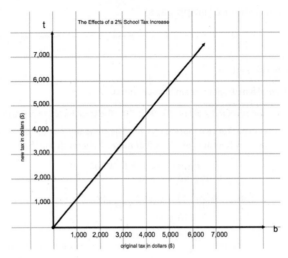

d.   Is the relationship proportional? Explain how you know.

Yes, the graph is a straight line through the point $(0, 0)$.

e.   What is the constant of proportionality? What does it mean in the context of the situation?

The constant of proportionality is the 1.02. *It means that after the* 2% *tax increase,* $\$1.02$ *will be paid for every dollar of tax paid before the increase.*

f.   If a tax payer's school taxes rose from $\$4,000$ to $\$4,020$, was there a 2% increase? Justify your answer using your graph, table, or equation.

No, the change represents less than a 2% *increase. On my graph, the point* $(4000, 4020)$ *does not fall on the line; it falls below the line, which means* $4,020$ *is too low for the second coordinate (the new tax amount).*

3.   The sports booster club sold candles as a fundraiser to support the new team. They earn a commission on their candle sales (which means they receive a certain percentage of the total dollar amount sold). If the club gets to keep 30% of the money from the candle sales, what would the club's total sales have to be in order to make at least $\$500$?

$$Part = Percent \cdot Whole$$
$$500 = 0.3\,W$$
$$500\left(\frac{1}{0.3}\right) = 0.3\left(\frac{1}{0.3}\right)W$$
$$1,666.67 \approx W$$

They will need candle sales totaling at least $\$1,666.67$.

4. Christian's mom works at the concession stand during sporting events. She told him they buy candy bars for $0.75 each and mark them up 40% to sell at the concession stand. What is the amount of the mark up? How much does the concession stand charge for each candy bar?

Let N represent the new price of a candy after the markup. Let M represent the percent or mark-up rate.

$N = M \cdot Whole$
$N = (100\% + 40\%)(0.75)$
$N = (1 + 0.4)(0.75)$
$N = 1.05$

The candy bars cost $1.05 at the concession stand. $1.05 − $0.75 = $0.30, so there is a markup of $0.30.

Exercise 5 (18 minutes)

Students work in cooperative learning groups of three or four students. Distribute one sheet of poster paper and markers to each group. Give students 15 minutes to answer the following two questions with their group and write their solutions on the poster paper. After 15 minutes, pair up student groups to explain, share, and critique their solutions.

Exercise 5

With your group, brainstorm solutions to the problems below. Prepare a poster that shows your solutions and math work. A calculator may be used for calculations.

5. For the next school year, the new soccer team will need to come up with $600.

a. Suppose the team earns $500 from the fundraiser at the start of the current school year, and the money is placed for one calendar year in a savings account earning 0.5% simple interest annually. How much money will the team still need to raise to meet next year's expenses?

Interest = Principal × Interest Rate × Time
Interest = $500 × 0.005 × 1
Interest = $2.50
Total Money Saved = Interest + Principal = $500.00 + $2.50 = $502.50
Total Money needed for next year = $600.00 − $502.50 = $97.50

The team will need to raise $97.50.

b. Jeff is a member of the new sports team. His dad owns a bakery. To help raise money for the team, Jeff's dad agrees to provide the team with cookies to sell at the concession stand for next year's opening game. The team must pay back the bakery $0.25 for each cookie it sells. The concession stand usually sells about 60 to 80 baked goods per game. Using your answer from part (a), determine a percent markup for the cookies the team plans to sell at next year's opening game. Justify your answer.

The team needs to raise $97.50. Based on past data for the typical number of baked goods sold, we estimate that we will sell 60 cookies, so we need to divide 97.50 by 60. 97.5 ÷ 60 is about 1.63. That means we need to make a profit of $1.63 per cookie after we pay back the bakery $0.25 per cookie. So, if we add $0.25 to $1.63, we arrive at a markup price of $1.88. We decide to round that up to $2.00 since we want to be sure we raise enough money. We may sell fewer than 60 cookies (especially if the data for the typical number of baked goods sold includes items other than cookies, such as cupcakes or muffins).

To find the percent markup, we used the following equation with $0.25 as the original price; since $2.00 − $0.25 = $1.75, then $1.75 is the markup.

$$Markup = Markup\ Rate \cdot Original\ Price$$
$$1.75 = Markup\ Rate \cdot (0.25)$$
$$1.75\left(\frac{1}{0.25}\right) = Markup\ Rate \cdot (0.25)\left(\frac{1}{0.25}\right)$$
$$7 = Markup\ Rate$$
$$7 = \frac{7}{1} = \frac{700}{100} = 700\%\ markup$$

c. Suppose the team ends up selling 78 cookies at next year's opening game. Find the percent error in the number of cookies that you estimated would be sold in your solution to part (b).

Percent Error $= \frac{|a-x|}{|x|} \cdot 100\%$, where x is the exact value and a is the approximate value.

We estimated 60 cookies would be sold, but if 78 are sold, then 78 is the actual value. Next, we used the percent error formula:

$$Percent\ Error = \frac{|a-x|}{|x|} \cdot 100\%$$
$$Percent\ Error = \frac{|60-78|}{|78|} \cdot 100\%$$
$$Percent\ Error = \frac{18}{78} \cdot 100\%$$
$$Percent\ Error \approx 23\%$$

There was about a 23% error in our estimate for the number of cookies sold.

Closing (1 minute)

- In what way is finding a 5% increase, commission, fee, and tax all the same?
- What types of real world problems can we solve if we understand percent?

Exit Ticket (5 minutes)

Name _____   Date _____

Lesson 11: Tax, Commissions, Fees, and Other Real-World Percent Problems

Exit Ticket

1. Lee works selling electronics. He earns a 5% commission on each sale he makes.

   a. Write an equation that shows the proportional relationship between the dollar amount of electronics Lee sells, d, and the amount of money he makes in commission, c.

   b. Express the constant of proportionality as a decimal.

   c. Explain what the constant of proportionality means in the context of this situation.

   d. If Lee wants to make $100 in commission, what is the dollar amount of electronics he must sell?

Exit Ticket Sample Solutions

1. Lee works selling electronics. He earns a 5% commission on each sale he makes.

   a. Write an equation that shows the proportional relationship between the dollar amount of electronics Lee sells, d, and the amount of money he makes in commission, c.

   $$c = \frac{1}{20} d$$

   b. Express the constant of proportionality as a decimal.

   0.05

   c. Explain what the constant of proportionality means in the context of this situation.

   The constant of proportionality of 0.05 means that Lee would earn five cents for every dollar of electronics that he sells.

   d. If Lee wants to make $100 in commission, what is the dollar amount of electronics he must sell?

   $$c = 0.05\,d$$
   $$100 = 0.05\,d$$
   $$\frac{1}{0.05}(100) = \frac{1}{0.05}(0.05)\,d$$
   $$2{,}000 = d$$

   Lee must sell $2,000 worth of electronics.

Problem Set Sample Solutions

1. A school district's property tax rate rises from 2.5% to 2.7% to cover a $300,000 budget deficit (shortage of money). What is the value of the property in the school district to the nearest dollar? (Note: Property is assessed at 100% of its value.)

   $$300{,}000 = 0.002\,W$$
   $$300{,}000\left(\frac{1}{0.002}\right) = 0.002\left(\frac{1}{0.002}\right)W$$
   $$150{,}000{,}000 = W$$

   The property is worth $150,000,000.

2. Jake's older brother Sam has a choice of two summer jobs. He can either work at an electronics store or at the school's bus garage. The electronics store would pay him to work 15 hours per week. He would make $8 per hour plus a 2% commission on his electronics sales. Sam could earn $300 per week working 15 hours cleaning buses. Sam wants to take the job that pays him the most. How much in electronics would Sam have to sell for the job at the electronics store to be the better choice for his summer job?

   Let S = the amount of electronics sales

   $$300 = 8(15) + 0.02(S)$$
   $$300 = 120 + 0.02S$$
   $$180 = 0.02S$$
   $$180\left(\frac{1}{0.02}\right) = 0.02\left(\frac{1}{0.02}\right)S$$
   $$9{,}000 = S$$

   Sam would have to sell more than $9,000 in electronics for the electronics store to be the better choice.

3. Sarah lost her science book. Her school charges a lost book fee equal to 75% of the cost of the book. Sarah received a notice stating she owed the school $60 for the lost book.

  a. Write an equation to represent the proportional relationship between the school's cost for the book and the amount a student must pay for a lost book. Let B represent the school's cost of the book in dollars and N represent the student's cost in dollars.

  $N = 0.75\,B$

  b. What is the constant or proportionality? What does it mean in the context of this situation?

  The constant of proportionality is $75\% = 0.75$. *It means that for every* $1 *the school spends to purchase a textbook, a student must pay* $0.75 *for a lost book.*

  c. How much did the school pay for the book?

  $$60 = 0.75\,B$$
  $$60\left(\frac{1}{0.75}\right) = 0.75\left(\frac{1}{0.75}\right)B$$
  $$\frac{60}{0.75} = B$$
  $$80 = B$$

  The school paid $80 *for the science book.*

4. In the month of May, a certain middle school has an average daily absentee rate of 8% each school day. The absentee rate is the percent of students who are absent from school each day.

  a. Write an equation that shows the proportional relationship between the number of students enrolled in the middle school and the average number of students absent each day. Let s represent the number of students enrolled in school, and let a represent the average number of students absent each day.

  $a = 0.08s$

  b. Use your equation to complete the table. List 5 possible values for s and a.

s	a
100	8
200	16
300	24
400	32
500	40

  c. Identify the constant of proportionality, and explain what it means in the context of this situation.

  The constant of proportionality is 0.08. $0.08 = 8\%$, *so on average, for every* 100 *students enrolled in school,* 8 *are absent from school.*

  d. Based on the absentee rate, determine the number of students absent on average from school if there are 350 students enrolled in the middle school.

  28 students.

  350 is halfway between 300 and 400. So, I used the table of values and looked at the numbers of students absent that correspond to 300 and 400 students at the school, which are 24 and 32. Halfway between 24 and 32 is 28.

5. The equation shown in the box below could relate to many different percent problems. Put an "X" next to each problem that could be represented by this equation. For any problem that does not match this equation, explain why it does not. $\boxed{Quantity = 1.05 \cdot Whole}$

_____   Find the amount of an investment after 1 year with 0.5% interest paid annually.

The equation should be: $Quantity = 1.005 \cdot Whole.$

___X___   Write an *equation* to show the amount paid for an item including tax, if the tax rate is 5%.

___X___   A proportional relationship has a constant of proportionality equal to 105%.

___X___
Whole	0	100	200	300	400	500
Quantity	0	105	210	315	420	525

_____   Mr. Hendrickson sells cars and earns a 5% commission on every car he sells. Write an equation to show the relationship between the price of a car Mr. Hendrickson sold and the amount of commission he earns.

The equation should be: $Quantity = 0.05 \cdot Whole.$

Name _____   Date _____

1. In New York State, sales tax rates vary by county. In Allegany County, the sales tax rate is $8\frac{1}{2}\%$.

   a. A book costs $12.99 and a video game costs $39.99. Rounded to the nearest cent, how much more is the tax on the video game than the tax on the book?

   b. Using n to represent the cost of an item before tax and t to represent the amount of sales tax for that item, write an equation to show the relationship between n and t.

   c. Using your equation, create a table that includes five possible pairs of solutions to the equation. Label each column appropriately.

d. Graph the relationship from parts (a) and (b) in the coordinate plane. Include a title and appropriate scales and labels for both axes.

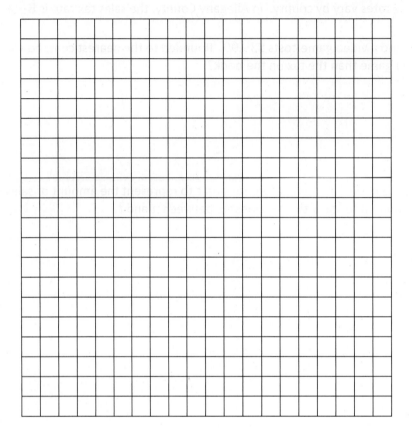

e. Is the relationship proportional? Why or why not? If so, what is the constant of proportionality? Explain.

f. In nearby Wyoming County, the sales tax rate is 8%. If you were to create an equation, graph, and table for this tax rate (similar to parts (a), (b), and (d) above), what would the points (0,0) and (1,0.08) represent? Explain their meaning in the context of this situation.

g. A customer returns an item to a toy store in Wyoming County. The toy store has another location in Allegany County, and the customer shops at both locations. The customer's receipt shows $2.12 tax was charged on a $24.99 item. Was the item purchased at the Wyoming County store or the Allegany County store? Explain and justify your answer by showing your math work.

2. Amy is baking her famous pies to sell at the Town Fall Festival. She uses $32\frac{1}{2}$ cups of flour for every 10 cups of sugar in order to make a dozen pies. Answer the following questions below and show your work.

a. Write an equation, in terms of f, representing the relationship between the number of cups of flour used and the number of cups of sugar used to make the pies.

b. Write the constant of proportionality as a percent. Explain what it means in the context of this situation.

c. To help sell more pies at the festival, Amy set the price for one pie at 40% less than what it would cost at her bakery. At the festival, she posts a sign that reads, "Amy's Famous Pies only $9.00/pie!" Using this information, what is the price of one pie at the bakery?

A Progression Toward Mastery

Assessment Task Item		STEP 1 Missing or incorrect answer and little evidence of reasoning or application of mathematics to solve the problem.	STEP 2 Missing or incorrect answer but evidence of some reasoning or application of mathematics to solve the problem.	STEP 3 A correct answer with some evidence of reasoning or application of mathematics to solve the problem, or an incorrect answer with substantial evidence of solid reasoning or application of mathematics to solve the problem.	STEP 4 A correct answer supported by substantial evidence of solid reasoning or application of mathematics to solve the problem.
1	**a** 7.RP.A.3 7.EE.B.3	Student is not able to compute the tax for either item correctly.	Student computes the tax rate for only one of the items correctly. OR Student computes both taxes correctly, but does not subtract the two tax values or does it incorrectly.	Student sets up and completes all computations correctly with no errors, but fails to round the difference to the nearest cent. OR Student sets up and completes all computations correctly with only one minor error.	Student sets up and completes all calculations correctly and correctly rounds the answer to the nearest cent.
	b 7.RP.A.2	Student does not answer the question.	Student has the incorrect answer because he or she writes an expression such as $0.85n$.	Student has the incorrect answer, but makes an attempt to write an equation. For example, the student incorrectly writes $t = 0.85n$.	Student has the correct answer: $t = 0.085n$.
	c 7.RP.A.2	Student attempts to answer the question, but does not construct a table or only provides one point. OR Student does not attempt to answer the question.	Student has the incorrect answer, but makes an attempt to construct a table. Fewer than four correct points are listed.	Student correctly calculates and lists five points, but the table is not labeled correctly. OR Student correctly calculates and lists four of the five points and the correctly labels the table.	Student has a correct table (with labeling) including five points that shows the cost of the item as the independent variable and amount of sales tax as the dependent variable. The student shows significant evidence of application of mathematics by multiplying each cost by 0.085 to get the amount of sales tax.

Module 4:   Percent and Proportional Relationships

163

d 7.RP.A.2 7.RP.A.3	Student makes an attempt to construct a graph, but the graph is incomplete, missing several components. OR Student does not attempt to construct a graph.	Student provides a graph that shows some evidence of understanding the proportional relationship, but the graph contains multiple errors. For example, the scale is incorrect and the axes are not labeled, the line is not straight, etc.	Student has a correct graph and uses an appropriate scale on each axis, but does not label the axes or provide a title for the graph. OR Student has a correct graph with one minor error, but provides a title for the graph and labels the axes correctly.	Student has a correct graph (with labeling and scale) showing a straight line through the origin. (Scales may vary.) The cost of the item is graphed along the x-axis and the amount of sales is graphed along the y-axis.
e 7.RP.A.2	Student may or may not state that the relationship is proportional, and provides little or no evidence of reasoning._ OR Student does not attempt to answer the question.	Student incorrectly states that the relationship is not proportional, but provides an explanation that demonstrates some understanding of proportional relationships. Student may or may not identify a correct constant of proportionality. OR Student correctly identifies the relationship as proportional, but states an incorrect constant of proportionality.	Student correctly states that the relationship is proportional, but provides an incomplete explanation to support the claim. For example, student only includes "because the graph is a straight line" and does not state that it passes through the origin. The student correctly identifies the constant of proportionality but may or may not explain its meaning. OR Student states the relationship is proportional but bases the answer on an incorrect graph from part (c). The constant of proportionality stated is based on the incorrect graph.	Student correctly states that the relationship is proportional and provides a thorough explanation, which includes the following: (1) the graph is a straight line through the origin, and (2) the ratios of sales tax to cost all equal 0.085. The student correctly identifies the constant of proportionality and explains its meaning as the unit rate, identifying 0.085 as the amount of sales tax per dollar.
f 7.RP.A.1 7.RP.A.2	Student does not answer the question.	Student incorrectly explains what $(0, 0)$ and $(1, 0.08)$ mean in the context of the situation, but provides some evidence of reasoning.	Student shows solid evidence of reasoning in their explanation, but the answer is not complete. For example, the student explains that $(1, 0.08)$ represents the unit rate and that $(0,0)$ is the point where there are zero dollars spent so no tax is charged, but does not relate both points to the context of the situation.	Student correctly explains what both points $(0, 0)$ and $(1, 0.08)$ mean in the context of the situation. The explanation includes evidence of solid reasoning. For example, $(0, 0)$ shows nothing was purchased, so no tax has been applied, and $(1, 0.08)$ shows the unit rate, meaning for every increase of $1.00 the

				amount of tax will increase by $0.08.
g 7.RP.A.3 7.EE.B.3	Student may or may not answer Allegany County, and provides little or no evidence of reasoning. OR Student does not attempt to answer the question.	Student does not have the correct answer of Allegany County, but supports the answer with some evidence of reasoning. Multiple errors are made in the calculations to find the tax rate.	Student has the correct answer of Allegany County, but the math work or explanation is slightly incomplete or contains a minor error.	Student has the correct answer of Allegany County and supports the answer with a valid explanation and correct math work (or uses estimation) to show that the tax rate is about 8.5%.
2 **a** 7.RP.A.1 7.RP.A.2	Student does not attempt to answer the question.	Student writes an equation involving f and s, but the equation is incorrect and shows little evidence of understanding.	Student writes an equation involving f and s, and although the equation is incorrect, it demonstrates an understanding of the proportional relationship. For instance, the student writes the equation in terms of s, such as $s = \frac{1}{3.25}f$.	Student writes a correct equation in terms of f, such as: $f = 3\frac{1}{4}s$ or $f = 3.25s$ or $f = \frac{13}{4}s$. Student shows substantial evidence of understanding by dividing 32.5 by 10 to find the constant of proportionality.
b 7.RP.A.2	Student answers incorrectly and shows little or no evidence of understanding how to convert a fraction or decimal to a percent. OR Student does not attempt to answer the question.	Student answers incorrectly, but the math work and/or explanation shows some evidence of understanding how to convert a fraction or decimal to a percent. The student may or may not have correctly explained what the constant of proportionality means in the context of the situation.	Student correctly answers 325%, but the explanation and/or supporting work is not complete.	Student correctly answers 325% with adequate work shown AND correctly explains that the amount of flour used is 325% the amount of sugar used.
c 7.RP.A.3 7.EE.B.3	Student states an incorrect price for the pie, and shows little or no relevant work to support the answer. OR Student does not attempt to answer the question.	Student states an incorrect price for the pie, but the math work shows a partial understanding of the task involved.	Student states the correct price of $15 for one pie at the bakery, but the supporting math work is incomplete, or contains a minor error. OR Student states an incorrect price for the pie, but the answer is based on sound mathematical work that contains a minor error.	Student correctly arrives at a price of $15 per pie, and supports the answer with math work that indicates solid reasoning and correct calculations. For instance, the student may write and solve an equation such as $9 = (1 - 0.40)x$.

Name _____ Date _____

1. In New York State, sales tax rates vary by county. In Allegany County, the sales tax rate is $8\frac{1}{2}\%$.

   a. A book costs $12.99 and a video game costs $39.99. Rounded to the nearest cent, how much more is the tax on the video game than the tax on the book?

   $12.99\ (8.5\%) = 12.99\ (0.085) = 1.10415$

   $39.99\ (8.5\%) = 39.99\ (0.085) = 3.39915$

   $3.39915 - 1.10415 = 2.295$

   Answer: $2.30

   b. Using n to represent the cost of an item before tax and t to represent the amount of sales tax for that item, write an equation to show the relationship between n and t.

   $$t = .085n$$

   c. Using your equation, create a table that includes five possible pairs of solutions to the equation. Label each column appropriately.

Cost of Item (n)	Amount of Sales Tax (t)
0	0.00
1.00	0.085
2.00	0.17
3.00	0.255
4.00	0.34
5.00	0.425

d. Graph the relationship from parts (a) and (b) in the coordinate plane. Include a title and appropriate scales and labels for both axes.

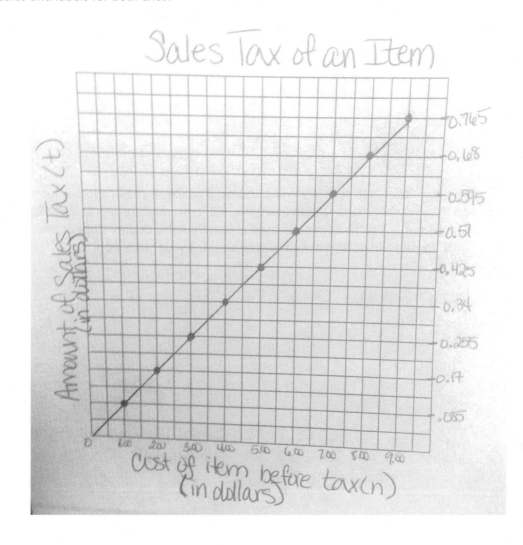

e. Is the relationship proportional? Why or why not? If so, what is the constant of proportionality? Explain.

Yes, the relationship is proportional because the graph of the equation is a straight line that touches the origin. Also, the table shows that the ratios of $\frac{\text{amount of sales tax}}{\text{cost of an item}}$ = 0.085.

$\frac{.085}{1} = \frac{.17}{2} = \frac{.255}{3} = \frac{.34}{4} = \frac{.425}{5}$

The constant of proportionality is .085 because that is the sales tax amount for $1.00, which is the unit rate.

f.   In nearby Wyoming County, the sales tax rate is 8%. If you were to create an equation, graph, and
     table for this tax rate (similar to parts (a), (b), and (d) above), what would the points (0,0) and
     (1,0.08) represent? Explain their meaning in the context of this situation.

> The point (0,0) [origin] means that no tax has been
> applied yet because nothing has been purchased.
> The point (1,0.08) is the unit rate or the constant
> of proportionality. It means that for an item
> that costs $1.00, the amount of tax applied
> is $0.08. The unit rate also shows that for every
> $1.00, the amount of tax will increase by $0.08.

g.   A customer returns an item to a toy store in Wyoming County. The toy store has another location in
     Allegany County, and the customer shops at both locations. The customer's receipt shows $2.12 tax
     was charged on a $24.99 item. Was the item purchased at the Wyoming County store or the
     Allegany County store? Explain and justify your answer by showing your math work.

> The item was purchased
> in Allegany
>
> $\frac{2.12}{24.99}$ is about $\frac{2.12 \times 4}{25 \times 4} = \frac{8.48}{100}$
>
> which is 8.48% or about 8.5%

2. Amy is baking her famous pies to sell at the Town Fall Festival. She uses $32\frac{1}{2}$ cups of flour for every 10 cups of sugar in order to make a dozen pies. Answer the following questions below and show your work.

a. Write an equation, in terms of f, representing the relationship between the number of cups of flour used and the number of cups of sugar used to make the pies.

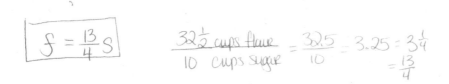

$$\boxed{f = \frac{13}{4}s}$$

$$\frac{32\frac{1}{2} \text{ cups flour}}{10 \text{ cups sugar}} = \frac{32.5}{10} = 3.25 = 3\frac{1}{4}$$
$$= \frac{13}{4}$$

b. Write the constant of proportionality as a percent. Explain what it means in the context of this situation.

$$3.25 = \frac{325}{100} = 325\%$$

A constant of proportionality of 325% means that the amount of flour used to make the pies is 325% the amount of sugar used.

c. To help sell more pies at the festival, Amy set the price for one pie at 40% less than what it would cost at her bakery. She posts a sign that reads, "Amy's Famous Pies only $9.00/pie!" Using this information, what is the price of one pie at the bakery?

$$x - 0.4x = 9$$
$$\frac{0.6x}{0.6} = \frac{9}{0.6}$$
$$x = 15$$

$$\begin{array}{r} 15.00 \\ 6\overline{)90} \\ \underline{-6} \\ 30 \end{array}$$

The price of one pie at the bakery costs $15.00.

Mathematics Curriculum

7
GRADE

Topic C:

Scale Drawings

7.RP.A.2b, 7.G.A.1

Focus Standard:	7.RP.A.2b	Recognize and represent proportional relationships between quantities.
		b. Identify the constant of proportionality (unit rate) in tables, graphs, equations, diagrams, and verbal descriptions of proportional relationships.
	7.G.A.1	Solve problems involving scale drawings of geometric figures, including computing actual lengths and areas from a scale drawing and reproducing a scale drawing at a different scale.
Instructional Days:	4	
Lesson 12:	The Scale Factor as a Percent for a Scale Drawing (P)[1]	
Lesson 13:	Changing Scales (E)	
Lesson 14:	Computing Actual Lengths from a Scale Drawing (P)	
Lesson 15:	Solving Area Problems Using Scale Drawings (P)	

In Lesson 12, students extend their understanding of scale factor from Module 1 to include scale factors represented as percents. Students know the scale factor to be the constant of proportionality, and they create scale drawings when given horizontal and vertical scale factors in the form of percents (**7.G.A.1**, **7.RP.A.2b**). In Lesson 13, students recognize that if Drawing B is a scale drawing of Drawing A, that one could also view Drawing A as being a scale drawing of Drawing B; they compute the scale factor from Drawing B to Drawing A and express it as a percentage. Also in this lesson, students are presented with three similar drawings – an original drawing, a reduction, and an enlargement – and, given the scale factor for the reduction (as a percentage of the original) and the scale factor for the enlargement (as a percentage of the original), students compute the scale factor between the reduced image and the enlarged image, and vice-versa, expressing each scale factor as a percentage. In Lesson 14, students compute the actual dimensions when given a scale drawing and the scale factor as a percent. To solve area problems related to scale drawings, in Lesson 15 students use the fact that an area, A', of a scale drawing is k^2 times the corresponding

---

[1] Lesson Structure Key: **P**-Problem Set Lesson, **M**-Modeling Cycle Lesson, **E**-Exploration Lesson, **S**-Socratic Lesson

Topic C: Scale Drawings

area, A, in the original picture (where k is the scale factor). For instance, given a scale factor of 25%, students convert to its fractional representation of $\frac{1}{4}$ and know that the area of the scale drawing will be $\left(\frac{1}{4}\right)^2$ or $\frac{1}{16}$ the area of the original picture and use that fact to problem solve.

Lesson 12: The Scale Factor as a Percent for a Scale Drawing

Student Outcomes

- Given a scale factor as a percent, students make a scale drawing of a picture or geometric figure using that scale, recognizing that the enlarged or reduced distances in a scale drawing are proportional to the corresponding distances in the original picture.
- Students understand scale factor to be the constant of proportionality.
- Students make scale drawings in which the horizontal and vertical scales are different.

Lesson Notes

In Module 1, students were introduced to proportional relationships within the context of scale drawings. Given a scale drawing, students identified the scale factor as the constant of proportionality. They compared the scale drawing with the original drawing to determine whether the scale drawing is a reduction or an enlargement of the original drawing by interpreting the scale factor. Students calculated the actual lengths and areas of objects in the scale drawing by using the scale factor.

In this module, Lessons 12–15 build on what students learned in Module 1. These lessons require students to create scale drawings when given a scale factor as a percent or to determine the scale factor as a percent when given the original drawing and the scale drawing. Students make scale drawings in which the horizontal and vertical scales are different. Students compute the scale factor of several drawings with different scales, determine actual lengths from scale drawings, and solve area problems using scale drawings. The outcomes may seem similar to the outcomes covered in Module 1; however, Module 4 emphasizes giving the scale factor as a written percent once it is determined. It is also important to note that the scale factor may still be written as a ratio, as in "1: 5," "1 to 5" or "one inch represents five inches."

Note: This module includes an examination of horizontal and vertical scale factors. It is important to note that if only a "scale factor" is named, we conventionally apply it both vertically and horizontally.

Classwork

Opening (7 minutes)

Review the definitions of scale drawing, reduction, enlargement, and scale factor from Module 1, Lessons 16–17. To review such definitions, refer to the drawing below and engage the students in a discussion about each definition.

> **Scaffolding:**
>
> The word *scale* has several meanings (mostly nouns) that might cause confusion. To make this new definition of the word clear, show visuals of the other meanings of the word.

Opening

Review the definitions of scale drawing, reduction, enlargement, and scale factor from Module 1, Lessons 16–17.

Compare the corresponding lengths of Figure A to the original octagon in the middle. This is an example of a particular type of <u>scale drawing</u> called a *reduction.* Explain why it is called that.

A scale drawing is a <u>reduction</u> of the original drawing when the corresponding lengths of the scale drawing are smaller than the lengths in the original drawing.

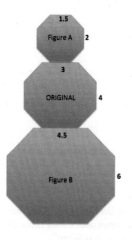

Compare the corresponding lengths of Figure B to the original octagon in the middle. This is an example of a particular type of <u>scale drawing</u> called an *enlargement.* Explain why it is called that.

A scale drawing is an <u>enlargement</u> of the original drawing when the corresponding lengths of the scale drawing are larger than the lengths in the original drawing.

The <u>scale factor</u> is the quotient of any length in the scale drawing and its corresponding length in the original drawing.

Use what you recall from Module 1 to determine the scale factors between the original figure and Figure A and the original figure and Figure B.

Scale Factor between original and Figure A: $\dfrac{1.5}{3} = \dfrac{1}{2}$

Scale Factor between original and Figure B: $\dfrac{4.5}{3} = \dfrac{3}{2}$

Using the diagram, complete the chart to determine the horizontal and vertical scale factors. Write answers as a percent and as a concluding statement using the previously learned reduction and enlargement vocabulary.

	Horizontal Measurement in Scale Drawing	Vertical Measurement in Scale Drawing	Concluding Statement
Figure A	$\dfrac{1.5}{3} = \dfrac{1}{2} = 50\%$	$\dfrac{2}{4} = \dfrac{1}{2} = 50\%$	*Figure A is a reduction of the original figure. A length in Figure A is 50% of the corresponding length in the original drawing.*
Figure B	$\dfrac{4.5}{3} = \dfrac{1.5}{1} = 150\%$	$\dfrac{6}{4} = \dfrac{1.5}{1} = 150\%$	*Figure B is an enlargement of the original figure. A length in Figure B is 150% of the corresponding length in the original drawing.*

Example 1 (10 minutes)

Example 1

Create a snowman on the accompanying grid. Use the octagon given as the middle of the snowman with the following conditions:

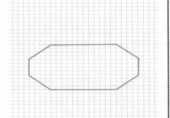

a. Calculate the width, neck, and height for the figure at the right.

> *Width:*   **20**
>
> *Neck:*   **12**
>
> *Height:*   **12**

b. To create the head of the snowman, make a scale drawing of the middle of the snowman with a scale factor of 75%. Calculate the new lengths for the width, neck, and height.

> *Width:* $75\%(20) = (0.75)(20) = 15$
>
> *Neck:* $75\%(12) = (0.75)(12) = 9$
>
> *Height:* $75\%(12) = (0.75)(12) = 9$

c. To create the bottom of the snowman, make a scale drawing of the middle of the snowman with a scale factor of 125%. Calculate the new lengths for the width, neck, and height.

> *Width:* $125\%(20) = (1.25)(20) = 25$
>
> *Waist:* $125\%(12) = (1.25)(12) = 15$
>
> *Height:* $125\%(12) = (1.25)(12) = 15$

d. Is the head a reduction or enlargement of the middle?

> *The head is a reduction of the middle since the lengths of the sides are smaller than the lengths in the original drawing.*

e. Is the bottom a reduction or enlargement of the middle?

> *The bottom is an enlargement of the middle since the lengths of the scale drawing are larger than the lengths in the original drawing.*

f. What is the significance of the scale factor as it relates to 100%? What happens when such scale factors are applied?

> *A scale factor of 100% would be the original drawing, and it would be neither an enlargement nor reduction. A scale factor of less than 100% results in a scale drawing that is a reduction of the original drawing. A scale factor of greater than 100% results in a scale drawing that is an enlargement of the original drawing.*

MP.3

Scaffolding:

As necessary, give students specific instructions on creating a scale drawing.

First, determine the original lengths for any horizontal or vertical distance that can be obtained by counting the boxes in the coordinate grid. Using the scale factor, determine the new corresponding lengths in the scale drawing. Draw new segments based on the calculations from the original segments. There may be more than one correct drawing. The head and bottom may be the correct lengths but may be off-center. To ensure the drawing is not off-center, the corresponding length needs to align with the original drawing. A corresponding length, such as 9, may need to be drawn in half-unit segment increments followed by 8 units, followed by a half-unit. This would offer an equal number of boxes from each endpoint of the scale drawing. Lastly, any diagonal segment should be drawn by connecting the vertical and horizontal corresponding segments.

Answer:

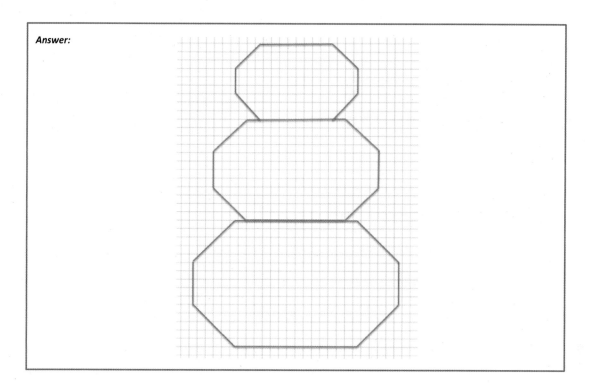

Discussion

- Recall that when working with percents, the percent must be converted to a decimal or fraction for use in calculating the scale drawing lengths. How do we convert a percent or fraction to a decimal? How do we convert a fractional percent to a decimal?

  > *Scaffolding:*
  >
  > Review the meanings of the words: *horizontal, vertical,* and *diagonal.* Have each student hold an arm up in the air to model each word's meaning as it relates to the orientation of a line segment.

    - *To convert a percent to a decimal, divide the percent by* 100 *and express the quotient as a decimal. Also, the percent can be written as decimal by moving the decimal point two places to the left. To convert a fractional percent to a decimal, divide the percent by* 100*; e.g.,* $5\frac{1}{3}\% = \frac{16}{3}\% = \frac{16}{3} \div 100 = \frac{16}{300} = \frac{4}{75} = 0.053\overline{3}$.

- How are the diagonal corresponding segments drawn in the scale drawings?

    - *Once the horizontal and vertical segment lengths of the scale drawing are calculated and drawn, then any diagonal lengths can be drawn by connecting the horizontal and vertical segments.*

- How are scale factor, unit rate, and constant of proportionality used?

    - *They are the same; the scale factor is the unit rate or constant of proportionality. When every length of the original drawing is multiplied by the scale factor, the corresponding length in the scale drawing is obtained.*

- Summarize the effects of the scale factor as a percent of a scale drawing.

    - *The scale factor is the number that determines whether the new drawing is an enlargement or a reduction of the original. If the scale factor is greater than* 100%*, then the resulting drawing will be an enlargement of the original drawing. If the scale factor is less than* 100%*, then the resulting drawing will be a reduction of the original drawing. The resulting enlarged or reduced distances are proportional to the original distances.*

Example 2 (4 minutes)

Example 2

Create a scale drawing of the arrow below using a scale factor of 150%.

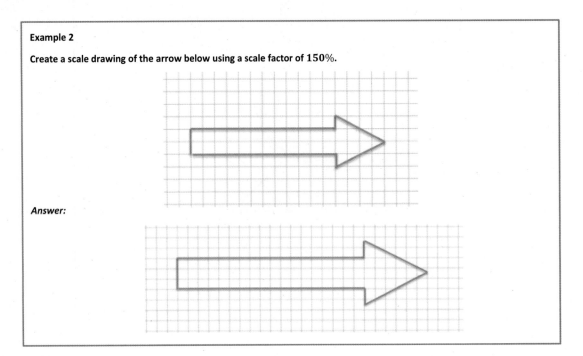

Answer:

Example 3 (4 minutes): Scale Drawings where the Horizontal and Vertical Scale Factors are Different

Example 3: Scale Drawings where the Horizontal and Vertical Scale Factors are Different

Sometimes it is helpful to make a scale drawing where the horizontal and vertical scale factors are different, such as when creating diagrams in the field of engineering. Having differing scale factors may distort some drawings. For example, when you are working with a very large horizontal scale, you sometimes must exaggerate the vertical scale in order to make it readable. This can be accomplished by creating a drawing with two scales. Unlike the scale drawings with just one scale factor, these types of scale drawings may look distorted. Next to the drawing below is a scale drawing with a horizontal scale factor of 50% and vertical scale factor of 25% (given in two steps). Explain how each drawing is created.

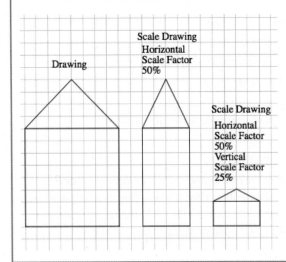

Each horizontal distance in the scale drawing is 50% (or half) of the corresponding length in the original drawing. Each vertical distance in the scale drawing is 25% (or one-fourth) of the corresponding length in the original drawing.

Horizontal Distance:

$$8(0.50) = 8\left(\frac{1}{2}\right) = 4$$

Vertical Distance of House:

$$8(0.25) = 8\left(\frac{1}{4}\right) = 2$$

Vertical Distance of Top of House:

$$4(0.25) = 4\left(\frac{1}{4}\right) = 1$$

Exercise 1 (5 Minutes)

Exercise 1

Create a scale drawing of the following drawing using a horizontal scale factor of $183\frac{1}{3}\%$ and a vertical scale factor of 25%.

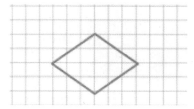

Horizontal Scale Factor: $\dfrac{183\frac{1}{3} \cdot 3}{100 \cdot 3} = \dfrac{550}{300} = \dfrac{11}{6}$

Horizontal Distance: $6\left(\dfrac{11}{6}\right) = 11$

Vertical Scale Factor: $\dfrac{25}{100} = \dfrac{1}{4}$

Vertical Distance: $4\left(\dfrac{1}{4}\right) = 1$

New Sketch:

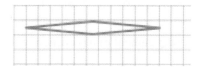

- When a scale factor is given as a percent, why is it best to convert the percent to a fraction?
  - *All percents can be written as fractions by dividing the percent by 100. This strategy is particularly helpful when the percent is a fractional percent. Also, sometimes the percent written as a decimal would be a repeating decimal, which may result in an approximate answer. Therefore, writing the percent as a fraction will ensure a precise answer.*

- To do this, the percent is divided by 100. When the percent is a fractional percent, the quotient is written as a complex fraction. How do you find an equivalent simple fraction?
  - *You convert all mixed numbers to improper fractions, then multiply both the numerator and denominator by the reciprocal of the denominator, and follow the rules of multiplying fractions. Another option is to write the fractional percent divided by 100 and multiply both the numerator and denominator by the denominator of the fractional percent, reducing the answer. For example,*

  $152\frac{1}{3}\%$ *can be written as* $\dfrac{152\frac{1}{3}}{100} = \dfrac{\frac{457}{3}}{100} = \dfrac{457}{3} \times \dfrac{1}{100} = \dfrac{457}{300}$ *or* $\dfrac{152\frac{1}{3}\times 3}{100\times 3} = \dfrac{457}{300}.$

Exercise 2 (3 Minutes)

Exercise 2

Chris is building a rectangular pen for his dog. The dimensions are 12 units long and 5 units wide.

12 Units

5 Units

Chris is building a second pen that is 60% the length of the original and 125% the width of the original. Write equations to determine the length and width of the second pen.

Length: $12 \times 0.60 = 7.2$

The length of the second pen is 7.2 *units.*

Width: $5 \times 1.25 = 6.25$

The width of the second pen is 6.25 *units.*

Closing (4 minutes)

- Note: To clarify, when a scale factor is mentioned, assume that it refers to both vertical and horizontal factors. It will be noted if the horizontal and vertical factors are intended to be different.

- How do you determine if a scale drawing is an enlargement or a reduction of the original if the scale factor is given as a percent?

- Can a scale drawing have different horizontal and vertical scale factors? If it can, how do you create a scale drawing with different horizontal and vertical scale factors?

- How are the corresponding lengths in a scale drawing and an original drawing related?

- How does the scale factor relate to the "constant of proportionality" that we have been studying?

Lesson Summary

The scale factor is the number that determines whether the new drawing is an enlargement or a reduction of the original. If the scale factor is greater than 100%, then the resulting drawing will be an enlargement of the original drawing. If the scale factor is less than 100%, then the resulting drawing will be a reduction of the original drawing.

When a scale factor is mentioned, assume that it refers to both vertical and horizontal factors. It will be noted if the horizontal and vertical factors are intended to be different.

To create a scale drawing with both the same vertical and horizontal factors, determine the horizontal and vertical distances of the original drawing. Using the given scale factor, determine the new corresponding lengths in the scale drawing by writing a numerical equation that requires the scale factor to be multiplied by the original length. Draw new segments based on the calculations from the original segments. If the scale factors are different, determine the new corresponding lengths the same way but use the unique given scale factor for both the horizontal length and vertical length.

Exit Ticket (8 minutes)

Name _____   Date _____

Lesson 12: The Scale Factor as a Percent for a Scale Drawing

Exit Ticket

1. Create a scale drawing of the picture below using a scale factor of 60%. Write three equations that show how you determined the lengths of three different parts of the resulting picture.

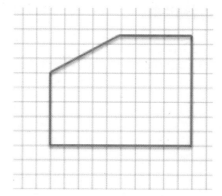

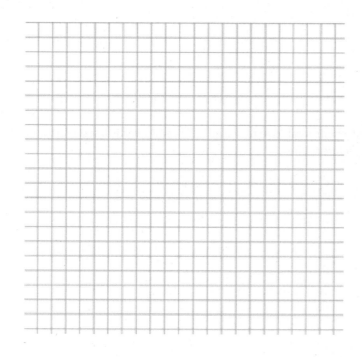

2. Sue wants to make two picture frames with lengths and widths that are proportional to the ones given below. Note: The illustration shown below is not drawn to scale.

8 inches

12 inches

a. Sketch a scale drawing using a horizontal scale factor of 50% and a vertical scale factor of 75%. Determine the dimensions of the new picture frame.

b. Sketch a scale drawing using a horizontal scale factor of 125% and a vertical scale factor of 140%. Determine the dimensions of the new picture frame.

Exit Ticket Sample Solutions

1. Create a scale drawing of the picture below using a scale factor of 60%. Write three equations that show how you determined the lengths of three different parts of the resulting picture.

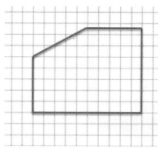

Scale Factor: $60\% = \dfrac{60}{100} = \dfrac{3}{5}$

Horizontal Distances: $10\left(\dfrac{3}{5}\right) = 6$

$5\left(\dfrac{3}{5}\right) = 3$

Vertical Distances: $5\left(\dfrac{3}{5}\right) = 3$

$7\dfrac{1}{2}\left(\dfrac{3}{5}\right) = \dfrac{15}{2}\left(\dfrac{3}{5}\right) = \dfrac{9}{2} = 4.5$

Scale Drawing:

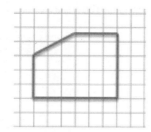

Equations:

Left Vertical Distance:	$5 \times 0.60 = 3$
Right Vertical Distance:	$7.5 \times 0.60 = 4.5$
Top Horizontal Distance:	$5 \times 0.60 = 3$
Bottom Horizontal Distance:	$10 \times 0.60 = 6$

2. Sue wants to make two picture frames like the one given below.

8

12

a. Sketch a scale drawing using a horizontal scale factor of 50% and a vertical scale factor of 75%. Determine the dimensions of the new picture frame.

Horizontal Measurement: $8(0.50) = 4$

Vertical Measurement: $12(0.75) = 9$

4 units by 9 units

b. Sketch a scale drawing using a horizontal scale factor of 125% and a vertical scale factor of 140%. Determine the dimensions of the new picture frame.

Horizontal Measurement: $8(1.25) = 10$

Vertical Measurement: $12(1.40) = 16.8$

10 units by 16.8 units

Problem Set Sample Solutions

1. Use the diagram below to create a scale drawing using a scale factor of $133\frac{1}{3}\%$. Write numerical equations to find the horizontal and vertical distances in the scale drawing.

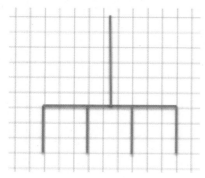

Scale Factor:

$$\frac{133\frac{1}{3} \cdot 3}{100 \cdot 3} = \frac{400}{300} = \frac{4}{3}$$

Horizontal Distance: $9\left(\frac{4}{3}\right) = 12$

Vertical Distance Forks: $3\left(\frac{4}{3}\right) = 4$

Vertical Distance Handle: $6\left(\frac{4}{3}\right) = 8$

Scale Drawing:

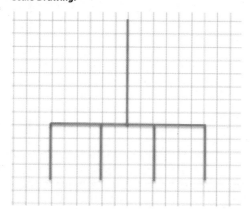

2. Create a scale drawing of the original drawing given below using a horizontal scale factor of 80% and a vertical scale factor of 175%. Write numerical equations to find the horizontal and vertical distances.

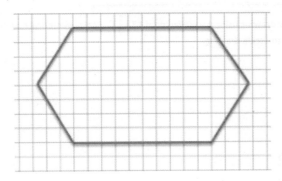

Horizontal Scale Factor: $80\% = \frac{80}{100} = \frac{4}{5}$

Horizontal Segment Lengths: $10(0.80) = 8$ *or* $10\left(\frac{4}{5}\right) = 8$

Horizontal Distance: $15\left(\frac{4}{5}\right) = 12$

Vertical Scale Factor: $175\% = \frac{175}{100} = \frac{7}{4}$

Vertical Distance: $8\left(\frac{7}{4}\right) = 14$

Scale Drawing:

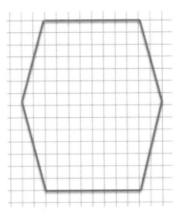

3. The accompanying diagram shows that the length of a pencil from its eraser to its tip is 7 units and that the eraser is 1.5 units wide. The picture was placed on a photocopy machine and reduced to $66\frac{2}{3}\%$. Find the new size of the pencil and sketch a drawing. Write numerical equations to find the new dimensions.

1.5 units

-------------------------7 units -------------------------

Scale Factor: $66\frac{2}{3}\% = \dfrac{66\frac{2}{3} \cdot 3}{100 \cdot 3} = \dfrac{200}{300} = \dfrac{2}{3}$

Pencil Length: $7\left(\dfrac{2}{3}\right) = 4\dfrac{2}{3}$

Eraser: $\left(1\dfrac{1}{2}\right)\left(\dfrac{2}{3}\right) = \left(\dfrac{3}{2}\right)\left(\dfrac{2}{3}\right) = 1$

4. Use the diagram to answer each question that follows.

    a. What are the corresponding horizontal and vertical distances in a scale drawing if the scale factor is 25%? Use numerical equations to find your answers.

       Horizontal Distance on Original Drawing: 14

       Vertical Distance on Original Drawing: 10

       Scale Drawing:

       Scale Factor: 25%

                             $\dfrac{25}{100} = \dfrac{1}{4}$

       Horizontal Distance: $14\left(\dfrac{1}{4}\right) = 3.5$

       Vertical Distance: $10\left(\dfrac{1}{4}\right) = 2.5$

    b. What are the corresponding horizontal and vertical distances in a scale drawing if the scale factor is 160%? Use a numerical equation to find your answers.

       Horizontal Distance on Original Drawing: 14

       Vertical Distance on Original Drawing: 10

       Scale Drawing:

       Scale Factor: 160%

                             $\dfrac{160}{100} = \dfrac{8}{5}$

       Horizontal Distance: $14\left(\dfrac{8}{5}\right) = 22.4$

       Vertical Distance: $10\left(\dfrac{8}{5}\right) = 16$

5. Create a scale drawing of the original drawing below using a horizontal scale factor of 200% and a vertical scale factor of 250%.

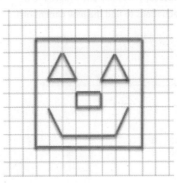

Answer:

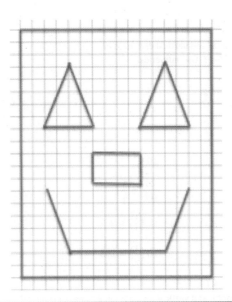

6. Using the diagram below, on grid paper sketch the same drawing using a horizontal scale factor of 50% and a vertical scale factor of 150%.

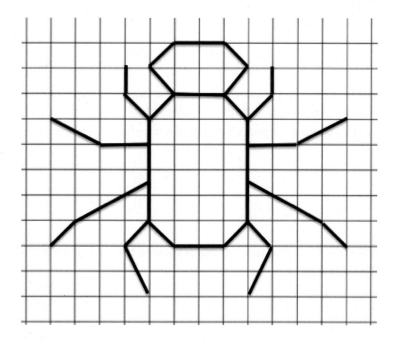

Answer:

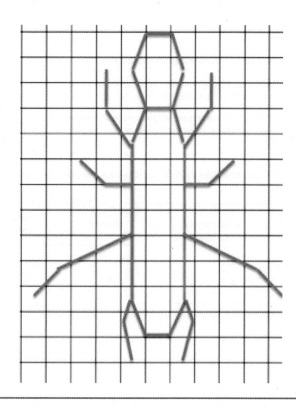

Lesson 13: Changing Scales

Student Outcomes

- Given Drawing 1 and Drawing 2 (a scale model of Drawing 1 with scale factor), students understand that Drawing 1 is also a scale model of Drawing 2 and compute the scale factor.
- Given three drawings that are scale drawings of each other and two scale factors, students compute the other related scale factor.

Classwork

Opening Exercise (8 minutes)

Students compare two drawings and determine the scale factor of one drawing to the second drawing and also decide whether one drawing is an enlargement of the original drawing or a reduction.

MP.2

Scaffolding:

To assist in determining the difference between a reduction and enlargement, fill in the blanks.

A scale drawing is a reduction of the actual drawing when the corresponding lengths of the scale drawing are _smaller_ than the lengths in the actual drawing and when the scale factor is _less_ than 100%.

A scale drawing is an enlargement of the actual drawing when the corresponding lengths of the scale drawing are _larger_ than the lengths in the actual drawing and when the scale factor is _greater_ than 100%.

Opening Exercise

Scale Factor: $\dfrac{length\ in\ SCALE\ DRAWING}{Corresponding\ length\ in\ ORIGINAL\ DRAWING}$

Describe, using percentages, the difference between a reduction and an enlargement.

A scale drawing is a reduction of the original drawing when the lengths of the scale drawing are smaller than the lengths in the original drawing. The scale factor is less than 100%.

A scale drawing is an enlargement of the original drawing when the lengths of the scale drawing are greater than the lengths in the original drawing. The scale factor is greater than 100%.

Use the two drawings below to complete the chart. Calculate the first row (Drawing 1 to Drawing 2) only.

	Quotient of Corresponding Horizontal Distances	Quotient of Corresponding Vertical Distances	Scale Factor as a Percent	Reduction or Enlargement?
Drawing 1 To Drawing 2	$\dfrac{3.92}{2.45} = 1.6$	$\dfrac{2.4}{1.5} = 1.6$	$1.6 = \dfrac{160}{100} = 160\%$	*Enlargement*
Drawing 2 to Drawing 1				

Compare Drawing 2 to Drawing 1. Using the completed work in the first row, make a conjecture (statement) about what the second row of the chart will be. Justify your conjecture without computing the second row.

Drawing 1 will be a reduction of Drawing 2. I know this because the corresponding lengths in Drawing 1 are smaller than the corresponding lengths in Drawing 2. Therefore, the scale factor from Drawing 2 to Drawing 1 would be less than 100%. Since Drawing 2 increased by 60% from Drawing 1, students may incorrectly assume the second row is 60% from the percent increase and 40% from subtracting $100\% - 60\% = 40\%$.

Compute the second row of the chart. Was your conjecture proven true? Explain how you know.

The conjecture was true because the calculated scale factor from Drawing 2 to Drawing 1 was 62.5%. Since the scale factor is less than 100%, the scale drawing is indeed a reduction.

	Quotient of Corresponding Horizontal Distances	Quotient of Corresponding Vertical Distances	Scale Factor as a Percent	Reduction or Enlargement?
Drawing 1 To Drawing 2	$\dfrac{3.92}{2.45} = 1.6$	$\dfrac{2.4}{1.5} = 1.6$	$1.6 = \dfrac{160}{100} = 160\%$	*Enlargement*
Drawing 2 to Drawing 1	$\dfrac{2.45}{3.92} = 0.625$	$\dfrac{1.5}{2.40} = 0.625$	$0.625 = \dfrac{62.5}{100} = 62.5\%$	*Reduction*

2.45 inches

3.92 inches

1.5 inches

DRAWING 1

DRAWING 2

2.4 inches

Discussion (7 minutes)

- If Drawing 2 is a scale drawing of Drawing 1, would it be a reduction or an enlargement? How do you know?
  - *It would be an enlargement because the scale factor as a percent will be larger than 100%.*

If students do not use scale factor as part of their rationale, ask the following question:

- We were working with the same two figures. Why was one comparison a reduction and the other an enlargement?
  - *Drawing 1 is a reduction of Drawing 2 because the corresponding lengths in Drawing 1 are smaller than the corresponding lengths in Drawing 2. Drawing 2 is an enlargement of Drawing 1 because the corresponding lengths in Drawing 2 are larger than the corresponding lengths in Drawing 1.*

- If you reverse the order and compare Drawing 2 to Drawing 1, it appears Drawing 1 is smaller; therefore, it is a reduction. What do you know about the scale factor of a reduction?
  - *The scale factor as a percent would be smaller than 100%.*

EUREKA MATH™

Lesson 13:   Changing Scales

- Recall that the representation from earlier lessons was $Quantity = Percent \times Whole$. It is important to decide the whole in each problem. In every scale drawing problem the whole is different. Does the "whole" have to be a length in the larger drawing?
  - *No, the whole is a length in the original or actual drawing. It may be the larger drawing, but it does not have to be.*

So, it is fair to say the whole, in the representation $Quantity = Percent \times Whole$, is a length in the actual or original drawing.

- To go from Drawing 1 to Drawing 2, a length in Drawing 1 is the whole. Using this relationship, the scale factor of Drawing 1 to Drawing 2 was calculated to be 160%. Does this mean Drawing 2 is 60% larger than Drawing 1? Explain how you know.
  - *Yes, the original drawing, Drawing 1, is considered to have a scale factor of 100%. The scale factor of Drawing 1 to Drawing 2 is 160%. Since it is greater than 100%, the scale drawing is an enlargement of the original drawing. Drawing 2 is 60% larger than Drawing 1 since the scale factor is 60% larger than the scale factor of Drawing 1.*

- Since Drawing 2 is 60% larger than Drawing 1, can I conclude that Drawing 1 is 60% smaller than Drawing 2, meaning the scale factor is $100\% - 60\% = 40\%$? Is this correct? Why or why not?
  - *No. To go from Drawing 2 to Drawing 1, a length in Drawing 2 is "the whole." So, using the same relationship, a length in Drawing 1 = Percent · a corresponding length in Drawing 2. Therefore, $2.45 = P(3.92)$. When we solve, we get $\frac{2.45}{3.92} = P$, which becomes 62.5%, not 40%. To determine scale factors as percents, we should never add or subtract percents, they must be calculated using multiplication or division.*

- In this example, we used the given measurements to calculate the scale factors. How could we create a scale drawing of a figure given the scale factor?
  - *The original drawing represents 100% of the drawing. An enlargement drawing would have a scale factor greater than 100%, and a reduction would have a scale factor less than 100%. If you are given the scale factor, then the corresponding distances in the scale drawing can be found by multiplying the distances in the original drawing by the scale factor.*

- Using this method, how can you work backwards and find the scale factor from Drawing 2 to Drawing 1 when only the scale factor from Drawing 1 to Drawing 2 was given?
  - *Since the scale factor for Drawing 2 was given, you can divide 100% (the original drawing) by the scale factor for Drawing 2. This will determine the scale factor from Drawing 2 to Drawing 1.*

- Justify your reasoning by using the drawing above as an example.
  - *Drawing 1 to Drawing 2 Scale Factor is 160%. (Assume this is given.)*
  - *Drawing 1 represents 100%.*
  - *The scale factor from Drawing 2 to Drawing 1 would be:*

    length in Drawing 1= Percent $\times$ length in Drawing 2

    100% length in Drawing 1= Percent$\times$ 160% length in Drawing 2

    $100 \div 160 = 0.625 \; or \frac{625}{1000} = \frac{5}{8}$

- Why is it possible to substitute a percent in for the quantity, percent, and whole in the relationship $Quantity = Percent \times Whole$?

  □ *The percent, which is being substituted for the quantity or whole, is the scale factor. The scale factor is the quotient of a length of the scale drawing and the corresponding length of the actual drawing. The percent that is being substituted into the formula is often an equivalent fraction of the scale factor. For instance, the scale factor for Drawing 2 to Drawing 1 was calculated to be 62.5%. In the formula, we could substitute 62.5% for the length; however, any of the following equivalent fractions would also be true:*

$$\frac{62.5}{100} = \frac{625}{1,000} = \frac{125}{200} = \frac{25}{40} = \frac{2.45}{3.92} = \frac{245}{392} = \frac{5}{8}.$$

Example 1 (4 minutes)

Example 1

The scale factor from Drawing 1 to Drawing 2 is 60%. Find the scale factor from Drawing 2 to Drawing 1. Explain your reasoning.

The scale drawing from Drawing 2 to Drawing 1 will be an enlargement. Drawing 1 is represented by 100%, and Drawing 2, a reduction of Drawing 1, is represented by 60%. A length in Drawing 2 will be the whole, so the scale factor from Drawing 2 to 1 is length in Drawing 1 $= Percent \times$ length in Drawing 2

$100\% = Percent \times 60\%$

$$\frac{100\%}{60\%} = \frac{1}{0.60} = \frac{1}{\frac{3}{5}} = \frac{5}{3} = 166\frac{2}{3}\%$$

Example 2 (10 minutes)

As a continuation to the Opening Exercise, now the task is to find the scale factor, as a percent, for each of three drawings.

Example 2

A regular octagon is an eight-sided polygon with side lengths that are all equal. All three octagons are scale drawings of each other. Use the chart and the side lengths to compute each scale factor as a percent. How can we check our answers?

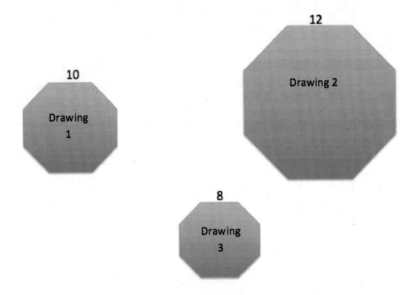

Actual Drawing to Scale Drawing	Scale Factor	Equation to Illustrate Relationship
Drawing 1 to Drawing 2	$Quantity = Percent \times Whole$ $length\ in\ Drawing\ 2 = Percent \times length\ in\ Drawing\ 1$ $12 = Percent \times 10$ $\dfrac{12}{10} = 1.20 = 120\%$	$10(1.2) = 12$
Drawing 1 to Drawing 3	$length\ in\ Drawing\ 3 = Percent \times length\ in\ Drawing\ 1$ $8 = Percent \times 10$ $\dfrac{8}{10} = 0.8 = 80\%$	$10(0.80) = 8$
Drawing 2 to Drawing 1	$length\ in\ Drawing\ 1 = Percent \times length\ in\ Drawing\ 2$ $10 = Percent \times 12$ $\dfrac{10}{12} = \dfrac{5}{6} = 83\dfrac{1}{3}\%$	$12(0.8\overline{3}) = 10$

Drawing 2 to Drawing 3	*length in Drawing 3 = Percent × length in Drawing 2* $8 = Percent \times 12$ $\frac{8}{12} = \frac{2}{3} = 66\frac{2}{3}\%$	$12(0.\overline{6}) = 8$
Drawing 3 to Drawing 1	*length in Drawing 1 = Percent × length in Drawing 3* $10 = Percent \times 8$ $\frac{10}{8} = 1.25 = 125\%$	$8(1.25) \ = \ 10$
Drawing 3 to Drawing 2	*length in Drawing 2 = Percent × length in Drawing 3* $12 = Percent \times 8$ $\frac{12}{8} = 1.5 = 150\%$	$8(1.5) \ = \ 12$

To check our answers, we can start with **10** *(the length of the original Drawing 1) and multiply by the scale factors we found to see whether we get the corresponding lengths in Drawings 2 and 3.*

Drawing 1 to 2: $\qquad 10(1.20) = 12$

Drawing 2 to 3: $\qquad 12\left(\frac{2}{3}\right) = 8$

▪ Why are all three octagons scale drawings of each other?

  ▫ *The octagons are scale drawings of each other because their corresponding side lengths are proportional to each other. Some of the drawings are reductions while others are enlargements. The drawing with side lengths that are larger than the other is considered an enlargement, whereas the drawings whose side lengths are smaller than the other are considered reductions. The ratio comparing these lengths is called the scale factor.*

Example 3 (5 minutes)

Example 3

The scale factor from Drawing 1 to Drawing 2 is 112%, and the scale factor from Drawing 1 to Drawing 3 is 84%. Drawing 2 is also a scale drawing of Drawing 3. Is Drawing 2 a reduction or an enlargement of Drawing 3? Justify your answer using the scale factor. The drawing is not necessarily drawn to scale.

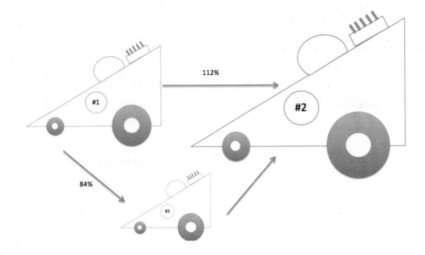

First, I needed to find the scale factor of Drawing 3 to Drawing 2 by using the relationship
$Quantity = Percent \times Whole.$

Drawing 3 is the whole. Therefore,

$$Drawing\ 2 = Percent \times Drawing\ 3$$

$$112\% = Percent \times 84\%$$

$$\frac{1.12}{0.84} = \frac{112}{84} = \frac{4}{3} = 133\frac{1}{3}\%$$

Since the scale factor is greater than 100%, *Drawing 2 is an enlargement of Drawing 3.*

Explain how you could use the scale factors from Drawing 1 to Drawing 2 (112%) and from Drawing 2 to Drawing 3 (75%) to show that the scale factor from Drawing 1 to Drawing 3 is 84%.

Since the scale factor from Drawing 1 to Drawing 2 is 112% *and the scale factor from Drawing 2 to Drawing 3 is* 75%, *I must first find* 75% *of* 112% *to get from Drawing 2 to Drawing 3.* $(0.75)(1.12) = 0.84.$ *Comparing this answer to the original problem, the resulting scale factor is indeed what was given as the scale factor from Drawing 1 to Drawing 3.*

> **Scaffolding:**
> - For all tasks involving scale drawings, consider modifying by (1) placing the drawings on grid paper and (2) using simpler figures, such as regular polygons or different quadrilaterals.

Closing (3 minutes)

- When given three drawings and only two scale factors, explain how to find the third scale factor.
- How are scale factors computed when two of the corresponding lengths are given?

Lesson Summary

To compute the scale factor from one drawing to another, use the representation:

$$Quantity\ =\ Percent\ \times\ Whole$$

where the whole is the length in the actual or original drawing and the quantity is the length in the scale drawing.

If the lengths of the sides are not provided but two scale factors are provided, use the same relationship but use the scale factors as the whole and quantity instead of the given measurements.

Exit Ticket (8 minutes)

Name _____   Date _____

Lesson 13: Changing Scales

Exit Ticket

1. Compute the scale factor, as a percent, of each given relationship. When necessary, round your answer to the nearest tenth of a percent.

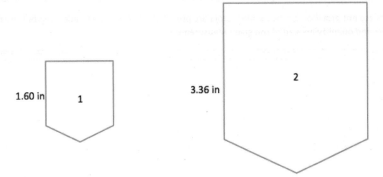

1.60 in   1

3.36 in   2

a.   Drawing 1 to Drawing 2

b.   Drawing 2 to Drawing 1

c.   Write two different equations that illustrate how each scale factor relates to the lengths in the diagram.

2. Drawings 2 and 3 are scale drawings of Drawing 1. The scale factor from Drawing 1 to Drawing 2 is 75%, and the scale factor from Drawing 2 to Drawing 3 is 50%. Find the scale factor from Drawing 1 to Drawing 3.

Exit Ticket Sample Solutions

1. Compute the scale factor, as a percent, of each given relationship. When necessary, round your answer to the nearest tenth of a percent.

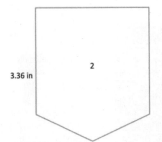

a. Drawing 1 to Drawing 2

   Drawing 2 = Percent × Drawing 1

   $3.36 = Percent \times 1.60$

   $\dfrac{3.36}{1.60} = 2.10 = 210\%$

b. Drawing 2 to Drawing 1

   Drawing 1 = Percent × Drawing 2

   $1.60 = Percent \times 3.36$

   $\dfrac{1.60}{3.36} = \dfrac{1}{2.10} \approx 0.476190476 \approx 47.6\%$

c. Write two different equations that illustrate how each scale factor relates to the lengths in the diagram.

   Drawing 1 to Drawing 2

   $1.60(2.10) = 3.36$

   Drawing 2 to Drawing 1

   $3.36(0.476) = 1.60$

2. Drawings 2 and 3 are scale drawings of Drawing 1. The scale factor from Drawing 1 to Drawing 2 is 75%, and the scale factor from Drawing 2 to Drawing 3 is 50%. Find the scale factor from Drawing 1 to Drawing 3.

   Drawing 1 to 2 is 75%. Drawing 2 to 3 is 50%. Therefore, Drawing 3 is 50% of 75%, so $(0.50)(0.75) = 0.375$. To determine the scale factor from Drawing 1 to Drawing 3, we went from 100% to 37.5%. Therefore, the scale factor is 37.5%. Using the relationship:

   $$Drawing\ 3 = Percent \times Drawing\ 1$$
   $$37.5\% = Percent \times 100\%$$
   $$0.375 = Percent$$
   $$= 37.5\%$$

Problem Set Sample Solutions

1. The scale factor from Drawing 1 to Drawing 2 is $41\frac{2}{3}\%$. Justify why Drawing 1 is a scale drawing of Drawing 2 and why it is an enlargement of Drawing 2. Include the scale factor in your justification.

Quantity = Percent × Whole

Length in Drawing 1 = Percent × Length in Drawing 2

$100\% = $ *Percent* $\times 41\frac{2}{3}\%$

$$\frac{100\%}{41\frac{2}{3}\%} = \frac{100 \cdot 3}{41\frac{2}{3} \cdot 3} = \frac{300}{125} = \frac{12}{5} = 2.40 = 240\%$$

Drawing 1 is a scale drawing of Drawing 2 because the lengths of Drawing 1 would be larger than the corresponding lengths of Drawing 2.

Since the scale factor is greater than 100%, the scale drawing is an enlargement of the original drawing.

2. The scale factor from Drawing 1 to Drawing 2 is 40%, and the scale factor from Drawing 2 to Drawing 3 is 37.5%. What is the scale factor from Drawing 1 to Drawing 3? Explain your reasoning, and check your answer using an example.

To find the scale factor from Drawing 1 to 3, I needed to find 37.5% of 40%, so $(0.375)(0.40) = 0.15$. The scale factor would be 15%.

To check, assume the length of Drawing 1 is 10. Then, using the scale factor for Drawing 2, Drawing 2 would be 4. Then, applying the scale factor to Drawing 3, Drawing 3 would be $4(0.375) = 1.5$. To go directly from Drawing 1 to Drawing 3, which was found to have a scale factor of 15%, then $10(0.15) = 1.5$.

3. Traci took a photograph and printed it to be a size of 4 units by 4 units as indicated in the diagram. She wanted to enlarge the original photograph to a size of 5 units by 5 units and 10 units by 10 units.

a. Sketch the different sizes of photographs.

4   5   10

b. What was the scale factor from the original photo to the photo that is 5 units by 5 units?

The scale factor from the original to the 5 by 5 enlargement is $\frac{5}{4} = 1.25 = 125\%$.

c. What was the scale factor from the original photo to the photo that is 10 units by 10 units?

The scale factor from the original to the 10 by 10 photo is $\frac{10}{4} = 2.5 = 250\%$.

d. What was the scale factor from the 5×5 photo to the 10×10 photo?

The scale factor from the 5×5 photo to the 10×10 photo is $\frac{10}{5} = 2 = 200\%$.

e. Write an equation to verify how the scale factor from the original photo to the enlarged 10×10 photo can be calculated using the scale factors from the original to the 5×5 and then from the 5×5 to the 10×10.

Scale Factor Original to 5×5: (125%)

Scale Factor 5×5 *to* 10×10: (200%)

$4(1.25) = 5$

$5(2.00) = 10$

Original to 10×10, *scale factor* $= 250\%$

$4(2.50) = 10$

The true equation $4(1.25)(2.00) = 4(2.50)$ *verifies that a single scale factor of* 250% *is equivalent to a scale factor of* 125% *followed by a scale factor of* 200%.

4. The scale factor from Drawing 1 to Drawing 2 is 30%, and the scale factor from Drawing 1 to Drawing 3 is 175%. What are the scale factors from the following:

a. Drawing 2 to Drawing 3

The scale factor from Drawing 2 to Drawing 3 is
$\frac{175\%}{30\%} = \frac{1.75}{0.30} = \frac{175}{30} = \frac{35}{6} = 55\frac{5}{6} = 583\frac{1}{3}\%$.

b. Drawing 3 to Drawing 1

The scale factor from Drawing 3 to Drawing 1 is
$\frac{1}{1.75} = \frac{100}{175} = \frac{4}{7} \approx 57.14\%$

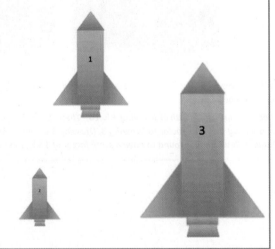

c. Drawing 3 to Drawing 2

The scale factor from Drawing 3 to Drawing 2 is $\dfrac{0.3}{1.75} = \dfrac{30}{175} = \dfrac{6}{35} \approx 17.14\%$

d. How can you check your answers?

To check my answers I can work backwards and multiply the scale factor from Drawing 1 to Drawing 3 of 175% to the scale factor from Drawing 3 to Drawing 2, and I should get the scale factor from Drawing 1 to Drawing 2.

$(1.75)(0.1714) \approx 0.29995 \approx 0.30 = 30\%$

Lesson 14: Computing Actual Lengths from a Scale Drawing

Student Outcomes

- Given a scale drawing, students compute the lengths in the actual picture using the scale factor.

Lesson Notes

The first example is an opportunity to highlight MP.1, as students work through a challenging problem to develop an understanding of how to use a scale drawing to determine the scale factor. Consider asking students to attempt the problem on their own or in groups. Then discuss and compare reasoning and methods.

Classwork

Example 1 (8 minutes)

Scaffolding:

- Consider modifying this task to involve simpler figures, such as rectangles, on grid paper.

Example 1

The distance around the entire small boat is 28. 4 units. The larger figure is a scale drawing of the smaller drawing of the boat. State the scale factor as a percent, and then use the scale factor to find the distance around the scale drawing.

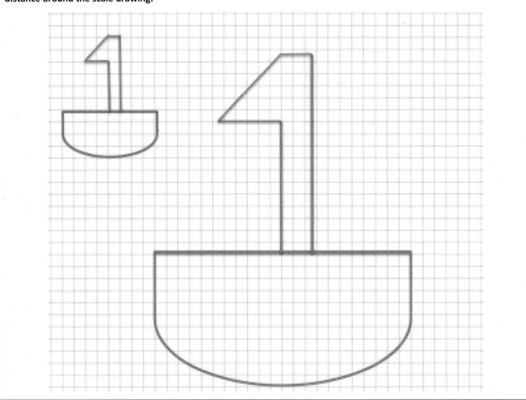

Scale Factor:

Horizontal distance of the smaller boat: 8 *units*　　*Vertical sail distance of smaller boat:* 6 *units*

Horizontal distance of the larger boat: 22 *units*　　*Vertical sail distance of larger boat:* 16.5 *units*

Scale Factor: $\textbf{\textit{Quantity}} = \textbf{\textit{Percent}} \times \textbf{\textit{Whole}}$

Smaller Boat is the whole.

Length in Larger $=$ *Percent* $\times$ *Length in Smaller*　　　　*Length in Larger* $=$ *Percent* $\times$ *Length in Smaller*

$$22 = P \times 8$$
$$\frac{22}{8} = 2.75 = 275\%$$

$$16.5 = P \times 6$$
$$\frac{16.5}{6} = 2.75 = 275\%$$

Total Distance:

Distance around small sailboat $= 28.4$

Distance around large sailboat $= 28.4(275\%) = 28.4(2.75) = 78.1$

The distance around the large sailboat is 78.1 *units.*

Discussion

- Recall the definition of the scale factor of a scale drawing.
  - □ *The scale factor is the quotient of any length of the scale drawing and the corresponding length of the actual drawing.*
- Since the scale factor is not given, how can the given diagrams be used to determine the scale factor?
  - □ *We can use the gridlines on the coordinate plane to determine the lengths of the corresponding sides.*
- Which corresponding parts did you choose to compare when calculating the scale factor, and why did you choose them?
  - □ *The horizontal segments representing the deck of the sailboat are the only segments where all four endpoints fall on grid lines. Therefore, we can compare these lengths using whole numbers.*
- If we knew the measures of all of the corresponding parts in both figures, would it matter which two we compare to calculate the scale factor? Should we always get the same value for the scale factor?
  - □ *Yes. There is no indication in the problem that the horizontal scale factor is different than the vertical scale factor, so the entire drawing is the same scale of the original drawing.*
- Since the scale drawing is an enlargement of the original drawing, what percent should the scale factor be?
  - □ *Since it is an enlargement, the scale factor should be larger than 100%.*
- How did we use the scale factor to determine the total distance around the scale drawing (the larger figure)?
  - □ *Once we know the scale factor, we can find the total distance around the larger sailboat by multiplying the total distance around the smaller sailboat by the scale factor.*

Exercise 1 (5 minutes)

Exercise 1

The length of the longer path is 32.4 units. The shorter path is a scale drawing of the longer path. Find the length of the shorter path and explain how you arrived at your answer.

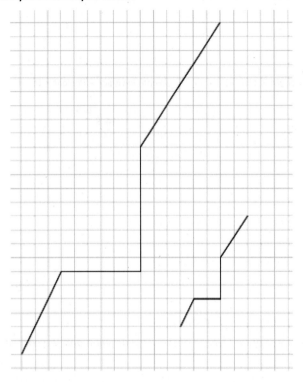

First, determine the scale factor. Since the smaller path is a reduction of the original drawing, the scale factor should be less than 100%. Since the smaller path is a scale drawing of the larger, the larger is the whole in the relationship.

$$Quantity = Percent \times Whole.$$

To determine the scale factor, compare the horizontal segments of the smaller path to the larger path.

$$Smaller = Percent \times Larger$$

$$2 = Percent \times 6$$

$$\frac{2}{6} = \frac{1}{3} = 33\frac{1}{3}\%.$$

To determine the length of the smaller path, multiply the length of the larger path by the scale factor.

$$32.4\left(\frac{1}{3}\right) = 10.8$$

The length of the shorter path is 10.8 units.

Example 2 (14 minutes): Time to Garden

Example 2

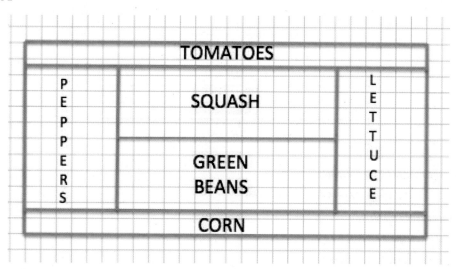

Sherry designed her garden as shown in the diagram above. The distance between any two consecutive vertical grid lines is 1 foot, and the distance between any two consecutive horizontal grid lines is also 1 foot. Therefore, each grid square has an area of one square foot. After designing the garden, Sherry decides to actually build the garden 75% of the size represented in the diagram.

a.   What are the outside dimensions shown in the blueprint?

Blueprint dimensions: *Length:* 26 *boxes* = 26 *ft.*

                              Width: 12 *boxes* = 12 *ft.*

b.   What will the overall dimensions be in the actual garden? Write an equation to find the dimensions. How does the problem relate to the scale factor?

Actual Garden Dimensions (75% of blueprint):   19. 5 *ft.* × 9 *ft.*

        Length: (26)(0. 75) = 19. 5 *ft.*

        Width: (12)(0. 75) = 9 *ft.*

Since the scale factor was given as 75%, *each dimension of the actual garden should be* 75% *of the original corresponding dimension. The found length of* 19. 5 *is* 75% *of* 26, *and the found width of* 9 *is* 75% *of* 12.

c.   If Sherry plans to use a wire fence to divide each section of the garden, how much fence does she need?

Dimensions of the blueprint:

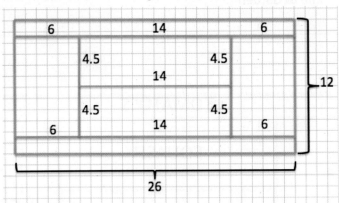

Total amount of wire needed for the blueprint:

$$26(4) + 12(2) + 4.5(4) + 14 = 160$$

The amount of wire needed is 160 ft.

New dimensions of actual garden:

    Length: *19.5 ft. (from part 2)*

    Width: *9 ft. (from part 2)*

    Inside Borders: *4.5(0.75) = 3.375, 3.375 ft.*

                      14(0.75) = 10.5, 10.5 ft.

The dimensions of the inside borders are 3.375 ft. by 10.5 ft.

Total wire with new dimensions:

$$19.5(4) + 9(2) + 3.375(4) + 10.5 = 120$$

OR

$$160(0.75) = 120$$

Total wire with new dimensions is 120 ft.

Simpler Way: 75% of 160 ft. = 120 ft.

d.   If the fence costs $3.25 per foot plus 7% sales tax, how much would the fence cost in total?

    $3.25(120) = 390$

    $390(1.07) = 417.30$

    The total cost is $417.30.

Discussion

- Why is the actual garden a reduction of the garden represented in the blueprint?

  □ *The given scale factor was less than* 100%, *which results in a reduction.*

- Does it matter if we find the total fencing needed for the garden in the blueprint and multiply the total by the scale factor versus finding each dimension of the actual garden using the scale factor and then determining the total fencing needed by finding the sum of the dimensions? Why or why not? What mathematical property is being illustrated?

  □ *No, it does not matter. If you determine each measurement of the actual garden first by using the scale factor and then add them together, the result is the same as if you were to find the total first and then multiply it by the scale factor. If you find the corresponding side lengths first, then you are using the property to distribute the scale factor to every measurement.*

    - $(0.75)(104 + 24 + 18 + 14) = 78 + 18 + 13.5 + 10.5$
    - $(0.75)(160) = 120$
    - $120 = 120$

- By the distributive property, the expressions $(0.75)(104 + 24 + 18 + 14)$ and $(0.75)(160)$ are equivalent, but each reveals different information. The first expression implies 75% of a collection of lengths, while the second is 75% of the total of the lengths.

- If we found the total cost, including tax, for one foot of fence and then multiplied that cost by the total amount of feet needed, would we get the same result as if we were to first find the total cost of the fence, and then calculate the sales tax on the total? Justify your reasoning with evidence. How does precision play an important role in the problem?

  □ *It should not matter; however, if we were to calculate the price first, including tax, per foot, the answer would be* $(3.25)(1.07) = 3.4775$. *When we solve a problem involving money, we often round to two decimal places; doing so in this case, gives us a price of* $3.48 *per foot. Then, to determine the total cost, we multiply the price per foot by the total amount, giving us* $(3.48)(120) = $417.60. *If the before-tax total is calculated, then we would get* $417.30, *leaving a difference of* $0.30. *Rounding in the problem early on is what caused the discrepancy. Therefore, to obtain the correct, precise answer, we should not round in the problem until the very final answer. If we did not round the price per foot, then the answers would have agreed.*

  $$(3.4775)(120) = 417.30$$

- Rounding aside, what is an equation that shows that it does not matter which method we use to calculate the total cost? What property justifies the equivalence?

  □ $(3.25)(1.07)(120) = (120)(3.25)(1.07)$. *These expressions are equivalent due to the commutative property.*

Exercise 2 (5 minutes)

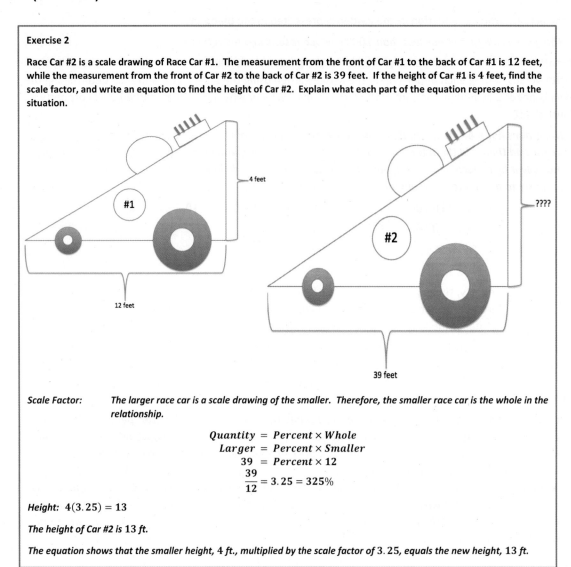

Exercise 2

Race Car #2 is a scale drawing of Race Car #1. The measurement from the front of Car #1 to the back of Car #1 is 12 feet, while the measurement from the front of Car #2 to the back of Car #2 is 39 feet. If the height of Car #1 is 4 feet, find the scale factor, and write an equation to find the height of Car #2. Explain what each part of the equation represents in the situation.

4 feet

????

#1

#2

12 feet

39 feet

Scale Factor: *The larger race car is a scale drawing of the smaller. Therefore, the smaller race car is the whole in the relationship.*

$$Quantity = Percent \times Whole$$
$$Larger = Percent \times Smaller$$
$$39 = Percent \times 12$$
$$\frac{39}{12} = 3.25 = 325\%$$

Height: $4(3.25) = 13$

The height of Car #2 is 13 ft.

The equation shows that the smaller height, 4 ft., multiplied by the scale factor of 3.25, equals the new height, 13 ft.

Discussion

▪ By comparing the corresponding lengths of Race Car #2 to Race Car #1, we can conclude that Race Car #2 is an enlargement of Race Car #1. If Race Car #1 were a scale drawing of Race Car #2, how would the solution change? What differences would there be in the solution compared to the solution found above?

  ▫ *The final answer would still be the same. The corresponding work would be different—when Race Car #2 is a scale drawing of Race Car #1, the scale drawing is an enlargement, resulting in a scale factor greater than 100%. Once the scale factor is determined, we find the corresponding height of Race Car #2 by multiplying the height of Race Car #1 by the scale factor, which is greater than 100%. If Race Car #1 were a scale drawing of Race Car #2, the scale drawing would be a reduction of the original, and the scale factor would be less than 100%. Once we find the scale factor, we then find the corresponding height of Race Car #2 by dividing the height of Race Car #1 by the scale factor.*

Exercise 3 (4 minutes)

Exercise 3

Determine the scale factor and write an equation that relates the vertical heights of each drawing to the scale factor. Explain how the equation illustrates the relationship.

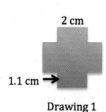

2 cm

1.1 cm →

Drawing 1

3.3 cm

Drawing 2

Equation: 1.1(scale factor) = vertical height in Drawing #2

First find the scale factor:

$$Quantity = Percent \times Whole$$
$$Drawing\ \#2 = Percent \times Drawing\ \#1$$
$$3.3 = Percent \times 2$$
$$\frac{3.3}{2} = 1.65 = 165\%$$

Equation: $(1.1)(1.65) = 1.815$

The vertical height of Drawing #2 is 1.815 cm.

Once we determine the scale, we can write an equation to find the unknown vertical distance by multiplying the scale factor by the corresponding distance in the original drawing.

Exercise 4 (2 minutes)

Exercise 4

The length of a rectangular picture is 8 inches, and the picture is to be reduced to be $45\frac{1}{2}\%$ of the original picture. Write an equation that relates the lengths of each picture. Explain how the equation illustrates the relationship.

$$8(0.455) = 3.64$$

The length of the reduced picture is 3.64 inches. The equation shows that the length of the reduced picture, 3.64, is equal to the original length, 8, multiplied by the scale factor, 0.455.

Closing (2 minutes)

- How do you compute the scale factor when given a figure and a scale drawing of that figure?
- How do you use the scale factor to compute the lengths of segments in the scale drawing and the original figure?

Exit Ticket (5 minutes)

Name _____   Date _____

Lesson 14: Computing Actual Lengths from a Scale Drawing

Exit Ticket

Each of the designs shown below is going to be displayed in a window using strands of white lights. The smaller design requires 225 feet of lights. How many feet of lights does the enlarged design require?

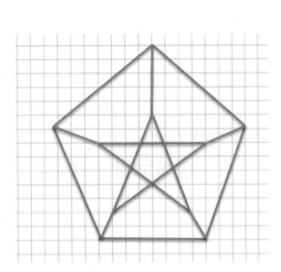

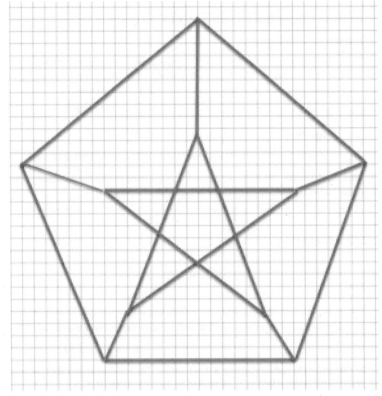

Exit Ticket Sample Solutions

Each of the designs shown below is to be displayed in a window using strands of white lights. The smaller design requires 225 feet of lights. How many feet of lights does the enlarged design require? Support your answer by showing all work and stating the scale factor used in your solution.

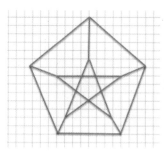
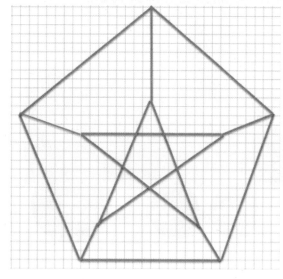

Scale Factor:

Bottom Horizontal Distance of the smaller design: 8

Bottom Horizontal Distance of the larger design: 16

Whole is the smaller design since we are going from the smaller to the larger.

$$Quantity = Percent \times Whole$$
$$Larger = Percent \times Smaller$$
$$16 = Percent \times 8$$
$$Scale\ Factor: \frac{16}{8} = 2 = 200\%$$

Number of feet of lights needed for the larger design:

$$225(200\%) = 225(2) = 450\ feet.$$

Problem Set Sample Solutions

1. The smaller train is a scale drawing of the larger train. If the length of the tire rod connecting the three tires of the larger train as shown below is 36 inches, write an equation to find the length of the tire rod of the smaller train. Interpret your solution in the context of the problem.

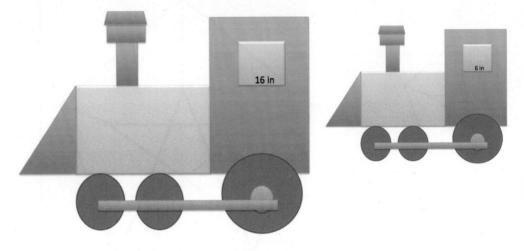

16 in

6 in

Scale Factor:

$$Smaller = Percent \times Larger$$
$$6 = Percent \times 16$$
$$\frac{6}{16} = 0.375 = 37.5\%$$

Tire rod of small train: $(36)(0.375) = 13.5$

The length of the tire rod of the small train is 13.5 *in.*

Since the scale drawing is smaller than the original, the corresponding tire rod is the same percent smaller as the windows. Therefore, finding the scale factor using the windows of the trains allows us to then use the scale factor to find all other corresponding lengths.

2. The larger arrow is a scale drawing of the smaller arrow. If the distance around the smaller arrow is 28 units, what is the distance around the larger arrow? Use an equation to find the distance and interpret your solution in the context of the problem.

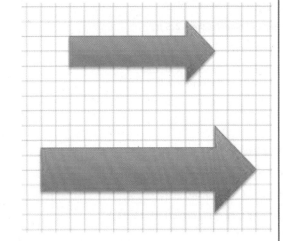

Horizontal Distance of Small Arrow: 8

Horizontal Distance of Larger Arrow: 12

Scale Factor:

$$Larger = Percent \times Smaller$$
$$12 = Percent \times 8$$
$$\frac{12}{8} = 1.5 = 150\%$$

Distance Around Larger Arrow:

$$(28)(1.5) = 42$$

The distance around the larger arrow is 42 units.

Using an equation where the distance of the smaller arrow is multiplied by the scale factor finds the distance around the larger arrow.

3. The smaller drawing below is a scale drawing of the larger. The distance around the larger drawing is 39.3 units. Using an equation, find the distance around the smaller drawing.

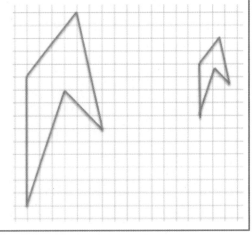

Vertical Distance of Large Drawing: 10 units

Vertical Distance of Small Drawing: 4 units

Scale Factor:

$$Smaller = Percent \times Larger$$
$$4 = Percent \times 10$$
$$Scale\ Factor: \frac{4}{10} = 0.4 = 40\%$$

Total Distance:

$$(39.3)(0.4) = 15.72$$

The total distance around the smaller drawing is 15.72 units.

4.   The figure is a diagram of a model rocket. The length of a model rocket is 2.5 feet, and the wing span is 1.25 feet. If the length of an actual rocket is 184 feet, use an equation to find the wing span of the actual rocket.

Length actual rocket: 184 *ft.*

Length of model rocket: 2.5 *ft.*

Scale Factor:

$$Actual = Percent \times Model$$
$$184 = Percent \times 2.5$$
$$\frac{184}{2.5} = 73.60 = 7,360\%$$

Wing Span:

Model Rocket Wing Span: 1.25 *ft.*

Actual: $(1.25)(73.60) = 92$

The wing span of the actual rocket is 92 ft.

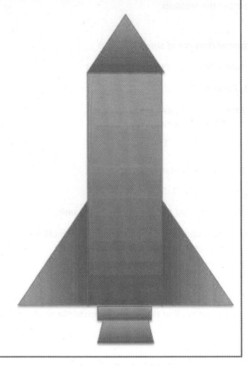

Lesson 15: Solving Area Problems Using Scale Drawings

Student Outcomes

- Students solve area problems related to scale drawings and percent by using the fact that an area, A', of a scale drawing is k^2 times the corresponding area, A, in the original drawing, where k is the scale factor.

Lesson Notes

The first three exercises in this lesson employ MP.8. Students will calculate the area in scale drawings and, through repeated calculations, generalize about the relationship between the area and the scale factor.

> *Scaffolding:*
>
> - Consider modifying the first three tasks to consist only of rectangles, and using grid paper to allow students to calculate area by counting square units. Additionally, using sentence frames, such as, "The area of Drawing 1 is _____ times the area of Drawing 2," may help students better understand the relationship.

Classwork

Opening Exercise (10 minutes)

Opening Exercise

For each diagram, Drawing 2 is a scale drawing of Drawing 1. Complete the accompanying charts. For each drawing: identify the side lengths, determine the area, and compute the scale factor. Convert each scale factor into a fraction and percent, examine the results, and write a conclusion relating scale factors to area.

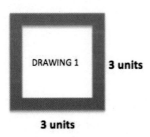

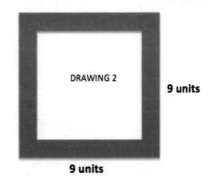

	Drawing 1	Drawing 2	Scale Factor as a Fraction and Percent
Side	3 units	9 units	Quantity = Percent × Whole Drawing 2 = Percent × Drawing 1 9 = Percent × 3 $\frac{9}{3} = \frac{3}{1} = 3 = 300\%$
Area	$A = lw$ $A = 3 \cdot 3$ sq. units $A = 9$ sq. units	$A = lw$ $A = 9 \cdot 9$ sq. units $A = 81$ sq. units	Quantity = Percent × Whole Drawing 2 Area = Percent × Drawing 1 Area 81 = Percent × 9 $\frac{81}{9} = \frac{9}{1} = 9 = 900\%$

Scale Factor: __3__   Quotient of Areas: __9__

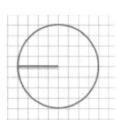

DRAWING 1

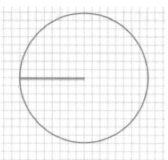

DRAWING 2

	Drawing 1	Drawing 2	Scale Factor as a Percent
Side	4 *units*	8 *units*	*Quantity = Percent × Whole* *Drawing 2 = Percent × Drawing 1* $8 = Percent × 4$ $\frac{8}{4} = \frac{2}{1} = 200\%$
Area	$A = \pi r^2$ $A = \pi(4)^2$ $A = 16\pi$ sq. units	$A = \pi r^2$ $A = \pi(8)^2$ $A = 64\pi$ sq. units	*Quantity = Percent × Whole* *Drawing 2 Area = Percent × Drawing 1 Area* $64\pi = Percent × 16\pi$ $\frac{64\pi}{16\pi} = \frac{4}{1} = 4 = 400\%$

Scale Factor: __2__   Quotient of Areas: __4__

The length of each side in Drawing 1 is 12 units, and the length of each side in Drawing 2 is 6 units.

Drawing 1

Drawing 2

	Drawing 1	Drawing 2	Scale Factor as a Percent
Side	12 *units*	6 *units*	*Quantity = Percent × Whole* *Drawing 2 = Percent × Drawing 1* $6 = Percent × 12$ $\frac{6}{12} = \frac{1}{2} = 50\%$
Area	$A = lw$ $A = 12(12)$ $A = 44$ sq. units	$A = lw$ $A = 6(6)$ $A = 36$ sq. units	*Quantity = Percent × Whole* *Drawing 2 Area = Percent × Drawing 1 Area* $36 = Percent × 144$ $\frac{36}{144} = \frac{1}{4} = 25\%$

Scale Factor: $\frac{1}{2}$ Quotient of Areas: $\frac{1}{4}$

Conclusion: $\left(\frac{1}{2}\right)\left(\frac{1}{2}\right) = \left(\frac{1}{2}\right)^2 = \frac{1}{4}$

The quotient of the areas is equal to the square of the scale factor.

Key Points: Overall Conclusion

If the scale factor is represented by k, then the area of the scale drawing is k^2 times the corresponding area of the original drawing.

Discussion

- Is it necessary to find the area of each drawing to determine the ratio of areas of the scale drawing to the original drawing, if the scale factor is known?
  - □ *No, once the scale factor of the corresponding sides is determined, the ratio of the area of the scale drawing to the original is the square of the scale factor.*

- Why is the scale factor often given as a percent or asked for as a percent but the area relationship is calculated as a fraction? Why can't a percent be used for this calculation?
  - □ *A scale factor given or calculated as a percent allows us to see if the scale drawing is an enlargement or reduction of the original drawing. However, in order to use the percent in a calculation it must be converted to an equivalent decimal or fraction form.*

- How is this relationship useful?
  - □ *If none of the side lengths are provided but instead a scale factor is provided, the relationship between the areas can be determined without needing to find the actual area of each drawing. For instance, if only the scale factor and the area of the original drawing are provided, the area of the scale drawing can be determined. (Similarly, if only the scale factor and area of the scale drawing are given, the area of the original drawing can be found.)*

- Why do you think this relationship exists?
  - □ *If area is determined by the product of two linear measures and each measure is increased by a factor of k, then it stands to reason that the area will increase by a factor of k^2.*

Example 1 (2 minutes)

Example 1	
What percent of the area of the large square is the area of the small square?	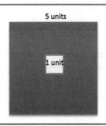
Scale Factor Small to Large Square: $\dfrac{1}{5}$	
Area of Small to Large: $\left(\dfrac{1}{5}\right)^2 = \dfrac{1}{25} = 0.04 = 4\%$	

Example 2 (4 minutes)

Example 2

What percent of the area of the large disk lies outside the smaller disk?

Radius of Small Disk $= 2$

Radius of Large Disk $= 4$

Scale Factor of Shaded Disk: $\dfrac{2}{4} = \dfrac{1}{2}$

Area of Shaded Disk to Large Disk:

$$\left(\dfrac{1}{2}\right)^2 = \dfrac{1}{4} = 25\%$$

Area Outside Shaded Disk: $\dfrac{3}{4} = 75\%$

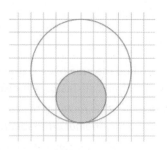

- Why does this work?
  - *The relationship between the scale factor and area has already been determined. So, determining the percent of the area outside the shaded region requires going a step further and subtracting the percent within the shaded region from 100%.*

Example 3 (4 minutes)

Example 3

If the area of the shaded region in the larger figure is approximately 21.5 square inches, write an equation that relates the areas using scale factor and explain what each quantity represents. Determine the area of the shaded region in the smaller scale drawing.

Scale Factor of Corresponding Sides:

$$\dfrac{6}{10} = \dfrac{3}{5} = 60\%$$

Area of Shaded Region of Smaller Figure: Assume A is the area of the shaded region of the larger figure.

$$\left(\dfrac{3}{5}\right)^2 A = \dfrac{9}{25} A$$
$$\left(\dfrac{3}{5}\right)^2 (21.5) = \dfrac{9}{25} A$$
$$\dfrac{9}{25} (21.5) = 7.74$$

10 inches   6 inches

In this equation, the square of the scale factor, $\left(\dfrac{3}{5}\right)^2$, multiplied by the area of the shaded region in the larger figure, 21.5 sq. in., is equal to the area of the shaded region of the smaller figure, 7.74 sq. in.

The area of shaded region of the smaller scale drawing is about 7.74 sq. in.

Example 4 (4 minutes)

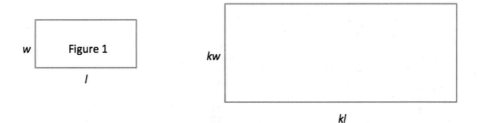

Example 4

Use Figure 1 below and the enlarged scale drawing to justify why the area of the scale drawing is k^2 times the area of the original figure.

Area of Figure 1:

    $Area = lw$

Area of Scale Drawing:

    $Area = lw$

    $Area = (kl)(kw)$

    $Area = k^2 lw$

Since the area of Figure 1 is lw, the area of the scale drawing is k^2 multiplied by the area of Figure 1.

Explain why the expressions $(kl)(kw)$ and $k^2 lw$ are equivalent. How do the expressions reveal different information about this situation?

$(kl)(kw)$ *is equivalent to* $klkw$ *by the associative property, which can be written* $kklw$ *using the commutative property. This is sometimes known as "any order, any grouping."* $kklw$ *is equal to* $k^2 lw$ *because* $k \times k = k^2$. $(kl)(kw)$ *shows the area as the product of each scaled dimension, while* $k^2 lw$ *shows the area as the square factor squared, times the original area (lw).*

Exercises (14 minutes)

Complete each part of the exercise together as a class to reinforce the skills learned in this lesson and the three lessons preceding it.

Exercise 1

1. The Lake Smith basketball team had a team picture taken of the players, the coaches, and the trophies from the season. The picture was 4 inches by 6 inches. The team decides to have the picture enlarged to a poster and then enlarged again to a banner measuring 48 inches by 72 inches.

    a.   Sketch drawings to illustrate the original picture and enlargements.

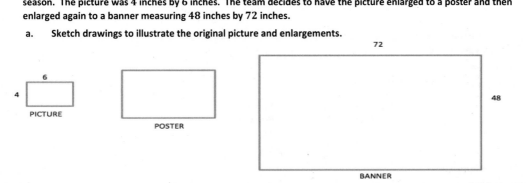

b. If the scale factor from the picture to the poster is 500%, determine the dimensions of the poster.

$Quantity = Percent \times Whole$
$Poster\ height = Percent \times Picture\ height$
$Poster\ height = 500\% \times 4\ in.$
$Poster\ height = (5.00)(4)\ in.$
$Poster\ height = 20\ in.$

$Quantity = Percent \times Whole$
$Poster\ width = Percent \times Picture\ width$
$Poster\ width = 500\% \times 6\ in.$
$Poster\ width = (5.00)(6)\ in.$
$Poster\ width = 30\ in.$

The dimensions of the poster are 20 in. by 30 in.

c. What scale factor is used to create the banner from the picture?

$Quantity = Percent \times Whole$
$Banner\ width = Percent \times Picture\ width$
$72 = Percent \times 6$
$\dfrac{72}{6} = Percent$
$12 = 1,200\%$

$Quantity = Percent \times Whole$
$Banner\ height = Percent \times Picture\ height$
$48 = Percent \times 4$
$\dfrac{48}{4} = Percent$
$12 = 1,200\%$

The scale factor used to create the banner from the picture is $1,200\%$.

d. What percent of the area of the picture is the area of the poster? Justify your answer using the scale factor AND by finding the actual areas.

Area of Picture:
$A = lw$
$A = (4)(6)$
$A = 24$
$Area = 24\ sq.\ in.$

Area of Poster:
$A = lw$
$A = (20)(30)$
$A = 600$
$Area = 600\ sq.\ in.$

$Quantity = Percent \times Whole$
$Area\ of\ Poster = Percent \times Area\ of\ Picture$
$600 = Percent \times 24$
$\dfrac{600}{24} = Percent$
$25 = 2500\%$

Using scale factor:

Scale factor from Picture to Poster was given earlier in the problem as $500\% = \dfrac{500}{100} = 5$.

The area of the poster is the square of the scale factor times the corresponding area of the picture. So, the area of the poster is 2500% the area of the original picture.

e. Write an equation involving the scale factor that relates the area of the poster to the area of the picture.

$Quantity = Percent \times Whole$
$Area\ of\ Poster = Percent \times Area\ of\ Picture$
$A = 2500\%\ p$
$A = 25p$

f. Assume you started with the banner and wanted to reduce it to the size of the poster. What would the scale factor as a percent be?

Banner dimensions: $48" \times 72"$

Poster dimensions: $20" \times 30"$

$Quantity = Percent \times Whole$
$Poster = Percent \times Banner$
$30 = Percent \times 72$
$\dfrac{30}{72} = \dfrac{5}{12} = \dfrac{5}{12} \times 100\% = 41\dfrac{2}{3}\%$

g.   **What scale factor would be used to reduce the poster to the size of the picture?**

Poster Dimensions: $20" \times 30"$

Picture Dimensions: $4" \times 6"$

$$Quantity = Percent\ x\ Whole$$
$$Picture\ width = Percent\ x\ Poster\ width$$
$$6 = Percent\ x\ 30$$
$$\frac{6}{30} = \frac{1}{5} = 0.2 = 20\%$$

Closing (3 minutes)

- If you know a length in a scale drawing and its corresponding length in the original drawing, how can you determine the relationship between the areas of the drawings?

- Given a scale factor of 25%, would the quotient of the area of the scale drawing to the area of the original drawing be $\frac{1}{4}$?

> **Lesson Summary**
>
> If the scale factor is represented by k, then the area of the scale drawing is k^2 times the corresponding area of the original drawing.

Exit Ticket (4 minutes)

Name _____   Date _____

Lesson 15: Solving Area Problems Using Scale Drawings

Exit Ticket

Write an equation relating the area of the original (larger) drawing to its smaller scale drawing. Explain how you determined the equation. What percent of the area of the larger drawing is the smaller scale drawing?

15 units

12 units

6 units

4.8 units

Exit Ticket Sample Solutions

Write an equation relating the area of the original (larger) drawing to its smaller scale drawing. Explain how you determined the equation. What percent of the area of the larger drawing is the smaller scale drawing?

15 units

12 units

6 units

4.8 units

Scale Factor:

$$Quantity = Percent \times Whole$$
$$Scale\ Drawing\ Length = Percent \times Original\ Length$$
$$6 = Percent \times 15$$
$$\frac{6}{15} = \frac{2}{5} = 0.4$$

The area of the scale drawing is equal to the square of the scale factor times the area of the original drawing. Using A to represent the area of the original drawing, then the area of the scale is:

$$\left(\frac{2}{5}\right)^2 A = \frac{4}{25}A$$

As a percent:
$$\frac{4}{25}A = \frac{16}{100}A = 0.16A$$

Therefore, the area of the scale drawing is 16% *of the area of the original drawing.*

Problem Set Sample Solutions

1. What percent of the area of the larger circle is shaded?

   a. Solve this problem using scale factors.

   Scale Factors:

   Shaded Small Circle: *radius* $= 1$ *unit*

   Shaded Medium Circle: *radius* $= 2$ *units*

   Large Circle: *radius* $= 3$ *units, area* $= A$

   Area of Small Circle: $\left(\frac{1}{3}\right)^2 A = \frac{1}{9}A$

   Area of Medium Circle: $\left(\frac{2}{3}\right)^2 A = \frac{4}{9}A$

   Area of Shaded Region: $\frac{1}{9}A + \frac{4}{9}A = \frac{5}{9}A = \frac{5}{9} \times 100\%, A = 55\frac{5}{9}\%A$

   The area of the shaded region is $55\frac{5}{9}\%$ *of the area of the entire circle.*

b. Verify your work in part *a* by finding the actual areas.

Areas:

Small Circle: $A = \pi r^2$

$A = \pi(1)^2$ *square units*

$A = 1\pi$ *square units*

Medium Circle: $A = \pi r^2$

$A = \pi(2)^2$ *square units*

$A = 4\pi$ *square units*

Area of Shaded Circles: $1\pi + 4\pi = 5\pi$

Large Circle: $A = \pi r^2$

$A = \pi(3)^2$ *square units*

$A = 9\pi$ *square units*

Percent of Shaded to Large Circle: $\dfrac{5\pi}{9\pi} = \dfrac{5}{9} = \dfrac{5}{9} \times 100\% = 55\dfrac{5}{9}\%$

2. The area of the large disk is 50.24 units^2.

   a. Find the area of the shaded region.

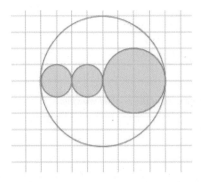

Radius of Small Shaded Circles $= 1$ *unit*

Radius of Larger Shaded Circle $= 2$ *units*

Radius of Large Disk $= 4$ *units*

Scale Factor of Shaded Region:

Small Shaded Circles: $\dfrac{1}{4}$

Large Shaded Circle: $\dfrac{2}{4}$

If A represents the area of the large disk, then the Total Shaded Area: $\left(\dfrac{1}{4}\right)^2 A + \left(\dfrac{1}{4}\right)^2 A + \left(\dfrac{2}{4}\right)^2 A$

$$\dfrac{1}{16}A + \dfrac{1}{16}A + \dfrac{4}{16}A = \dfrac{6}{16}A$$
$$\dfrac{6}{16}A = \dfrac{6}{16}(50.24)\ units^2$$

The area of the shaded region is 18.84 *units^2.*

b.   What percent of the large circular region is unshaded?

Area of the shaded region is 18.84 square units. Area of Total is 50.24 square units. Area of the unshaded region is 31.40 square units. Percent of large circular region that is unshaded is

$$\frac{31.4}{50.24} = \frac{5}{8} = 0.625 = 62.5\%$$

3.   Ben cut the following rockets out of cardboard. The height from the base to the tip of the smaller rocket is 20 cm. The height from the base to the tip of the larger rocket is 120 cm. What percent of the area of the smaller rocket is the area of the larger rocket?

Height of smaller rocket: 20 cm

Height of larger rocket: 120 cm

Scale Factor:

$$Quantity = Percent \times Whole$$
$$Actual\ height\ of\ larger\ rocket = Percent \times height\ of\ smaller\ rocket$$
$$120 = Percent \times 20$$
$$6 = Percent$$

$$600\%$$

Area of Larger Rocket:

$$(scale\ factor)^2(area\ of\ smaller\ rocket)$$

$$(6)^2(area\ of\ smaller\ rocket)$$

$$36A$$

$$36 = 36 \times 100\% = 3,600\%$$

The area of the larger rocket is 3,600% the area of the smaller rocket.

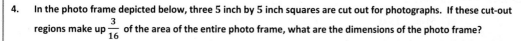

4.   In the photo frame depicted below, three 5 inch by 5 inch squares are cut out for photographs. If these cut-out regions make up $\frac{3}{16}$ of the area of the entire photo frame, what are the dimensions of the photo frame?

Since the cut-out regions make up $\frac{3}{16}$ of the entire photo frame, then each cut-out region makes up $\frac{\frac{3}{16}}{3} = \frac{1}{16}$ of the entire photo frame.

The relationship between the area of the scale drawing is (square factor)^2 × area of original drawing.

The area of each cut-out is $\frac{1}{16}$ of the area of the original photo frame. Therefore, the square of the scale factor is $\frac{1}{16}$. Since $\left(\frac{1}{4}\right)^2 = \frac{1}{16}$, the scale factor that relates the cut-out to the entire photo frame is $\frac{1}{4}$, or 25%.

To find the dimensions of the square photo frame: $Quantity = Percent\ x\ Whole$

$$Small\ square\ side\ length = Percent \times photo\ frame\ side\ length$$
$$5\ inches = 25\% \times photo\ frame\ side\ length$$
$$5\ inches = \frac{1}{4} \times photo\ frame\ side\ length$$
$$4(5)\ inches = 4\left(\frac{1}{4}\right) \times photo\ frame\ side\ length$$
$$20\ inches = photo\ frame\ side\ length$$

The dimensions of the square photo frame are 20 in. by 20 in.

5. Kelly was online shopping for envelopes for party invitations and saw these images on a website.

 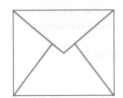 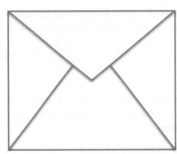

The website listed the dimensions of the small envelope as 6 in. by 8 in. and the medium envelope as 10 in. by $13\frac{1}{3}$ in.

a. Compare the dimensions of the small and medium envelopes. If the medium envelope is a scale drawing of the small envelope, what is the scale factor?

To find the scale factor:

$Quantity = Percent \times Whole$

$Medium\ height = Percent \times small\ height$

$$10 = Percent \times 6$$

$$\frac{10}{6} = \frac{5}{3} = \frac{5}{3} \times 100\% = 166\frac{2}{3}\%$$

$Quantity = Percent \times Whole$

$Medium\ width = Percent \times small\ width$

$$13\frac{1}{3} = Percent\ x\ 8$$

$$\frac{13\frac{1}{3}}{8} = \frac{5}{3} = \frac{5}{3} \times 100\% = 166\frac{2}{3}\%$$

b. If the large envelope was created based on the dimensions of the small envelope using a scale factor of 250%, find the dimensions of the large envelope.

Scale Factor is 250%, so multiply each dimension of the small envelope by 2.50.

Large envelope dimensions are:

$$6(2.5)\ in. = 15\ in. \qquad\qquad 8(2.5)\ in. = 20\ in.$$

c. If the medium envelope was created based on the dimensions of the large envelope, what scale factor was used to create the medium envelope?

Scale factor:

$Quantity = Percent \times Whole$

$Medium = Percent \times Large$

$$10 = Percent \times 15$$

$$\frac{10}{15} = Percent$$

$$\frac{2}{3} = \frac{2}{3} \times 100\% = 66\frac{2}{3}\%$$

$Medium = Percent \times Large$

$Medium = Percent \times Large$

$$13\frac{1}{3} = Percent \times 20$$

$$\frac{13\frac{1}{3}}{20} = Percent$$

$$\frac{2}{3} = \frac{2}{3} \times 100\% = 66\frac{2}{3}\%$$

d. What percent of the area of the larger envelope is the area of the medium envelope?

Scale Factor of larger to medium: $66\frac{2}{3}\% = \frac{2}{3}$

Area: $\left(\frac{2}{3}\right)^2 = \frac{4}{9} = \frac{4}{9} \times 100\% = 44\frac{4}{9}\%$

The area of the medium envelope is $44\frac{4}{9}\%$ of the larger envelope.

Mathematics Curriculum

7
GRADE

Topic D:

Population, Mixture, and Counting Problems Involving Percents

7.RP.A.2c, 7.RP.A.3, 7.EE.B.3

Focus Standard:	7.RP.A.2c	Recognize and represent proportional relationships between quantities.
	c.	Represent proportional relationships by equations. *For example, if total cost t is proportional to the number n of items purchased at a constant price p, the relationship between the total cost and the number of items can be expressed as t = pn.*
	7.RP.A.3	Use proportional relationships to solve multi-step ratio and percent problems. *Examples: simple interest, tax, markups and markdowns, gratuities and commissions, fees, percent increase and decrease, percent error.*
	7.EE.B.3	Solve multi-step real-life and mathematical problems posed with positive and negative rational numbers in any form (whole numbers, fractions, and decimals), using tools strategically. Apply properties of operations to calculate with numbers in any form; convert between forms as appropriate; and assess the reasonableness of answers using mental computation and estimation strategies. *For example: If a woman making $25 an hour gets a 10% raise, she will make an additional 1/10 of her salary an hour, or $2.50, for a new salary of $27.50. If you want to place a towel bar 9 3/4 inches long in the center of a door that is 27 1/2 inches wide, you will need to place the bar about 9 inches from each edge; this estimate can be used as a check on the exact computation.*
Instructional Days:	3	
Lesson 16:	Population Problems (P)[1]	
Lesson 17:	Mixture Problems (P)	
Lesson 18:	Counting Problems (P)	

---

[1] Lesson Structure Key: **P**-Problem Set Lesson, **M**-Modeling Cycle Lesson, **E**-Exploration Lesson, **S**-Socratic Lesson

EUREKA MATH™

Topic D: Population, Mixture, and Counting Problems Involving Percents

Topic D provides students with additional experience solving word problems related to percents. Students see the relevance and purpose of their algebraic work in Module 3, as they use it to efficiently solve multi-step word problems involving percents (**7.RP.A.3**, **7.EE.B.3**). They also see percent applied to other areas of math and science. In Lessons 16 and 17, students represent and solve population and mixture problems using algebraic expressions and equations, along with their foundational understanding from Topic A of the expression $Quantity = Percent \times Whole$ (**7.RP.A.2c**). Topic D concludes with Lesson 18, where students solve counting problems involving percents, preparing them for future work with probability.

Lesson 16: Population Problems

Student Outcomes

- Students write and use algebraic expressions and equations to solve percent word problems related to populations of people and compilations.

Lesson Notes

In Module 4, students have been deepening their understanding of ratios and proportional relationships by solving a variety of multi-step percent problems using algebraic equations, expressions, and visual models. The concept relating 100% as "a whole" is a foundation that students applied in problems including percent increase and decrease, percent error, markups, markdowns, commission, and scale drawings.

Lessons 16–18 provide students with further applications related to percents—specifically, problems involving populations, mixtures, and counting. From Module 3, students will apply their knowledge of algebra to solve multi-step percent word problems. In Lessons 16 and 17, students will use the equation $quantity = percent \times whole$ to solve mixture and population problems. Lesson 18 concludes Topic D with counting problems involving percents, which prepares students for probability.

Classwork

Opening Exercise (5 minutes)

Students will work with partners to fill in the information in the table.

Opening Exercise

Number of girls in classroom:	Number of boys in classroom:	Total number of students in classroom:
Percent of the total number of students that are girls:	Percent of the total number of students that are boys:	Percent of boys and girls in the classroom:
Number of girls whose names start with a vowel:	Number of boys whose names start with a vowel:	Number of students whose names start with a vowel:
Percent of girls whose names start with a vowel:	Percent of boys whose names start with a vowel:	
Percent of the total number of students that are girls whose names start with a vowel:	Percent of the total number of students that are boys whose names start with a vowel:	Percent of students whose names start with a vowel:

Discussion (5 minutes)

- How did you calculate the percent of boys in the class? How did you calculate the percent of girls in the class?
    - *Take the number of each gender group, divide by the total number of students in the class, then multiply by 100%.*
- What is the difference between the percent of girls whose names begin with a vowel and the percent of students who are girls whose names begin with a vowel?
    - *The first is the number of girls whose names begin with a vowel divided by the total number of girls, as opposed to the number of girls whose names begin with a vowel divided by the total number of students.*
- Is there a relationship between the two?
    - *Yes, if you multiply the percent of students who are girls and the percent of girls whose names begin with a vowel, it equals the percent of students who are girls and whose names begin with a vowel.*
- If the percent of boys whose names start with a vowel and percent of girls whose names start with a vowel were given and you were to find out the percent of all students whose names start with a vowel, what other information would be necessary?
    - *You would need to know the percent of the total number of students that are boys or the percent of the total number of students that are girls.*

Scaffolding:

- Consider offering pre-made tape diagrams for students. Additionally, consider modifying to begin with tasks that are both simpler and more concrete, such as, "Out of 100 people, 60% are girls, and 20% of the girls wear glasses. How many of the total are girls that wear glasses?" Relating the visual models to simpler examples will lead towards success with more complex problems.

Example 1 (5 minutes)

Individually, students will read and make sense of the word problem. Class will reconvene to work out the problem together.

MP.1

Example 1

A school has 60% girls and 40% boys. If 20% of the girls wear glasses and 40% of the boys wear glasses, what percent of all students wears glasses?

Let n represent the number of students in the school.

The number of girls is $0.6n$. The number of boys is $0.4n$.

100%

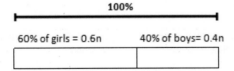

60% of girls = 0.6n   40% of boys= 0.4n

The number of girls wearing glasses is as follows:
$0.2(0.6n) = 0.12n.$

100%

20% of 60% of n = 0.2 × 0.6n = 0.12n

The number of boys wearing glasses is as follows:
$0.4(0.4n) = 0.16n.$

100%

40% of 40% of n = 0.4 × 0.4n = 0.16n

The total number of students wearing glasses is as follows: $0.12n + 0.16n = 0.28n.$ $0.28 = 28\%$, so 28% of the students wear glasses.

- Can you explain the reasonableness of the answer?
  - *Yes, if we assume there are 100 students, 20% of 60 girls is 12 girls, and 40% of 40 boys is 16 boys. The number of students who wear glasses would be 28 out of 100 or 28%.*

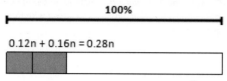

Exercises 1–2 (5 minutes)

Exercises 1–2

1. How does the percent of students who wear glasses change if the percent of girls and boys remains the same (that is, 60% girls and 40% boys) but 20% of the boys wear glasses and 40% of the girls wear glasses?

    Let n represent the number of students in the school.

    The number of girls is $0.6n$. The number of boys is $0.4n$.

    100%

60% of girls = 0.6n	40% of boys= 0.4n

    Girls who wear glasses: *Boys who wear glasses:*

    40% of 60% of n = 0.4 × 0.6n = 0.24n   20% of 40% of n = 0.2 × 0.4n = 0.08n

    Students who wear glasses:

    100%

    40% of 60% of n = 0.4 x 0.6n   20% of 40% of n= 0.2 x 0.4n

    0.24n + 0.08n = 0.32n

    32% of students wear glasses.

2. How would the percent of students who wear glasses change if the percent of girls is 40% of the school and the percent of boys is 60% of the school, and 40% of the girls wear glasses and 20% of the boys wear glasses? Why?

The number of students wearing glasses would be equal to the answer for Example 1 because all of the percents remain the same except that a swap is made between the boys and girls. So, the number of boys wearing glasses is swapped with the number of girls and the number of girls wearing glasses is swapped with the number of boys, but the total number of students wearing glasses is the same.

Let n represent the number of students in the school.

The number of boys is $0.6n$. The number of girls is $0.4n$.

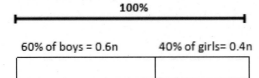

Boys who wear glasses:

Girls who wear glasses:

Students who wear glasses:

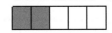

- Explain why the expressions $0.12n + 0.16n$ and $0.28n$ are equivalent. Also, explain how they reveal different information about the situation.

    □ *The equivalence can be shown using the distributive property; $0.12n$ represents the fact that 12% of the total are girls that wear glasses; $0.16n$ represents the fact that 16% of the total are boys that wear glasses; $0.28n$ represents the fact that 28% of the total wear glasses.*

MP.2
&
MP.7

Example 2 (5 minutes)

Give students time to set up the problem using a tape diagram. Work out the example as a class.

Example 2

The weight of the first of three containers is 12% more than the second, and the third container is 20% lighter than the second. The first container is heavier than the third container by what percent?

Let n represent the weight of the second container. (The tape diagram representation for the second container is divided into five equal parts to show 20%. This will be useful when drawing a representation for the third container and also when sketching a 12% portion for the first container since it will be slightly bigger than half of the 20% portion created.)

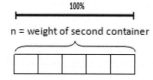

The weight of the first container is $(1.12)n$.

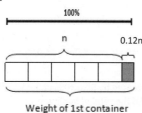

The weight of the third container is $(0.80)n$.

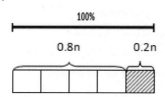

The following represents the difference in weight between the first and third container:

$$1.12n - 0.80n = 0.32n$$

Recall that the weight of the third container is $0.8n$

$0.32n \div 0.8n = 0.4$. The first container is 40% heavier than the third container.

or also $1.4 \times 100\% = 140\%$. This also shows that the first container is 40% heavier than the third container.

- How can we represent the weight of the third container using another expression (besides $0.8n$)?
    - $n - 0.20n$
- Compare these two expressions and what they tell us.
    - *$n - 0.20n$ tells us that the third container is 20% less than the second container, while $0.8n$ shows that the third container is 80% of the second container. Both are equivalent.*
- After rereading the problem, can you explain the reasonableness of the answer?
    - *If the second container weighed 100 lb., then the first container weighs 112 lb., and the third container weighs 80 lb. $112 \div 80 = 1.4$. So, the first container is 40% more than the third.*

- What is the importance of the second container?

  □ *It is the point of reference for both the first and third containers, and both expressions are written in terms of the second container.*

Exercise 3 (3 minutes)

Exercise 3

3. Matthew's pet dog is 7% heavier than Harrison's pet dog, and Janice's pet dog is 20% lighter than Harrison's. By what percent is Matthew's dog heavier than Janice's?

   Let h represent the weight of Harrison's dog.

   Matthew's dog is $1.07h$, and Janice's dog is $0.8h$.

   Since $1.07 \div 0.8 = \frac{107}{80} = 1.3375$, Mathew's dog is 33.75% heavier than Janice's dog.

Example 3 (5 minutes)

Example 3

In one year's time, 20% of Ms. McElroy's investments increased by 5%, 30% of her investments decreased by 5%, and 50% of investments increased by 3%. By what percent did the total of her investments increase?

Let n represent the dollar amount of Ms. McElroy's investments before the changes occurred during the year.

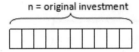

After the changes, the following represents the dollar amount of her investments:

$0.2n(1.05) + 0.3n(0.95) + 0.5n(1.03)$

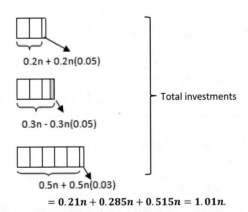

$$= 0.21n + 0.285n + 0.515n = 1.01n.$$

Since $1.01 = 101\%$, Ms. McElroy's total investments increased by 1%.

- How is an increase of 5% denoted in the equation?
  - *The result of a* 5% *increase is the whole* $(100\% = 1)$ *plus another* 5%*, which is five hundredths, and* $1 + 0.05 = 1.05$*, which is multiplied by* n*, Ms. McElroy's original investments.*
- How else can the increase of 5% be written in the equation?
  - *It can be written as the sum of the original amount and the original amount multiplied by* 0.05.
- Why is the 5% decrease denoted as (0.95) and an increase of 5% denoted as 1.05?
  - *The decrease is* 5% *less than* 100%*, so* $100\% - 5\% = 95\%$*. In decimal form it is* 0.95*. An increase is* 5% *more than* 100%*. The decimal for it is* 1.05.

Exercise 4 (5 minutes)

Exercise 4

4. A concert had 6,000 audience members in attendance on the first night and the same on the second night. On the first night the concert exceeded expected attendance by 20% while the second night was below the expected attendance by 20%. What was the difference in percent of concert attendees and expected attendees for both nights combined?

Let x represent the expected number of attendees on the first night and y represent the number expected on the second night.

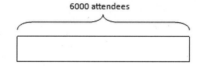

First night: $x + 0.2x = 6,000$

Second night: $y - 0.2y = 6,000$

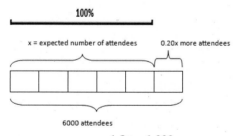

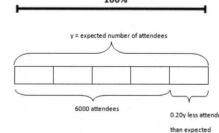

$$1.2x = 6,000$$
$$x = 5,000$$
$$6,000 - 5,000 = 1,000$$

The first night was attended by 1,000 *more people than expected.*

$$0.8y = 6,000$$
$$y = 7,500$$
$$7,500 - 6,000 = 1,500$$

The second night was attended by 1,500 *less people than expected.*

$$5,000 + 7,500 = 12,500$$

12,500 *people were expected in total on both nights.*

$1,500 - 1,000 = 500.$ $\dfrac{500}{12,500} \times 100\% = 4\%$*. The concert missed its expected attendance by* 4%*.*

Closing (4 minutes)

- What is the importance of defining the variable for percent population problems?

  - *We solve for and set up expressions and equations around the variable. The variable gives us a reference of what the whole (100%) is to help us figure out the parts or percents that are unknown.*

- How do tape diagrams help to solve for percent population problems?

  - *It is a visual or manipulative, which helps us understand the problem and set up an equation. Coupled with the 100% bar, it tells us whether or not our answers are reasonable.*

- Give examples of equivalent expressions from this lesson, and explain how they reveal different information about the situation.

  - *Answers may vary. For example, in Exercise 3, the first night's attendance is expressed as $x + 0.2x$. This expression shows that there were 20% more attendees than expected. The equivalent expression would be $1.2x$.*

Exit Ticket (7 minutes)

Name _____   Date _____

Lesson 16: Population Problems

Exit Ticket

1. Jodie spent 25% less buying her English reading book than Claudia. Gianna spent 9% less than Claudia. Gianna spent more than Jodie by what percent?

2. Mr. Ellis is a teacher who tutors students after school. Of the students he tutors, 30% need help in computer science and the rest need assistance in math. Of the students who need help in computer science, 40% are enrolled in Mr. Ellis's class during the school day. Of the students who need help in math, 25% are enrolled in his class during the school day. What percent of the after-school students are enrolled in Mr. Ellis's classes?

Exit Ticket Sample Solutions

1. Jodie spent 25% less buying her English reading book than Claudia. Gianna spent 9% less than Claudia. Gianna spent more than Jodie by what percent?

   Let c = amount Claudia spent in dollars. The number of dollars Jodie spent was $0.75c$, and the number of dollars

   Gianna spent was $0.91c$. $0.91c \div 0.75c = \frac{91}{75} \times 100\% = 121\frac{1}{3}\%$. Gianna spent $21\frac{1}{3}\%$ more than Jodie.

2. Mr. Ellis is a teacher who tutors students after school. Of the students he tutors, 30% need help in computer science and the rest need assistance in math. Of the students who need help in computer science, 40% are enrolled in Mr. Ellis's class during the school day. Of the students who need help in math, 25% are enrolled in his class during the school day. What percent of the after-school students are enrolled in Mr. Ellis's classes?

   Let t represent the after-school students tutored by Mr. Ellis.

   Computer science after-school students: $0.3t$

   Math after-school students : $0.7t$

   After-school computer science students who are also Mr. Ellis's students: $0.4 \times 0.3t = 0.12t$

   After-school math students who are also Mr. Ellis's students: $0.25 \times 0.7t = 0.175t$

   Number of after-school students who are enrolled in Mr. Ellis's classes: $0.12t + 0.175t = 0.295t$

   Out of all the students Mr. Ellis tutors, 29.5% of the tutees are enrolled in his classes.

Problem Set Sample Solutions

1. A first container is filled with a mixture that is 30% acid. A second container is filled with a mixture that is 50% acid. The second container is 50% larger than the first, and the two containers are emptied into a third container. What percent of acid is the third container?

   Let t be the amount of mixture in the first container. Then the second container has $1.5t$, and the third container has $2.5t$.

   The amount of acid in the first container is $0.3t$, the amount of acid in the second container is $0.5(1.5t) = 0.75t$, and the amount of acid in the third container is $1.05t$. The percent of acid in the third container is

   $\frac{1.05}{2.5} \times 100\% = 42\%$.

2. The store's markup on a wholesale item is 40%. The store is currently having a sale, and the item sells for 25% off the retail price. What is the percent of profit made by the store?

   Let w represent the wholesale price of an item.

   Retail price: $1.4w$

   Sale price: $1.4w - (1.4w \times 0.25) = 1.05w$

   The store still makes a 5% profit on a sold item that is on sale.

3. During lunch hour at a local restaurant, 90% of customers order a meat entrée and 10% order a vegetarian entrée. Of the customers who order a meat entrée, 80% order a drink. Of the customers who order a vegetarian entrée, 40% order a drink. What is the percent of customers who order a drink with their entrée?

Let e represent lunch entrées.

Meat entrées: $0.9e$

Vegetarian entrées: $0.1e$

Meet entrées with drinks: $0.9e \times 0.8 = 0.72e$

Vegetarian entrées with drinks: $0.1e \times 0.4 = 0.04e$

Entrées with drinks: $0.72e + 0.04e = 0.76e$. *Seventy six percent of lunch entrées are ordered with a drink.*

4. Last year's spell-a-thon spelling test for a first grade class had 15% more words with four or more letters than this year's spelling test, and next year, there will be 5% less than this year. What percent more words have four or more letters in last year's test than next year's?

Let t represent this year's amount of spell-a-thon words with four letters or more.

Last year: $1.15t$

Next year: $0.95t$

$1.15\,t \div 0.95t \times 100\% \approx 121\%$. *There were about 21% more words with four or more letters last year than there will be next year.*

5. An ice cream shop sells 75% less ice cream in December than in June. Twenty percent more ice cream is sold in July than in June. By what percent did ice cream sales increase from December to July?

Let j represent sales in June.

December: $0.25j$

July: $1.20\,j$

$1.20 \div 0.25 = 4.8 \times 100\% = 480\%$. *Ice cream sales in July increase by 380% from ice cream sales in December.*

6. The livestock on a small farm the prior year consisted of 40% goats, 10% cows, and 50% chickens. This year, there is a 5% decrease in goats, 9% increase in cows, and 15% increase in chickens. What is the percent increase of livestock this year?

Let l represent the number of livestock the prior year.

goats decrease: $0.4l - (0.4l \times 0.05) = 0.38l$ or $0.95(0.4l) = 0.38l$

cows increase: $0.1\,l + (0.1l \times 0.09) = 0.109l$ or $1.09(0.1l) = 0.109l$

chickens increase: $0.5k + (0.5k \times 0.15) = 0.575l$ or $1.15(0.5l) = 0.575l$

$0.38l + 0.109l + 0.575l = 1.064l$. *There is an increase of 6.4% in livestock.*

7. In a pet shelter that is occupied by 55% dogs and 45% cats, 60% of the animals are brought in by concerned people who found these animals in the streets. If 90% of the dogs are brought in by concerned people, what is the percent of cats that are brought in by concerned people?

Let c represent the percent of cats brought in by concerned people.

$$0.55(0.9) + (0.45)(c) = 1(0.6)$$
$$0.495 + 0.45c = 0.6$$
$$0.495 - 0.495 + 0.45c = 0.6 - 0.495$$
$$0.45c = 0.105$$
$$0.45c \div 0.45 = 0.105 \div 0.45$$
$$c \approx 0.233$$

About 23% of the cats brought into the shelter are brought in by concerned people.

8. An artist wants to make a particular teal color paint by mixing a 75% blue hue and 25% yellow hue. He mixes a blue hue that has 85% pure blue pigment and a yellow hue that has 60% of pure yellow pigment. What is the percent of pure pigment that is in the resulting teal color paint?

Let p represent the teal color paint.

$$(0.75 \times 0.85p) + (0.25 \times 0.6p) = 0.7875p$$

78. 75% of pure pigment is in the resulting teal color paint.

9. On Mina's block, 65% of her neighbors do not have any pets, and 35% of her neighbors own at least one pet. If 25% of the neighbors have children but no pets, and 60% of the neighbors who have pets also have children, what percent of the neighbors have children?

Let n represent the number of Mina's neighbors.

Neighbors who do not have pets: $0.65n$

Neighbors who own at least one pet: $0.35n$

Neighbors who have children but no pets: $0.25 \times 0.65n = 0.1625n$

Neighbors who have children and pets: $0.6 \times 0.35n = 0.21n$

Percent of neighbors who have children: $0.1625n + 0.21n = 0.3725n.$

37. 25% of Mina's neighbors have children.

Lesson 17: Mixture Problems

Student Outcomes

- Students write and use algebraic expressions and equations to solve percent word problems related to mixtures.

Scaffolding:

Doing an actual, physical demonstration with containers of water and juice to illustrate the Opening Exercise will aid in understanding. Additionally, using visuals to show examples of customary measurement units will help students that may be unfamiliar with these terms (ounce, cup, pint, quart, gallon).

Classwork

Opening Exercises (10 minutes)

In pairs, students will use their knowledge of percents to complete the charts and answer mixture problems. To highlight MP.1, consider asking students to attempt to make sense of and solve the Opening Exercise without the chart, then explain the solution methods they developed.

Opening Exercise

Imagine you have two equally sized containers. One is pure water, and the other is 50% water and 50% juice. If you combined them, what percent of juice would be the result?

	1st liquid	2nd liquid	Resulting liquid
Amount of liquid (gallons)	1	1	2
Amount of pure juice (gallons)	$0 = 1 \times 0$ *quantity = percent × whole*	$0.5 = 0.5 \times 1$ *quantity = percent × whole*	$0.5 = x \times 2$ *quantity = percent × whole*

25% of the resulting mixture is juice because $\dfrac{0.5}{2} = \dfrac{1}{4}$.

If a 2-gallon container of pure juice is added to 3 gallons of water, what percent of the mixture is pure juice?

Let x represent the percent of pure juice in the resulting juice mixture.

	1st liquid	2nd liquid	Resulting liquid
Amount of liquid (gallons)	2	3	5
Amount of pure juice (gallons)	$2.0 = 1.0 \times 2$ *quantity = percent × whole*	$0 = 0 \times 3$ *quantity = percent × whole*	$2.0 = x \times 5$ *quantity = percent × whole*

- What is the percent of pure juice in water?
  - *Zero percent.*
- How much pure juice will be in the resulting mixture?
  - *2 gallons because the only pure juice to be added is the first liquid.*
- What percent is pure juice out of the resulting mixture?
  - *40%*

If a 2-gallon container of juice mixture that is 40% pure juice is added to 3 gallons of water, what percent of the mixture is pure juice?

	1st liquid	2nd liquid	Resulting liquid
Amount of liquid (gallons)	2	3	5
Amount of pure juice (gallons)	$0.8 = 0.4 \times 2$ *quantity = percent × whole*	$0 = 0 \times 3$ *quantity = percent × whole*	$0.8 = x \times 5$ *quantity = percent × whole*

- How many gallons of the juice mixture is pure juice?
  - $2(0.40) = 0.8$ *gallons*
- What percent is pure juice out of the resulting mixture?
  - 16%
- Does this make sense relative to the prior problem?
  - *Yes, because the mixture should have less juice than the prior problem.*

If a 2-gallon juice cocktail that is 40% pure juice is added to 3 gallons of pure juice, what percent of the resulting mixture is pure juice?

	1st liquid	2nd liquid	Resulting liquid
Amount of liquid (gallons)	2	3	5
Amount of pure juice (gallons)	$0.8 = 0.4 \times 2$ *quantity = percent × whole*	$3 = 1.00 \times 3$ *quantity = percent × whole*	$3.8 = x \times 5$ *quantity = percent × whole*

- What is the difference between this problem and the previous one?
  - *Instead of adding water to the two gallons of juice mixture, pure juice is added, so the resulting liquid contains 3.8 gallons of pure juice.*
- What percent is pure juice out of the resulting mixture?
  - *Let x represent the percent of pure juice in the resulting mixture.*
  $$x(5) = 40\%(2) + 100\%(3)$$
  $$5x = 0.8 + 3$$
  $$5x = 3.8$$
  $$x = 0.76$$
  The mixture is 76% pure juice.

Discussion (5 minutes)

- What pattern do you see in setting up the equations?
  - *Quantity = percent × whole. The sum of parts or mixtures is equal to the resulting mixture. For each juice mixture, you multiply the percent of pure juice by the total amount of juice.*
- How is the form of the expressions and equations in the mixture problems similar to population problems from the previous lesson (for example, finding out how many boys and girls wear glasses)?

MP.7

  - *Just as you would multiply the sub-populations (such as girls or boys) by the given category (students wearing glasses) to find the percent in the whole population, mixture problems parallel the structure of population problems. In mixture problems, the sub-populations are the different mixtures, and the category is the potency of a given element. In this problem the element is pure juice.*

EUREKA MATH™   Lesson 17:   Mixture Problems

Example 1 (5 minutes)

Allow students to answer the problems independently and reconvene as a class to discuss the example.

Example 1

A 5-gallon container of trail mix is 20% nuts. Another trail mix is added to it, resulting in a 12-gallon container of trail mix that is 40% nuts.

a. Write an equation to describe the relationships in this situation.

  Let j represent the percent of nuts in the second trail mix that is added to the first trail mix to create the resulting 12-gallon container of trail mix.

$$0.4\,(12) = 0.2(5) + j(12 - 5)$$

b. Explain in words how each part of the equation relates to the situation.

  Quantity = Percent × Whole

  Resulting gallons of trail mix (resulting % of nuts) = 1st trail mix in gallons (% of nuts) + 2nd trail mix in gallons (% of nuts)

c. What percent of the second trail mix is nuts?

$$4.8 = 1 + 7j$$
$$4.8 - 1 = 1 - 1 + j$$
$$3.8 = 7j$$
$$j \approx 0.5429$$

  About 54% of the second trail mix is nuts.

- What information is missing from this problem?
  - *The amount of the second trail mix, but we can calculate it easily because it is the difference of the total trail mix and the first trail mix.*
- How is this problem different from the Opening Exercises?
  - *Instead of juice, the problem is about trail mix. Mathematically, this example is not asking for the percent of a certain quantity in the resulting mixture but rather asking for the percent composition of one of the trail mixes being added.*
- How is the problem similar to the Opening Exercises?
  - *We are still using quantity = percent × whole.*
- Is the answer reasonable?
  - *Yes, because the second percent of nuts in the trail mix should be a percent bigger than 40% since the first trail mix is 20% nuts.*

Exercise 1 (10 minutes)

Exercise 1

Represent each situation using an equation, and show all steps in the solution process.

a. A 6-pint 25% oil mixture is added to a 3-pint 40% oil mixture. What percent of the resulting mixture is oil?

Let x represent the percent of oil in the resulting mixture.

$$0.25(6) + 0.40(3) = x(9)$$
$$1.5 + 1.2 = 9x$$
$$2.7 = 9x$$

$x = 0.3$; the resulting mixture is 9 pints of 30% oil.

b. An 11-ounce gold chain of 24% gold was made from a melted down 4-ounce charm of 50% gold and a golden locket. What percent of the locket was pure gold?

Let x represent the percent of pure gold in the locket.

$$0.5(4) + (x)(7) = 0.24(11)$$
$$2 + 7x = 2.64$$
$$2 - 2 + 7x = 2.64 - 2$$
$$\frac{7x}{7} = \frac{0.64}{7}$$
$$x \approx 0.0914$$

The locket was about 9% gold.

c. In a science lab, two containers are filled with mixtures. The first container is filled with a mixture that is 30% acid. The second container is filled with a mixture that is 50% acid, and the second container is 50% larger than the first. The first and second containers are then emptied into a third container. What percent of acid is in the third container?

Let m represent the total amount of mixture in the first container.

$0.3m$ is the amount of acid in the first container.

$0.5(m + 0.5m)$ is the amount of acid in the second container.

$0.3m + 0.5(m + 0.5m) = 0.3m + 0.5(1.5m) = 1.05m$ is the amount of acid in the mixture in the third container.

$m + 1.5m = 2.5m$ is the amount of mixture in the third container. So, $\frac{1.05m}{2.5m} = 0.42 = 42\%$ is the percent of acid in the third container.

Example 2 (5 minutes)

Encourage students to find the missing information and set up the equation with the help of other classmates. Review the process with the whole class by soliciting student responses.

Example 2

Soil that contains 30% clay is added to soil that contains 70% clay to create 10 gallons of soil containing 50% clay. How much of each of the soils was combined?

Let x be the amount of soil with 30% clay.

1st soil amount (% of clay) + 2nd soil amount (% of clay) = resulting amount (resulting % of clay)

$$(0.3)(x) + (0.7)(10 - x) = (0.5)(10)$$
$$0.3x + 7 - 0.7x = 5$$
$$-0.4x + 7 - 7 = 5 - 7$$
$$-0.4x = -2$$
$$x = 5$$

5 gallons of the 30% clay soil and $10 - 5 = 5$, so 5 gallons of the 70% clay soil must be mixed to make 10 gallons of 50% clay soil.

Exercise 2 (5 minutes)

Exercise 2

The equation: $(0.2)(x) + (0.8)(6 - x) = (0.4)(6)$ is used to model a mixture problem.

a. How many units are in the total mixture?

   6 units

b. What percents relate to the two solutions that are combined to make the final mixture?

   20% and 80%

c. The two solutions combine to make six units of what percent solution?

   40%

d. When the amount of a resulting solution is given (for instance 4 gallons) but the amounts of the mixing solutions are unknown, how are the amounts of the mixing solutions represented?

   If the amount of gallons of the first mixing solution is represented by the variable, x, then the amount of gallons of the second mixing solution is $4 - x$.

Closing (5 minutes)

MP.7

- What is the general structure of the expressions for mixture problems?

  - *The general equation looks like the following:*
    Whole quantity = part + part.

  - *Utilizing this structure makes an equation that looks like the following:*
    % of resulting quantity (amount of the resulting quantity) = % of 1st quantity (amount of 1st quantity) + % of 2nd quantity (amount of 2nd quantity).

- How do mixture and population problems compare?

  - *These problems both utilize the equation quantity = percent x whole. Mixture problems deal with quantities of solutions and mixtures as well as potencies while population problems deal with sub-groups and categories.*

Exit Ticket (5 minutes)

Name _____   Date _____

Lesson 17: Mixture Problems

Exit Ticket

A 25% vinegar solution is combined with triple the amount of a 45% vinegar solution and a 5% vinegar solution resulting in 20 milliliters of a 30% vinegar solution.

1. Determine an equation that models this situation, and explain what each part represents in the situation.

2. Solve the equation and find the amount of each of the solutions that were combined.

Exit Ticket Sample Solutions

A 25% vinegar solution is combined with triple the amount of a 45% vinegar solution and a 5% vinegar solution resulting in 20 milliliters of a 30% vinegar solution.

2. Determine an equation that models this situation, and explain what each part represents in the situation.

Let s represent the number of milliliters of the 1st vinegar solution.

$$(0.25)(s) + (0.45)(3s) + (0.05)(20 - 4s) = (0.3)(20)$$

3. Solve the equation, and find the amount of each of the solutions that were combined.

$$0.25s + 1.35s + 1 - 0.2s = 6$$
$$1.6s - 0.2s + 1 = 6$$
$$1.4s + 1 - 1 = 6 - 1$$
$$1.4s \div 1.4 = 5 \div 1.4$$
$$s \approx 3.57$$
$$3s \approx 3(3.57) = 10.71$$
$$20 - 4s \approx 20 - 4(3.57) = 5.72$$

Around 3.57 ml of the 25% vinegar solution, 10.71 ml of the 45% vinegar solution and 5.72 ml of the 5% vinegar solution were combined to make 20 ml of the 30% vinegar solution.

Problem Set Sample Solutions

1. A 5-liter cleaning solution contains 30% bleach. A 3-liter cleaning solution contains 50% bleach. What percent of bleach is obtained by putting the two mixtures together?

Let x represent the percent of bleach in the resulting mixture.

$$0.3(5) + 0.5(3) = x(8)$$
$$1.5 + 1.5 = 8x$$
$$3 \div 8 = 8x \div 8$$
$$x = 0.375$$

The percent of bleach in the resulting cleaning solution is 37.5%.

2. A container is filled with 100 grams of bird feed that is 80% seed. How many grams of bird feed containing 5% seed must be added to get bird feed that is 40% seed?

Let x represent the amount of bird feed, in grams, to be added.

$$0.8(100) + 0.05x = 0.4(100 + x)$$
$$80 + 0.05x = 40 + 0.4x$$
$$80 - 40 + 0.05x = 40 - 40 + 0.4x$$
$$40 + 0.05x = 0.4x$$
$$40 + 0.05x - 0.05x = 0.4x - 0.05x$$
$$40 \div 0.35 = 0.35x \div 0.35$$
$$x \approx 114.3$$

About 114.3 grams of the bird seed containing 5% seed must be added.

3. A container is filled with 100 grams of bird feed that is 80% seed. Tom and Sally want to mix the 100 grams with bird feed that is 5% seed to get a mixture that is 40% seed. Tom wants to add 114 grams of the 5% seed and Sally wants to add 115 grams of the 5% seed mix. What will be the percent of seed if Tom adds 114 grams? What will be the percent of seed if Sally adds 115 grams? How much do you think should be added to get 40% seed?

    If Tom adds 114 grams, then let x be the percent of seed in his new mixture. $214x = 0.8(100) + 0.05(114)$. Solving, we get the following:

    $$x = \frac{80 + 5.7}{214} = \frac{85.7}{214} \approx 0.4005 = 40.05\%.$$

    If Sally adds 115 grams, then let y be the percent of seed in her new mixture. $215y = 0.8(100) + 0.05(115)$. Solving, we get the following:

    $$y = \frac{80 + 5.75}{215} = \frac{85.75}{215} \approx 0.3988 = 39.88\%.$$

    The amount to be added should be between 114 and 115 grams. It should probably be closer to 114 because 40.05% is closer to 40% than 39.88%.

4. Jeanie likes mixing leftover salad dressings together to make new dressings. She combined 0.55 L of a 90% vinegar salad dressing with 0.45 L of another dressing to make 1 L of salad dressing that is 60% vinegar. What percent of the second salad dressing was vinegar?

    Let c represent the percent of vinegar in the second salad dressing.

    $$0.55(0.9) + (0.45)(c) = 1(0.6)$$
    $$0.495 + 0.45c = 0.6$$
    $$0.495 - 0.495 + 0.45c = 0.6 - 0.495$$
    $$0.45c = 0.105$$
    $$0.45c \div 0.45 = 0.105 \div 0.45$$
    $$c \approx 0.233$$

    The second salad dressing was around 23% vinegar.

5. Anna wants to make 30 ml of a 60% salt solution by mixing together a 72% salt solution and a 54% salt solution. How much of each solution must she use?

    Let s represent the amount, in ml, of the first salt solution.

    $$0.72(s) + 0.54(30 - s) = 0.60(30)$$
    $$0.72s + 16.2 - 0.54s = 18$$
    $$0.18s + 16.2 = 18$$
    $$0.18s + 16.2 - 16.2 = 18 - 16.2$$
    $$0.18s = 1.8$$
    $$s = 10$$

    Anna needs 10 ml of the 72% solution and 20 ml of the 54% solution.

6. A mixed bag of candy is 25% chocolate bars and 75% other filler candy. Of the chocolate bars, 50% of them contain caramel. Of the other filler candy, 10% of them contain caramel. What percent of candy that contains caramel?

    Let c represent the percent of candy containing caramel in the mixed bag of candy.

    $$0.25(0.50) + (0.75)(0.10) = 1(c)$$
    $$0.125 + 0.075 = c$$
    $$0.2 = c$$

    In the mixed bag of candy, 20% of the candy contains caramel.

7. A local fish market receives the daily catch of two local fishermen. The first fisherman's catch was 84% fish while the rest was other non-fish items. The second fisherman's catch was 76% fish while the rest was other non-fish items. If the fish market receives 75% of its catch from the first fisherman and 25% from the second, what was the percent of other non-fish items the local fish market bought from the fishermen altogether?

Let n represent the percent of non-fish items of the total market items.

$$0.75(0.16) + 0.25(0.24) = n$$
$$0.12 + 0.06 = n$$
$$0.18 = n$$

The percent of non-fish items in the local fish market is 18%.

Lesson 18: Counting Problems

Student Outcomes

- Students solve counting problems related to computing percents.

Lesson Notes

Students will continue to apply their understanding of percents to problem solve counting problems. The problems in this lesson lend themselves to the concept of probability without formal computations of combinations and permutations.

Classwork

Opening Exercise (5 minutes)

Opening Exercise

You are about to switch out your books from your locker but forget the order of your locker combination. You know that there are a 3, 16, and 21 in some order. What is the percent of locker combinations that start with 3?

Locker Combination Possibilities:

3, 16, 21

21, 16, 3

16, 21, 3

21, 3, 16

16, 3, 21

3, 21, 16

$$\frac{2}{6} = \frac{1}{3} = 0.33\overline{3} = 33.\overline{3}\%$$

> *Scaffolding:*
>
> For all problems that involve determining a number of combinations, consider using manipulatives to allow students to create different physical arrangements. Additionally, in cases where numbers or letters will cause further confusion, consider modifying tasks to involve arranging pictures or colors.

Discussion (3 minutes)

- What amounts did you use to find the percent of locker combinations that start with 3?
  - *Since there are only 2 locker combinations that start with a 3 and a total of 6 locker combinations, we used 2 and 6.*
- What amounts would you use to find the percent of locker combinations that end with a 3?
  - *There are only 2 locker combinations that end with a 3 and a total of 6 locker combinations; we would use 2 and 6.*
- Allow opportunity for students to share other solution methods and reflections with one another.

Example 1 (5 minutes)

Have students answer questions in this example independently. Reconvene as a class to share out and model solutions.

Example 1

All of the 3-letter passwords that can be formed using the letters "A" and "B" are as follows:

AAA, AAB, ABA, ABB, BAA, BAB, BBA, BBB.

    a.   **What percent of passwords contain at least two "B's"?**

         There are four passwords that contain at least two "B's": ABB, BAB, BBA, and BBB. There are eight passwords total.

$$\frac{4}{8} = \frac{1}{2} = 50\%, \text{ so } 50\% \text{ of the passwords contain at least two "B's".}$$

    b.   **What percent of passwords contain no "A's"?**

         There is 1 password that contains no "A's". There are 8 passwords total.

$$\frac{1}{8} = 0.125 = 12.5\%, \text{ so } 12.5\% \text{ of the passwords contain no "A's".}$$

- What is another way of saying "passwords containing at least two 'B's'"?
  - *Passwords that have one or no "A's". Passwords that have two or more "B's".*
- Would the percent of passwords containing one or no "A's" be equal to the percent of passwords containing at least two "B's"?
  - *Yes, because they represent the same group of passwords.*
- What is another way of saying, "passwords containing no 'A's'"?
  - *A password that contains all "B's".*

Exercises 1–2 (5 minutes)

Students may work individually or in pairs to complete Exercises 1–2.

Exercises 1–2

1. **How many 4-letter passwords can be formed using the letters "A" and "B"?**

     16: AAAA, AAAB, AABB, ABBB, AABA, ABAA, ABAB, ABBA, BBBB, BBBA, BBAA, BAAA, BBAB, BABB, BABA, BAAB

2. **What percent of the 4-letter passwords contain**

    a.   **no "A's"?**

         6.25%

    b.   **exactly one "A"?**

         25%

    c.   **exactly two "A's"?**

         37.5%

---

    d.   **exactly three "A's"?**

        25%

    e.   **four "A's"?**

        6.25%

    f.   **the same number of "A's" and "B's"?**

        37.5%

- Which percents are equal?
  - *No "A's" and four "A's" have the same percent. Exactly one "A" and exactly three "A's" have the same percents. Exactly two "A's" and the same number of "A's" and "B's" also have the same percents.*
- Why do you think they are equal?
  - *Four "A's" is the same as saying no "B's", and since there are only two letters, no "B's" is the same as no "A's". The same reasoning is for exactly one "A" and exactly three "A's". If there are exactly three "A's", then this would mean that there is exactly one "B", and since there are only two letters, exactly one "B" is the same as exactly one "A". Finally, exactly two "A's" and the same number of "A's" and "B's" are the same because the same amount of "A's" and "B's" would be two.*

Example 2 (5 minutes)

Example 2

In a set of 3-letter passwords, 40% of the passwords contain the letter B and two of another letter. Which of the two sets below meet the criteria? Explain how you arrived at your answer.

Set 1				Set 2	
BBB	AAA	CAC		CEB	BBB
CBC	ABA	CCC		EBE	CCC
BBC	CCB	CAB		CCC	EEE
AAB	AAC	BAA		EEB	CBC
ACB	BAC	BCC		CCB	ECE

For each set, I counted how many passwords have the letter "B" and two of another letter. Then I checked to see if that quantity equaled 40% of the total number of passwords in the set.

In Set 1, CBC, AAB, ABA, CCB, BAA, and BCC are the passwords that contain a "B" and two of another letter. Set 1 meets the criteria since there are 15 passwords total and 40% of 15 is 6.

$$quantity = percent \times whole$$
$$6 = 0.4(15)$$
$$6 = 6 \rightarrow True$$

In Set 2, EBE, EEB, CCB, and CBC are the only passwords that contain a "B" and two other of the same letter. Set 2 meets the criteria since there are 10 passwords total and 40% of 10 is 4.

$$quantity = percent \times whole$$
$$4 = 0.4(10)$$
$$4 = 4 \rightarrow True$$

So, both Sets 1 and 2 meet the criteria.

Exercises 3–4 (5 minutes)

Exercises 3–4

3. Shana read the following problem:

    "How many letter arrangements can be formed from the word "triangle" that have two vowels and two consonants (order does not matter)?"

    She answered that there are 30 letter arrangements.

    Twenty percent of the letter arrangements that began with a vowel actually had an English definition. How many letter arrangements that begin with a vowel have an English definition?

    $$0.20 \times 30 = 6$$

    Six have a formal English definition.

4. Using three different keys on a piano, a songwriter makes the beginning of his melody with three notes, C, E, and G:
    CCE, EEE, EGC, GCE, CEG, GEE, CGE, GGE, EGG, EGE, GCG, EEC, ECC, ECG, GGG, GEC, CCG, CEE, CCC, GEG, CGC

    a. From the list above, what is the percent of melodies with all three notes that are different?

    $$\frac{6}{21} \approx 28.6\%$$

    b. From the list above, what is the percent of melodies that have three of the same notes?

    $$\frac{3}{21} \approx 14.3\%$$

Example 3 (10 minutes)

Example 3

Look at the 36 points on the coordinate plane with whole number coordinates between 1 and 6, inclusive.

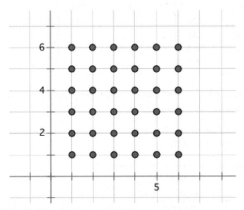

a. Draw a line through each of the points which have an x-coordinate and y-coordinate sum of 7.

    Draw a line through each of the points which have an x-coordinate and y-coordinate sum of 6.

    Draw a line through each of the points which have an x-coordinate and y-coordinate sum of 5.

    Draw a line through each of the points which have an x-coordinate and y-coordinate sum of 4.

    Draw a line through each of the points which have an x-coordinate and y-coordinate sum of 3.

Draw a line through each of the points which have an x-coordinate and y-coordinate sum of 2.

Draw a line through each of the points which have an x-coordinate and y-coordinate sum of 8.

Draw a line through each of the points which have an x-coordinate and y-coordinate sum of 9.

Draw a line through each of the points which have an x-coordinate and y-coordinate sum of 10.

Draw a line through each of the points which have an x-coordinate and y-coordinate sum of 11.

Draw a line through each of the points which have an x-coordinate and y-coordinate sum of 12.

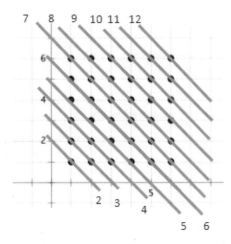

b. What percent of the 36 points have a coordinate sum of 7?

$16\frac{2}{3}\%$

c. Write a numerical expression that could be used to determine the percent of the 36 points that have a coordinate sum of 7.

There are six coordinate points in which the sum of the x-coordinate and the y-coordinate is 7. So,

$$\frac{6}{36} \times 100 = 16\frac{2}{3}\%$$

d. What percent of the 36 points have a coordinate sum of 5 or less?

$27\frac{7}{9}\%$

e. What percent of the 36 points have a coordinate sum of 4 or 10?

$16\frac{2}{3}\%$

Closing (3 minutes)

- What information must be known to find the percent of possible outcomes for a counting problem?
  - *To decipher percents, the total number of possible outcomes needs to be known as well as the different outcomes.*

Exit Ticket (5 minutes)

Lesson 18:   Counting Problems

Name _____   Date _____

Lesson 18: Counting Problems

Exit Ticket

1. There are a van and a bus transporting students on a student camping trip. Arriving at the site, there are 3 parking spots. Let v represent the van and b represent the bus. The chart shows the different ways the vehicles can park.

a. In what percent of arrangements are the vehicles separated by an empty parking space?

	Parking Space 1	Parking Space2	Parking Space 3
Option 1	V	B	
Option 2	V		B
Option 3	B	V	
Option 4	B		V
Option 5		V	B
Option 6		B	V

b. In what percent of arrangements are the vehicles parked next to each other?

c. In what percent of arrangements does the left or right parking space remain vacant?

Exit Ticket Sample Solutions

1. There are a van and a bus transporting students on a student camping trip. Arriving at the site, there are 3 parking spots. Let v represent the van and b represent the bus. The chart shows the different ways the vehicles can park.

    a. In what percent of arrangements are the vehicles separated by an empty parking space?

    $$\frac{2}{6} = 33\frac{1}{3}\%$$

    b. In what percent of arrangements are the vehicles parked next to each other?

    $$\frac{4}{6} = 66\frac{2}{3}\%$$

    c. In what percent of arrangements does the left or right parking space remain vacant?

    $$\frac{4}{6} = 66\frac{2}{3}\%$$

	Parking Space 1	Parking Space 2	Parking Space 3
Option 1	V	B	
Option 2	V		B
Option 3	B	V	
Option 4	B		V
Option 5		V	B
Option 6		B	V

Problem Set Sample Solutions

1. A six-sided die (singular for dice) is thrown twice. The different rolls are as follows:

    1 and 1, 1 and 2, 1 and 3, 1 and 4, 1 and 5, 1 and 6,

    2 and 1, 2 and 2, 2 and 3, 2 and 4, 2 and 5, 2 and 6,

    3 and 1, 3 and 2, 3 and 3, 3 and 4, 3 and 5, 3 and 6,

    4 and 1, 4 and 2, 4 and 3, 4 and 4, 4 and 5, 4 and 6,

    5 and 1, 5 and 2, 5 and 3, 5 and 4, 5 and 5, 5 and 6,

    6 and 1, 6 and 2, 6 and 3, 6 and 4, 6 and 5, 6 and 6.

    a. What is the percent that both throws will be even numbers?

    $$\frac{9}{36} = 25\%$$

    b. What is the percent that the second throw is a 5?

    $$\frac{6}{36} = 16\frac{2}{3}\%$$

    c. What is the percent that the first throw is lower than a 6?

    $$\frac{30}{36} = 83\frac{1}{3}\%$$

2. You have the ability to choose three of your own classes, art, language, and physical education. There are three art classes (A1, A2, A3), two language classes (L1, L2), and two P.E. classes (P1, P2) to choose from (order does not matter and you must choose one from each subject).

A1, L1, P1	A2, L1, P1	A3, L1, P1
A1, L1, P2	A2, L1, P2	A3, L1, P2
A1, L2, P1	A2, L2, P1	A3, L2, P1
A1, L2, P2	A2, L2, P2	A3, L2, P2

Compare the percent of possibilities with A1 in your schedule to the percent of possibilities with L1 in your schedule.

A1: $\dfrac{4}{12} = 33\dfrac{1}{3}\%$ *L1:* $\dfrac{6}{12} = 50\%$

There is a greater percent with L1 in my schedule.

3. Fridays are selected to show your school pride. The colors of your school are orange, blue, and white, and you can show your spirit by wearing a top, a bottom, and an accessory with the colors of your school. During lunch, 11 students are chosen to play for a prize on stage. The table charts what the students wore:

Top	W	O	W	O	B	W	B	B	W	W	W
Bottom	B	O	B	B	O	B	B	B	O	W	B
Accessory	W	O	B	W	B	O	B	W	O	O	O

a. What is the percent of outfits that are one color?

$\dfrac{2}{11} = 18\dfrac{2}{11}\%$

b. What is the percent of outfits that include orange accessories?

$\dfrac{5}{11} = 45\dfrac{5}{11}\%$

4. Shana wears two rings (G represents gold, and S represents silver) at all times on her hand. She likes fiddling with them and places them on different fingers (pinky, ring, middle, index) when she gets restless. The chart is tracking the movement of her rings.

	Pinky Finger	Ring Finger	Middle Finger	Index Finger
Position 1		G	S	
Position 2			S	G
Position 3	G		S	
Position 4				S,G
Position 5	S	G		
Position 6	G	S		
Position 7	S		G	
Position 8	G		S	
Position 9		S,G		
Position 10		G	S	
Position 11			G	S
Position 12		S		G
Position 13	S,G			
Position 14			S,G	

a. What percent of the positions shows the gold ring on her pinky finger?

$$\frac{4}{14} \approx 28.57\%$$

b. What percent of the positions shows she wears both rings on one finger?

$$\frac{4}{14} = 28\frac{4}{7}\%$$

5. Use the coordinate plane below to answer the following questions:

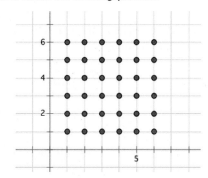

a. What is the percent of the 36 points whose quotient of $\frac{x-coordinate}{y-coordinate}$ is greater than one?

$$\frac{15}{36} = 41\frac{2}{3}\%$$

b. What is the percent of the 36 points whose coordinate quotient is equal to one?

$$\frac{6}{36} = 16\frac{2}{3}\%$$

Name _____   Date _____

DAY ONE: CALCULATOR ACTIVE

You may use a calculator for this part of the assessment. Show your work to receive full credit.

1. Kara works at a fine jewelry store and earns commission on her total sales for the week. Her weekly paycheck was in the amount of $6,500, including her salary of $1,000. Her sales for the week totaled $45,000. Express her rate of commission as a percent, rounded to the nearest whole number.

2. Kacey and her three friends went out for lunch, and they wanted to leave a 15% tip. The receipt shown below lists the lunch total before tax and tip. The tip is on the cost of the food plus tax. The sales tax rate in Pleasantville is 8.75%.

   a. Use mental math to estimate the approximate total cost of the bill including tax and tip to the nearest dollar. Explain how you arrived at your answer.

```
        SAM'S WORLD FAMOUS BURGER
              1522 OAK ROAD
            PLEASANTVILLE, USA

BBQ BURGER W/CHEESE           9.99
CHICKEN FINGER BASKE          8.99
MUSHROOM BURGER              10.99
CHILI CHEESE FRIES            8.99

                   TOTAL: $38.96

         THANKS FOR YOUR BUSINESS.
            FOLLOW US ONLINE!

          WWW.CUSTOMRECEIPT.COM
```

b.   Find the actual total of the bill including tax and tip. If Kacey and her three friends split the bill equally, how much will each person pay including tax and tip?

3.   Cool Tees is having a Back to School sale where all t-shirts are discounted by 15%. Joshua wants to buy five shirts: one costs $9.99, two cost $11.99 each, and two others cost $21.00 each.

    a.   What is the total cost of the shirts including the discount?

b. By law, sales tax is calculated on the discounted price of the shirts. Would the total cost of the shirts including the 6.5% sales tax be greater if the tax was applied before a 15% discount is taken, rather than after a 15% discount is taken? Explain.

c. Joshua remembered he had a coupon in his pocket that would take an additional 30% off the price of the shirts. Calculate the new total cost of the shirts including the sales tax.

d. If the price of each shirt is 120% of the store's cost price, write an equation and find the store's cost price for a $21 shirt.

4. Tierra, Cameron, and Justice wrote equations to calculate the amount of money in a savings account after one year with $\frac{1}{2}$% interest paid annually on a balance of M dollars. Let T represent the total amount of money saved.

$$\text{Tiara's Equation:} \qquad T = 1.05M$$

$$\text{Cameron's Equation:} \qquad T = M + 0.005M$$

$$\text{Justice's Equation:} \qquad T = M(1 + 0.005)$$

a. The three students decided to see if their equations would give the same answer by using a $100 balance. Find the total amount of money in the savings account using each student's equation. Show your work.

b. Explain why their equations will or will not give the same answer.

5. A printing company is enlarging the image on a postcard to make a greeting card. The enlargement of the postcard's rectangular image is done using a scale factor of 125%. Be sure to show all other related math work.

a. Represent a scale factor of 125% as a fraction and decimal.

b. The postcard's dimensions are 7 inches by 5 inches. What are the dimensions of the greeting card?

c. If the printing company makes a poster by enlarging the postcard image, and the poster's dimensions are 28 inches by 20 inches, represent the scale factor as a percent.

d. Write an equation, in terms of the scale factor, that shows the relationship between the areas of the postcard and poster. Explain your equation.

e. Suppose the printing company wanted to start with the greeting card's image and reduce it to create the postcard's image. What scale factor would they use? Represent this scale factor as a percent.

f.   In math class, students had to create a scale drawing that was smaller than the postcard image. Azra used a scale factor of 60% to create the smaller image. She stated the dimensions of her smaller image as: $4\frac{1}{6}$ inches by 3 inches. Azra's math teacher did not give her full credit for her answer. Why? Explain Azra's error, and write the answer correctly.

Name _____   Date _____

DAY TWO: CALCULATOR INACTIVE

You will now complete the remainder of the assessment without the use of a calculator.

6. A $100 MP3 player is marked up by 10% and then marked down by 10%. What is the final price? Explain your answer.

7. The water level in a swimming pool increased from 4.5 feet to 6 feet. What is the percent increase in the water level rounded to the nearest tenth of a percent? Show your work.

8. A 5-gallon mixture contains 40% acid. A 3-gallon mixture contains 50% acid. What percent acid is obtained by putting the two mixtures together? Show your work.

9. In Mr. Johnson's third and fourth period classes, 30% of the students scored a 95% or higher on a quiz. Let n be the total number of students in Mr. Johnson's classes. Answer the following questions, and show your work to support your answers.

   a. If 15 students scored a 95% or higher, write an equation involving n that relates the number of students who scored a 95% or higher to the total number of students in Mr. Johnson's third and fourth period classes.

   b. Solve your equation in part (a) to find how many students are in Mr. Johnson's third and fourth period classes.

   c. Of the students who scored below 95%, 40% of them are girls. How many boys scored below 95%?

A Progression Toward Mastery

Assessment Task Item		STEP 1 Missing or incorrect answer and little evidence of reasoning or application of mathematics to solve the problem.	STEP 2 Missing or incorrect answer but evidence of some reasoning or application of mathematics to solve the problem.	STEP 3 A correct answer with some evidence of reasoning or application of mathematics to solve the problem or an incorrect answer with substantial evidence of solid reasoning or application of mathematics to solve the problem.	STEP 4 A correct answer supported by substantial evidence of solid reasoning or application of mathematics to solve the problem.
1	7.RP.A.3	Student answers incorrectly and provides little or no evidence of understanding how to find the rate of commission as a percent. OR Student does not attempt to answer the question.	Student answers incorrectly but provides some evidence of understanding percents, although multiple errors are made.	Student states a correct answer of 12%, but the work shown does not support the answer. OR Student answer is incorrect due to a calculation error (with or without the use of a calculator); however, a correct process for arriving at the answer is shown. OR Student does not round the answer or rounds incorrectly to state the answer as 12.$\overline{2}$% or 12.2% but provides adequate math work to support the answer.	Student correctly finds the rate of commission to be 12% when rounded to the nearest whole number percent. Substantial evidence of understanding is provided in the steps/work shown.
2	a 7.RP.A.3 7.EE.B.3	Student arrives at an answer that is substantially outside the range of $48–$51. The explanation provides little or no evidence of understanding how to estimate the tax and tip to arrive at the total	Student arrives at an answer that is substantially outside the range of $48–$51. However, the explanation demonstrates some understanding of percent and how to use mental math and	Student arrives at an answer that is outside the range of $48–$51 but provides an explanation of a correct process, although a calculation error is made. OR Student states an	Student states an answer within the reasonable range of $48–$51 and provides a thorough explanation of how to arrive at the answer using mental math and estimation skills.

Module 4:   Percent and Proportional Relationships

		bill. OR Student does not attempt to answer the question.	estimation skills to find the total cost, although there are multiple errors.	answer that is within the range of $48–$51 for the total cost of the bill, but the explanation is incomplete.	
	b **7.RP.A.3**	Student answers incorrectly and provides little or no evidence of understanding how to find the tip, tax, or total bill. OR Student does not attempt to answer the question.	Student has an incorrect answer but provides math work that shows how to correctly find at least one of the following: the amount of the tax or the amount of the tip. Student divides the answer by 4 but states the answer incorrectly because of a rounding error and/or a missing dollar sign. AND Student does not check the answer to determine if the bill will be paid in full if each person pays the amount stated in the answer.	Student states a correct answer of $48.73 or $48.72 but does not support the answer with adequate work. AND Student divides the answer by 4 to arrive at the answer and rounds correctly but either does not include a dollar sign on the answer or does not check the answer to determine if the bill will be paid in full if each person pays the amount stated in the answer. OR Student has an incorrect answer but provides work that shows a correct process, despite making a calculation error.	Student states a correct answer of $48.73 for the total bill, providing substantial evidence of the steps taken to reach the correct answer. The student divides $48.73 by 4 and states that three people will pay $12.18 and one person will pay $12.19. If the student waited to round until the very end of the problem, another acceptable answer is $48.72. Thus, each person would pay exactly $12.18.
3	**a** **7.RP.A.3** **7.EE.B.3**	Student answers incorrectly and provides little or no evidence of understanding how to find the discount price. OR Student does not attempt to answer the question.	Student answers incorrectly, but the math work shown provides some evidence of understanding how to find the discount price, although there are multiple errors, or a step in the process is missing.	Student arrives at an incorrect answer due to a minor error, but the math work shown indicates a sound understanding of the steps involved. OR Student has the correct answer of $64.57 but does not show adequate work to support the answer.	Student has the correct answer of $64.57, and the math work shown includes finding the total costs of the shirts and correctly applying the discount.
	b **7.RP.A.3** **7.EE.B.3**	Student does not clearly answer yes or no, and the explanation is incomplete, ambiguous, and/or lacks sound reasoning. OR Student does not	Student incorrectly states that, yes, the total cost is greater if the tax is applied before the discount is taken. Student work is incomplete but shows some understanding of	Student correctly states that the total amount will be the same, $68.77, but does not adequately explain why. OR, due to a minor calculation error, student incorrectly	Student correctly states that the total amount will be the same, $68.77. The explanation shows substantial evidence of understanding. For example, by using the

		attempt to answer the question.	how to find the total cost with the tax and discount applied.	states that the total cost is greater if the tax is applied before the discount is taken and supporting work is shown.	commutative property of multiplication the student shows that: $75.97\,(0.85)(1.065) = 75.97\,(1.065)(0.85)$.
c 7.RP.A.3 7.EE.B.3		Student answer is incorrect and provides little or no evidence of understanding how to find the additional 30% discount and final discount price with tax. OR Student does not attempt to answer the question.	Student answer is incorrect, but the math work shown contains some evidence of a correct process, although it may be incomplete and/or contain multiple errors or at least one conceptual error. For instance, student finds the amount of an additional 30% discount but does not subtract it from $64.57.	Student states the correct answer of $48.14 but does not provide adequate math work to fully support the answer. OR Student arrives at an incorrect answer due to a calculation error (with or without the use of a calculator) but uses a sound process that indicates the steps necessary to find the new total cost of the shirts with tax.	Student states the correct answer of $48.14. Student supports the answer by showing the correct steps taken to arrive at the answer and makes no errors in the calculations.
d 7.RP.A.3 7.EE.B.4		Student does not provide a correct equation or solution. The math work shown provides little or no evidence of understanding how to find the store's cost price of the shirt. OR Student does not attempt to answer the question.	Student writes an incorrect equation but solves it correctly or demonstrates the correct process to solve it but makes a minor error. OR Student writes a correct equation but makes a conceptual error when solving it. For instance, student converts 120% to 1.20 and writes the equation $21 = 1.2c$ but then erroneously multiplies 1.2 by 21 to find the cost. OR Student arrives at the correct cost of the shirt, $17.50, but does so using another method and does not provide an equation.	Student writes a correct equation to find the store's cost price, such as $21 = 1.2c$, and demonstrates the correct process needed to solve the equation. However, a minor calculation error or rounding error (with or without the use of a calculator) causes the student to arrive at an incorrect answer. OR Student writes a correct equation to find the store's cost price of the shirt, such as $21 = 1.2c$ but incorrectly states the price as $17.05 or makes another type of rounding error, or does not use a dollar symbol in writing the final answer as 17.50. But the math work shows a correct process and the	Student writes a correct equation to find the store's cost price of the shirt, such as $21 = 1.2c$, and uses it to arrive at a correct answer of $17.50. Student supports the answer by showing the correct steps taken to arrive at the answer and makes no errors in the calculations.

				steps necessary to arrive at the correct answer.	
4	**a** 7.RP.A.3 7.EE.B.3	Student states an incorrect answer and does not use each of the three equations to find the total amount of money in the savings account. OR Student does not attempt to answer the question.	Student uses each of the three equations to determine the amount of money in the savings account but makes multiple errors.	Student states the correct answers of $105 (Tiara) and $100.50 (Cameron and Justice) but does not show adequate supporting work. OR Student answers incorrectly due to a calculation error (with or without the use of a calculator) but shows correct work substituting 100 into each equation and performs the correct order of operations.	Student states the correct answers of $105 (Tiara) and $100.50 (Cameron and Justice). Student shows the correct math work by substituting 100 into each equation and performing the operations correctly.
	b 7.RP.A.3 7.EE.B.3	Student attempts to provide a written explanation but does not explain whether or not the equations will yield the same answer. OR Student does not attempt to answer the question.	Student incorrectly states that the equations will yield the same answer.	Student correctly states that the equations will not yield the same answer but does not provide an adequate explanation to support the claim.	Student correctly states that the equations will not yield the same answer. The explanation is sound and complete. For instance, *Cameron and Justice have the same answers because they correctly converted $\frac{1}{2}$% to a decimal and used the distributive property, whereas Tiara performed her conversion incorrectly by representing $\frac{1}{2}$% as 5%.*
5	**a** 7.RP.A.1 7.RP.A.2	Student provides incorrect answers for both the decimal and fractional representations of 125%. OR Student does not attempt to answer the question.	Student incorrectly states both the decimal and fractional representations of 125%, although the math work shown indicates some understanding of how to convert a percent to a decimal and fraction.	Student correctly states 125% as both a fraction and decimal but does not provide any math work to support the answers. OR Student correctly states 125% as either a fraction or decimal but not both.	Student correctly represents 125% as $\frac{5}{4}$, 1.25, or $\frac{125}{100}$. Student supports the answer by showing the correct steps taken to convert the percent to a decimal and fraction.

b 7.RP.A.3 7.EE.B.3 7.G.A.1	Student incorrectly states the dimensions of the greeting card and provides little or no sound mathematical work related to the task. OR Student does not attempt to answer the question.	Student correctly states only one dimension of the greeting card (either 8.75 *inches* or 6.25 *inches*) with or without relevant math work shown. OR Student does not state the correct dimensions of the greeting card, but the math work shown indicates some understanding of the process involved.	Student correctly states the dimensions of the greeting card to be 8.75 *inches* and 6.25 *inches* but does not provide adequate math work to support the answers. OR Student demonstrates a correct process to find the dimensions of the greeting card, but a calculation error is made (with or without the use of a calculator), which causes one or both answers to be stated incorrectly. OR Student correctly states only one dimension of the greeting card (either 8.75 inches or 6.25 inches); however, relevant math work is shown for *both* dimensions.	Student correctly states the dimensions of the greeting card to be 8.75 *inches* and 6.25 *inches*, or $8\frac{3}{4}$ inches by $6\frac{1}{4}$ inches, and provides adequate math work to support the answer.
c 7.RP.A.3 7.EE.B.3 7.G.A.1	Student does not correctly represent the scale factor as a percent, and the math work provided indicates little or no understanding of the task involved. OR Student does not attempt to answer the question.	Student does not correctly state the scale factor as a percent, but the math work provided indicates some understanding of finding the ratio of the corresponding side lengths. The ratios may or may not be stated correctly, and the work does not indicate a scale factor of 4.	Student correctly represents the scale factor as 400%, but the math work provided does not adequately support the answer. OR Student does not correctly state the scale factor as 400% but the math work provided demonstrates a correct process of finding the scale factor, and shows the scale factor to be 4.	Student correctly represents the scale factor as 400%, and the math work provided demonstrates a correct process of finding the scale factor and converting it to a percent.
d 7.RP.A.3 7.EE.B.3 7.G.A.1	Student attempts to answer the question by finding both areas but does not write an equation to show the relationship between them. (This may or may not include calculation errors.)	Student provides a written expression and, while it may be incomplete, shows some evidence of understanding the relationship that exists. For instance, student writes 16c but does not	Student correctly gives an equation in the form: $P = 16c$. The student shows a comparison of the areas of the postcard and poster, but the work contains a minor error and/or the claim is not fully supported with an	Student correctly gives an equation in the form: $P = 16c$, where P is the area of the poster, c is the area of the post card, and 16 is the scale factor. Student explanation provides adequate support for

		OR Student does not attempt to answer the question.	include an equal sign or explain the meaning of the expression.	explanation. **OR** Student makes an error in the equation, but the work and explanation provided correctly shows otherwise. For example, student gives an equation of $P = 1600c$.	the equation, such as finding the areas of the poster (560 sq. in.) and post card (35 sq. in.), and finding the ratio of those areas to be 16 to 1 or 1600%.
	e **7.RP.A.3**	Student attempts to answer the question but does not provide a scale factor in the form of a percent, and the scale factor provided is not equivalent to 80% or 125%. **OR** Student does not attempt to answer the question.	Student sets up the problem backwards to show an enlargement (as in the original problem) instead of a reduction. The math work provided represents the scale factor as $\frac{1.25}{1}$, and it may or may not be converted to a percent.	Student sets up the problem correctly (for instance, writes the scale factor as $\frac{1}{1.25}$) but incorrectly or never converts it to a percent (with or without the use of a calculator).	Student correctly states a scale factor of 80% and provides complete and correct supporting work to show that $\frac{1}{1.25} = 0.80 = 80\%$.
	f **7.RP.A.3** **7.EE.B.3** **7.G.A.1**	Student attempts to answer the question, but the explanation and/or math work is incorrect and incomplete and provides little or no evidence of understanding the error that occurred in Azra's answer. **OR** Student does not attempt to answer the question.	Student answer is vague and states that Azra's teacher did not give her full credit because the dimensions Azra stated are incorrect. However, some correct math work is shown, but it is not complete enough to arrive at the correct dimensions.	Student correctly explains that Azra's teacher did not give her full credit because the dimensions of the smaller image are $4\frac{1}{5}$ in. $\times$ 3 in. instead of $4\frac{1}{6}$ in. $\times$ 3 in. but does not support the claim with adequate math work. **OR** Student correctly states that Azra's teacher did not give her full credit because one of the dimensions of the smaller image is incorrect. Although the exact correct dimensions are never stated, the math work indicates the student computed them.	Student correctly explains that Azra's teacher did not give her full credit because the dimensions of the smaller image are $4\frac{1}{5}$ in. $\times$ 3 in. instead of $4\frac{1}{6}$ in. $\times$ 3 in. and supports the claim with math work showing that 60% of 7 is $4\frac{1}{5}$.
6	**7.RP.A.3**	Student states an incorrect final price and does not explain how to arrive at final price.	Student states an incorrect final price, but the explanation, although incomplete or	Student states a correct final price of $99, but the explanation provided does not fully support	Student states a correct final price of $99 and provides a complete and thorough explanation.

		OR Student does not attempt to answer the question.	only partially correct, indicates some understanding of markup or markdown and of the steps involved in solving the problem. **OR** Student states a correct final price of $99 but provides no supporting explanation of how to arrive at that price.	the answer. For instance, student explains the steps taken to find the 10% markup price but does not explain how to then take the 10% markdown to arrive at the final answer. **OR** Student states an incorrect answer due to a minor calculation error but provides a correct explanation that includes the correct steps to first find a 10% markup and then take a 10% markdown on that price.	For example, *First I multiplied* 100 *by* 1.10 *to find the price after the* 10% *markup. I arrived at* $110 *for the markup price. Then, I multiplied* 110 *by* 0.9 *to find the price after it was marked down by* 10%*. I arrived at* $99 *for the final price because* 110 (0.9) = 99.
7	**7.RP.A.3** **7.EE.B.3**	Student arrives at an incorrect percent increase in the water level and shows little or no relevant math work to support the answer. **OR** Student does not attempt to answer the question.	Student arrives at an incorrect percent increase in the water level, but the math work shown indicates a partial understanding of the necessary steps involved, although the math work is not entirely correct or complete.	Student correctly states a 33.3% *percent increase in the water level*, but the math work shown does not fully support the answer. **OR** Student states an incorrect answer (such as 33%) due to a minor calculation or rounding error but provides math work that shows the correct steps to find the percent increase in the water level.	Student correctly states a 33.3% *percent increase in the water level* and shows adequate supporting math work with no errors.
8	**7.RP.A.3**	Student arrives at an incorrect percent of acid in the combined mixtures and shows little or no relevant math work to support the answer. **OR** Student does not attempt to answer the question.	Student arrives at an incorrect percent of acid in the combined mixtures but shows some work that indicates a partial understanding of the steps involved, although there are multiple errors.	Student correctly states that the percent acid in the combined mixtures is 43.75%, or $43\frac{3}{4}$%, but the math work shown does not fully indicate how the student arrives at that answer. **OR** Student shows the correct math work that indicates the steps necessary to arrive at the correct answer, but a rounding or minor	Student correctly states that the percent acid in the combined mixtures is 43.75%, or $43\frac{3}{4}$%. Student work shows a thorough and correct understanding of the steps required to reach the answer, with no errors made through multiple steps.

Module 4:   Percent and Proportional Relationships

				calculation error is made resulting in an incorrect answer such as 43% or 44%. <u>OR</u> Student states an incorrect answer but is able to find the acid amounts for 3 and 5 gallons and shows the necessary work. However, a mistake is made when calculating the percent of acid in the 8-gallon solution.	
9	**a** **7.RP.A.3** **7.EE.B.3**	Student answer is not in the form of an equation, and the written work indicates little or no understanding of using an equation to represent the proportional relationship involving percent. <u>OR</u> Student does not attempt to answer the question.	Student attempts to write an equation, and although it is not an equation, the written work is relevant. For example, student only writes an expression such as $0.3n$. <u>OR</u> Student writes an equation involving n, but the equation does not show an adequate understanding of the proportional relationship that exists.	Student writes an equation involving n, of the form: $Part = Percent \times Whole$ (or an equivalent form), but when substituting the values into the equation, an error is made. For instance, the student mistakenly uses 95% instead of 30% in the equation and writes the relationship as $15 = 0.95n$ or some equivalent form.	Student writes a correct equation as $15 = 0.3n$ or in some equivalent form.
	b **7.RP.A.3** **7.EE.B.4**	Student has an incorrect answer and provides little or no evidence of understanding how to solve the equation. <u>OR</u> Student does not use the equation in part (a) to solve the problem. The answer provided may or may not be correct. <u>OR</u> Student does not attempt to answer the question.	Student provides an incorrect solution but attempts to solve the equation written in part (a), although there is a conceptual error in the solution process.	Student arrives at a correct answer of 50 *students* based on a correct equation written in part (a). However, student does not show adequate math work to indicate the process and steps taken to arrive at the answer. <u>OR</u> Student arrives at an incorrect solution using a correct equation from part (a), due to a minor calculation error. But student shows math work that indicates a sound understanding of the correct process and	Student arrives at a correct answer of 50 *students* using the correct equation from part (a). The math work provided indicates a sound understanding of the correct process and steps necessary to reach the correct answer, and calculations contain no errors.

Module 4:   Percent and Proportional Relationships

			steps necessary to reach the correct answer. <u>OR</u> Student arrives at a correct answer based on an incorrect equation written in part (a) and shows math work that indicates a sound understanding of the correct process and steps necessary to reach the correct answer.	
c **7.RP.A.3** **7.EE.B.3**	Student answers incorrectly and provides little or no evidence of understanding the steps involved in finding the number of boys who scored below 95%. <u>OR</u> Student does not attempt to answer the question.	Student arrives at an incorrect answer, but the math work shown provides some evidence of understanding the process involved. For instance, student shows how to find 60% of a quantity or 40% of a quantity (although it may not be the correct quantity) and/or how to arrive at the number of students who scored below a 95%, which is 35 *students*.	Student states the correct answer of 21 *boys*. However, student does not show adequate math work to indicate the process and steps taken to arrive at the answer. <u>OR</u> Student arrives at an incorrect answer due to a minor calculation error. However, the math work shown indicates a sound understanding of the correct process and steps necessary to reach the correct answer.	Student states the correct answer of 21 *boys*. The math work provided indicates a sound understanding of the correct process and steps necessary to reach the correct answer, and calculations contain no errors.

Name _____   Date _____

DAY ONE: CALCULATOR ACTIVE

You may use a calculator for this part of the assessment. Show your work to receive full credit.

1. Kara works at a fine jewelry store and earns commission on her total sales for the week. Her weekly paycheck was in the amount of $6,500, including her salary of $1,000. Her sales for the week totaled $45,000. Express her rate of commission as a percent. Round to the nearest whole number.

(Handwritten work:)

6500 − 1000 = 5500 in commission

r : commission rate

part = percent × whole

$$\frac{5500}{45000} = \frac{r(45000)}{45000}$$

$$\frac{5500}{45000} = r$$

.12 ≈ r

$.12 = \frac{12}{100} = 12\%$

(Long division:)

45000) 55000   .12
−45000
 100000
 −90000
 10000

The commission rate is 12%.

2. Kacey and her three friends went out for lunch, and they wanted to leave a 15% tip. The receipt shown lists the lunch total before tax and tip. The tip is on the cost of the food plus tax. The sales tax rate in Pleasantville is 8.75%.

   a. Use mental math to estimate the approximate total cost of the bill including tax and tip to the nearest dollar. Explain how you arrived at your answer.

(Handwritten answer:)

I think the bill will be about $50. I found my answer by rounding the total to $40. Then, I multiplied by .09, which is close to 8.75%. I got $3.60 in tax. I added that to $40 to get $43.60, which is close to $44.00. I know 10% of $44 is $4.40 and 5% would be $2.20. So the total plus a 15% tip is approximately $44 + $6.60 = $50.60.

(Receipt:)

```
SAM'S WORLD FAMOUS BURGER
       1522 OAK ROAD
    PLEASANTVILLE, USA

BBQ BURGER W/CHEESE        9.
CHICKEN FINGER BASKE       8.
MUSHROOM BURGER           10.
CHILI CHEESE FRIES         8.

            TOTAL: $38.

THANKS FOR YOUR BUSINESS.
    FOLLOW US ONLINE!

   WWW.CUSTOMRECEIPT.COM
```

b. Find the actual total of the bill including tax and tip. If Kacey and her three friends split the bill equally, how much will each person pay including tax and tip?

```
  38.96
x .0875
 3.409  sales tax
```

```
  38.96
+ 3.409
 42.369
    ↓
  $42.37  sales tax
        + total
```

```
  42.37
x  .15
 6.3555
    ↓
 $6.36 tip
```

```
     12.1825
4) 48.7300
  -4 6
  ...
```

```
  42.37
+ 6.36
 48.73  total plus tax
        and tip
```

$48.73

Three people will have to pay $12.18 and one person will have to pay $12.19.

3. Cool Tees is having a Back to School sale where all t-shirts are discounted by 15%. Joshua wants to buy five shirts: one costs $9.99, two cost $11.99 each, and two others cost $21.00 each.

a. What is the total cost of the shirts including the discount?

```
 11.99
x   2
 23.98
```

```
 21.00
x   2
 42.00
```

```
 23.98
 42.00
+ 9.99
 75.97
```

```
 75.97
x  .85
 64.57
```

```
 100%
- 15%
  85%
```

The total cost with the discount is $64.57.

b. By law, sales tax is calculated on the discounted price of the shirts. Would the total cost of the shirts including the 6.5% sales tax be greater if the tax was applied before a 15% discount is taken, rather than after a 15% discount is taken? Explain.

The total cost would be the same because of the commutative property of multiplication. Either way, the total cost including tax and discount is $68.77.

Tax applied after discount
Cost = Percent x Whole x Tax Rate
= (.85)(75.97)(1.065)
= 68.77

Tax applied before discount
Cost = Percent x Whole x Tax Rate
= (1.065)(75.97)(.85)
= 68.77

c. Joshua remembered he had a coupon in his pocket that would take an additional 30% off the price of the shirts. Calculate the new total cost of the shirts including the sales tax.

64.57
x .70
45.199
↓
$45.20 discount price
x .065
2.938
$2.94 sales tax

45.20
+ 2.94
$48.14

The new total cost of the shirts will be $48.14.

100% - 30% = 70%

d. If the price of each shirt is 120% of the store's cost price, write an equation and find the store's cost price for a $21 shirt.

1.2c = 21
$\frac{1.2c}{1.2} = \frac{21}{1.2}$
c = 17.5
The cost price is $17.50.

c is cost price
120% = 1.2

1.2)21.0
      17.5
12)210
   -12
     90
    -84
      60
     -60
       0

4. Tierra, Cameron, and Justice wrote equations to calculate the amount of money in a savings account after one year with $\frac{1}{2}$% interest paid annually on a balance of M dollars. Let T represent the total amount of money saved.

Tiara's Equation:	$T = 1.05M$
Cameron's Equation:	$T = M + 0.005M$
Justice's Equation:	$T = M(1 + 0.005)$

a. The three students decided to see if their equations would give the same answer by using a $100 balance. Find the total amount of money in the savings account using each student's equation. Show your work.

$$T = 1.05(100) = \$10\overline{5}$$
$$T = 100 + .005(100) = 100 + .5 = \$100.50$$
$$T = 100(1+.005) = 100(1.005) = \$100.50$$

b. Explain why their equations will or will not give the same answer.

Cameron's and Justice's equations give the same answers, but Tiara's does not. Tiara's equation is set up correctly, but she made a mistake when she changed ½% to a decimal. ½% = 0.5% = 0.005 Cameron and Justice both used the distributive property to solve their equations and the correct decimal of .005. This is why their answers are the same.

5. A printing company is enlarging the image on a postcard to make a greeting card. The enlargement of the postcard's rectangular image is done using a scale factor of 125%. Be sure to show all other related math work.

    a. Represent a scale factor of 125% as a fraction and decimal.

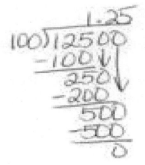

$$\frac{125\%}{100\%} = 1.25 \text{ decimal}$$

$$\frac{125 \div 25}{100 \div 25} = \frac{5}{4} \text{ fraction}$$

$$100\overline{)12500} \quad 1.25$$

    b. The postcard's dimensions are 7 inches by 5 inches. What are the dimensions of the greeting card?

$$\begin{array}{r} 1.25 \\ \times\ 7 \\ \hline 8.75 \end{array} \qquad \begin{array}{r} 1.25 \\ \times\ 5 \\ \hline 6.25 \end{array}$$

The dimensions of the greeting card are 8.75 inches by 6.25 inches.

    c. If the printing company makes a poster by enlarging the postcard image, and the poster's dimensions are 28 inches by 20 inches, represent the scale factor as a percent.

$$\frac{28 \div 4}{20 \div 4} = \frac{7}{5}$$

$$\frac{7}{5} = \frac{7}{5}$$

4 is the scale factor, which is 400%.

d. Write an equation, in terms of the scale factor, that shows the relationship between the areas of the postcard and poster. Explain your equation.

Area of Poster
$A = \ell w$
$= (28)(20)$
$= 560 \text{ in}^2$

Area of Post Card
$A = \ell w$
$= (7)(5)$
$= 35 \text{ in}^2$

$$
\begin{array}{r}
16 \\
35 \overline{)560} \\
-35 \\
\hline
210 \\
-210 \\
\hline
0
\end{array}
$$

The area of the poster is 16 times the area of the post card. The scale factor is 16 or 1600%. So my equation is P = 16c, where P is the area of the poster, 16 is the scale factor and c is the area of the post card.

e. Suppose the printing company wanted to start with the greeting card's image and reduce it to create the postcard's image. What scale factor would they use? Represent this scale factor as a percent.

PC → GC
scale factor: $\frac{5}{4}$

$\frac{8.75}{7} = \frac{6.25}{5}$

$1.25 = 1.25$

$\frac{5}{4}$

GC → PC
scale factor: $\frac{4}{5}$

$\frac{7}{8.75} = \frac{5}{6.25}$

$.8 = .8$

$\frac{4}{5} = 80\%$

$$
\begin{array}{r}
8 \\
5 \overline{)40} \\
-40 \\
\hline
0
\end{array}
$$

The scale factor is 80%

f. In math class, students had to create a scale drawing that was smaller than the postcard image.
    Azra used a scale factor of 60% to create the smaller image. She stated the dimensions of her
    smaller image as: $4\frac{1}{6}$ inches by 3 inches. Azra's math teacher did not give her full credit for her
    answer. Why? Explain Azra's error and write the answer correctly.

Azra did not receive full credit because she
made an error when changing her decimal
to a fraction. She wrote $4\frac{2}{10} = 4\frac{1}{6}$, but it
is $4\frac{2}{10} = 4\frac{1}{5}$ because 2 and 10 are divisible
by 2.

5in $\boxed{PC}$ $\xrightarrow{60\%}$ $\boxed{Azra}$ $\dfrac{7}{\times .6}{4.2}$ $\dfrac{5}{\times .6}{3.0}$ $60\% = .6$

7in

$$4.2 = 4\frac{2}{10} = 4\frac{1}{5}$$

The dimensions of her image are $4\frac{1}{5}$ inches
by 3 inches.

Name _____   Date _____

DAY TWO: CALCULATOR INACTIVE

You will now complete the remainder of the assessment without the use of a calculator.

6. A $100 MP3 player is marked up by 10% and then marked down by 10%. What is the final price? Explain your answer.

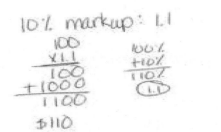

7. The water level in a swimming pool increased from 4.5 feet to 6 feet. What is the percent increase in the water level, rounded to the nearest tenth of a percent? Show your work.

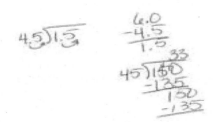

8. A 5-gallon mixture contains 40% acid. A 3-gallon mixture contains 50% acid. What percent acid is obtained by putting the two mixtures together? Show your work.

9. In Mr. Johnson's third and fourth period classes, 30% of the students scored a 95% or higher on a quiz. Let n be the total number of students in Mr. Johnson's classes. Answer the following questions, and show your work to support your answer.

   a. If 15 students scored a 95% or higher, write an equation involving n that relates the number of students who scored a 95% or higher to the total number of students in Mr. Johnson's third and fourth period classes.

   $$.3n = 15$$

   b. Solve your equation in part (a) to find how many students are in Mr. Johnson's third and fourth period classes.

   $$\frac{.3n}{.3} = \frac{15}{.3}$$

   $$\boxed{n = 50 \text{ students}}$$

   c. Of the students who scored below 95%, 40% of them are girls. How many boys scored below 95%?

   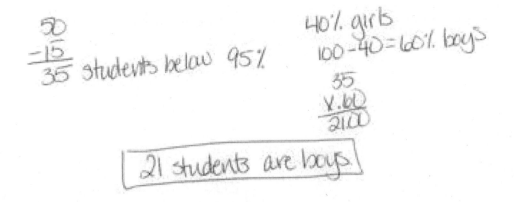

   $$\begin{array}{r} 50 \\ -15 \\ \hline 35 \end{array} \text{ students below } 95\%$$

   40% girls
   $100 - 40 = 60\%$ boys

   $$\begin{array}{r} 35 \\ \times .60 \\ \hline 2100 \end{array}$$

   $$\boxed{21 \text{ students are boys}}$$

Mathematics Curriculum

Student Material

Lesson 1: Percent

Classwork

Opening Exercise 1: Matching

Match the percents with the correct sentence clues.

25%	I am half of a half. 5 cubic inches of water filled in a 20 cubic inch bottle.
50%	I am less than $\frac{1}{100}$. 25 out of 5,000 contestants won a prize.
30%	The chance of birthing a boy or a girl. A flip of a coin.
1%	I am less than a half but more than one-fourth. 15 out of 50 play drums in a band.
10%	I am equal to 1. 35 question out of 35 questions were answered correctly.
100%	I am more than 1. Instead of the $1,200 expected to be raised, $3,600 was collected for the school's fundraiser.
300%	I am a tenth of a tenth. One penny out of one dollar.
$\frac{1}{2}$%	I am less than a fourth but more than a hundredth. $11 out of $110 earned is saved in the bank.

Opening Exercise 2

Color in the grids to represent the following fractions:

a. $\dfrac{30}{100}$ b. $\dfrac{3}{100}$ c. $\dfrac{\frac{1}{3}}{100}$

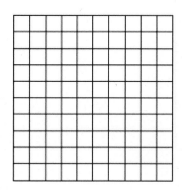   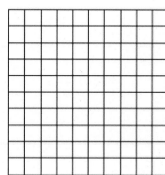   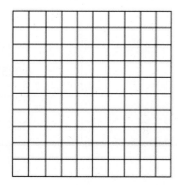

Example 1

Use the definition of the word "percent" to write each percent as a fraction and then a decimal.

Percent	Fraction	Decimal
37.5%		
100%		
110%		
1%		
$\dfrac{1}{2}\%$		

Example 2

Fill in the chart by converting between a fraction, decimal, and percent. Show your work in the space below.

Fraction	Decimal	Percent
		350%
	0.025	
$\frac{1}{8}$		

Exercise 1: Class Card Activity

Read your card to yourself (each student will have a different card) and work out the problem. When the exercise begins, listen carefully to the questions being read. When you have the card with the equivalent value, respond by reading your card aloud.

Examples:

0.22 should be read "twenty two-hundredths".

$\dfrac{\frac{1}{5}}{1000}$ should be read "one-fifth thousandths" or "one-fifth over one thousand".

$\dfrac{7}{300}$ should be read " seven-three hundredths" or "seven over three hundred".

$\dfrac{200}{100}$ should be read "two hundred-hundredths" or "two hundred over 100".

Lesson Summary

- *Percent* means "per hundred". P percent is the same as $\frac{P}{100}$. Write % as short for percent.
- Usually there are three ways to write a number: a percent, a fraction, and a decimal. Fractions and decimals are related to the ratio of percent over 100.

Problem Set

1. Use a visual model to represent the following percents:
    a. 90%
    b. 0.9%
    c. 900%
    d. $\frac{9}{10}$%

2. Benjamin believes that $\frac{1}{2}$% is equivalent to 50%. Is he correct? Why or why not?

3. Order the following from least to greatest:

    $100\%, \dfrac{1}{100}, 0.001\%, \dfrac{1}{10}, 0.001, 1.1, 10, \dfrac{10{,}000}{100}$

4. Fill in the chart by converting between a fraction, decimal, and percent. Show work in the space below.

Fraction	Decimal	Percent
		100%
	0.0825	
	6.25	
		$\frac{1}{8}$%
$\frac{2}{300}$		
		33.3%
$\frac{3\frac{}{4}}{100}$		
		250%
	0.005	
$\frac{150}{100}$		
$\frac{5\frac{1}{2}}{100}$	0.055	$5\frac{1}{2}$%

Lesson 2: Part of a Whole as a Percent

Classwork

Opening Exercise

a. What is the whole unit in each scenario?

Scenario	Whole Unit
15 is what percent of 90?	
What number is 10% of 56?	
90% of a number is 180.	
A bag of candy contains 300 pieces and 25% of the pieces in the bag are red.	
Seventy percent (70%) of the students earned a B on the test.	
The 20 girls in the class represented 55% of the students in the class.	

b. Read each problem and complete the table to record what you know.

Problem	Part	Percent	Whole
40% of the students on the field trip love the museum. If there are 20 students on the field trip, how many love the museum?			
40% of the students on the field trip love the museum. If 20 students love the museum, how many are on the field trip?			
20 students on the field trip love the museum. If there are 40 students on the field trip, what percent love the museum?			

Example 1: Visual Approaches to Finding a Part, Given a Percent of the Whole

In Ty's math class, 20% of students earned an A on a test. If there were 30 students in the class, how many got an A?

Exercise 1

In Ty's art class, 12% of the Flag Day art projects received a perfect score. There were 25 art projects turned in by Ty's class. How many of the art projects earned a perfect score? (Identify the whole.)

Example 2: A Numeric Approach to Finding a Part, Given a Percent of the Whole

In Ty's English class, 70% of the students completed an essay by the due date. There are 30 students in Ty's English class. How many completed the essay by the due date?

Example 3: An Algebraic Approach to Finding a Part, Given a Percent of the Whole

A bag of candy contains 300 pieces of which 28% are red. How many pieces are red?

Which quantity represents the whole?

Which of the terms in the percent equation is unknown? Define a letter (variable) to represent the unknown quantity.

Write an expression using the percent and the whole to represent the number of pieces of red candy.

Write and solve an equation to find the unknown quantity.

Exercise 2

A bag of candy contains 300 pieces of which 28% are red. How many pieces are *NOT* red?

    a.   Write an equation to represent the number of pieces that are not red, n.

    b.   Use your equation to find the number of pieces of candy that are not red.

    c.   Jah-Lil told his math teacher that he could use the answer from part (b) and mental math to find the number of pieces of candy that are not red. Explain what Jah-Lil meant by that.

Example 4: Comparing Part of a Whole to the Whole with the Percent Formula

Zoey inflated 24 balloons for decorations at the middle school dance. If Zoey inflated 15% of the balloons that are inflated for the dance, how many balloons are there in total? Solve the problem using the percent formula, and verify your answer using a visual model.

Example 5: Finding the Whole given a Part of the Whole and the Corresponding Percent

Haley is making admission tickets to the middle school dance. So far she has made 112 tickets, and her plan is to make 320 tickets. What percent of the admission tickets has Haley produced so far? Solve the problem using the percent formula, and verify your answer using a visual model.

Lesson Summary

- Visual models or numeric methods can be used to solve percent problems.
- Equations can be used to solve percent problems using the basic equation:

$$Part = Percent \times Whole.$$

Problem Set

1. Represent each situation using an equation. Check your answer with a visual model or numeric method.
   a. What number is 40% of 90?
   b. What number is 45% of 90?
   c. 27 is 30% of what number?
   d. 18 is 30% of what number?
   e. 25.5 is what percent of 85?
   f. 21 is what percent of 60?

2. Forty percent of the students on a field trip love the museum. If there are 20 students on the field trip, how many love the museum?

3. Maya spent 40% of her savings to pay for a bicycle that cost her $85.
   a. How much money was in her savings to begin with?
   b. How much money does she have left in her savings after buying the bicycle?

4. Curtis threw 15 darts at a dart board. 40% of his darts hit the bull's-eye. How many darts did not hit the bull's-eye?

5. A tool set is on sale for $424.15. The original price of the tool set was $499. What percent of the original price is the sale price?

6. Matthew's total points scored in basketball this season were 168 points. He scored 147 of those points in the regular season and the rest were scored in his only playoff game. What percent of his total points did he score in the playoff game?

7. Brad put 10 crickets in his pet lizard's cage. After one day, Brad's lizard had eaten 20% of the crickets he had put in the cage. By the end of the next day, the lizard had eaten 25% of the remaining crickets. How many crickets were left in the cage at the end of the second day?

---

8. A furnace used 40% of the fuel in its tank in the month of March, then used 25% of the remaining fuel in the month of April. At the beginning of March, there were 240 gallons of fuel in the tank. How much fuel (in gallons) was left at the end of April?

9. In Lewis County, there were 2,277 student athletes competing in spring sports in 2014. That was 110% of the number from 2013, which was 90% of the number from the year before. How many student athletes signed up for a spring sport in 2012?

10. Write a real world word problem that could be modeled by the equation below. Identify the elements of the percent equation and where they appear in your word problem, and then solve the problem.

$57.5 = p(250)$

Lesson 3: Comparing Quantities with Percent

Classwork

Opening Exercise

If each 10×10 unit square represents one whole, then what percent is represented by the shaded region?

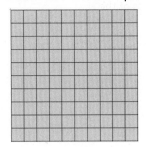 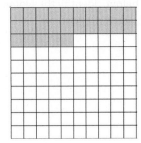

In the model above, 25% represents a quantity of 10 students. How many students does the shaded region represent?

Example 1

a.   The members of a club are making friendship bracelets to sell to raise money. Anna and Emily made 54 bracelets over the weekend. They need to produce 300 bracelets by the end of the week. What percent of the bracelets were they able to produce over the weekend?

b.   Anna produced 32 bracelets of the 54 bracelets produced by Emily and Anna over the weekend. Compare the number of bracelets that Emily produced as a percent of those that Anna produced.

c.   Compare the number of bracelets that Anna produced as a percent of those that Emily produced

Exercises 1–4

1.   There are 750 students in the 7th grade class and 625 students in the 8th grade class at Kent Middle School.

    a.   What percent is the 7th grade class of the 8th grade class at Kent Middle School?

    b.   The principal will have to increase the number of 8th grade teachers next year if the 7th grade enrollment exceeds 110% of the current 8th grade enrollment. Will she need to increase the number of teachers? Explain your reasoning.

2. At Kent Middle School, there are 104 students in the band and 80 students in the choir. What percent of the number of students in the choir is the number of students in the band?

3. At Kent Middle School, breakfast costs $1.25 and lunch costs $3.75. What percent of the cost of lunch is the cost of breakfast

4. Describe a real world situation that could be modeled using the equation: $398.4 = 0.83(x)$. Describe how the elements of the equation correspond with the real world quantities in your problem. Then solve your problem.

Lesson Summary

- Visual models or arithmetic methods can be used to solve problems that compare quantities with percents.

- Equations can be used to solve percent problems using the basic equation:
  $Quantity = Percent \times Whole$.

- "Quantity" in the new percent formula is the equivalent of "part" in the original percent formula.

Problem Set

1. Solve each problem using an equation.

   a. 49.5 is what percent of 33?

   b. 72 is what percent of 180?

   c. What percent of 80 is 90?

2. This year, Benny is 12 years old, and his mom is 48 years old.

   a. What percent of his mom's age is Benny's age?

   b. What percent of Benny's age is his mom's age?

   c. In two years, what percent of his age will Benny's mom's age be at that time?

   d. In 10 years, what percent will Benny's mom's age be of his age?

   e. In how many years will Benny be 50% of his mom's age?

   f. As Benny and his mom get older, Benny thinks they are getting closer in age. Do you agree or disagree? Explain your reasoning.

3. This year, Benny is 12 years old. His brother Lenny's age is 175% of Benny's age. How old is Lenny?

4. When Benny's sister Penny is 24, Benny's age will be 125% of her age.

   a. How old will Benny be then?

   b. If Benny is 12 years old now, how old is Penny now? Explain your reasoning.

5. Benny's age is currently 200% of his sister Jenny's age. What percent of Benny's age will Jenny's age be in 4 years?

6. At an animal shelter there are 15 dogs, 12 cats, 3 snakes, and 5 parakeets.

   a. What percent of the number of cats is the number of dogs?

   b. What percent of the number of cats is the number of snakes?

   c. What percent less parakeets are there than dogs?

   d. Which animal has 80% of the number of another animal?

   e. Which animal makes up approximately 14% of the animals in the shelter?

Lesson 3:   Comparing Quantities with Percent

7. Is 2 hours and 30 minutes more or less than 10% of a day? Explain your answer.

8. A club's membership increased from 25 to 30 members.
    a. Express the new membership as a percent of the old membership.
    b. Express the old membership as a percent of the new membership.

9. The number of boys in a school is 120% the number of girls at the school.
    a. Find the number of boys if there are 320 girls.
    b. Find the number of girls if there are 360 boys.

10. The price of a bicycle was increased from $300 to $450.
    a. What percent of the original price is the increased price?
    b. What percent of the increased price is the original price?

11. The population of Appleton is 175% of the population of Cherryton.
    a. Find the population in Appleton if the population in Cherryton is 4,000 people.
    b. Find the population in Cherryton if the population in Appleton is 10,500 people.

12. A statistics class collected data regarding the number of boys and the number of girls in each classroom at their school during homeroom. Some of their results are shown in the table below:
    a. Complete the blank cells of the table using your knowledge about percent.

Number of Boys (x)	Number of Girls (y)	Number of Girls as a Percent of the Number of Boys
10	5	
	1	25%
18	12	
5	10	
4		50%
20		90%
	10	250%
	6	60%
11		200%
	5	$33\frac{1}{3}\%$
15		20%
	15	75%
6	18	

25	10	
10		110%
	2	10%
16		75%
	7	50%
3		200%
12	10	

b. Using a coordinate plane and grid paper, locate and label the points representing the ordered pairs (x, y).

c. Locate all points on the graph that would represent classrooms in which the number of girls y is 100% of the number of boys x. Describe the pattern that these points make.

d. Which points represent the classrooms in which the number of girls is greater than 100% of the number of boys? Which points represent the classrooms in which the number of girls is less than 100% of the number of boys? Describe the locations of the points in relation to the points in part (c).

e. Find three ordered pairs from your table representing classrooms where the number of girls is the same percent of the number of boys. Do these points represent a proportional relationship? Explain your reasoning?

f. Show the relationship(s) from part (e) on the graph, and label them with the corresponding equation(s).

g. What is the constant of proportionality in your equation(s), and what does it tell us about the number of girls and the number of boys at each point on the graph that represents it? What does the constant of proportionality represent in the table in part (a)?

Lesson 4: Percent Increase and Decrease

Classwork

Opening Exercise

Cassandra likes jewelry. She has five rings in her jewelry box.

    a.   In the box below, sketch Cassandra's five rings.

    b.   Draw a double number line diagram relating the number of rings as a percent of the whole set of rings.

    c.   What percent is represented by the whole collection of rings? What percent of the collection does each ring represent?

Example 1: Finding a Percent Increase

Cassandra's aunt said she will buy Cassandra another ring for her birthday. If Cassandra gets the ring for her birthday, what will be the percent increase in her ring collection?

Exercise 1

a. Jon increased his trading card collection by 5 cards. He originally had 15 cards. What is the percent increase? Use the equation: $Quantity = Percent \; x \; Whole$ to arrive at your answer, and then justify your answer using a numeric or visual model.

b. Suppose instead of increasing the collection by 5 cards, John increased his 15-card collection by just 1 card. Will the percent increase be the same as when Cassandra's ring collection increased by 1 ring (in Example 1)? Why or why not? Explain.

c. Based on your answer to part (b) how is displaying change as a percent useful?

Discussion

"I will only pay 90% of my bill."	"10% of my bill will be subtracted from the original total."

Example 2: Percent Decrease

Ken said that he is going to reduce the number of calories that he eats during the day. Ken's trainer asked him to start off small and reduce the number of calories by no more than 7% . Ken estimated and consumed 2,200 calories per day instead of his normal 2,500 calories per day until his next visit with the trainer. Did Ken reduce his calorie intake by 7%? Justify your answer.

Exercise 2

Skylar is answering the following math problem:

"The value of an investment decreased by 10%. The original amount of the investment was $75. What is the current value of the investment?"

a. Skylar said 10% of $75 is $7.50, and since the investment decreased by that amount, you have to subtract $7.50 from $75 to arrive at the final answer of $67.50. Create one algebraic equation that can be used to arrive at the final answer of $67.50. Solve the equation to prove it results in an answer of $67.50. Be prepared to explain your thought process to the class.

b. Skylar wanted to show the proportional relationship between the dollar value of the original investment, x, and its value after a 10% decrease, y. He creates the table of values shown. Does it model the relationship? Explain. Then provide a correct equation for the relationship Skylar wants to model.

x	y
75	7.5
100	10
200	20
300	30
400	40

Lesson 4:   Percent Increase and Decrease

Example 3: Finding a Percent Increase or Decrease

Justin earned 8 badges in Scouts as of the Scout Master's last report. Justin wants to complete 2 more badges so that he will have a total of 10 badges earned before the Scout Master's next report.

   a.   If Justin completes the additional 2 badges, what will be the percent increase in badges?

   b.   Express the 10 badges as a percent of the 8 badges.

   c.   Does 100% plus your answer in part (a) equal your answer in part (b)? Why or why not?

Example 4: Finding the Original Amount Given a Percent Increase or Decrease

The population of cats in a rural neighborhood has declined in the past year by roughly 30%. Residents hypothesize that this is due to wild coyotes preying on the cats. The current cat population in the neighborhood is estimated to be 12. Approximately how many cats were there originally?

Example 5: Finding the Original Amount Given a Percent Increase or Decrease

Lu's math level on her achievement test in 7th grade was a level 650. Her math teacher told her that her test level went up by 25% from her 6th-grade test score level. What was Lu's test score level in 6th grade?

Closing

Phrase	Whole Unit (100%)
"Mary has 20% more money than John."	
"Anne has 15% less money than John."	
"What percent more (money) does Anne have than Bill?"	
"What percent less (money) does Bill have than Anne?	

Problem Set

1. A store advertises 15% off an item that regularly sells for $300.

   a. What is the sale price of the item?

   b. How is a 15% discount similar to a 15% decrease? Explain.

   c. If 8% sales tax is charged on the sale price, what is the total with tax?

   d. How is 8% sales tax like an 8% increase? Explain.

2. An item that was selling for $72 is reduced to $60. Find the percent decrease in price. Round your answer to the nearest tenth.

3. A baseball team had 80 players show up for tryouts last year and this year had 96 players show up for tryouts. Find the percent increase in players from last year to this year.

4. At a student council meeting, there were a total of 60 students present. Of those students, 35 were female.

   a. By what percent is the number of females greater than the number of males?

   b. By what percent is the number of males less than the number of females?

   c. Why are the percent increase and percent decrease in parts (a) and (b) different?

5. Once each day, Darlene writes in her personal diary and records whether the sun is shining or not. When she looked back though her diary she found that over a period of 600 days, the sun was shining 60% of the time. She kept recording for another 200 days and then found that the total number of sunny days dropped to 50%. How many of the final 200 days were sunny days?

6. Henry is considering purchasing a mountain bike. He likes two bikes: One costs $500 and the other costs $600. He tells his dad that the bike that is more expensive is 20% more than the cost of the other bike. Is he correct? Justify your answer.

7. State two numbers such that the lesser number is 25% less than the greater number.

8. State two numbers such that the greater number is 75% more than the lesser number.

9. Explain the difference in your thought process for Problems 7 and 8. Can you use the same numbers for each problem? Why or Why not?

| **Lesson 4:** | Percent Increase and Decrease |

10. In each of the following expressions, c represents the original cost of an item.

    i. $0.90c$

    ii. $0.10c$

    iii. $c - 0.10c$

  a. Circle the expression(s) that represents 10% of the original cost. If more than one answer is correct, explain why the expressions you chose are equivalent.

  b. Put a box around the expression(s) that represents the final cost of the item after a 10% decrease. If more than one is correct, explain why the expressions you chose are equivalent.

  c. Create a word problem involving a percent decrease, so that the answer can be represented by expression ii).

  d. Create a word problem involving a percent decrease, so that the answer can be represented by expression i).

  e. Tyler wants to know if it matters if he represents a situation involving a 25% decrease as $0.25x$ or $(1 - 0.25)x$. In the space below, write an explanation that would help Tyler understand how the context of a word problem often determines how to represent the situation.

Lesson 5: Find One Hundred Percent Given Another Percent

Classwork

Opening Exercise

What are the whole number factors of 100? What are the multiples of those factors? How many multiples are there of each factor (up to 100)?

Factors of 100	Multiples of the Factors of 100	Number of Multiples
100	100	1
50	50, 100	2
1	1, 2, 3, 4, 5, 6, … , 98, 99, 100	100

Example 1: Using a Modified Double Number Line with Percent

The 42 students who play wind instruments represent 75% of the students who are in band. How many students are in band?

Exercises 1–3

1. Bob's Tire Outlet sold a record number of tires last month. One salesman sold 165 tires, which was 60% of the tires sold in the month. What was the record number of tires sold?

2. Nick currently has 7,200 points in his fantasy baseball league, which is 20% more points than Adam. How many points does Adam have?

3. Kurt has driven 276 miles of his road trip but has 70% of the trip left to go. How many more miles does Kurt have to drive to get to his destination?

Example 2: Mental Math Using Factors of 100

Answer each part below using only mental math and describe your method.

    a.   If 39 is 1% of a number, what is that number? How did you find your answer?

    b.   If 39 is 10% of a number, what is that number? How did you find your answer?

    c.   If 39 is 5% of a number, what is that number? How did you find your answer?

    d.   If 39 is 15% of a number, what is that number? How did you find your answer?

    e.   If 39 is 25% of a number, what is that number? How did you find your answer?

Exercises 4–5

4. Derrick had a 0.250 batting average at the end of his last baseball season which means that he got a hit 25% of the times he was up to bat. If Derrick had 47 hits last season, how many times did he bat?

5. Nelson used 35% of his savings account for his class trip in May. If he used $140 from his savings account while on his class trip, how much money was in his savings account before the trip?

Problem Set

Use a double number line to answer Problems 1–5.

1. Tanner collected 360 cans and bottles while fundraising for his baseball team. This was 40% of what Reggie collected. How many cans and bottles did Reggie collect?

2. Emilio paid $287.50 in taxes to the school district that he lives in this year. This year's taxes were a 15% increase from last year. What did Emilio pay in school taxes last year?

3. A snowmobile manufacturer claims that its newest model is 15% lighter than last year's model. If this year's model weighs 799 lb., how much did last year's model weigh?

4. Student enrollment at a local school is concerning the community because the number of students has dropped to 504, which is a 20% decrease from the previous year. What was the student enrollment the previous year?

5. A color of paint used to paint a race car includes a mixture of yellow and green paint. Scotty wants to lighten the color by increasing the amount of yellow paint 30%. If a new mixture contains 3.9 liters of yellow paint, how many liters of yellow paint did he use in the previous mixture?

Use factors of 100 and mental math to answer Problems 6–10. Describe the method you used.

6. Alexis and Tasha challenged each other to a typing test. Alexis typed 54 words in 1-minute, which was 120% of what Tasha typed. How many words did Tasha type in 1-minute?

7. Yoshi is 5% taller today than she was one year ago. Her current height is 168 cm. How tall was she one year ago?

8. Toya can run one lap of the track in 1 min 3 sec., which is 90% of her younger sister Niki's time. What is Niki's time for one lap of the track?

9. An animal shelter houses only cats and dogs, and there are 25% more cats than dogs. If there are 40 cats, how many dogs are there, and how many animals are there total?

10. Angie scored 91 points on a test but only received a 65% grade on the test. How many points were possible on the test?

For Problems 11–17, find the answer using any appropriate method.

11. Robbie owns 15% more movies than Rebecca, and Rebecca owns 10% more movies than Joshua. If Rebecca owns 220 movies, how many movies do Robbie and Joshua each have?

12. 20% of the seventh grade students have math class in the morning. $16\frac{2}{3}\%$ of those students also have science class in the morning. If 30 seventh grade students have math class in the morning but not science class, find how many seventh grade students there are.

13. The school bookstore ordered three-ring notebooks. They put 75% of the order in the warehouse and sold 80% of the rest in the first week of school. There are 25 notebooks left in the store to sell. How many three-ring notebooks did they originally order?

14. In the first game of the year, the modified basketball team made 62.5% of their foul shot free throws. Matthew made all 6 of his free throws, which made up for 25% of the team's free throws. How many free throws did the team miss altogether?

15. Aiden's mom calculated that in the previous month, their family had used 40% of their monthly income for gasoline, and 63% of that gasoline was consumed by the family's SUV. If the family's SUV used $261.45 worth of gasoline last month, how much money was left after gasoline expenses?

16. Rectangle A is a scale drawing of Rectangle B and has 25% of its area. If Rectangle A has side lengths of 4 cm. and 5 cm., what are the side lengths of Rectangle B?

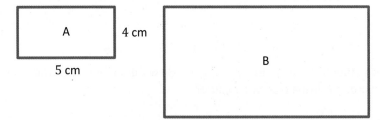

17. Ted is a supervisor and spends 20% of his typical work day in meetings and 20% of that meeting time in his daily team meeting. If he starts each day at 7: 30 a.m., and his daily team meeting is from 8: 00 a.m. to 8: 20 a.m., when does Ted's typical work day end?

Lesson 6: Fluency with Percents

Classwork

Opening Exercise

Solve the following problem using mental math only. Be prepared to discuss your method with your classmates.

Cory and Everett have collected model cars since the third grade. Cory has 80 model cars in his collection, which is 25% more than what Everett has. How many model cars does Everett have?

Example 1: Mental Math and Percents

   a.   75% of the students In Jesse's class are 60 inches or taller. If there are 20 students in her class, how many students are 60 inches or taller?

   b.   Bobbie wants to leave a tip for her waitress equal to 15% of her bill. Bobbie's bill for her lunch was $18. How much money represents 15% of the bill?

Exercises 1–6

1. Express 9 hours as a percentage of 3 days.

2. Richard works from $11\!:\!00$ a.m. to $3\!:\!00$ a.m. His dinner break is 75% of the way through his work shift. What time is Richard's dinner break?

3. At a playoff basketball game, there were 370 fans cheering for school A and 555 fans cheering for school B.

   a. Express the number of fans for school A as a percent of the number of fans for school B.

   b. Express the number of fans for school B as a percent of the number of fans for school A.

   c. What percent more fans were there for school B than for school A?

4. Rectangle A has a length of 8 cm. and a width of 16 cm. Rectangle B has the same area as the first, but its width is 62.5% of the length of the first rectangle. Express the width of Rectangle B as a percent of the area of Rectangle A. What percent more or less is the width Rectangle B than the width of Rectangle A?

5. A plant in Mikayla's garden was 40 inches tall one day and was 4 feet tall one week later. By what percent did the plant's height increase over one week?

6. Loren must obtain a minimum number of signatures on a petition before it can be submitted. She was able to obtain 672 signatures, which is 40% more than she needs. How many signatures does she need?

Problem Set

1. Micah has 294 songs stored in his phone which is 70% of the songs that Jorge has stored in his phone. How many songs are stored on Jorge's phone?

2. Lisa sold 81 magazine subscriptions, which was 27% of her class' fundraising goal. How many magazine subscriptions does her class hope to sell?

3. Theresa and Isaiah are comparing the number of pages that they read for pleasure over the summer. Theresa read 2210 pages, which was 85% of the number of pages that Isaiah read. How many pages did Isaiah read?

4. In a parking garage, the number of SUVs is 40% greater than the number of non-SUVs. Gina counted 98 SUVs in the parking garage. How many automobiles were parked in the garage?

5. The price of a tent was decreased by 15% and sold for $76.49. What was the original price of the tent in dollars?

6. 40% of the students at Rockledge Middle School are musicians. 75% of those musicians have to read sheet music when they play their instruments. If 38 of the students can play their instruments without reading sheet music, how many students are there at Rockledge Middle School?

7. At Longbridge Middle School, 240 students said that they are an only child, which is 48% of the school's student enrollment. How many students attend Longbridge Middle School?

8. Grace and her father spent $4\frac{1}{2}$ hours over the weekend restoring their fishing boat. This time makes up 6% of the time needed to fully restore the boat. How much total time is needed to fully restore the boat?

9. Bethany's mother was upset with her because Bethany's text messages from the previous month were 218% of the amount allowed at no extra cost under her phone plan. Her mother had to pay for each text message over the allowance. Bethany had 5,450 text messages last month. How many text messages is she allowed under her phone plan at no extra cost?

10. Harry used 84% of the money in his savings account to buy a used dirt bike that cost him $1,050. How much money is left in Harry's savings account?

11. 15% of the students in Mr. Riley's social studies classes watch the local news every night. Mr. Riley found that 136 of his students do not watch the local news. How many students are in Mr. Riley's social studies classes?

12. Grandma Bailey and her children represent about 9.1% of the Bailey family. If Grandma Bailey has 12 children, how many members are there in the Bailey family?

13. Shelley earned 20% more money waitressing this week than last week. This week she earned $72 waitressing. How much money did she earn last week?

14. Lucy's savings account has 35% more money than her sister Edy's. Together the girls have saved a total of $206.80. How much money has each girl saved?

15. Bella spent 15% of her paycheck at the mall, and 40% of that was spent at the movie theatre. Bella spent a total of $13.74 at the movie theater for her movie ticket, popcorn, and a soft drink. How much money was in Bella's paycheck?

16. On a road trip, Sara's brother drove 47.5% of the trip and Sara drove 80% of the remainder. If Sara drove for4 hours and 12 minutes, how long was the road trip?

Lesson 7: Markup and Markdown Problems

Example 1: A Video Game Markup

Games Galore Super Store buys the latest video game at a wholesale price of $30.00. The markup rate at Game's Galore Super Store is 40%. You use your allowance to purchase the game at the store. How much will you pay, not including tax?

    a.   Write an equation to find the price of the game at Games Galore Super Store. Explain your equation.

    b.   Solve the equation from part (a).

    c.   What was the total markup of the video game? Explain.

    d.   You and a friend are discussing markup rate. He says that an easier way to find the total markup is by multiplying the wholesale price of $30 by 40%. Do you agree with him? Why or why not?

Example 2: Black Friday

A $300 mountain bike is discounted by 30%, and then discounted an additional 10% for shoppers who arrive before 5:00 a.m.

a. Find the sales price of the bicycle.

b. In all, by how much has the bicycle been discounted in dollars? Explain.

c. After both discounts were taken, what was the total percent discount?

d. Instead of purchasing the bike for $300, how much would you save if you bought it before 5:00 a.m.?

Exercises 1–3

1. Sasha went shopping and decided to purchase a set of bracelets for 25% off of the regular price. If Sasha buys the bracelets today, she will receive an additional 5%. Find the sales price of the set of bracelets with both discounts. How much money will Sasha save if she buys the bracelets today?

$44.00

2. A golf store purchases a set of clubs at a wholesale price of $250. Mr. Edmond learned that the clubs were marked up 200%. Is it possible to have a percent increase greater than 100%? What is the retail price of the clubs?

3. Is a percent increase of a set of golf clubs from $250 to $750 the same as a markup rate of 200%? Explain.

Example 3: Working Backwards

A car that normally sells for $20,000 is on sale for $16,000. The sales tax is 7.5%.

    a.   What percent of the original price of the car is the final price?

    b.   Find the discount rate.

    c.   By law, sales tax has to be applied to the discount price. Would it be better for the consumer if the 7.5% sales tax were calculated before the 20% discount was applied? Why or why not?

    d.   Write an equation applying the commutative property to support your answer to part (c).

Exercise 4

a. Write an equation to determine the selling price, p, on an item that is originally priced s dollars after a markup of 25%.

b. Create a table (and label it) showing five possible pairs of solutions to the equation.

c. Create a graph (and label it) of the equation.

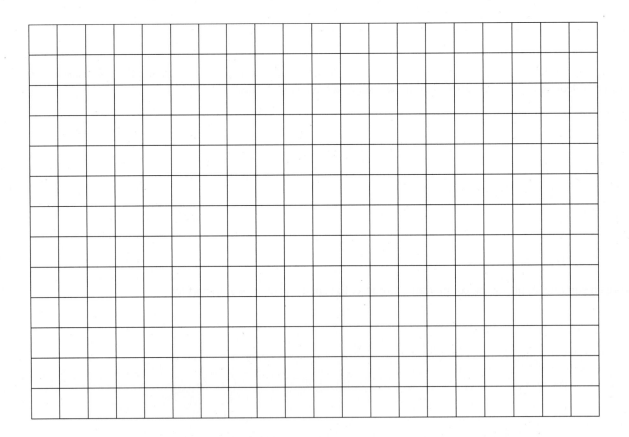

d.   Interpret the points $(0,0)$ and $(1,r)$.

Exercise 5

Use the following table to calculate the markup or markdown rate. Show your work. Is the relationship between the original price and selling price proportional or not? Explain.

Original Price, m (in dollars)	Selling Price, p (in dollars)
$1,750	$1,400
$1,500	$1,200
$1,250	$1,000
$1,000	$800
750	600

Problem Set

1. You have a coupon for an additional 25% off the price of any sale item at a store. The store has put a robotics kit on sale for 15% off the original price of $40. What is the price of the robotics kit after both discounts?

2. A sign says that the price marked on all music equipment is 30% off the original price. You buy an electric guitar for the sale price of $315.
   a. What is the original price?
   b. How much money did you save off the original price of the guitar?
   c. What percent of the original price is the sale price?

3. The cost of a New York Yankees baseball cap is $24.00. The local sporting goods store sells it for $30.00. Find the markup rate.

4. Write an equation to determine the selling price, p, on an item that is originally priced s dollars after a markdown of 15%.
   a. Create a table (and label it) showing five possible pairs of solutions to the equation.
   b. Create a graph (and label it) of the equation.

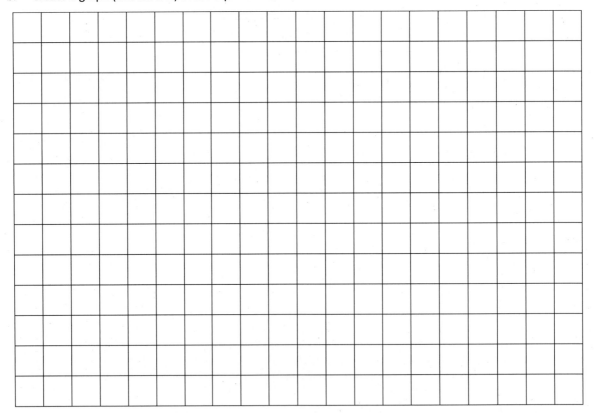

   c. Interpret the points $(0,0)$ and $(1, r)$.

5. At the amusement park, Laura paid $6.00 for a small cotton candy. Her older brother works at the park, and he told her they mark up the cotton candy by 300%. Laura does not think that is mathematically possible. Is it possible, and if so, what is the price of the cotton candy before the markup?

6. A store advertises that customers can take 25% off the original price and then take an extra 10% off. Is this 35% off? Explain.

7. An item that costs $50 is marked 20% off. Sales tax for the item is 8%. What is the final price, including tax?
    a. Solve the problem with the discount applied before the sales tax.
    b. Solve the problem with discount applied after the sales tax.
    c. Compare your answers in parts (a) and (b). Explain.

8. The sale price for a bicycle is $315 dollars. The original price was first discounted by 50% and then discounted an additional 10%. Find the original price of the bicycle.

9. A ski shop has a markup rate of 50%. Find the selling price of skis that cost the storeowner $300.

10. A tennis supply store pays a wholesaler $90 for a tennis racquet and sells it for $144. What is the markup rate?

11. A shoe store is selling a pair of shoes for $60 that has been discounted by 25%. What was the original selling price?

12. A shoe store has a markup rate of 75% and is selling a pair of shoes for $133. Find the price the store paid for the shoes.

13. Write $5\frac{1}{4}\%$ as a simple fraction.

14. Write $\frac{3}{8}$ as a percent.

15. If 20% of the 70 faculty members at John F. Kennedy Middle School are male, what is the number of male faculty members?

16. If a bag contains 400 coins, and $33\frac{1}{2}\%$ are nickels, how many nickels are there? What percent of the coins are not nickels?

Lesson 8: Percent Error Problems

Classwork

Example 1: How Far Off

Find the absolute error for the following problems. Explain what the absolute error means in context.

    a.   Taylor's Measurement 1

    b.   Connor's Measurement 1

    c.   Jordan's Measurement 2

Example 2: How Right is Wrong?

    a.   Find the percent error for Taylor's Measurement 1. What does this mean?

b. From Example 1, part (b), find the percent error for Connor's Measurement 1. What does this mean?

c. From Example 1, part (c), find the percent error for Jordan's Measurement 2. What does it mean?

d. What is the purpose of finding percent error?

Exercises 1–3

Calculate the percent error for Problems 1–3. Leave your final answer in fraction form, if necessary.

1. A realtor expected 18 people to show up for an open house, but 25 attended.

2. In science class, Mrs. Moore's students were directed to weigh a 300 gram mass on the balance scale. Tina weighed the object and reported 328 grams.

3. Darwin's coach recorded that he had bowled 250 points out of 300 in a bowling tournament. However, the official scoreboard showed that Darwin actually bowled 225 points out of 300.

Example 3: Estimating Percent Error

The attendance at a musical event was counted several times. All counts were between 573 and 589. If the actual attendance number is between 573 and 589, inclusive, what is the most the percent error could be? Explain your answer.

Problem Set

1. The odometer in Mr. Washington's car does not work correctly. The odometer recorded 13.2 miles for his last trip
    to the hardware store, but he knows the distance traveled is 15 miles. What is the percent error? Use a calculator
    and the percent error formula to help find the answer. Show your steps.

2. The actual length of a soccer field is 500 feet. A measuring instrument shows the length to be 493 feet. The actual
    width of the field is 250 feet, but the recorded width is 246.5 feet. Answer the following questions based on this
    information. Round all decimals to the nearest tenth.

    a. Find the percent error for the length of the soccer field.

    b. Find the percent error of the area of the soccer field.

    c. Explain why the values from parts (a) and (b) are different.

250 feet

500 feet

3. Kayla's class went on a field trip to an aquarium. One tank had 30 clown fish. She miscounted the total number of
    clown fish in the tank and recorded it as 24 fish. What is Kayla's percent error?

4. Sid used geometry software to draw a circle of radius 4 units on a grid. He estimated the area of the circle by
    counting the squares that were mostly inside the circle and got an answer of 52 square units.

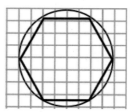

    a. Is his estimate too large or too small?

    b. Find the percent error in Sid's estimation to the nearest hundredth using the π key on your calculator.

5. The exact value for the density of aluminum is 2.699 g/cm^3. Working in the science lab at school, Joseph finds the
    density of a piece of aluminum to be 2.75 g/cm^3. What is Joseph's percent error? (Round to the nearest
    hundredths.)

6. The world's largest marathon, The New York City Marathon, is held on the first Sunday in November each year. It is
    estimated that anywhere between 2 million and 2.5 million spectators will line the streets to cheer on Marathon
    runners. At most, what is the percent error?

7. A circle is inscribed inside a square, which has a side length of 12.6 cm. Jared estimates the area of the circle to be about 80% of the area of the square and comes up with an estimate of 127 cm^2.

12.6 cm

   a. Find the absolute error from Jared's estimate to two decimal places.

   b. Find the percent error of Jared's estimate to two decimal places.

   c. Do you think Jared's estimate was reasonable?

   d. Would this method of computing the area of a circle always be too large?

8. In a school library, 52% of the books are paperback. If there are 2,658 books in the library, how many of them are not paperback to the nearest whole number?

9. Shaniqua has 25% less money than her older sister Jennifer. If Shaniqua has $180, how much money does Jennifer have?

10. An item that was selling for $1,102 is reduced to $806. To the nearest whole, what is the percent decrease?

11. If 60 calories from fat is 75% of the total number of calories in a bag of chips, find the total number of calories in the bag of chips.

Lesson 9: Problem Solving when the Percent Changes

Classwork

Example 1

Tom's money is 75% of Sally's money. After Sally spent $120 and Tom saved all his money, Tom's money is 50% more than Sally's. How much money did each have at the beginning? Use a visual model and a percent line to solve the problem.

Example 2

Erin and Sasha went to a candy shop. Sasha bought 50% more candies than Erin. After Erin bought 8 more candies, Sasha had 20% more. How many candies did Erin and Sasha have at first?

   a.   Model the situation using a visual model.

b. How many candies did Erin have at first? Explain.

Example 3

Kimberly and Mike have an equal amount of money. After Kimberly spent $50 and Mike spent $25, Mike's money is 50% more than Kimberly's. How much did Kimberly and Mike have at first?

a. Use an equation to solve the problem.

b. Use a visual model to solve the problem.

c. Which method do you prefer and why?

Exercise

Todd has 250% more video games than Jaylon. Todd has 56 video games in his collection. He gives Jaylon 8 of his games. How many video games did Todd and Jaylon have in the beginning? How many do they have now?

Problem Set

1. Solve each problem using an equation.

   a. What is 150% of 625?

   b. 90 is 40% of what number?

   c. What percent of 520 is 40? Round to the nearest hundredth of a percent.

2. The actual length of a machine is 12.25 cm. The measured length is 12.2 cm. Round to the nearest hundredth of a percent.

   a. Find the absolute error.   b. Find the percent error.

3. A rowing club has 600 members. 60% of them are women. After 200 new members joined the club, the percentage of women was reduced to 50%. How many of the new members are women?

4. 40% of the marbles in a bag are yellow. The rest are orange and green. The ratio of the number of orange to the number of green is 4: 5. If there are 30 green marbles, how many yellow marbles are there? Use a visual model to show your answer.

5. Susan has 50% more books than Michael. Michael has 40 books. If Michael buys 8 more books, will Susan have more or less books? What percent more or less will Susan's books be? Use any method to solve the problem.

6. Harry's money is 75% of Kayla's money. After Harry earned $30 and Kayla earned 25% more of her money, Harry's money is 80% of Kayla's money. How much money did each have at the beginning? Use a visual model to solve the problem.

Lesson 10: Simple Interest

Classwork

$$Interest = Principal \times Rate \times Time$$

$$I = P \times r \times t$$
$$I = Prt$$

- r is the percent of the principal that is paid over a period of time (usually per year).
- t is the time.
- r and t must be compatible. For example, if r is an annual interst rate, then t must be written in years.

Example 1: Can Money Grow? A Look at Simple Interest

Larry invests \$100 in a savings plan. The plan pays $4\frac{1}{2}\%$ interest each year on his \$100 account balance.

a. How much money will Larry earn in interest after 3 years? After 5 years?

b. How can you find the balance of Larry's account at the end of 5 years?

Exercise 1

Find the balance of a savings account at the end of 10 years if the interest earned each year is 7.5%. The principal is $500.

Example 2: Time Other Than One Year

A $1,000 savings bond earns simple interest at the rate of 3% each year. The interest is paid at the end of every month. How much interest will the bond have earned after three months?

Example 3: Solving for P, r, or t

Mrs. Williams wants to know how long it will take an investment of $450 to earn $200 in interest if the yearly interest rate is 6.5%, paid at the end of each year.

Exercises 2

Write an equation to find the amount of simple interest, A, earned on a $600 investment after $1\frac{1}{2}$ years, if the semi-annual (six month) interest rate is 2%.

Exercise 3

A $1,500 loan has an annual interest rate of $4\frac{1}{4}$% on the amount borrowed. How much time has elapsed if the interest is now $127.50?

Problem Set

1. Enrique takes out a student loan to pay for his college tuition this year. Find the interest on the loan if he borrowed $2,500 at an annual interest rate of 6% for 15 years.

2. Your family plans to start a small business in your neighborhood. Your father borrows $10,000 from the bank at an annual interest rate of 8% rate for 36 months. What is the amount of interest he will pay on this loan?

3. Mr. Rodriguez invests $2,000 in a savings plan. The savings account pays an annual interest rate of 5.75% on the amount he put in at the end of each year.

    a. How much will Mr. Rodriguez earn if he leaves his money in the savings plan for 10 years?

    b. How much money will be in his savings plan at the end of 10 years?

    c. Create (and label) a graph in the coordinate plane to show the relationship between time and the amount of interest earned for 10 years. Is the relationship proportional? Why or why not? If so, what is the constant of proportionality?

    d. Explain what the points $(0, 0)$ and $(1, 115)$ mean on the graph.

    e. Using the graph, find the balance of the savings plan at the end of seven years.

    f. After how many years will Mr. Rodriguez have increased his original investment by more than 50%? Show your work to support your answer.

4. Use a table to prove that the relationship between time and the balance is or is not proportional. Explain your reasoning.

5. Without actually graphing, describe the graph of the relationship between the time and the balance.

Challenge Problem

6. George went on a game show and won $60,000. He wanted to invest it and found two funds that he liked. Fund 250 earns 15% interest annually, and Fund 100 earns 8% interest annually. George does not want to earn more than $7,500 in interest income this year. He made the table below to show how he could invest the money.

	I	P	r	t
Fund 100		x	0.08	1
Fund 250		$60,000 - x$	0.15	1
Total	7,500	60,000	■■■■	

    a. Explain what value x is in this situation.

    b. Explain what the expression $60,000 - x$ represents in this situation.

    c. Using the simple interest formula, complete the table for the amount of interest earned.

    d. Write an equation to show the total amount of interest earned from both funds.

    e. Use algebraic properties to solve the equation for x and the principal, in dollars, George could invest in Fund 100. Show your work.

f.   Use your answer from part (e) to determine how much George could invest in Fund 250.

g.   Using your answers to parts (e) and (f), how much interest would George earn from each fund?

Lesson 11: Tax, Commissions, Fees, and Other Real-World Percent Problems

Classwork

Opening Exercise

How are each of the following percent applications different, and how are they the same? First, describe how percents are used to solve each of the following problems. Then, solve each problem. Finally, compare your solution process for each.

    a.   Silvio earns 10% for each car sale he makes while working at a used car dealership. If he sells a used car for $2,000, what is his commission?

    b.   Tu's family stayed at a hotel for 10 nights on their vacation. The hotel charged a 10% room tax, per night. How much did they pay in room taxes if the room cost $200 per night?

    c.   Eric bought a new computer and printer online. He had to pay 10% in shipping fees. The items totaled $2,000. How much did the shipping cost?

    d.   Selena had her wedding rehearsal dinner at a restaurant. The restaurant's policy is that gratuity is included in the bill for large parties. Her father said the food and service were exceptional, so he wanted to leave an extra 10% tip on the total amount of the bill. If the dinner bill totaled $2,000, how much money did her father leave as the extra tip?

Exercises 1–4

Show all work; a calculator may be used for calculations.

The school board has approved the addition of a new sports team at your school.

1. The district ordered 30 team uniforms and received a bill for $2,992.50. The total included a 5% discount.

    a. The school needs to place another order for two more uniforms. The company said the discount will not apply because the discount only applies to orders of $1,000 or more. How much will the two uniforms cost?

    b. The school district does not have to pay the 8% sales tax on the $2,992.50 purchase. Estimate the amount of sales tax the district saved on the $2,992.50 purchase. Explain how you arrived at your estimate.

    c. A student who loses a uniform must pay a fee equal to 75% of the school's cost of the uniform. For a uniform that cost the school $105, will the student owe more or less than $75 for the lost uniform? Explain how to use mental math to determine the answer.

    d. Write an equation to represent the proportional relationship between the school's cost of a uniform and the amount a student must pay for a lost uniform. Use u to represent the uniform cost and s to represent the amount a student must pay for a lost uniform. What is the constant of proportionality?

2. A taxpayer claims the new sports team caused his school taxes to increase by 2%.

   a. Write an equation to show the relationship between the school taxes before and after a 2% increase. Use b to represent the dollar amount of school tax before the 2% increase and t to represent the dollar amount of school tax after the 2% increase.

   b. Use your equation to complete the table below, listing at least 5 pairs of values.

b	t
1,000	
2,000	
	3,060
	6,120

   c. On graph paper, graph the relationship modeled by the equation in part (a). Be sure to label the axes and scale.

   d. Is the relationship proportional? Explain how you know.

   e. What is the constant of proportionality? What does it mean in the context of the situation?

   f. If a tax payer's school taxes rose from $4,000 to $4,020, was there a 2% increase? Justify your answer using your graph, table, or equation.

3. The sports booster club sold candles as a fundraiser to support the new team. They earn a commission on their candle sales (which means they receive a certain percentage of the total dollar amount sold). If the club gets to keep 30% of the money from the candle sales, what would the club's total sales have to be in order to make at least $500?

4. Christian's mom works at the concession stand during sporting events. She told him they buy candy bars for $0.75 each and mark them up 40% to sell at the concession stand. What is the amount of the mark up? How much does the concession stand charge for each candy bar?

With your group, brainstorm solutions to the problems below. Prepare a poster that shows your solutions and math work. A calculator may be used for calculations.

5. For the next school year, the new soccer team will need to come up with $600.

   a. Suppose the team earns $500 from the fundraiser at the start of the current school year, and the money is placed for one calendar year in a savings account earning 0.5% simple interest annually. How much money will the team still need to raise to meet next year's expenses?

b. Jeff is a member of the new sports team. His dad owns a bakery. To help raise money for the team, Jeff's dad agrees to provide the team with cookies to sell at the concession stand for next year's opening game. The team must pay back the bakery $0.25 for each cookie it sells. The concession stand usually sells about 60 to 80 baked goods per game. Using your answer from part (a), determine a percent markup for the cookies the team plans to sell at next year's opening game. Justify your answer.

c. Suppose the team ends up selling 78 cookies at next year's opening game. Find the percent error in the number of cookies that you estimated would be sold in your solution to part (b).

$$\text{Percent Error} = \frac{|a-x|}{|x|} \cdot 100\%, \text{ where } x \text{ is the exact value and } a \text{ is the approximate value.}$$

Problem Set

1. A school district's property tax rate rises from 2.5% to 2.7% to cover a $300,000 budget deficit (shortage of money). What is the value of the property in the school district to the nearest dollar? (Note: Property is assessed at 100% of its value.)

2. Jake's older brother Sam has a choice of two summer jobs. He can either work at an electronics store or at the school's bus garage. The electronics store would pay him to work 15 hours per week. He would make $8 per hour plus a 2% commission on his electronics sales. Sam could earn $300 per week working 15 hours cleaning buses. Sam wants to take the job that pays him the most. How much in electronics would Sam have to sell for the job at the electronics store to be the better choice for his summer job?

3. Sarah lost her science book. Her school charges a lost book fee equal to 75% of the cost of the book. Sarah received a notice stating she owed the school $60 for the lost book.

    a. Write an equation to represent the proportional relationship between the school's cost for the book and the amount a student must pay for a lost book.

    b. What is the constant or proportionality? What does it mean in the context of this situation?

    c. How much did the school pay for the book?

4. In the month of May, a certain middle school has an average daily absentee rate of 8% each school day. The absentee rate is the percent of students who are absent from school each day.

    a. Write an equation that shows the proportional relationship between the number of students enrolled in the middle school and the average number of students absent each day. Let s represent the number of

    b. Use your equation to complete the table. List **5** possible values for s and a.

s	a

    c. Identify the constant of proportionality, and explain what it means in the context of this situation.

    d. Based on the absentee rate, determine the number of students absent on average from school if there are **350** students enrolled in the middle school.

5. The equation shown in the box below could relate to many different percent problems. Put an "X" next to each
    problem that could be represented by this equation. For any problem that does not match this equation, explain
    why it does not. $\boxed{Quantity = 1.05 \cdot Whole}$

_____   Find the amount of an investment after 1 year with 0.5% interest paid annually.

_____   Write an equation to show the amount paid for an item including tax, if the tax rate is 5%.

_____   A proportional relationship has a constant of proportionality equal to 105%.

_____

Whole	0	100	200	300	400	500
Quantity	0	105	210	315	420	525

_____   Mr. Hendrickson sells cars and earns a 5% commission on every car he sells. Write an
               equation to show the relationship between the price of a car Mr. Hendrickson sold and the
               amount of commission he earns.

Lesson 12: The Scale Factor as a Percent for a Scale Drawing

Classwork

Review the definitions of scale drawing, reduction, enlargement, and scale factor from Module 1, Lessons 16–17.

Compare the corresponding lengths of Figure A to the original octagon in the middle. This is an example of a particular type of <u>scale drawing</u> called a_____. Explain why it is called that.

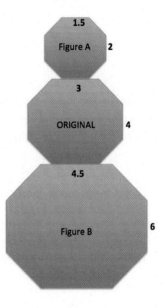

Compare the corresponding lengths of Figure B to the original octagon in the middle. This is an example of a particular type of <u>scale drawing</u> called an _____. Explain why it is called that.

The <u>scale factor</u> is the quotient of any length in the scale drawing to its corresponding length in the actual drawing.

Use what you recall from Module 1 to determine the scale factors between the original figure and Figure A, and the original figure and Figure B.

Using the diagram, complete the chart to determine the horizontal and vertical scale factors. Write answers as a percent, and as a concluding statement using the previously learned reduction and enlargement vocabulary.

	Horizontal Measurement in Scale Drawing	Vertical Measurement in Scale Drawing	Concluding Statement
Figure A			
Figure B			

Example 1

Create a snowman on the accompanying grid. Use the octagon given as the middle of the snowman with the following conditions:

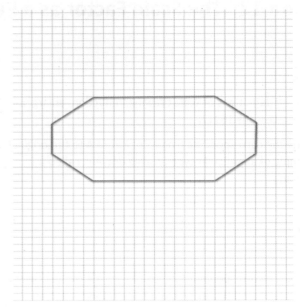

a. Calculate the width, neck, and height for the figure at the right.

b. To create the head of the snowman, make a scale drawing of the middle of the snowman with a scale factor of 75%. Calculate the new lengths for the width, neck, and height.

c. To create the bottom of the snowman, make a scale drawing of the middle of the snowman with a scale factor of 125%. Calculate the new lengths for the width, neck, and height.

d. Is the head a reduction or enlargement of the middle?

e. Is the bottom a reduction or enlargement of the middle?

f. What is the significance of the scale factor as it relates to 100%? What happens when such scale factors are applied?

Example 2

Create a scale drawing of the arrow below using a scale factor of 150%.

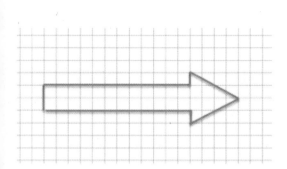

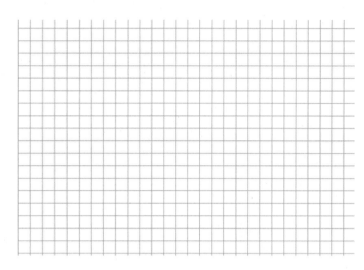

Example 3: Scale Drawing where the Horizontal and Vertical Scale Factors are Different

Sometimes it is helpful to make a scale drawing where the horizontal and vertical scale factors are different, such as when creating diagrams in the field of engineering. Having differing scale factors may distort some drawings. For example, when you are working with a very large horizontal scale, you sometimes must exaggerate the vertical scale in order to make it readable. This can be accomplished by creating a drawing with two scales. Unlike the scale drawings with just one scale factor, these types of scale drawings may look distorted. Next to the drawing below is a scale drawing with a horizontal scale factor of 50% and vertical scale factor of 25% (given in two steps). Explain how each drawing is created.

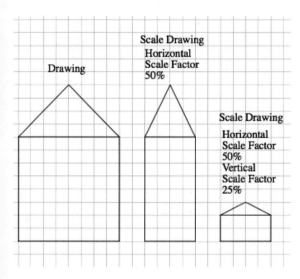

Exercise 1

Create a scale drawing of the following drawing using a horizontal scale factor of $183\frac{1}{3}\%$ and a vertical scale factor of 25%.

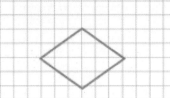

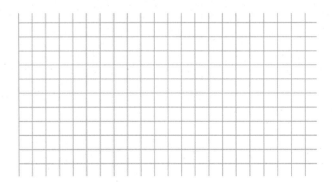

Exercise 2

Chris is building a rectangular pen for his dog. The dimensions are 12 units long and 5 units wide.

12 Units

5 Units

Chris is building a second pen that is 60% the length of the original and 125% the width of the original. Write equations to determine the length and width of the second pen.

Lesson Summary

The scale factor is the number that determines whether the new drawing is an enlargement or a reduction of the original. If the scale factor is greater than 100%, then the resulting drawing will be an enlargement of the original drawing. If the scale factor is less than 100%, then the resulting drawing will be a reduction of the original drawing.

When a scale factor is mentioned, assume that it refers to both vertical and horizontal factors. It will be noted if the horizontal and vertical factors are intended to be different.

To create a scale drawing with both the same vertical and horizontal factors, determine the horizontal and vertical distances of the original drawing. Using the given scale factor, determine the new corresponding lengths in the scale drawing by writing a numerical equation that requires the scale factor to be multiplied by the original length. Draw new segments based on the calculations from the original segments. If the scale factors are different, determine the new corresponding lengths the same way but use the unique given scale factor for both the horizontal length and vertical length.

Problem Set

1. Use the diagram below to create a scale drawing using a scale factor of $133\frac{1}{3}\%$. Write numerical equations to find the horizontal and vertical distances in the scale drawing.

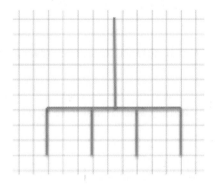

2. Create a scale drawing of the original drawing given below using a horizontal scale factor of 80% and a vertical scale factor of 175%. Write numerical equations to find the horizontal and vertical distances.

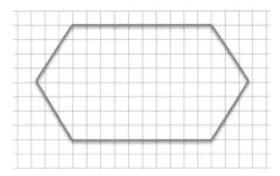

---

3. The accompanying diagram shows that the length of a pencil from its eraser to its tip is 7 units and that the eraser is 1.5 units wide. The picture was placed on a photocopy machine and reduced to $66\frac{2}{3}$%. Find the new size of the pencil and sketch a drawing. Write numerical equations to find the new dimensions.

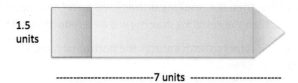

4. Use the diagram to answer each question that follows.

    a. What are the corresponding horizontal and vertical distances in a scale drawing if the scale factor is 25%? Use numerical equations to find your answers.

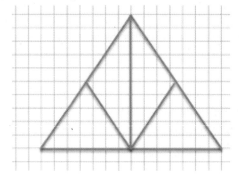

    b. What are the corresponding horizontal and vertical distances in a scale drawing if the scale factor is 160%? Use a numerical equation to find your answers.

5. Create a scale drawing of the original drawing below using a horizontal scale factor of 200% and a vertical scale factor of 250%.

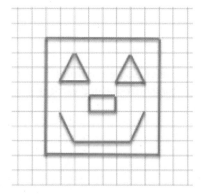

6. Using the diagram below, on grid paper sketch the same drawing using a horizontal scale factor of 50% and a vertical scale factor of 150%.

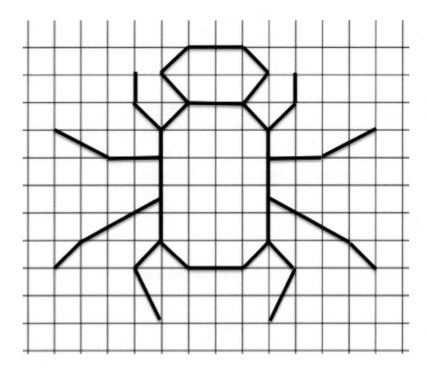

Lesson 13: Changing Scales

Classwork

Classwork

Opening Exercise

Scale Factor: $\dfrac{length\ in\ SCALE\ DRAWING}{Corresponding\ length\ in\ ORIGINAL\ DRAWING}$

Describe, using percentages, the difference between a reduction and an enlargement.

Use the two drawings below to complete the chart. Calculate the first row (Drawing 1 to Drawing 2) only.

2.45 inches

1.5 inches

DRAWING 1

3.92 inches

DRAWING 2

2.4 inches

	Quotient of Corresponding Horizontal Distances	Quotient of Corresponding Vertical Distances	Scale Factor as a Percent	Reduction or Enlargement?
Drawing 1 To Drawing 2				
Drawing 2 to Drawing 1				

Compare Drawing 2 to Drawing 1. Using the completed work in the first row, make a conjecture (statement) about what the second row of the chart will be. Justify your conjecture without computing the second row.

Compute the second row of the chart. Was your conjecture proven true? Explain how you know.

Example 1

The scale factor from Drawing 1 to Drawing 2 is 60%. Find the scale factor from Drawing 2 to Drawing 1. Explain your reasoning.

Example 2

A regular octagon is an eight-sided polygon with side lengths that are all equal. All three octagons are scale drawings of each other. Use the chart and the side lengths to compute each scale factor as a percent. How can we check our answers?

Actual Drawing to Scale Drawing	Scale Factor	Equation to Illustrate Relationship
Drawing 1 to Drawing 2		
Drawing 1 to Drawing 3		
Drawing 2 to Drawing 1		
Drawing 2 to Drawing 3		
Drawing 3 to Drawing 1		
Drawing 3 to Drawing 2		

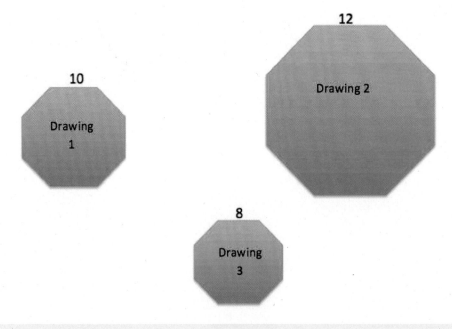

Example 3

The scale factor from Drawing 1 to Drawing 2 is 112%, and the scale factor from Drawing 1 to Drawing 3 is 84%. Drawing 2 is also a scale drawing of Drawing 3. Is Drawing 2 a reduction or an enlargement of Drawing 3? Justify your answer using the scale factor. The drawing is not necessarily drawn to scale.

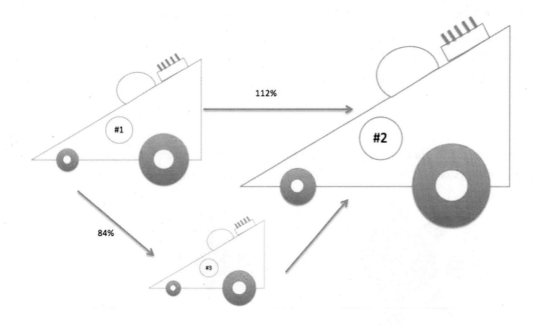

Explain how you could use the scale factors from Drawing 1 to Drawing 2 (112%) and from Drawing 2 to Drawing 3 (75%) to show that the scale factor from Drawing 1 to Drawing 3 is 84%.

Lesson Summary

To compute the scale factor from one drawing to another, use the representation:

$$Quantity = Percent \times Whole$$

where the whole is the length in the actual or original drawing and the quantity is the length in the scale drawing.

If the lengths of the sides are not provided but two scale factors are provided, use the same relationship but use the scale factors as the whole and quantity instead of the given measurements.

Problem Set

1. The scale factor from Drawing 1 to Drawing 2 is $41\frac{2}{3}\%$. Justify why Drawing 1 is a scale drawing of Drawing 2 and why it is an enlargement of Drawing 2. Include the scale factor in your justification.

2. The scale factor from Drawing 1 to Drawing 2 is 40% and the scale factor from Drawing 2 to Drawing 3 is 37.5%. What is the scale factor from Drawing 1 to Drawing 3? Explain your reasoning, and check your answer using an example.

3. Traci took a photograph and printed it to be a size of 4 units by 4 units as indicated in the diagram. She wanted to enlarge the original photograph to a size of 5 units by 5 units and 10 units by 10 units.
   a. Sketch the different sizes of photographs.
   b. What was the scale factor from the original photo to the photo that is 5 units by 5 units?
   c. What was the scale factor from the original photo to the photo that is 10 units by 10 units?
   d. What was the scale factor from the 5 x 5 photo to the 10 x 10 photo?
   e. Write an equation to verify how the scale factor from the original photo to the enlarged 10 x 10 photo can be calculated using the scale factors from the original to the 5 x 5, and then from the 5 x 5 to the 10 x 10.

---

4. The scale factor from Drawing 1 to Drawing 2 is 30%, and the scale factor from Drawing 1 to Drawing 3 is 175%. What are the scale factors from the following:

    a. Drawing 2 to Drawing 3

    b. Drawing 3 to Drawing 1

    c. Drawing 3 to Drawing 2

    d. How can you check your answers?

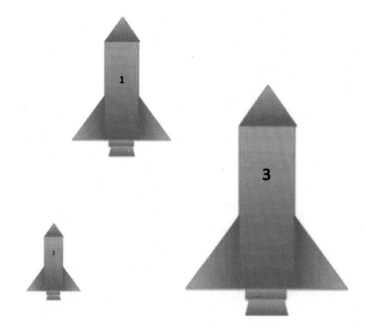

Lesson 14: Computing Actual Lengths from a Scale Drawing

Classwork

Example 1

The distance around the entire small boat is 28.4 units. The larger figure is a scale drawing of the smaller drawing of the boat. State the scale factor as a percent, and then use the scale factor to find the distance around the scale drawing.

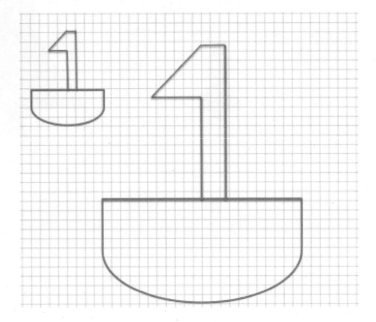

Exercise 1

The length of the longer path is 32.4 units. The shorter path is a scale drawing of the longer path. Find the length of the shorter path and explain how you arrived at your answer.

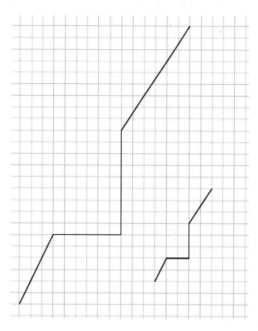

Example 2

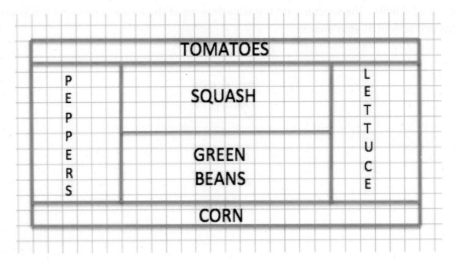

Sherry designed her garden as shown in the diagram above. The distance between any two consecutive vertical grid lines is 1 foot, and the distance between any two consecutive horizontal grid lines is also 1 foot. Therefore, each grid square has an area of one square foot. After designing the garden, Sherry decides to actually build the garden 75% of the size represented in the diagram.

a. What are the outside dimensions shown in the blueprint?

b. What will the overall dimensions be in the actual garden? Write an equation to find the dimensions. How does the problem relate to the scale factor?

c. If Sherry plans to use a wire fence to divide each section of the garden, how much fence does she need?

d.   If the fence costs $3.25 per foot plus 7% sales tax, how much would the fence cost in total?

Exercise 2

Race Car #2 is a scale drawing of Race Car #1. The measurement from the front of Car #1 to the back of Car #1 is 12 feet, while the measurement from the front of Car #2 to the back of Car #2 is 39 feet. If the height of Car #1 is 4 feet, find the scale factor, and write an equation to find the height of Car #2. Explain what each part of the equation represents in the situation.

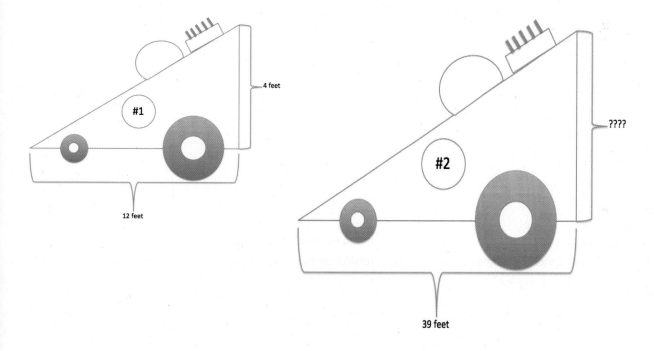

Exercise 3

Determine the scale factor and write an equation that relates the vertical heights of each drawing to the scale factor. Explain how the equation illustrates the relationship.

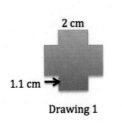

2 cm

1.1 cm →

Drawing 1

3.3 cm

Drawing 2

Exercise 4

The length of a rectangular picture is 8 inches, and the picture is to be reduced to be $45\frac{1}{2}\%$ of the original picture. Write an equation that relates the lengths of each picture. Explain how the equation illustrates the relationship.

Problem Set

1. The smaller train is a scale drawing of the larger train. If the length of the tire rod connecting the three tires of the larger train as shown below is 36 inches, write an equation to find the length of the tire rod of the smaller train. Interpret your solution in the context of the problem.

2. The larger arrow is a scale drawing of the smaller arrow. The distance around the smaller arrow is 28 units, what is the distance around the larger arrow? Use an equation to find the distance and interpret your solution in the context of the problem.

3. The smaller drawing below is a scale drawing of the larger. The distance around the larger drawing is 39.3 units. Using an equation, find the distance around the smaller drawing.

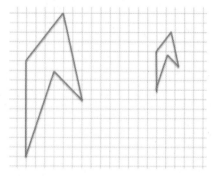

4. The figure is a diagram of a model rocket. The length of a model rocket is 2.5 feet, and the wing span is 1.25 feet. If the length of an actual rocket is 184 feet, use an equation to find the wing span of the actual rocket.

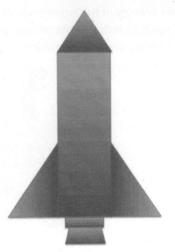

Lesson 15: Solving Area Problems Using Scale Drawings

Classwork

Opening Exercise

For each diagram, Drawing 2 is a scale drawing of Drawing 1. Complete the accompanying charts. For each drawing: identify the side lengths, determine the area, and compute the scale factor. Convert each scale factor into a fraction and percent, examine the results, and write a conclusion relating scale factors to area.

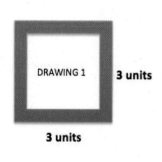

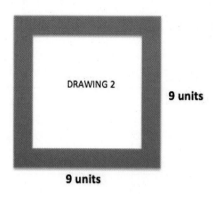

	Drawing 1	Drawing 2	Scale Factor as a Fraction and Percent
Side			
Area			

Scale Factor: _____   Quotient of Areas: _____

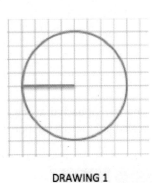

DRAWING 1

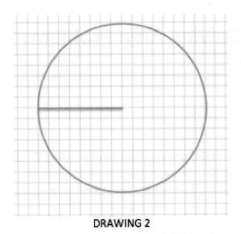

DRAWING 2

	Drawing 1	Drawing 2	Scale Factor as a Fraction and Percent
Side			
Area			

Scale Factor: _____   Quotient of Areas: _____

The length of each side in Drawing 1 is 12 units, and the length of each side in Drawing 2 is 6 units.

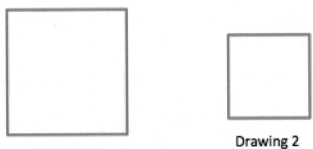

Drawing 1   Drawing 2

	Drawing 1	Drawing 2	Scale Factor as a Fraction and Percent
Side			
Area			

Scale Factor: _____   Quotient of Areas: _____

Conclusion:

Example 1

What percent of the area of the large square is the area of the small square?

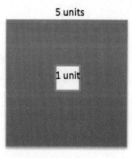

Example 2

What percent of the area of the large disk lies outside the smaller disk?

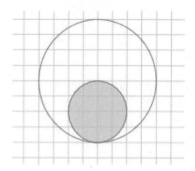

Example 3

If the area of the shaded region in the larger figure is approximately 21.5 square inches, write an equation that relates the areas using scale factor and explain what each quantity represents. Determine the area of the shaded region in the smaller scale drawing.

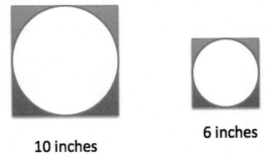

10 inches   6 inches

Example 4

Use Figure 1 below and the enlarged scale drawing to justify why the area of the scale drawing is k^2 times the area of the original figure.

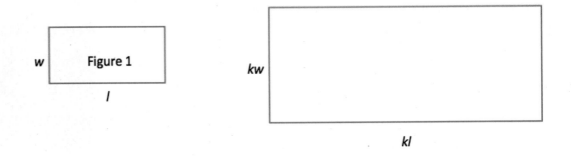

Explain why the expressions $(kl)(kw)$ and k^2lw are equivalent. How do the expressions reveal different information about this situation?

EUREKA
MATH™

Exercises

1. The Lake Smith basketball team had a team picture taken of the players, the coaches, and the trophies from the season. The picture was 4 inches by 6 inches. The team decides to have the picture enlarged to a poster and then enlarged again to a banner measuring 48 inches by 72 inches.

   a. Sketch drawings to illustrate the original picture and enlargements.

   b. If the scale factor from the picture to the poster is 500%, determine the dimensions of the poster.

   c. What scale factor is used to create the banner from the picture?

d. What percent of the area of the picture is the area of the poster? Justify your answer using the scale factor AND by finding the actual areas.

e. Write an equation involving the scale factor that relates the area of the poster to the area of the picture.

f. Assume you started with the banner and wanted to reduce it to the size of the poster. What would the scale factor as a percent be?

g. What scale factor would be used to reduce the poster to the size of the picture?

Problem Set

1. What percent of the area of the larger circle is shaded?

   a. Solve this problem using scale factors.

   b. Verify your work in part a by finding the actual areas.

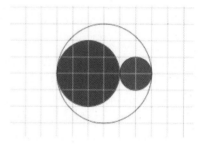

2. The area of the large disk is 50.24 units^2.

   a. Find the area of the shaded region.

   b. What percent of the large circular region is unshaded?

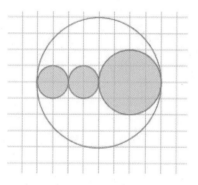

3. Ben cut the following rockets out of cardboard. The height from the base to the tip of the smaller rocket is 20 cm. The height from the base to the tip of the larger rocket is 120 cm. What percent of the area of the smaller rocket is the area of the larger rocket?

4. In the photo frame depicted below, three 5 inch by 5 inch squares are cut out for photographs. If these cut-out regions make up $\frac{3}{16}$ of the area of the entire photo frame, what are the dimensions of the photo frame?

5. Kelly was online shopping for envelopes for party invitations and saw these images on a website.

 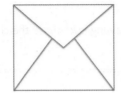 

The website listed the dimensions of the small envelope as 6 in. by 8 in. and the medium envelope as 10 in. by $13\frac{1}{3}$ in.

a. Compare the dimensions of the small and medium envelopes. If the medium envelope is a scale drawing of the small envelope, what is the scale factor?

b. If the large envelope was created based on the dimensions of the small envelope using a scale factor of 250%, find the dimensions of the large envelope.

c. If the medium envelope was created based on the dimensions of the large envelope, what scale factor was used to create the medium envelope?

d. What percent of the area of the larger envelope is the area of the medium envelope?

Lesson 16: Population Problems

Classwork

Opening Exercise

Number of girls in classroom:	Number of boys in classroom:	Total number of students in classroom:
Percent of the total number of students that are girls:	Percent of the total number of students that are boys:	Percent of boys and girls in the classroom:
Number of girls whose names start with a vowel:	Number of boys whose names start with a vowel:	Number of students whose names start with a vowel:
Percent of girls whose names start with a vowel:	Percent of boys whose names start with a vowel:	
Percent of the total number of students that are girls whose names start with a vowel:	Percent of the total number of students that are boys whose names start with a vowel:	Percent of students whose names start with a vowel:

Example 1

A school has 60% girls and 40% boys. If 20% of the girls wear glasses and 40% of the boys wear glasses, what percent of all students wears glasses?

Exercises 1–2

1. How does the percent of students who wear glasses change if the percent of girls and boys remains the same (that is, 60% girls and 40% boys) but 20% of the boys wear glasses and 40% of the girls wear glasses?

2. How would the percent of students who wear glasses change if the percent of girls is 40% of the school and the percent of boys is 60% of the school, and 40% of the girls wear glasses and 20% of the boys wear glasses? Why?

Example 2

The weight of the first of three containers is 12% more than the second, and the third container is 20% lighter than the second. The first container is heavier than the third container by what percent?

Exercise 3

3. Matthew's pet dog is 7% heavier than Harrison's pet dog, and Janice's pet dog is 20% lighter than Harrison's. By what percent is Matthew's dog heavier than Janice's?

Example 3

In one year's time, 20% of Ms. McElroy's investments increased by 5%, 30% of her investments decreased by 5%, and 50% of investments increased by 3%. By what percent did the total of her investments increase?

Exercise 4

4. A concert had 6,000 audience members in attendance on the first night and the same on the second night. On the first night the concert exceeded expected attendance by 20% while the second night was below the expected attendance by 20%. What was the difference in percent of concert attendees and the percent expected attendees for both nights combined?

Problem Set

1. A first container is filled with a mixture that is 30% acid. A second container is filled with a mixture that is 50% acid. The second container is 50% larger than the first, and the two containers are emptied into a third container. What percent of acid is the third container?

2. The store's markup on a wholesale item is 40%. The store is currently having a sale, and the item sells for 25% off the retail price. What is the percent of profit made by the store?

3. During lunch hour at a local restaurant, 90% of customers order a meat entrée and 10% order a vegetarian entrée. Of the customers who order a meat entrée, 80% order a drink. Of the customers who order a vegetarian entrée, 40% order a drink. What is the percent of customers who order a drink with their entrée?

4. Last year's spell-a-thon spelling test for a first grade class had 15% more words with four or more letters than this year's spelling test; and next year, there will be 5 percent less than this year. What percent more words have four or more letters in last year's test than next year's?

5. An ice cream shop sells 75% less ice cream in December than in June. Twenty percent more ice cream is sold in July than in June. By what percent did ice cream sales increase from December to July?

6. The livestock on a small farm the prior year consisted of 40% goats, 10% cows, and 50% chickens. This year, there is a 5% decrease in goats, 9% increase in cows, and 15% increase in chickens. What is the percent increase of livestock this year?

7. In a pet shelter that is occupied by 55% dogs and 45% cats, 60% of the animals are brought in by concerned people who found these animals in the streets. If 90% of the dogs are brought in by concerned people, what is the percent of cats that are brought in by concerned people?

8. An artist wants to make a particular teal color paint by mixing a 75% blue hue and 25% yellow hue. He mixes a blue hue that has 85% pure blue pigment and a yellow hue that has 60% of pure yellow pigment. What is the percent of pure pigment that is in the resulting teal color paint?

9. On Mina's block, 65% of her neighbors do not have any pets, and 35% of her neighbors own at least one pet. If 25% of the neighbors have children but no pets, and 60% of the neighbors who have pets also have children, what percent of the neighbors have children?

Lesson 17: Mixture Problems

Opening Exercise

Imagine you have two equally sized containers. One is pure water, and the other is 50% water and 50% juice. If you combined them, what percent of juice would be the result?

	1st liquid	2nd liquid	Resulting liquid
Amount of liquid (gallons)			
Amount of pure juice (gallons)			

If a 2-gallon container of pure juice is added to 3 gallons of water, what percent of the mixture is pure juice?

	1st liquid	2nd liquid	Resulting liquid
Amount of liquid (gallons)			
Amount of pure juice (gallons)			

If a 2-gallon container of juice mixture that is 40% pure juice is added to 3 gallons of water, what percent of the mixture is pure juice?

	1st liquid	2nd liquid	Resulting liquid
Amount of liquid (gallons)			
Amount of pure juice (gallons)			

If a 2-gallon juice cocktail that is 40% pure juice is added to 3 gallons of pure juice, what percent of the resulting mixture is pure juice?

	1st liquid	2nd liquid	Resulting liquid
Amount of liquid (gallons)			
Amount of pure juice (gallons)			

Example 1

A 5-gallon container of trail mix is 20% nuts. Another trail mix is added to it, resulting in a 12-gallon container of trail mix that is 40% nuts.

a. Write an equation to describe the relationships in this situation.

b. Explain in words how each part of the equation relates to the situation.

c. What percent of the second trail mix is nuts?

Exercise 1

Represent each situation using an equation, and show all steps in the solution process.

a.   A 6-pint 25% oil mixture is added to a 3-pint 40% oil mixture. What percent of the resulting mixture is oil?

b.   An 11-ounce gold chain of 24% gold was made from a melted down 4-ounce charm of 50% gold and a golden
     locket. What percent of the locket was pure gold?

c.   In a science lab, two containers are filled with mixtures. The first container is filled with a mixture that is 30% acid.
     The second container is filled with a mixture that is 50% acid, and the second container is 50% larger than the
     first. The first and second containers are then emptied into a third container. What percent of acid is in the third
     container?

Example 2

Soil that contains 30% clay is added to soil that contains 70% clay to create 10 gallons of soil containing 50% clay. How much of each of the soils was combined?

Exercise 2

The equation: $(0.2)(x) + (0.8)(6 - x) = (0.4)(6)$ is used to model a mixture problem.

a. How many units are in the total mixture?

b. What percents relate to the two solutions that are combined to make the final mixture?

c. The two solutions combine to make six units of what percent solution?

d. When the amount of a resulting solution is given (for instance 4 gallons) but the amounts of the mixing solutions are unknown, how are the amounts of the mixing solutions represented?

Problem Set

1. A 5-liter cleaning solution contains 30% bleach. A 3-liter cleaning solution contains 50% bleach. What percent of bleach is obtained by putting the two mixtures together?

2. A container is filled with 100 grams of bird feed that is 80% seed. How many grams of bird feed containing 5% seed must be added to get bird feed that is 40% seed?

3. A container is filled with 100 grams of bird feed that is 80% seed. Tom and Sally want to mix the 100 grams with bird feed that is 5% seed to get a mixture that is 40% seed. Tom wants to add 114 grams of the 5% seed and Sally wants to add 115 grams of the 5% mix. What will be the percent of seed if Tom adds 114 grams? What will be the percent of seed if Sally adds 115 grams? How much do you think should be added to get 40% seed?

4. Jeanie likes mixing left-over salad dressings together to make new dressings. She combined 0.55 L of a 90% vinegar salad dressing with 0.45 L of another dressing to make 1 L of salad dressing that is 60% vinegar. What percent of the second salad dressing was vinegar?

5. Anna wants to make 30 ml of a 60% salt solution by mixing together a 72% salt solution and a 54% salt solution. How much of each solution must she use?

6. A mixed bag of candy is 25% chocolate bars and 75% other filler candy. Of the chocolate bars, 50% of them contains caramel. Of the other filler candy, 10% of them contain caramel. What percent of candy that contains caramel?

7. A local fish market receives the daily catch of two local fishermen. The first fisherman's catch was 84% fish while the rest was other non-fish items. The second fisherman's catch was 76% fish while the rest was other non-fish items. If the fish market receives 75% of its catch from the first fisherman and 25% from the second, what was the percent of other non-fish items the local fish market bought from the fishermen altogether?

Lesson 18: Counting Problems

Opening Exercise

You are about to switch out your books from your locker during passing period but forget the order of your locker combination. You know that there is a 3, 16, and 21 in some order. What is the percent of locker combinations that start with 3?

Locker Combination Possibilities:

3, 16, 21

21, 16, 3

16, 21, 3

21, 3, 16

16, 3, 21

3, 21, 16

Example 1

All of the 3-letter passwords that can be formed using the letters "A" and "B" are as follows:

AAA, AAB, ABA, ABB, BAA, BAB, BBA, BBB.

   a. What percent of passwords contain at least two "B's"?

   b. What percent of passwords contain no "A's"?

Exercises 1–2

1. How many 4-letter passwords can be formed using the letters "A" and "B"?

2. What percent of the 4-letter passwords contain
    a. no "A's"?

    b. exactly one "A"?

    c. exactly two "A's"?

    d. exactly three "A's"?

    e. four "A's"

    f. the same number of "A's" and "B's"?

Example 2

In a set of 3-letter passwords, 40% of the passwords contain the letter B and two of another letter. Which of the two sets below meet the criteria? Explain how you arrived at your answer.

Set 1

BBB	AAA	CAC
CBC	ABA	CCC
BBC	CCB	CAB
AAB	AAC	BAA
ACB	BAC	BCC

Set 2

CEB	BBB
EBE	CCC
CCC	EEE
EEB	CBC
CCB	ECE

Exercises 3–4

3. Shana read the following problem:

   "How many letter arrangements can be formed from the word "triangle" that have two vowels and two consonants (order does not matter)?"

   She answered that there are 30 letter arrangements.

   Twenty percent of the letter arrangements that began with a vowel actually had an English definition. How many letter arrangements that begin with a vowel have an English definition?

4. Using three different keys on a piano, a songwriter makes the beginning of his melody with three notes, C, E, and G:

   CCE, EEE, EGC, GCE, CEG, GEE, CGE, GGE, EGG, EGE, GCG, EEC, ECC, ECG, GGG, GEC, CCG, CEE, CCC, GEG, CGC

   a. From the list above, what is the percent of melodies with all three notes that are different?

   b. From the list above, what is the percent of melodies that have three of the same notes?

Example 3

Look at the 36 points on the coordinate plane with whole number coordinates between 1 and 6, inclusive.

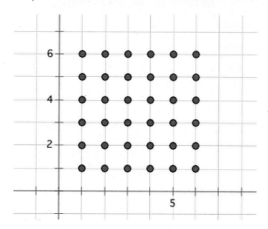

a. Draw a line through each of the points which have an x-coordinate and y-coordinate sum of 7.
    Draw a line through each of the points which have an x-coordinate and y-coordinate sum of 6.
    Draw a line through each of the points which have an x-coordinate and y-coordinate sum of 5.
    Draw a line through each of the points which have an x-coordinate and y-coordinate sum of 4.
    Draw a line through each of the points which have an x-coordinate and y-coordinate sum of 3.
    Draw a line through each of the points which have an x-coordinate and y-coordinate sum of 2.
    Draw a line through each of the points which have an x-coordinate and y-coordinate sum of 8.
    Draw a line through each of the points which have an x-coordinate and y-coordinate sum of 9.
    Draw a line through each of the points which have an x-coordinate and y-coordinate sum of 10.
    Draw a line through each of the points which have an x-coordinate and y-coordinate sum of 11.
    Draw a line through each of the points which have an x-coordinate and y-coordinate sum of 12.

b. What percent of the 36 points have coordinate sum 7?

c. Write a numerical expression that could be used to determine the percent of the 36 points that have a coordinate sum of 7.

d. What percent of the 36 points have coordinate sum 5 or less?

e. What percent of the 36 points have coordinate sum 4 or 10?

Problem Set

1. A six-sided die (singular for dice) is thrown twice. The different rolls are as follows:

    1 and 1, 1 and 2, 1 and 3, 1 and 4, 1 and 5, 1 and 6,

    2 and 1, 2 and 2, 2 and 3, 2 and 4, 2 and 5, 2 and 6,

    3 and 1, 3 and 2, 3 and 3, 3 and 4, 3 and 5, 3 and 6,

    4 and 1, 4 and 2, 4 and 3, 4 and 4, 4 and 5, 4 and 6,

    5 and 1, 5 and 2, 5 and 3, 5 and 4, 5 and 5, 5 and 6,

    6 and 1, 6 and 2, 6 and 3, 6 and 4, 6 and 5, 6 and 6.

    a. What is the percent that both throws will be even numbers?
    b. What is the percent that the second throw is a 5?
    c. What is the percent that the first throw is lower than a 6?

2. You have the ability to choose three of your own classes, art, language, and physical education. There are three art classes (A1, A2, A3), two language classes (L1, L2), and two P.E. classes (P1, P2) to choose from (order does not matter and you must choose one from each subject).

A1, L1, P1	A2, L1, P1	A3, L1, P1
A1, L1, P2	A2, L1, P2	A3, L1, P2
A1, L2, P1	A2, L2, P1	A3, L2, P1
A1, L2, P2	A2, L2, P2	A3, L2, P2

    Compare the percent of possibilities with A1 in your schedule to the percent of possibilities with L1 in your schedule.

3. Fridays are selected to show your school pride. The colors of your school are orange, blue, and white, and you can show your spirit by wearing a top, a bottom, and an accessory with the colors of your school. During lunch, 11 students are chosen to play for a prize on stage. The table charts what the students wore:

Top	W	O	W	O	B	W	B	B	W	W	W
Bottom	B	O	B	B	O	B	B	B	O	W	B
Accessory	W	O	B	W	B	O	B	W	O	O	O

    a. What is the percent of outfits that are one color?
    b. What is the percent of outfits that include orange accessories?

4. Shana wears two rings (G represents gold, and S represents silver) at all times on her hand. She likes fiddling with them and places them on different fingers (pinky, ring, middle, index) when she gets restless. The chart is tracking the movement of her rings.

	Pinky Finger	Ring Finger	Middle Finger	Index Finger
Position 1		G	S	
Position 2			S	G
Position 3	G		S	
Position 4				S,G
Position 5	S	G		
Position 6	G	S		
Position 7	S		G	
Position 8	G		S	
Position 9		S,G		
Position 10		G	S	
Position 11			G	S
Position 12		S		G
Position 13	S,G			
Position 14			S,G	

a. What percent of the positions shows the gold ring on her pinky finger?

b. What percent of the positions shows she wears both rings on one finger?

5. Use the coordinate plane below to answer the following questions:

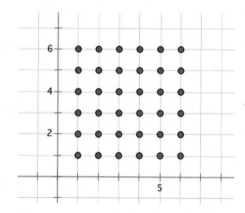

a. What is the percent of the 36 points whose quotient of $\dfrac{x-coordinate}{y-coordinate}$ is greater than one?

b. What is the percent of the 36 points whose coordinate quotient is equal to one?

Mathematics Curriculum

Copy Ready Material

Name _____ Date _____

Lesson 1: Percent

Exit Ticket

1. Fill in the chart converting between fractions, decimals and percents. Show work in the space provided.

Fraction	Decimal	Percent
$\dfrac{1}{8}$		
	1.125	
		$\dfrac{2}{5}\%$

2. Using the values from the chart in Problem 1, which is the least and which is the greatest? Explain how you arrived at your answers.

Exercise 1 Cards

I have the equivalent value 0.11. Who has the card equivalent to 350%?	I have the equivalent value 3.5. Who has the card equivalent to $\frac{3}{8}$?	I have the equivalent value 37.5%. Who has the card equivalent to $\frac{\frac{1}{4}}{100}$?	I have the equivalent value 0.0025%. Who has the card equivalent to 5?	I have the equivalent value 500%. Who has the card equivalent to $1\frac{2}{5}$?
I have the equivalent value $.4\%$. Who has the card equivalent to $\frac{1}{5}\%$?	I have the equivalent value 0.002. Who has the card equivalent to 100%?	I have the equivalent value 1. Who has the card equivalent to $\frac{210}{100}$?	I have the equivalent value 210%. Who has the card equivalent to $\frac{\frac{3}{4}}{100}$?	I have the equivalent value 0.75%. Who has the card equivalent to $35\frac{1}{2}\%$?
I have the equivalent value 0.355. Who has the card equivalent to 2%?	I have the equivalent value $\frac{1}{50}$. Who has the card equivalent to 0.5%?	I have the equivalent value $\frac{1}{200}$. Who has the card equivalent to 0.37?	I have the equivalent value 37%. Who has the card equivalent to 90%?	I have the equivalent value $\frac{9}{10}$. Who has the card equivalent to $\frac{\frac{1}{10}}{100}$?
I have the equivalent value 0.10%. Who has the card equivalent to $\frac{1}{2}$?	I have the equivalent value 50%. Who has the card equivalent to 300?	I have the equivalent value $30,000\%$. Who has the card equivalent to $\frac{3}{5}\%$?	I have the equivalent value $\frac{3}{500}$. Who has the card equivalent to 75%?	I have the equivalent value $\frac{3}{4}$. Who has the card equivalent to $\frac{180}{100}$?
I have the equivalent value 180%. Who has the card equivalent to 5%?	I have the equivalent value 0.05. Who has the card equivalent to $\frac{1}{100}\%$?	I have the equivalent value $\frac{1}{10,000}$. Who has the card equivalent to 1.1?	I have the equivalent value 110%. Who has the card equivalent to 250%?	I have the equivalent value 2.5. Who has the card equivalent to 18%?
I have the equivalent value $\frac{9}{50}$. Who has the card equivalent to $\frac{15}{4}$?	I have the equivalent value 375%. Who has the card equivalent to 0.06?	I have the equivalent value 6%. Who has the card equivalent to 0.4?	I have the equivalent value $\%$. Who has the card equivalent to 1.5%?	I have the equivalent value $\frac{3}{200}$. Who has the card equivalent to 11%?

Sprint: Fractions, Decimals, and Percents – Round 1

Number Correct: _____

Directions: Write each number in the alternate form indicated.

1.	$\dfrac{20}{100}$ as a percent	
2.	$\dfrac{40}{100}$ as a percent	
3.	$\dfrac{80}{100}$ as a percent	
4.	$\dfrac{85}{100}$ as a percent	
5.	$\dfrac{95}{100}$ as a percent	
6.	$\dfrac{100}{100}$ as a percent	
7.	$\dfrac{10}{10}$ as a percent	
8.	$\dfrac{1}{1}$ as a percent	
9.	$\dfrac{1}{10}$ as a percent	
10.	$\dfrac{2}{10}$ as a percent	
11.	$\dfrac{4}{10}$ as a percent	
12.	75% as a decimal	
13.	25% as a decimal	
14.	15% as a decimal	
15.	10% as a decimal	
16.	5% as a decimal	
17.	30% as a fraction	
18.	60% as a fraction	
19.	90% as a fraction	
20.	50% as a fraction	
21.	25% as a fraction	
22.	20% as a fraction	

23.	$\dfrac{9}{10}$ as a percent	
24.	$\dfrac{9}{20}$ as a percent	
25.	$\dfrac{9}{25}$ as a percent	
26.	$\dfrac{9}{50}$ as a percent	
27.	$\dfrac{9}{75}$ as a percent	
28.	$\dfrac{18}{75}$ as a percent	
29.	$\dfrac{36}{75}$ as a percent	
30.	96% as a fraction	
31.	92% as a fraction	
32.	88% as a fraction	
33.	44% as a fraction	
34.	22% as a fraction	
35.	3% as a decimal	
36.	30% as a decimal	
37.	33% as a decimal	
38.	33.3% as a decimal	
39.	3.3% as a decimal	
40.	0.3% as a decimal	
41.	$\dfrac{1}{3}$ as a percent	
42.	$\dfrac{1}{9}$ as a percent	
43.	$\dfrac{2}{9}$ as a percent	
44.	$\dfrac{8}{9}$ as a percent	

EUREKA MATH™

Lesson 1:   Percent

3

Sprint: Fractions, Decimals, and Percents – Round 2

Number Correct: _____

Directions: Write each number in the alternate form indicated.

Improvement: _____

1.	$\dfrac{30}{100}$ as a percent	
2.	$\dfrac{60}{100}$ as a percent	
3.	$\dfrac{70}{100}$ as a percent	
4.	$\dfrac{75}{100}$ as a percent	
5.	$\dfrac{90}{100}$ as a percent	
6.	$\dfrac{50}{100}$ as a percent	
7.	$\dfrac{5}{10}$ as a percent	
8.	$\dfrac{1}{2}$ as a percent	
9.	$\dfrac{1}{4}$ as a percent	
10.	$\dfrac{1}{8}$ as a percent	
11.	$\dfrac{3}{8}$ as a percent	
12.	60% as a decimal	
13.	45% as a decimal	
14.	30% as a decimal	
15.	6% as a decimal	
16.	3% as a decimal	
17.	3% as a fraction	
18.	6% as a fraction	
19.	60% as a fraction	
20.	30% as a fraction	
21.	45% as a fraction	
22.	15% as a fraction	

23.	$\dfrac{6}{10}$ as a percent	
24.	$\dfrac{6}{20}$ as a percent	
25.	$\dfrac{6}{25}$ as a percent	
26.	$\dfrac{6}{50}$ as a percent	
27.	$\dfrac{6}{75}$ as a percent	
28.	$\dfrac{12}{75}$ as a percent	
29.	$\dfrac{24}{75}$ as a percent	
30.	64% as a fraction	
31.	60% as a fraction	
32.	56% as a fraction	
33.	28% as a fraction	
34.	14% as a fraction	
35.	9% as a decimal	
36.	90% as a decimal	
37.	99% as a decimal	
38.	99.9% as a decimal	
39.	9.9% as a decimal	
40.	0.9% as a decimal	
41.	$\dfrac{4}{9}$ as a percent	
42.	$\dfrac{5}{9}$ as a percent	
43.	$\dfrac{2}{3}$ as a percent	
44.	$\dfrac{1}{6}$ as a percent	

Name _____   Date _____

Lesson 2: Part of a Whole as Percent

Exit Ticket

1. On a recent survey, 60% of those surveyed indicated that they preferred walking to running.

   a. If 540 people preferred walking, how many people were surveyed?

   b. How many people preferred running?

2. Which is greater: 25% of 15 or 15% of 25? Explain your reasoning using algebraic representations or visual models.

Name _____   Date _____

Lesson 3: Comparing Quantities with Percent

Exit Ticket

Solve each problem below using at least two different approaches.

1. Jenny's great grandmother is 90 years old. Jenny is 12 years old. What percent of Jenny's great grandmother's age is Jenny's age?

2. Jenny's mom is 36 years old. What percent of Jenny's mother's age is Jenny's great grandmother's age?

Sprint: Part, Whole, or Percent – Round 1

Number Correct: _____

Directions: Find each missing value.

1.	1% of 100 is?	
2.	2% of 100 is?	
3.	3% of 100 is?	
4.	4% of 100 is?	
5.	5% of 100 is?	
6.	9% of 100 is?	
7.	10% of 100 is?	
8.	10% of 200 is?	
9.	10% of 300 is?	
10.	10% of 500 is?	
11.	10% of 550 is?	
12.	10% of 570 is?	
13.	10% of 470 is?	
14.	10% of 170 is?	
15.	10% of 70 is?	
16.	10% of 40 is?	
17.	10% of 20 is?	
18.	10% of 25 is?	
19.	10% of 35 is?	
20.	10% of 36 is?	
21.	10% of 37 is?	
22.	10% of 37.5 is?	

23.	10% of 22 is?	
24.	20% of 22 is?	
25.	30% of 22 is?	
26.	50% of 22 is?	
27.	25% of 22 is?	
28.	75% of 22 is?	
29.	80% of 22 is?	
30.	85% of 22 is?	
31.	90% of 22 is?	
32.	95% of 22 is?	
33.	5% of 22 is?	
34.	15% of 80 is?	
35.	15% of 60 is?	
36.	15% of 40 is?	
37.	30% of 40 is?	
38.	30% of 70 is?	
39.	30% of 60 is?	
40.	45% of 80 is?	
41.	45% of 120 is?	
42.	120% of 40 is?	
43.	120% of 50 is?	
44.	120% of 55 is?	

EUREKA
MATH™

Lesson 3:   Comparing Quantities with Percent

Sprint: Part, Whole, or Percent – Round 2

Number Correct: _____

Directions: Find each missing value.

Improvement: _____

1.	20% of 100 is?		23.	10% of 4 is?	
2.	21% of 100 is?		24.	20% of 4 is?	
3.	22% of 100 is?		25.	30% of 4 is?	
4.	23% of 100 is?		26.	50% of 4 is?	
5.	25% of 100 is?		27.	25% of 4 is?	
6.	25% of 200 is?		28.	75% of 4 is?	
7.	25% of 300 is?		29.	80% of 4 is?	
8.	25% of 400 is?		30.	85% of 4 is?	
9.	25% of 4000 is?		31.	90% of 4 is?	
10.	50% of 4000 is?		32.	95% of 4 is?	
11.	10% of 4000 is?		33.	5% of 4 is?	
12.	10% of 4700 is?		34.	15% of 40 is?	
13.	10% of 4600 is?		35.	15% of 30 is?	
14.	10% of 4630 is?		36.	15% of 20 is?	
15.	10% of 463 is?		37.	30% of 20 is?	
16.	10% of 46.3 is?		38.	30% of 50 is?	
17.	10% of 18 is?		39.	30% of 90 is?	
18.	10% of 24 is?		40.	45% of 90 is?	
19.	10% of 3.63 is?		41.	90% of 120 is?	
20.	10% of 0.336 is?		42.	125% of 40 is?	
21.	10% of 37 is?		43.	125% of 50 is?	
22.	10% of 37.5 is?		44.	120% of 60 is?	

Name _____   Date _____

Lesson 4: Percent Increase and Decrease

Exit Ticket

Erin wants to raise her math grade to a 95 to improve her chances of winning a math scholarship. Her math average for the last marking period was an 81. Erin decides she must raise her math average by 15% to meet her goal. Do you agree? Why or why not? Support your written answer by showing your math work.

Name _____   Date _____

Lesson 5: Finding One Hundred Percent Given Another Percent

Exit Ticket

1. A tank that is 40% full contains 648 gallons of water. Use a double number line to find the capacity of the water tank.

2. Loretta picks apples for her grandfather to make apple cider. She brings him her cart with 420 apples. Her grandfather smiles at her and says, "Thank you Loretta. That is 35% of the apples that we need."

   Use mental math to find how many apples Loretta's grandfather needs. Describe your method.

Name _____   Date _____

Lesson 6: Fluency with Percents

Exit Ticket

1. Parker was able to pay for 44% of his college tuition with his scholarship. The remaining $10,054.52 he paid for with a student loan. What was the cost of Parker's tuition?

2. Two bags contain marbles. Bag A contains 112 marbles and Bag B contains 140 marbles. What percent fewer marbles does Bag A have than Bag B?

3. There are 42 students on a large bus and the rest are on a smaller bus. If 40% of the students are on the smaller bus, how many total students are on the two buses?

Sprint: Percent More or Less – Round 1

Number Correct: _____

Directions: Find each missing value.

1.	100% of 10 is ___?	
2.	10% of 10 is ___?	
3.	10% more than 10 is ___?	
4.	11 is ___ % more than 10?	
5.	11 is ___% of 10?	
6.	11 is 10% more than ___ ?	
7.	110% of 10 is ___?	
8.	10% less than 10 *is* ___?	
9.	9 is ___% less than 10?	
10.	9 is ___% of 10?	
11.	9 is 10% less than ___?	
12.	10% of 50 is ___?	
13.	10% more than 50 is ___?	
14.	55 is ___% of 50?	
15.	55 is ___% more than 50?	
16.	55 is 10% more than ___?	
17.	110% of 50 is ___?	
18.	10% less than 50 is ___?	
19.	45 is ___% of 50?	
20.	45 is ___% less than 50?	
21.	45 is 10% less than ___?	
22.	40 is ___% less than 50?	

23.	15% of 80 is ___?	
24.	15% more than 80 is ___?	
25.	What is 115% of 80?	
26.	92 is 115% of ___?	
27.	92 is ___% more than 80?	
28.	115% of 80 is ___?	
29.	What is 15% less than 80?	
30.	What % of 80 is 68?	
31.	What % less than 80 is 68?	
32.	What % less than 80 is 56?	
33.	What % of 80 is 56?	
34.	What is 20% more than 50?	
35.	What is 30% more than 50?	
36.	What is 140% of 50?	
37.	What % of 50 is 85?	
38.	What % more than 50 is 85?	
39.	What % less than 50 is 35?	
40.	What % of 50 is 35?	
41.	1 is what % of 50?	
42.	6 is what % of 50?	
43.	24% of 50 is?	
44.	24% more than 50 is?	

Sprint: Percent More or Less – Round 2

Number Correct: _____

Directions: Find each missing value.

Improvement: _____

1.	100% of 20 is ___?	
2.	10% of 20 is ___?	
3.	10% more than 20 is ___?	
4.	22 is ___ % more than 20?	
5.	22 is ___% of 20?	
6.	22 is 10% more than ___ ?	
7.	110% of 20 is ___?	
8.	10% less than 20 is ___?	
9.	18 is ___% less than 20?	
10.	18 is ___% of 20?	
11.	18 is 10% less than ___?	
12.	10% of 200 is ___?	
13.	10% more than 200 is ___?	
14.	220 is ___% of 200?	
15.	220 is ___% more than 200?	
16.	220 is 10% more than ___?	
17.	110% of 200 is ___?	
18.	10% less than 200 is ___?	
19.	180 is ___% of 200?	
20.	180 is ___% less than 200?	
21.	180 is 10% less than ___?	
22.	160 is ___% less than 200?	

23.	15% of 60 is ___?	
24.	15% more than 60 is ___?	
25.	What is 115% of 60?	
26.	69 is 115% of ___?	
27.	69 is ___% more than 60?	
28.	115% of 60 is ___?	
29.	What is 15% less than 60?	
30.	What % of 60 is 51?	
31.	What % less than 60 is 51?	
32.	What % less than 60 is 42?	
33.	What % of 60 is 42?	
34.	What is 20% more than 80?	
35.	What is 30% more than 80?	
36.	What is 140% of 80?	
37.	What % of 80 is 104?	
38.	What % more than 80 is 104?	
39.	What % less than 80 is 56?	
40.	What % of 80 is 56?	
41.	1 is what % of 200?	
42.	6 is what % of 200?	
43.	24% of 200 is?	
44.	24% more than 200 is?	

Lesson 6:   Fluency with Percents

13

Name _____   Date _____

Lesson 7: Markup and Markdown Problems

Exit Ticket

1. A store that sells skis buys them from a manufacturer at a wholesale price of $57. The store's markup rate is 50%.

    a. What price does the store charge its customers for the skis?

    b. What percent of the original price is the final price? Show your work.

    c. What is the percent increase from the original price to the final price?

Name _____   Date _____

Lesson 8: Percent Error Problems

Exit Ticket

1. The veterinarian weighed Oliver's new puppy, Boaz, on a defective scale. He weighed 36 pounds. However, Boaz weighs exactly 34.5 pounds. What is the percent of error in measurement of the defective scale to the nearest tenth?

2. Use the π key on a scientific or graphing calculator to compute the percent of error of the approximation of pi, 3.14, to the value π. Show your steps, and round your answer to the nearest hundredth of a percent.

3. Connor and Angie helped take attendance during their school's practice fire drill. If the actual count was between 77 and 89, inclusive, what is the most the absolute error could be? What is the most the percent error could be? Round your answer to the nearest tenth of a percent.

Name _____   Date _____

Lesson 9: Problem Solving When the Percent Changes

Exit Ticket

Terrence and Lee were selling magazines for a charity. In the first week, Terrance sold 30% more than Lee. In the second week, Terrance sold 8 magazines, but Lee did not sell any. If Terrance sold 50% more than Lee by the end of the second week, how many magazines did Lee sell?

Choose any model to solve the problem. Show your work to justify your answer.

Name _____   Date _____

Lesson 10: Simple Interest

Exit Ticket

1. Erica's parents gave her $500 for her high school graduation. She put the money into a savings account that earned 7.5% annual interest. She left the money in the account for nine months before she withdrew it. How much interest did the account earn if interest is paid monthly?

2. If she would have left the money in the account for another nine months before withdrawing, how much interest would the account have earned?

3. About how many years and months would she have to leave the money in the account if she wants to reach her goal of saving $750?

Sprint: Fractional Percents – Round 1

Number Correct: _____

Directions: Find the part that corresponds with each percent.

1.	1% of 100	
2.	1% of 200	
3.	1% of 400	
4.	1% of 800	
5.	1% of 1,600	
6.	1% of 3,200	
7.	1% of 5,000	
8.	1% of 10,000	
9.	1% of 20,000	
10.	1% of 40,000	
11.	1% of 80,000	
12.	$\frac{1}{2}$% of 100	
13.	$\frac{1}{2}$% of 200	
14.	$\frac{1}{2}$% of 400	
15.	$\frac{1}{2}$% of 800	
16.	$\frac{1}{2}$% of 1,600	
17.	$\frac{1}{2}$% of 3,200	
18.	$\frac{1}{2}$% of 5,000	
19.	$\frac{1}{2}$% of 10,000	
20.	$\frac{1}{2}$% of 20,000	
21.	$\frac{1}{2}$% of 40,000	
22.	$\frac{1}{2}$% of 80,000	

23.	$\frac{1}{4}$% of 100	
24.	$\frac{1}{4}$% of 200	
25.	$\frac{1}{4}$% of 400	
26.	$\frac{1}{4}$% of 800	
27.	$\frac{1}{4}$% of 1,600	
28.	$\frac{1}{4}$% of 3,200	
29.	$\frac{1}{4}$% of 5,000	
30.	$\frac{1}{4}$% of 10,000	
31.	$\frac{1}{4}$% of 20,000	
32.	$\frac{1}{4}$% of 40,000	
33.	$\frac{1}{4}$% of 80,000	
34.	1% of 1,000	
35.	$\frac{1}{2}$% of 1,000	
36.	$\frac{1}{4}$% of 1,000	
37.	1% of 4,000	
38.	$\frac{1}{2}$% of 4,000	
39.	$\frac{1}{4}$% of 4,000	
40.	1% of 2,000	
41.	$\frac{1}{2}$% of 2,000	
42.	$\frac{1}{4}$% of 2,000	
43.	$\frac{1}{2}$% of 6,000	
44.	$\frac{1}{4}$% of 6,000	

Sprint: Fractional Percents – Round 2

Number Correct: _____

Improvement: _____

Directions: Find the part that corresponds with each percent.

1.	10% of 30	
2.	10% of 60	
3.	10% of 90	
4.	10% of 120	
5.	10% of 150	
6.	10% of 180	
7.	10% of 210	
8.	20% of 30	
9.	20% of 60	
10.	20% of 90	
11.	20% of 120	
12.	5% of 50	
13.	5% of 100	
14.	5% of 200	
15.	5% of 400	
16.	5% of 800	
17.	5% of 1,600	
18.	5% of 3,200	
19.	5% of 6,400	
20.	5% of 600	
21.	10% of 600	
22.	20% of 600	

23.	$10\frac{1}{2}$% of 100	
24.	$10\frac{1}{2}$% of 200	
25.	$10\frac{1}{2}$% of 400	
26.	$10\frac{1}{2}$% of 800	
27.	$10\frac{1}{2}$% of 1,600	
28.	$10\frac{1}{2}$% of 3,200	
29.	$10\frac{1}{2}$% of 6,400	
30.	$10\frac{1}{4}$% of 400	
31.	$10\frac{1}{4}$% of 800	
32.	$10\frac{1}{4}$% of 1,600	
33.	$10\frac{1}{4}$% of 3,200	
34.	10% of 1,000	
35.	$10\frac{1}{2}$% of 1,000	
36.	$10\frac{1}{4}$% of 1,000	
37.	10% of 2,000	
38.	$10\frac{1}{2}$% of 2,000	
39.	$10\frac{1}{4}$% of 2,000	
40.	10% of 4,000	
41.	$10\frac{1}{2}$% of 4,000	
42.	$10\frac{1}{4}$% of 4,000	
43.	10% of 5,000	
44.	$10\frac{1}{2}$% of 5,000	

Name _____   Date _____

Lesson 11: Tax, Commissions, Fees, and Other Real-World Percent Problems

Exit Ticket

1. Lee works selling electronics. He earns a 5% commission on each sale he makes.

   a. Write an equation that shows the proportional relationship between the dollar amount of electronics Lee sells, d, and the amount of money he makes in commission, c.

   b. Express the constant of proportionality as a decimal.

   c. Explain what the constant of proportionality means in the context of this situation.

   d. If Lee wants to make $100 in commission, what is the dollar amount of electronics he must sell?

Name _____   Date _____

1. In New York State, sales tax rates vary by county. In Allegany County, the sales tax rate is $8\frac{1}{2}\%$.

    a. A book costs $12.99 and a video game costs $39.99. Rounded to the nearest cent, how much more is the tax on the video game than the tax on the book?

    b. Using n to represent the cost of an item before tax and t to represent the amount of sales tax for that item, write an equation to show the relationship between n and t.

    c. Using your equation, create a table that includes five possible pairs of solutions to the equation. Label each column appropriately.

d. Graph the relationship from parts (a) and (b) in the coordinate plane. Include a title and appropriate scales and labels for both axes.

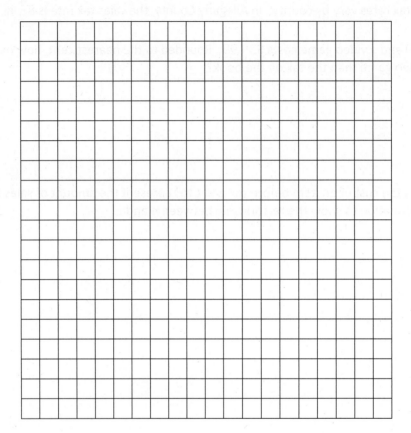

e. Is the relationship proportional? Why or why not? If so, what is the constant of proportionality? Explain.

f. In nearby Wyoming County, the sales tax rate is 8%. If you were to create an equation, graph, and table for this tax rate (similar to parts (a), (b), and (d) above), what would the points (0,0) and (1,0.08) represent? Explain their meaning in the context of this situation.

g. A customer returns an item to a toy store in Wyoming County. The toy store has another location in Allegany County, and the customer shops at both locations. The customer's receipt shows $2.12 tax was charged on a $24.99 item. Was the item purchased at the Wyoming County store or the Allegany County store? Explain and justify your answer by showing your math work.

2. Amy is baking her famous pies to sell at the Town Fall Festival. She uses $32\frac{1}{2}$ cups of flour for every 10 cups of sugar in order to make a dozen pies. Answer the following questions below and show your work.

    a. Write an equation, in terms of f, representing the relationship between the number of cups of flour used and the number of cups of sugar used to make the pies.

    b. Write the constant of proportionality as a percent. Explain what it means in the context of this situation.

    c. To help sell more pies at the festival, Amy set the price for one pie at 40% less than what it would cost at her bakery. At the festival, she posts a sign that reads, "Amy's Famous Pies only $9.00/pie!" Using this information, what is the price of one pie at the bakery?

Name _____   Date _____

Lesson 12: The Scale Factor as a Percent for a Scale Drawing

1. Create a scale drawing of the picture below using a scale factor of 60%. Write three equations that show how you determined the lengths of three different parts of the resulting picture.

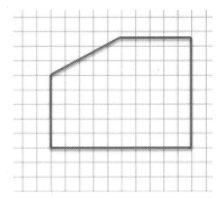

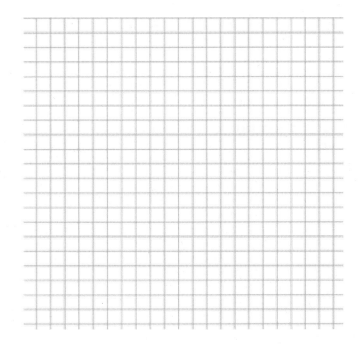

2. Sue wants to make two picture frames with lengths and widths that are proportional to the ones given below. Note: The illustration shown below is not drawn to scale.

8 inches

12 inches

a. Sketch a scale drawing using a horizontal scale factor of 50% and a vertical scale factor of 75%. Determine the dimensions of the new picture frame.

b. Sketch a scale drawing using a horizontal scale factor of 125% and a vertical scale factor of 140%. Determine the dimensions of the new picture frame.

Name _____   Date _____

Lesson 13: Changing Scales

1. Compute the scale factor, as a percent, of each given relationship. When necessary, round your answer to the nearest tenth of a percent.

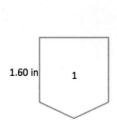

1.60 in

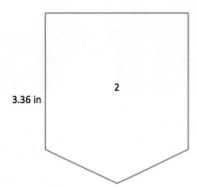

3.36 in

a.   Drawing 1 to Drawing 2

b.   Drawing 2 to Drawing 1

c.   Write two different equations that illustrate how each scale factor relates to the lengths in the diagram.

2. Drawings 2 and 3 are scale drawings of Drawing 1. The scale factor from Drawing 1 to Drawing 2 is 75%, and the scale factor from Drawing 2 to Drawing 3 is 50%. Find the scale factor from Drawing 1 to Drawing 3.

Name _____   Date _____

Lesson 14: Computing Actual Lengths from a Scale Drawing

Exit Ticket

Each of the designs shown below is going to be displayed in a window using strands of white lights. The smaller design requires 225 feet of lights. How many feet of lights does the enlarged design require?

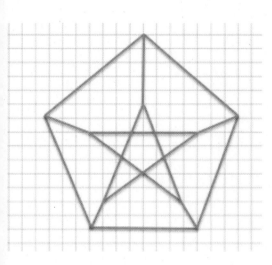
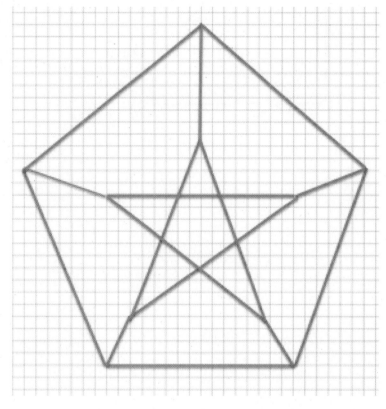

Name _____   Date _____

Lesson 15: Solving Area Problems Using Scale Drawings

Exit Ticket

Write an equation relating the area of the original (larger) drawing to its smaller scale drawing. Explain how you determined the equation. What percent of the area of the larger drawing is the smaller scale drawing?

15 units

12 units

6 units

4.8 units

Name _____   Date _____

Lesson 16: Population Problems

Exit Ticket

1. Jodie spent 25% less buying her English reading book than Claudia. Gianna spent 9% less than Claudia. Gianna spent more than Jodie by what percent?

2. Mr. Ellis is a teacher who tutors students after school. Of the students he tutors, 30% need help in computer science and the rest need assistance in math. Of the students who need help in computer science, 40% are enrolled in Mr. Ellis's class during the school day. Of the students who need help in math, 25% are enrolled in his class during the school day. What percent of the after-school students are enrolled in Mr. Ellis's classes?

Name _____   Date _____

Lesson 17: Mixture Problems

Exit Ticket

A 25% vinegar solution is combined with triple the amount of a 45% vinegar solution and a 5% vinegar solution resulting in 20 milliliters of a 30% vinegar solution.

1.   Determine an equation that models this situation, and explain what each part represents in the situation.

2.   Solve the equation and find the amount of each of the solutions that were combined.

Name _____   Date _____

Lesson 18: Counting Problems

Exit Ticket

1. There are a van and a bus transporting students on a student camping trip. Arriving at the site, there are 3 parking spots. Let v represent the van and b represent the bus. The chart shows the different ways the vehicles can park.

   a. In what percent of arrangements are the vehicles separated by an empty parking space?

	Parking Space 1	Parking Space2	Parking Space 3
Option 1	V	B	
Option 2	V		B
Option 3	B	V	
Option 4	B		V
Option 5		V	B
Option 6		B	V

   b. In what percent of arrangements are the vehicles parked next to each other?

   c. In what percent of arrangements does the left or right parking space remain vacant?

Name _____   Date _____

DAY ONE: CALCULATOR ACTIVE

You may use a calculator for this part of the assessment. Show your work to receive full credit.

1. Kara works at a fine jewelry store and earns commission on her total sales for the week. Her weekly paycheck was in the amount of $6,500, including her salary of $1,000. Her sales for the week totaled $45,000. Express her rate of commission as a percent, rounded to the nearest whole number.

2. Kacey and her three friends went out for lunch, and they wanted to leave a 15% tip. The receipt shown below lists the lunch total before tax and tip. The tip is on the cost of the food plus tax. The sales tax rate in Pleasantville is 8.75%.

    a. Use mental math to estimate the approximate total cost of the bill including tax and tip to the nearest dollar. Explain how you arrived at your answer.

    ```
          SAM'S WORLD FAMOUS BURGER
                 1522 OAK ROAD
              PLEASANTVILLE, USA


    BBQ BURGER W/CHEESE          9.99
    CHICKEN FINGER BASKE         8.99
    MUSHROOM BURGER             10.99
    CHILI CHEESE FRIES           8.99

                      TOTAL: $38.96

       THANKS FOR YOUR BUSINESS.
          FOLLOW US ONLINE!

           WWW.CUSTOMRECEIPT.COM
    ```

b.   Find the actual total of the bill including tax and tip. If Kacey and her three friends split the bill equally, how much will each person pay including tax and tip?

3.   Cool Tees is having a Back to School sale where all t-shirts are discounted by 15%. Joshua wants to buy five shirts: one costs $9.99, two cost $11.99 each, and two others cost $21.00 each.

   a.   What is the total cost of the shirts including the discount?

b. By law, sales tax is calculated on the discounted price of the shirts. Would the total cost of the shirts including the 6.5% sales tax be greater if the tax was applied before a 15% discount is taken, rather than after a 15% discount is taken? Explain.

c. Joshua remembered he had a coupon in his pocket that would take an additional 30% off the price of the shirts. Calculate the new total cost of the shirts including the sales tax.

d. If the price of each shirt is 120% of the store's cost price, write an equation and find the store's cost price for a $21 shirt.

4. Tierra, Cameron, and Justice wrote equations to calculate the amount of money in a savings account after one year with $\frac{1}{2}\%$ interest paid annually on a balance of M dollars. Let T represent the total amount of money saved.

         Tiara's Equation: $T = 1.05M$

         Cameron's Equation: $T = M + 0.005M$

         Justice's Equation: $T = M(1 + 0.005)$

a. The three students decided to see if their equations would give the same answer by using a $100 balance. Find the total amount of money in the savings account using each student's equation. Show your work.

b. Explain why their equations will or will not give the same answer.

5. A printing company is enlarging the image on a postcard to make a greeting card. The enlargement of the postcard's rectangular image is done using a scale factor of 125%. Be sure to show all other related math work.

   a. Represent a scale factor of 125% as a fraction and decimal.

   b. The postcard's dimensions are 7 inches by 5 inches. What are the dimensions of the greeting card?

   c. If the printing company makes a poster by enlarging the postcard image, and the poster's dimensions are 28 inches by 20 inches, represent the scale factor as a percent.

d. Write an equation, in terms of the scale factor, that shows the relationship between the areas of the postcard and poster. Explain your equation.

e. Suppose the printing company wanted to start with the greeting card's image and reduce it to create the postcard's image. What scale factor would they use? Represent this scale factor as a percent.

f.   In math class, students had to create a scale drawing that was smaller than the postcard image. Azra used a scale factor of 60% to create the smaller image. She stated the dimensions of her smaller image as: $4\frac{1}{6}$ inches by 3 inches. Azra's math teacher did not give her full credit for her answer. Why? Explain Azra's error, and write the answer correctly.

Name _____   Date _____

DAY TWO: CALCULATOR INACTIVE

You will now complete the remainder of the assessment without the use of a calculator.

6. A $100 MP3 player is marked up by 10% and then marked down by 10%. What is the final price?
    Explain your answer.

7. The water level in a swimming pool increased from 4.5 feet to 6 feet. What is the percent increase in the
    water level rounded to the nearest tenth of a percent? Show your work.

8. A 5-gallon mixture contains 40% acid. A 3-gallon mixture contains 50% acid. What percent acid is
    obtained by putting the two mixtures together? Show your work.

9. In Mr. Johnson's third and fourth period classes, 30% of the students scored a 95% or higher on a quiz. Let n be the total number of students in Mr. Johnson's classes. Answer the following questions, and show your work to support your answers.

   a. If 15 students scored a 95% or higher, write an equation involving n that relates the number of students who scored a 95% or higher to the total number of students in Mr. Johnson's third and fourth period classes.

   b. Solve your equation in part (a) to find how many students are in Mr. Johnson's third and fourth period classes.

   c. Of the students who scored below 95%, 40% of them are girls. How many boys scored below 95%?

Staff

Nashrah Ahmed, Coordinator of User Experience

Deirdre Bey, Formatter

Thomas Brasdefer, Formatter

Brenda Bryant, Program Operations Associate

Adrienne Burgess, Project Associate – Website Content

Alyson Burgess, Associate Director of Administration

Rose Calloway, Document Specialist

Adam Cardais, Copy Editor

Jamie Carruth, Formatter

Lauren Chapalee, Professional Learning Manager – English

Gregar Chapin, Website Project Coordinator

Chris Clary, Director of Branding and Marketing

Katelyn Colacino, Formatter

Julia Cooper, Formatter

Barbara Davidson, Deputy Director

Karen Elkins, Formatter

Jennifer George, Formatter

Erin Glover, Formatter

Laurie Gonsoulin, Formatter

Eric Halley, Formatter

Candice Hartley, Formatter

Thomas Haynes, Copy Editor

Robert Hunsicker, Program Operations Associate

Jennifer Hutchinson, Copy Editor

Anne Ireland, Print Edition Coordinator

Maggie Kay, Copy Editor

Liz LeBarron, Program Operations and Support Associate

Jeff LeBel, XML Developer

Tam Le, Document Production Manager

Natanya Levioff, Director of Program Operations and Support

Siena Mazero, Project Associate – Website Content

Stacie McClintock, XML Developer

Cindy Medici, Copy Editor

Elisabeth Mox, Executive Assistant to the President

Lynne Munson, President and Executive Director

Sarah Oyler, Document Specialist

Diego Quiroga, Accounts Specialist

Becky Robinson, Program Operations Associate

Amy Rome, Copy Editor

Rachel Rooney, Program Manager – English/History

Neela Roy, Print Edition Associate

Tim Shen, Customer Relations Associate

Kathleen Smith, Formatter

Leigh Sterten, Project Associate – Web Content

Wendy Taylor, Copy Editor

Megan Wall, Formatter

Marjani Warren, Account Manager

Sam Wertheim, Product Delivery Manager

Amy Wierzbicki, Assets and Permissions Manager

Sarah Woodard, Associate Director – English/History

Eureka Math: A Story of Ratios **Contributors**

Michael Allwood, Curriculum Writer
Tiah Alphonso, Program Manager – Curriculum Production
Catriona Anderson, Program Manager – Implementation Support
Beau Bailey, Curriculum Writer
Scott Baldridge, Lead Mathematician and Lead Curriculum Writer
Bonnie Bergstresser, Math Auditor
Gail Burrill, Curriculum Writer
Beth Chance, Statistician
Joanne Choi, Curriculum Writer
Jill Diniz, Program Director
Lori Fanning, Curriculum Writer
Ellen Fort, Math Auditor
Kathy Fritz, Curriculum Writer
Glenn Gebhard, Curriculum Writer
Krysta Gibbs, Curriculum Writer
Winnie Gilbert, Lead Curriculum Writer / Editor, Grade 8
Pam Goodner, Math Auditor
Debby Grawn, Curriculum Writer
Bonnie Hart, Curriculum Writer
Stefanie Hassan, Lead Curriculum Writer / Editor, Grade 8
Sherri Hernandez, Math Auditor
Patrick Hopfensperger, Curriculum Writer
Sunil Koswatta, Mathematician, Grade 8

Brian Kotz, Curriculum Writer
Henry Kranendonk, Statistics Lead Curriculum Writer / Editor
Connie Laughlin, Math Auditor
Jennifer Loftin, Program Manager – Professional Development
Abby Mattern, Math Auditor
Nell McAnelly, Project Director
Saki Milton, Curriculum Writer
Pia Mohsen, Curriculum Writer
Jerry Moreno, Statistician
Ann Netter, Lead Curriculum Writer / Editor, Grades 6-7
Roxy Peck, Statistician, Statistics Lead Curriculum Writer / Editor
Terrie Poehl, Math Auditor
Spencer Roby, Math Auditor
Kathleen Scholand, Math Auditor
Erika Silva, Lead Curriculum Writer / Editor, Grade 6-7
Hester Sutton, Advisor / Reviewer Grades 6-7
Shannon Vinson, Statistics Lead Curriculum Writer / Editor
Julie Wortmann, Lead Curriculum Writer / Editor, Grade 7
David Wright, Mathematician, Lead Curriculum Writer / Editor, Grades 6-7
Kristen Zimmerman, Document Production Manager